CAST OF CHARACTERS

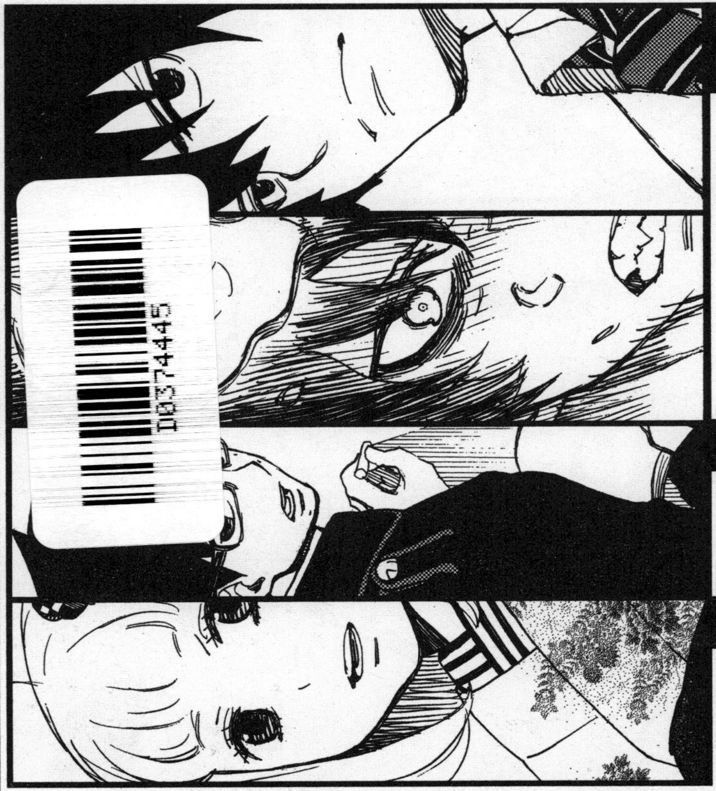

RIN OKUMURA

Born of a human mother and Satan, the God of Demons, Rin Okumura has powers he can barely control. After Satan kills Father Fujimoto, Rin's foster father, Rin decides to become an Exorcist so he can someday defeat Satan. Now a first-year student at True Cross Academy and an Exwire at the Exorcism Cram School, he hopes to someday become a Knight. When he draws the Koma Sword, he manifests his infernal power in the form of blue flames.

YUKIO OKUMURA

Rin's brother. Hoping to become a doctor, he's a genius who is the youngest student ever to become an instructor at the Exorcism Cram School. An instructor in Demon Pharmaceuticals, he possesses the titles of Doctor and Dragoon.

SHIEMI MORIYAMA

Daughter of the owner of Futsumaya, an exorcist supply shop. Inspired by Rin and Yukio, she became an Exwire and hopes to someday become an Exorcist. She has the ability to become a Tamer and can summon a baby Greenman.

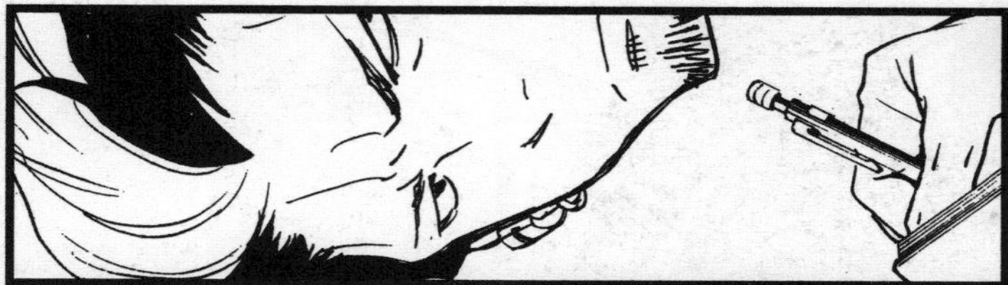

Ryuji Suguro

Heir to a venerable temple in Kyoto. After the Blue Night, he became an Exwire and hopes to become an Exorcist someday. He wants to achieve the titles of Dragoon and Aria.

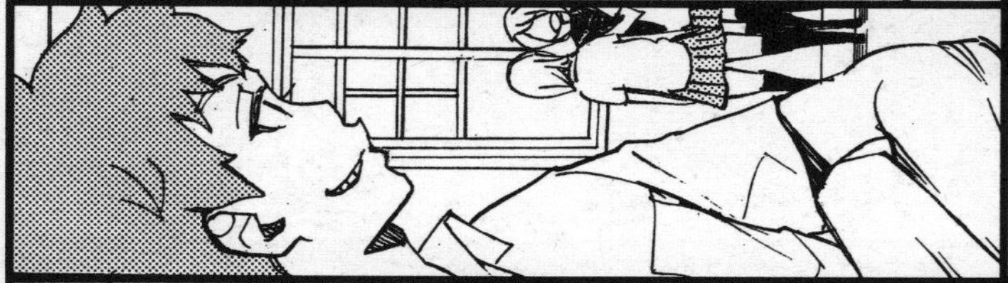

Renzo Shima

Once a pupil of Suguro's father and now Suguro's friend. He's an Exwire who wants to become an Aria. He has an easygoing personality and is totally girl-crazy.

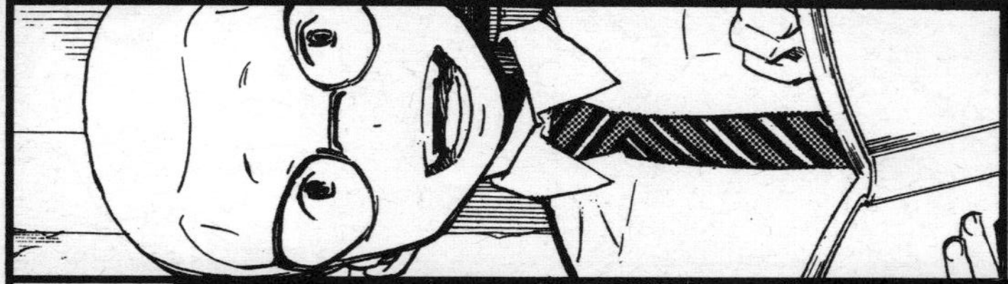

Konekomaru Miwa

Like Shima, he was once a pupil of Suguro's father and is now Suguro's friend. He's an Exwire who hopes to become an Aria someday. He is small in size and has a quiet and composed personality.

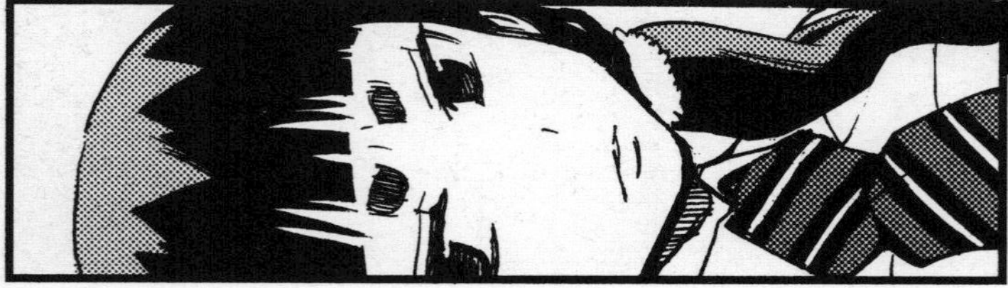

Izumo Kamiki

An Exwire with the blood of shrine maidens. She has the ability to become a Tamer and can summon two white foxes. Her friend Paku quit school, but Izumo has continued attending.

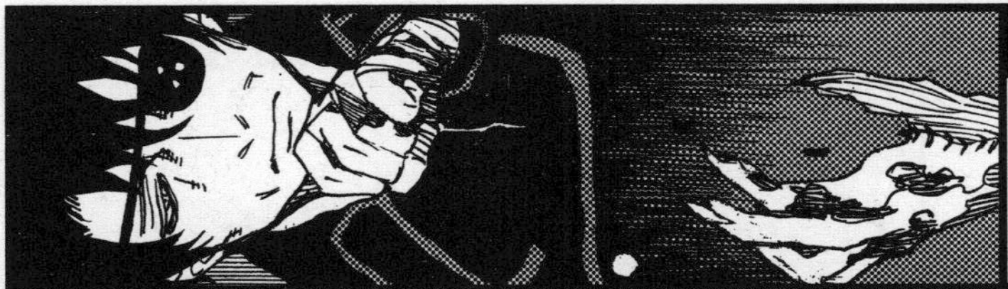

IGOR NEUHAUS

A Senior Exorcist First Class who holds the titles of Tamer, Doctor and Aria. He teaches magic circles and seals at the Exorcism Cram School. Little else is known about him.

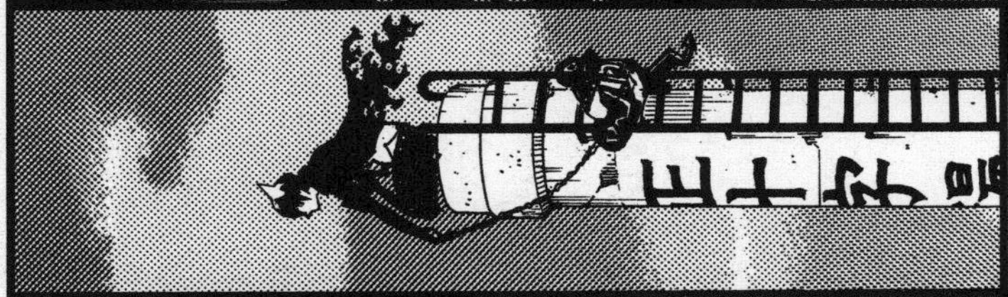

AMAIMON

Mephisto Pheles's younger brother. Mephisto ordered him to come to True Cross Academy. Little else is known about him as well.

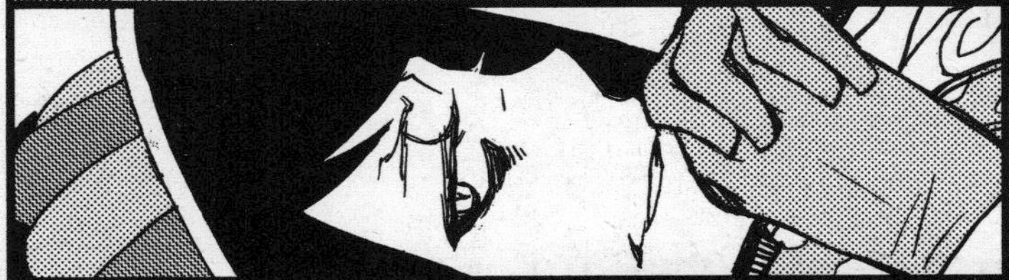

MEPHISTO PHELES

President of True Cross Academy and head of the Exorcism Cram School. He was Father Fujimoto's friend, and now he is Rin and Yukio's guardian. His behavior is suspicious, and all details about his true identity are shrouded in mystery.

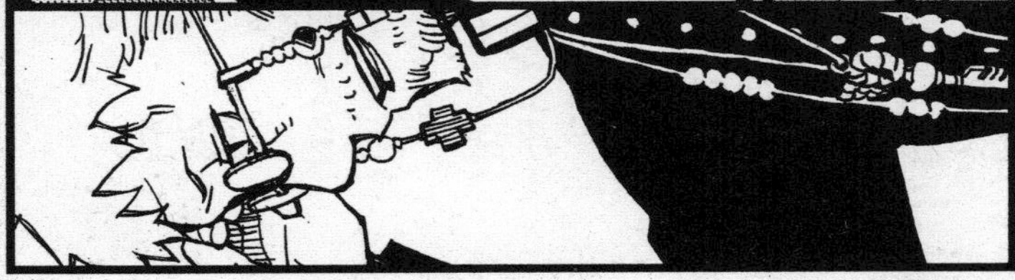

SHIRO FUJIMOTO

The man who raised Rin and Yukio. He was a priest at True Cross Church and a famous Exorcist. He held the rank of Paladin and once taught Demon Pharmaceuticals. Satan possessed him and he gave his life defending Rin.

✺ THE STORY SO FAR ✺

UNKNOWN TO RIN OKUMURA, BOTH HUMAN AND DEMON BLOOD RUNS IN HIS VEINS. IN AN ARGUMENT WITH HIS FOSTER FATHER, FATHER FUJIMOTO, RIN LEARNS THAT SATAN IS HIS TRUE FATHER. SATAN SUDDENLY APPEARS AND TRIES TO DRAG RIN DOWN TO GEHENNA BECAUSE RIN HAS INHERITED HIS POWER. FATHER FUJIMOTO FIGHTS TO DEFEND RIN, BUT DIES IN THE PROCESS. RIN DECIDES TO BECOME AN EXORCIST SO HE CAN SOMEDAY DEFEAT SATAN AND BEGINS STUDYING AT THE EXORCISM CRAM SCHOOL UNDER THE INSTRUCTION OF HIS TWIN BROTHER YUKIO, WHO IS ALREADY AN EXORCIST.

RIN AND YUKIO MEET A YOUNG GIRL NAMED SHIEMI MORIYAMA AT FUTSUMAYA, AN EXORCISM SUPPLY SHOP. SHIEMI CAN'T WALK BECAUSE OF A DEMONIC INFECTION IN HER LEGS. AFTER THE BROTHERS SAVE HER FROM HER AFFLICTION, SHE DECIDES SHE WANTS TO SEE THE OUTSIDE WORLD AND BEGINS WALKING ON HER OWN. SHE BEGINS ATTENDING THE EXORCISM CRAM SCHOOL SO SHE CAN BECOME A STRONGER PERSON.

◉ THE STORY SO FAR ◉

—BEFORE SUMMER BREAK

IN PREPARATION FOR THE EXWIRE CERTIFICATION EXAM, THE TRAINEES—ALSO KNOWN AS PAGES—PARTICIPATE IN AN INTENSIVE STUDY CAMP. A DEMON LOOKING FOR RIN ATTACKS THE OTHER STUDENTS, BUT SHIEMI, WHO HAS A STRONG DESIRE TO BE HELPFUL TO EVERYONE, IS INSTRUMENTAL IN SAVING THEM ALL.

AFTER BARELY ESCAPING THE DANGER, MEPHISTO PHELES REVEALS THAT HE PLANNED THE WHOLE INCIDENT AS THE EXWIRE CERTIFICATION EXAM. ALL THE STUDENTS ADVANCE TO THE RANK OF EXWIRE, BUT THEIR NEXT TRIAL AWAITS!!

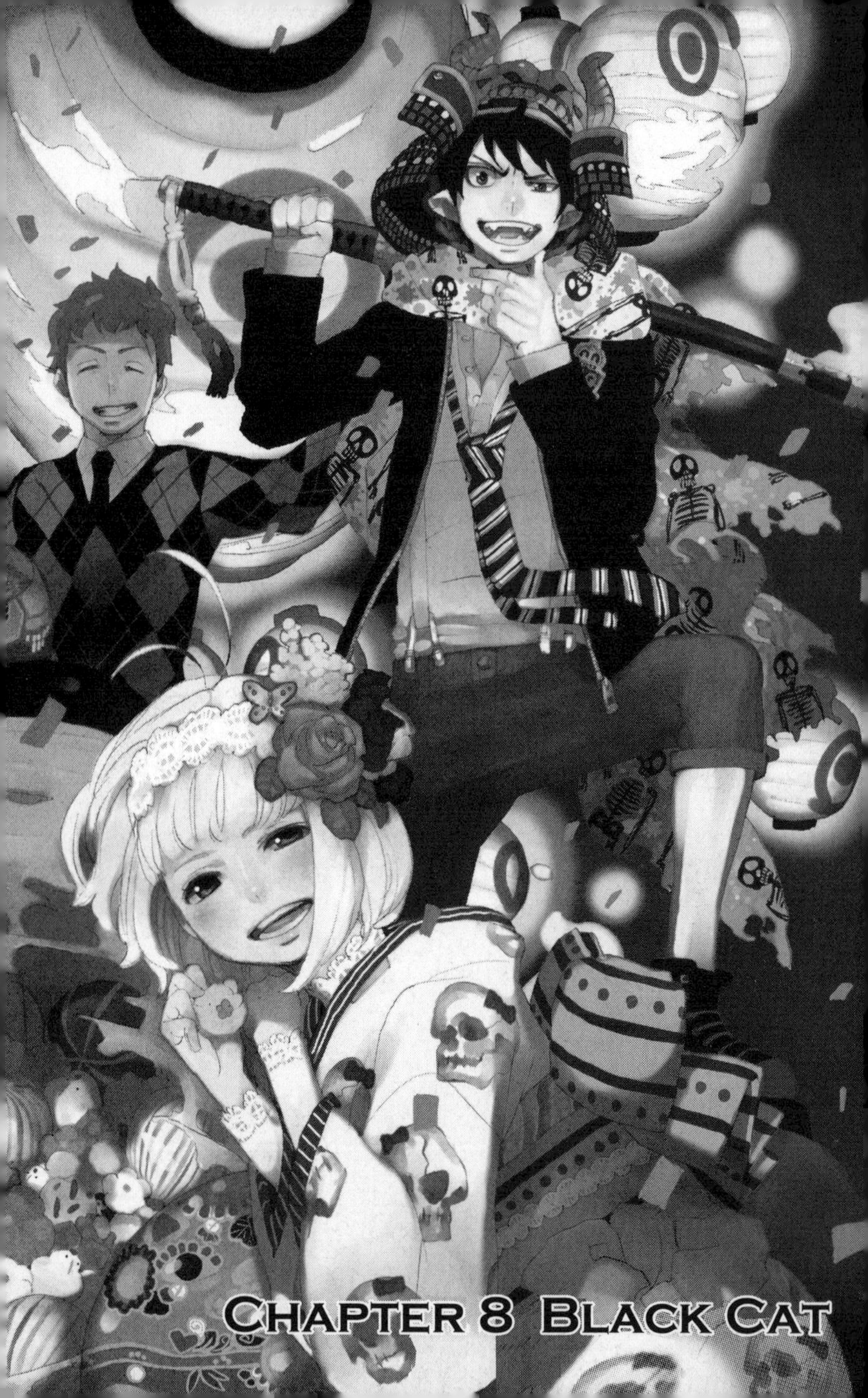
Chapter 8 Black Cat

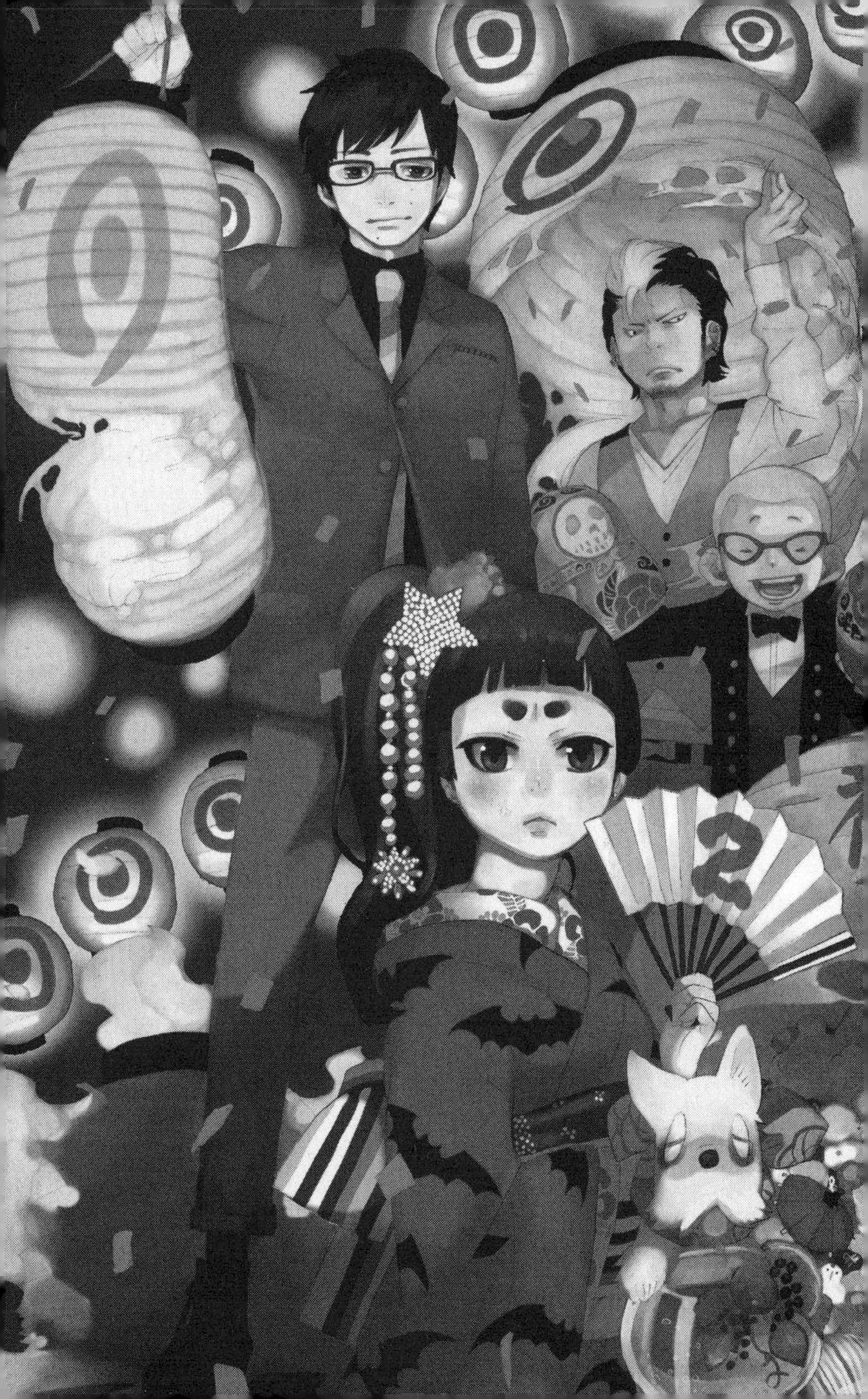

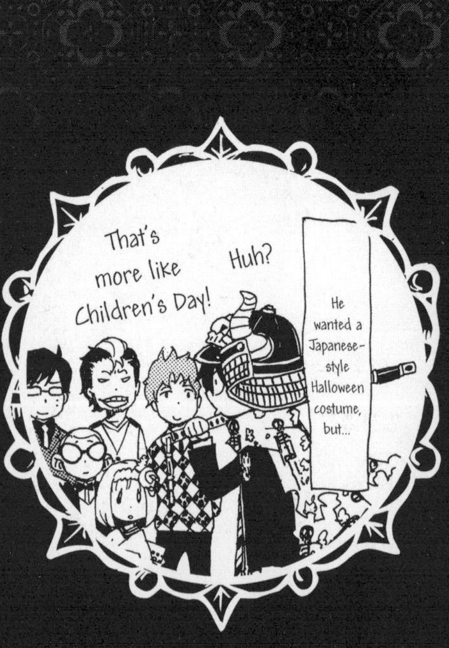
He wanted a Japanese-style Halloween costume, but...
Huh?
That's more like Children's Day!

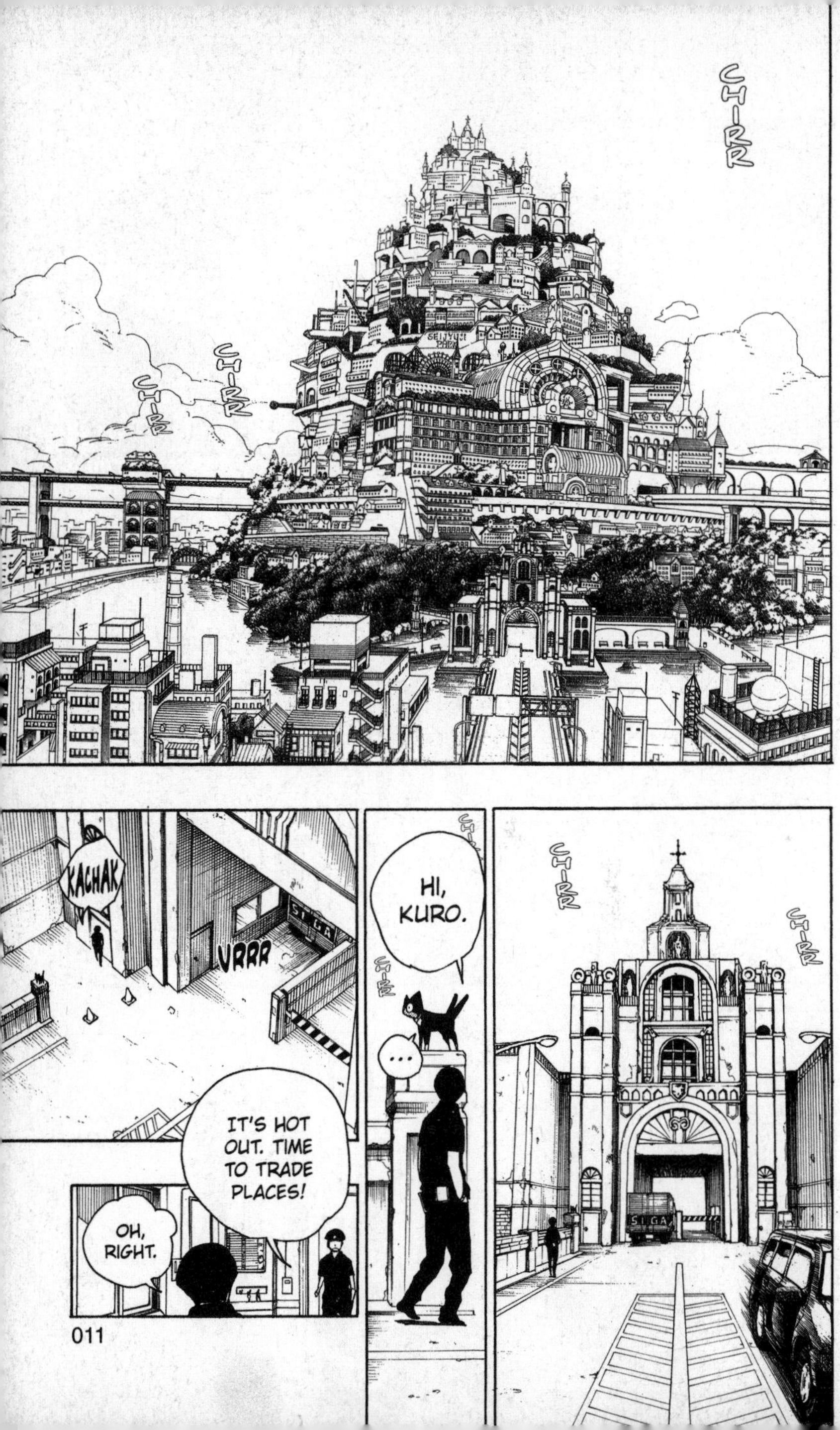
CHIRR
CHIRR
CHIRR
CHIRR
CHIRR
HI, KURO.
CHIRR
...
KACHAK
SIGA
VRRR
IT'S HOT OUT. TIME TO TRADE PLACES!
OH, RIGHT.
SIGA

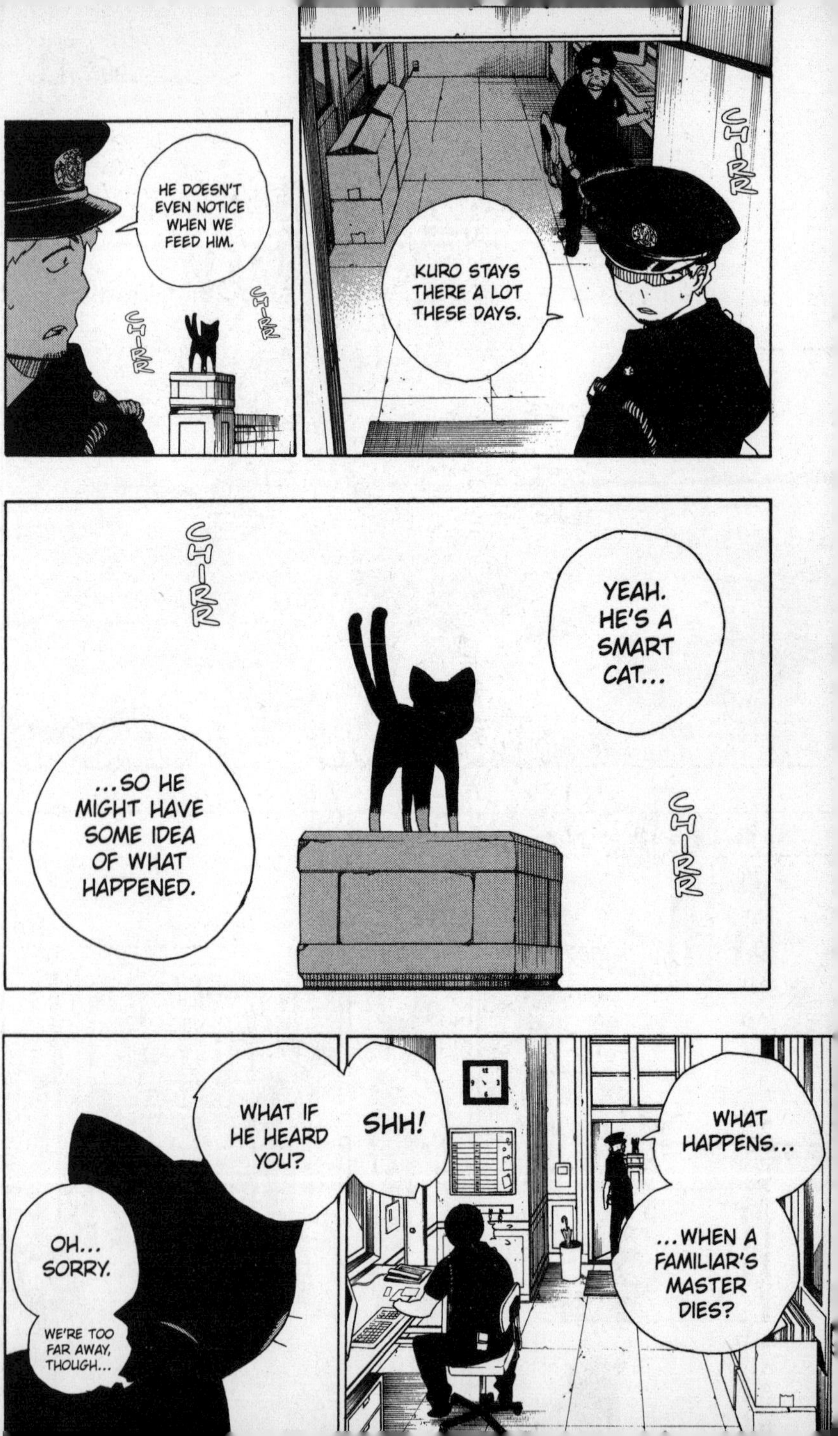
CHIRR
KURO STAYS THERE A LOT THESE DAYS.
HE DOESN'T EVEN NOTICE WHEN WE FEED HIM.
CHIRR
CHIRR
YEAH. HE'S A SMART CAT...
CHIRR
...SO HE MIGHT HAVE SOME IDEA OF WHAT HAPPENED.
CHIRR
WHAT HAPPENS...
...WHEN A FAMILIAR'S MASTER DIES?
SHH!
WHAT IF HE HEARD YOU?
OH... SORRY.
WE'RE TOO FAR AWAY, THOUGH...

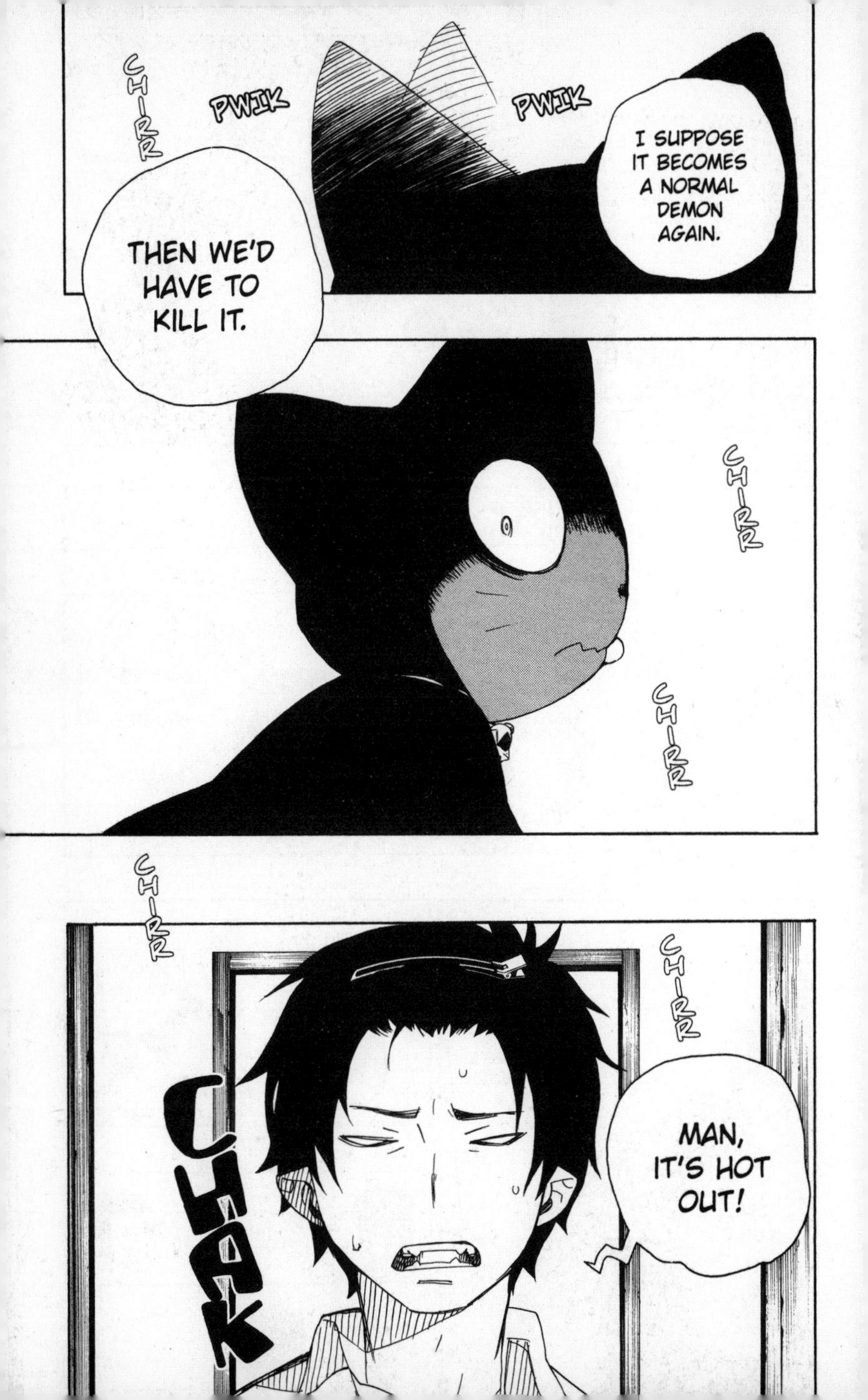
PWIK
I SUPPOSE IT BECOMES A NORMAL DEMON AGAIN.
PWIK
CHIRR
THEN WE'D HAVE TO KILL IT.
CHIRR
CHIRR
CHIRR
CHIRR
MAN, IT'S HOT OUT!
CHAK

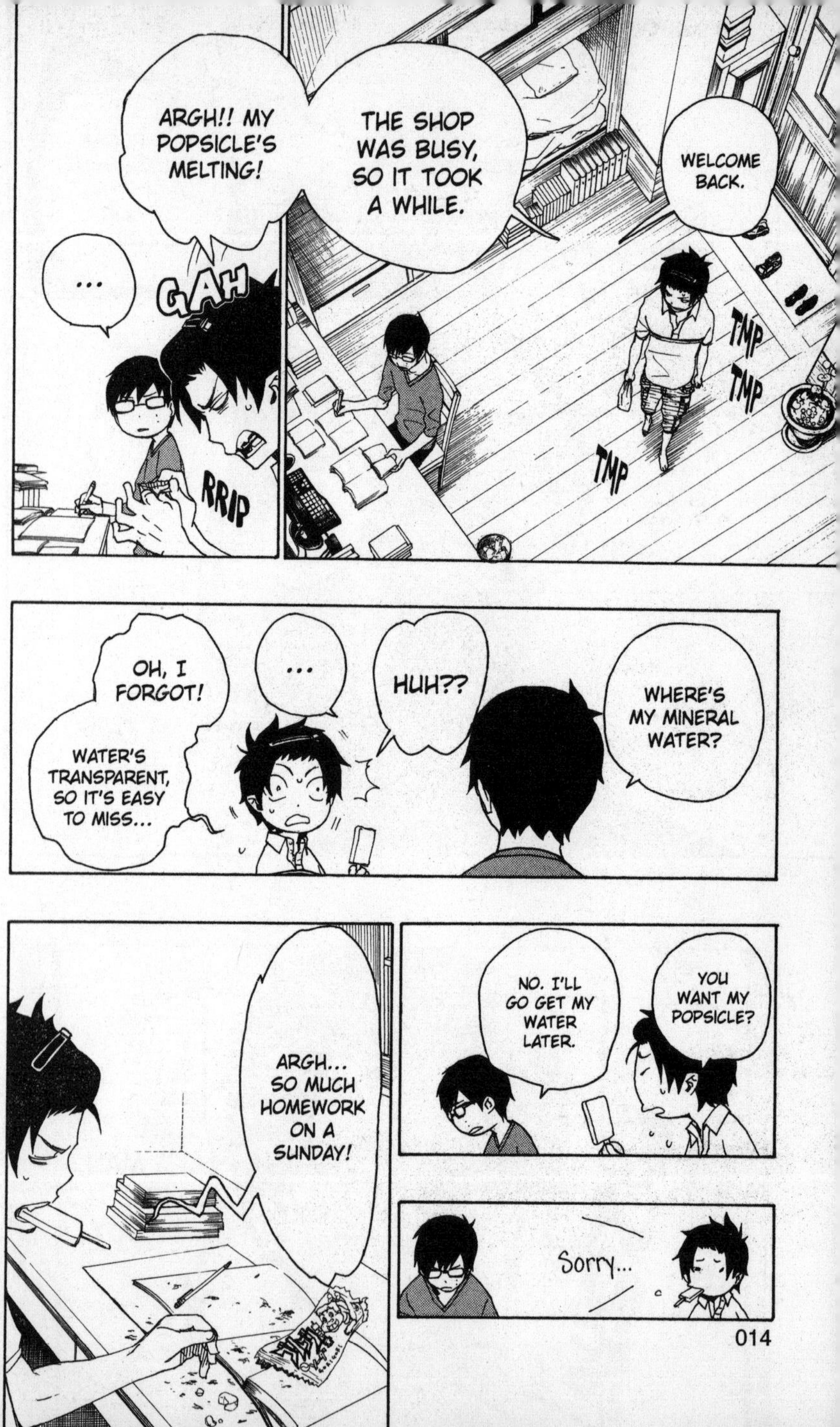
WELCOME BACK.
THE SHOP WAS BUSY, SO IT TOOK A WHILE.
TMP
TMP
TMP
ARGH!! MY POPSICLE'S MELTING!
GAH
...
RRIP
WHERE'S MY MINERAL WATER?
HUH??
...
OH, I FORGOT!
WATER'S TRANSPARENT, SO IT'S EASY TO MISS...
YOU WANT MY POPSICLE?
NO. I'LL GO GET MY WATER LATER.
Sorry...
ARGH... SO MUCH HOMEWORK ON A SUNDAY!

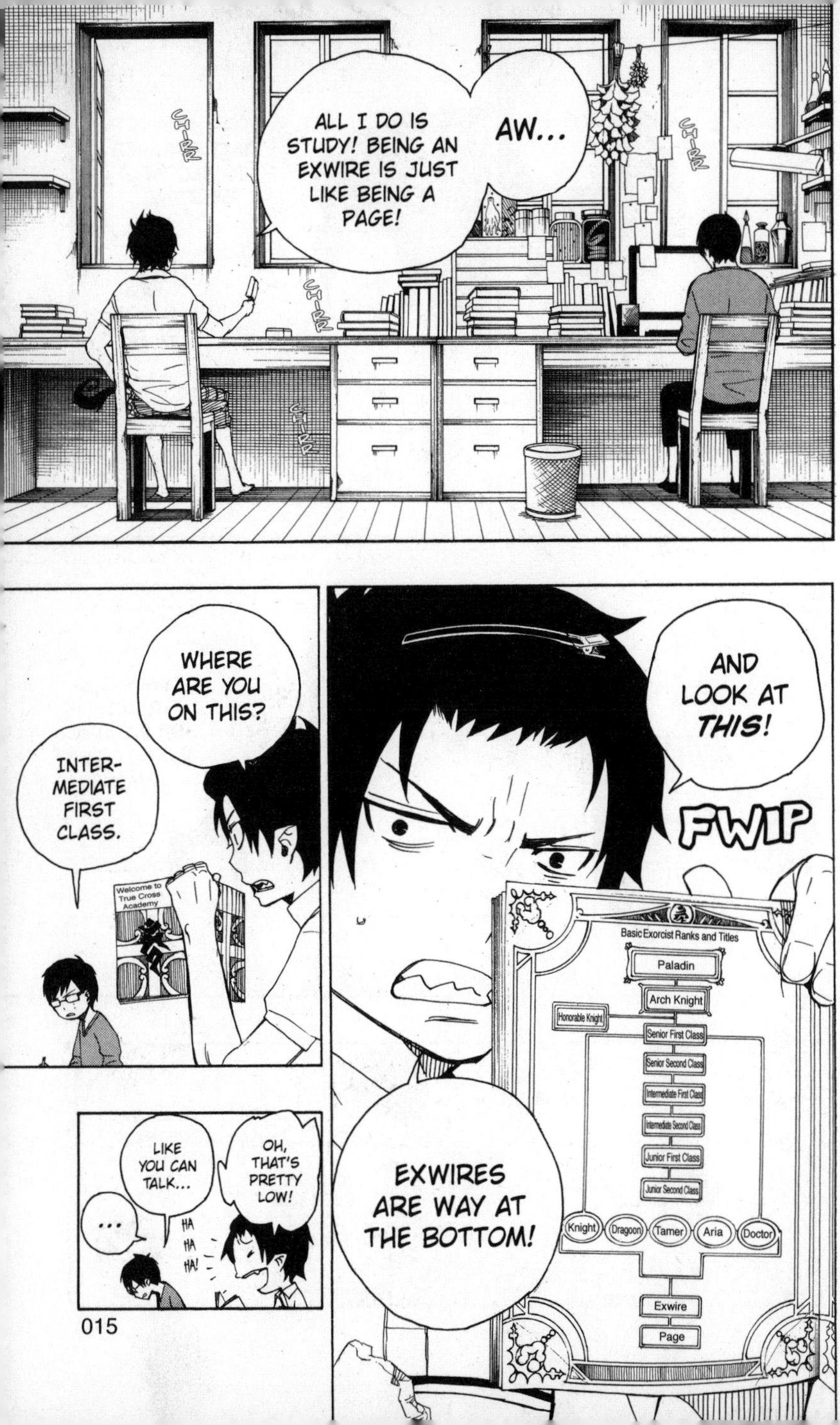
AW...
ALL I DO IS STUDY! BEING AN EXWIRE IS JUST LIKE BEING A PAGE!
CHIRP
CHIRP
CHIRP
CHIRP
AND LOOK AT THIS!
FWIP
Basic Exorcist Ranks and Titles
Paladin
Arch Knight
Honorable Knight
Senior First Class
Senior Second Class
Intermediate First Class
Intermediate Second Class
Junior First Class
Junior Second Class
Knight
Dragoon
Tamer
Aria
Doctor
Exwire
Page
EXWIRES ARE WAY AT THE BOTTOM!
WHERE ARE YOU ON THIS?
INTER-MEDIATE FIRST CLASS.
Welcome to True Cross Academy
OH, THAT'S PRETTY LOW!
LIKE YOU CAN TALK...
HA HA HA!
...

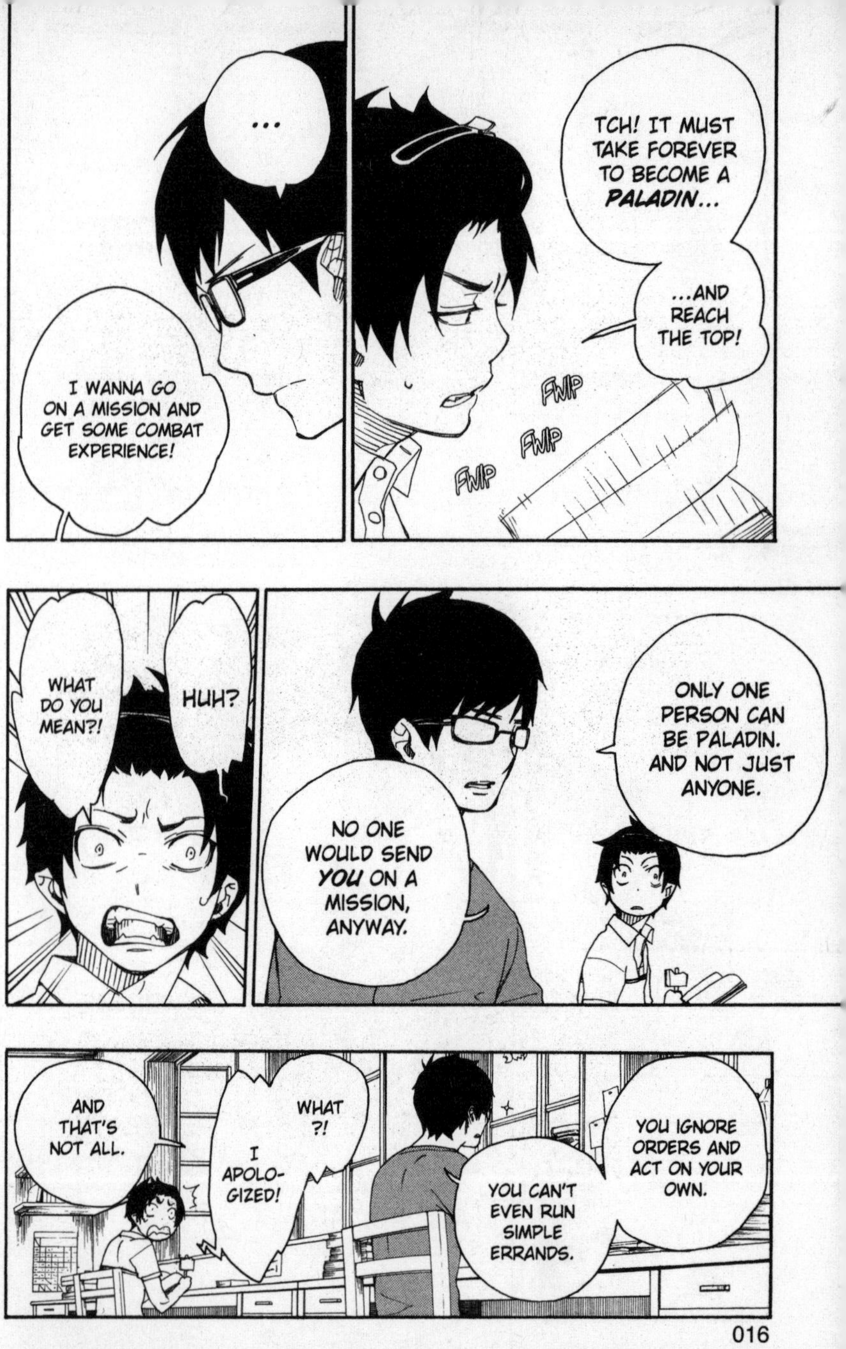
TCH! IT MUST TAKE FOREVER TO BECOME A PALADIN...
...AND REACH THE TOP!
FWIP
FWIP
FWIP
...
I WANNA GO ON A MISSION AND GET SOME COMBAT EXPERIENCE!
ONLY ONE PERSON CAN BE PALADIN. AND NOT JUST ANYONE.
NO ONE WOULD SEND YOU ON A MISSION, ANYWAY.
HUH?
WHAT DO YOU MEAN?!
YOU IGNORE ORDERS AND ACT ON YOUR OWN.
YOU CAN'T EVEN RUN SIMPLE ERRANDS.
WHAT?!
I APOLOGIZED!
AND THAT'S NOT ALL.

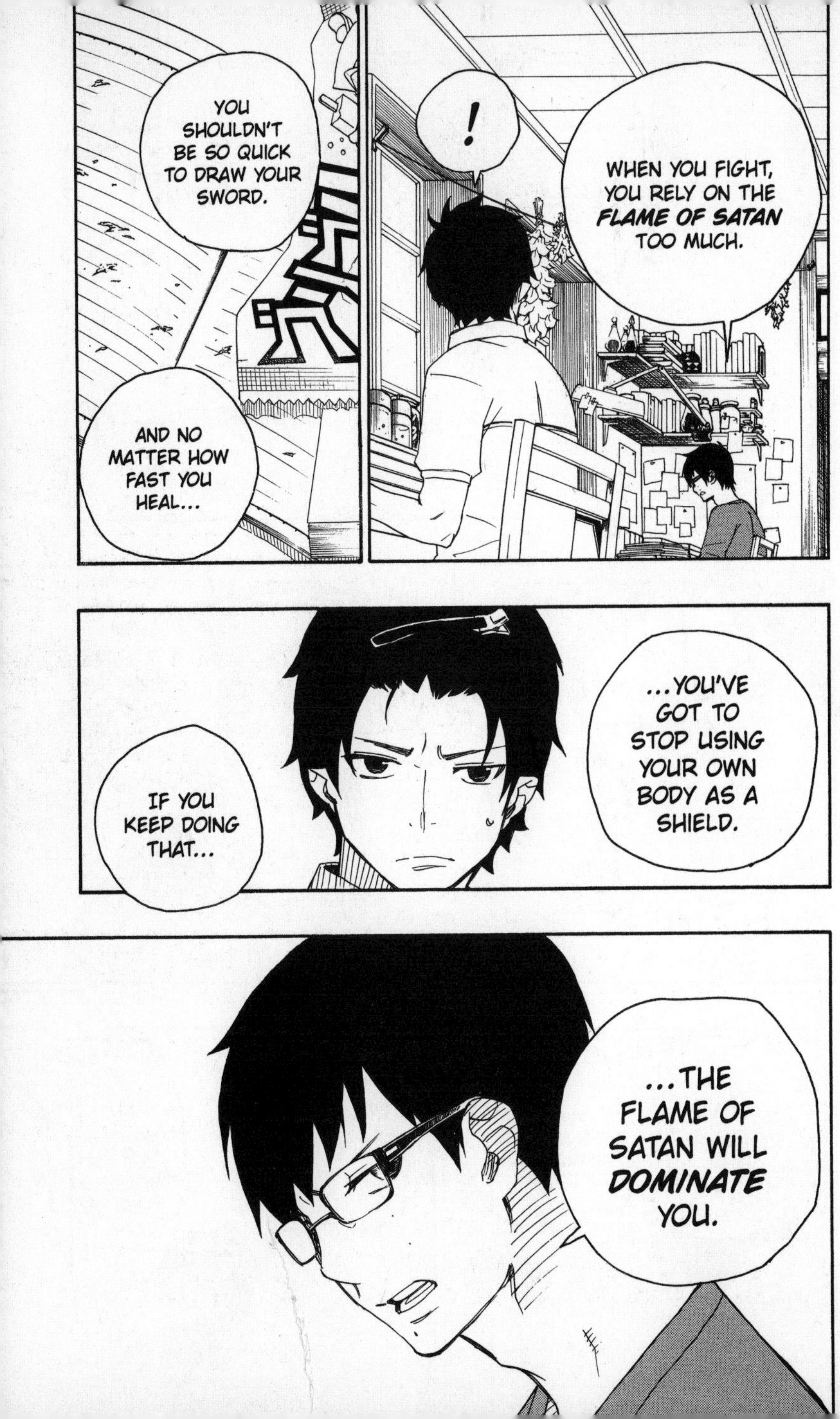
WHEN YOU FIGHT, YOU RELY ON THE *FLAME OF SATAN* TOO MUCH.
!
YOU SHOULDN'T BE SO QUICK TO DRAW YOUR SWORD.
AND NO MATTER HOW FAST YOU HEAL...
...YOU'VE GOT TO STOP USING YOUR OWN BODY AS A SHIELD.
IF YOU KEEP DOING THAT...
...THE FLAME OF SATAN WILL *DOMINATE* YOU.

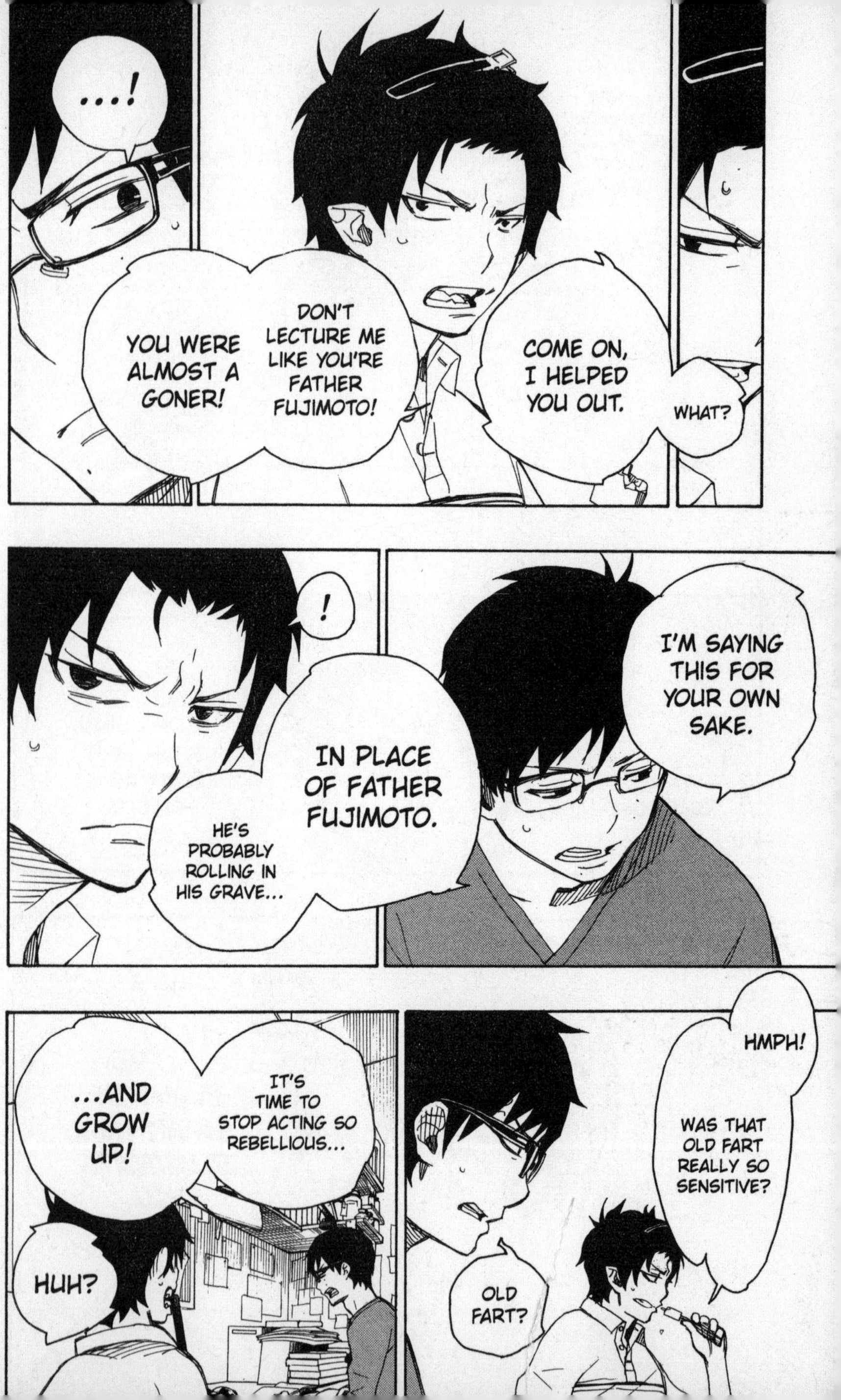
WHAT?
COME ON, I HELPED YOU OUT.
DON'T LECTURE ME LIKE YOU'RE FATHER FUJIMOTO!
YOU WERE ALMOST A GONER!
...!
I'M SAYING THIS FOR YOUR OWN SAKE.
IN PLACE OF FATHER FUJIMOTO.
!
HE'S PROBABLY ROLLING IN HIS GRAVE...
HMPH!
WAS THAT OLD FART REALLY SO SENSITIVE?
OLD FART?
IT'S TIME TO STOP ACTING SO REBELLIOUS...
...AND GROW UP!
HUH?

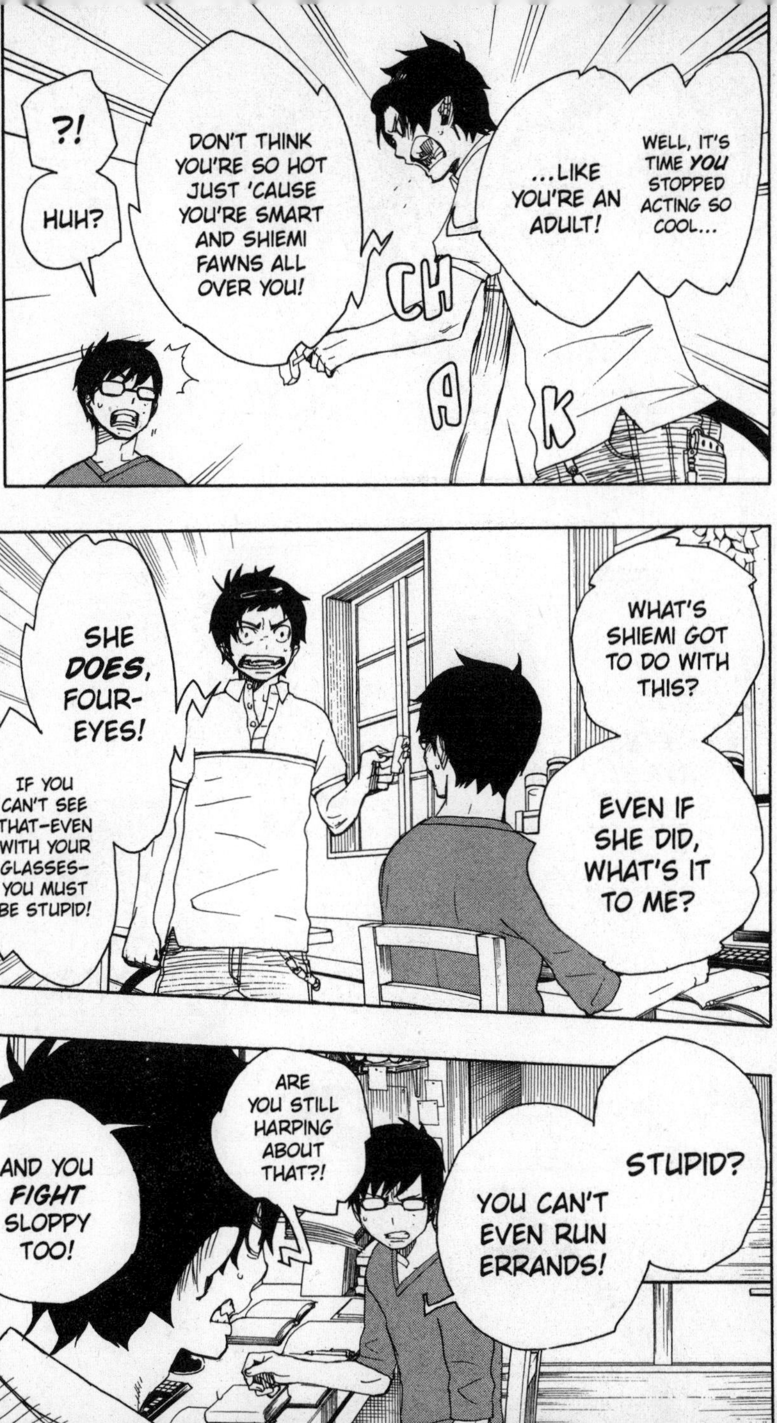
WELL, IT'S TIME *YOU* STOPPED ACTING SO COOL...
...LIKE YOU'RE AN ADULT!
CHAK
DON'T THINK YOU'RE SO HOT JUST 'CAUSE YOU'RE SMART AND SHIEMI FAWNS ALL OVER YOU!
?!
HUH?
WHAT'S SHIEMI GOT TO DO WITH THIS?
EVEN IF SHE DID, WHAT'S IT TO ME?
SHE *DOES*, FOUR-EYES!
IF YOU CAN'T SEE THAT–EVEN WITH YOUR GLASSES–YOU MUST BE STUPID!
STUPID?
YOU CAN'T EVEN RUN ERRANDS!
ARE YOU STILL HARPING ABOUT THAT?!
AND YOU *FIGHT* SLOPPY TOO!

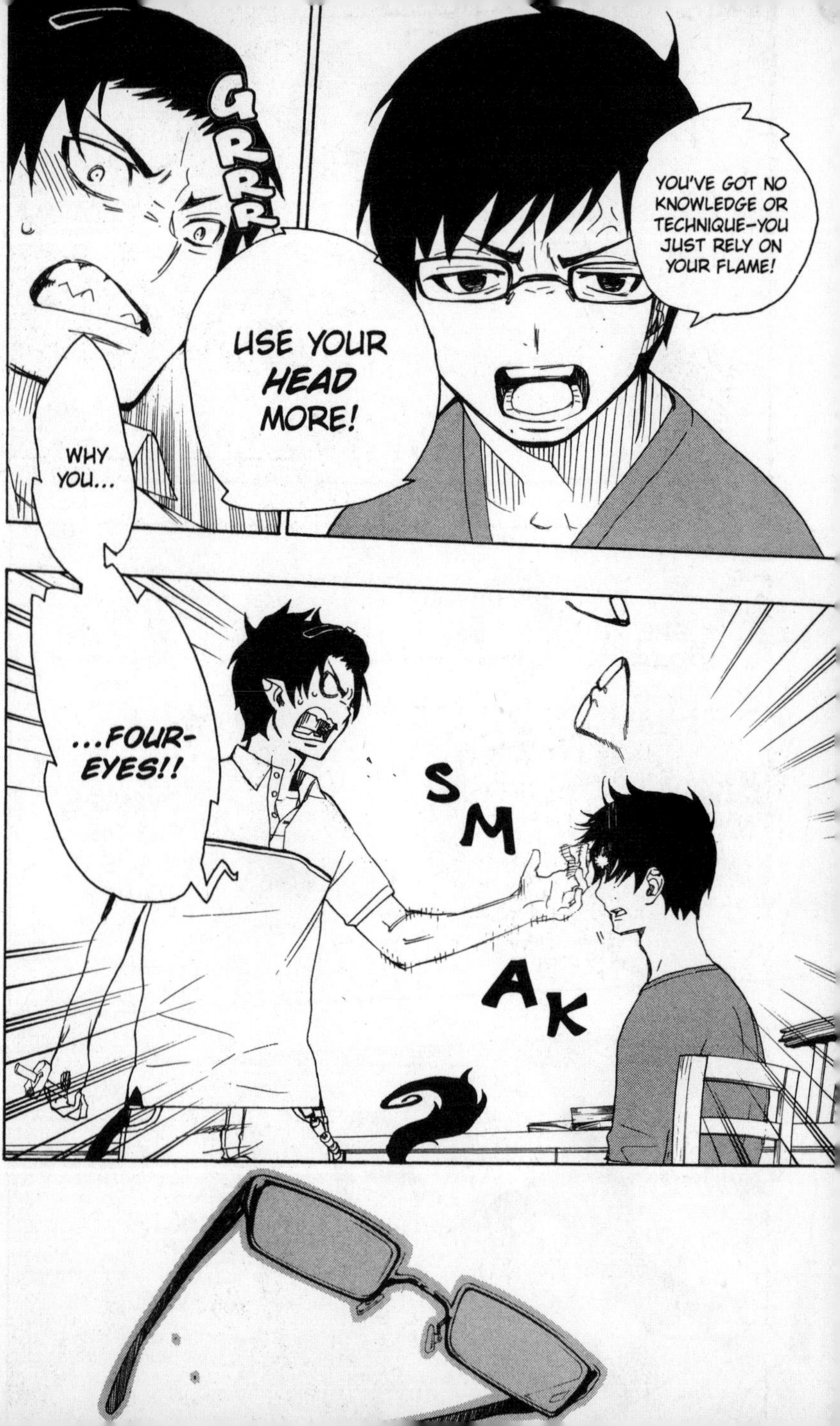
YOU'VE GOT NO KNOWLEDGE OR TECHNIQUE—YOU JUST RELY ON YOUR FLAME!
USE YOUR HEAD MORE!
GRRR
WHY YOU...
...FOUR-EYES!!
SMAK

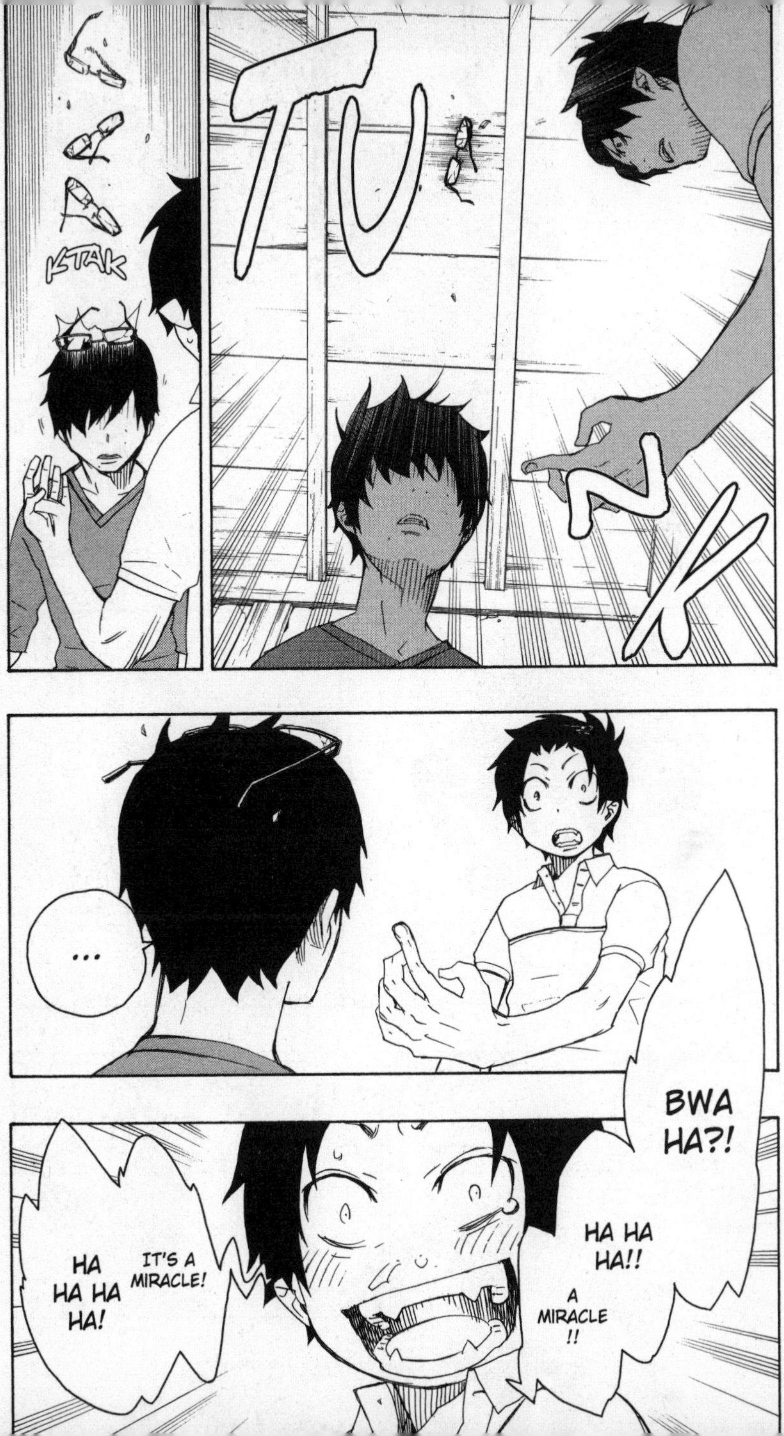
TUNK
KTAK
...
BWA HA?!
HA HA HA!!
A MIRACLE !!
IT'S A MIRACLE!
HA HA HA HA!

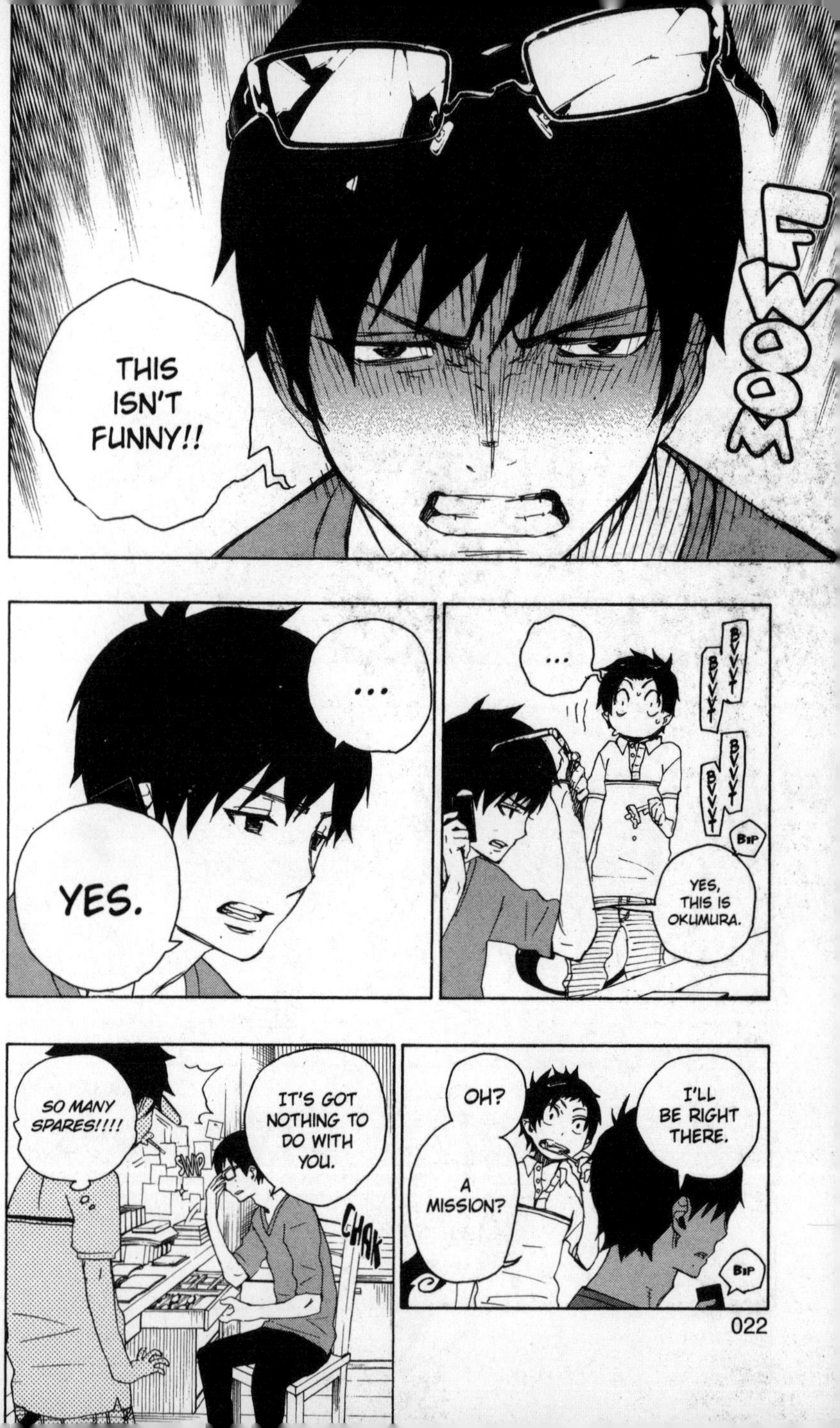
FWOOM
THIS ISN'T FUNNY!!
BVVVT BVVVT
BVVVT BVVVT
...
BIP
YES, THIS IS OKUMURA.
...
YES.
I'LL BE RIGHT THERE.
OH?
A MISSION?
BIP
CHAK
IT'S GOT NOTHING TO DO WITH YOU.
SO MANY SPARES!!!!

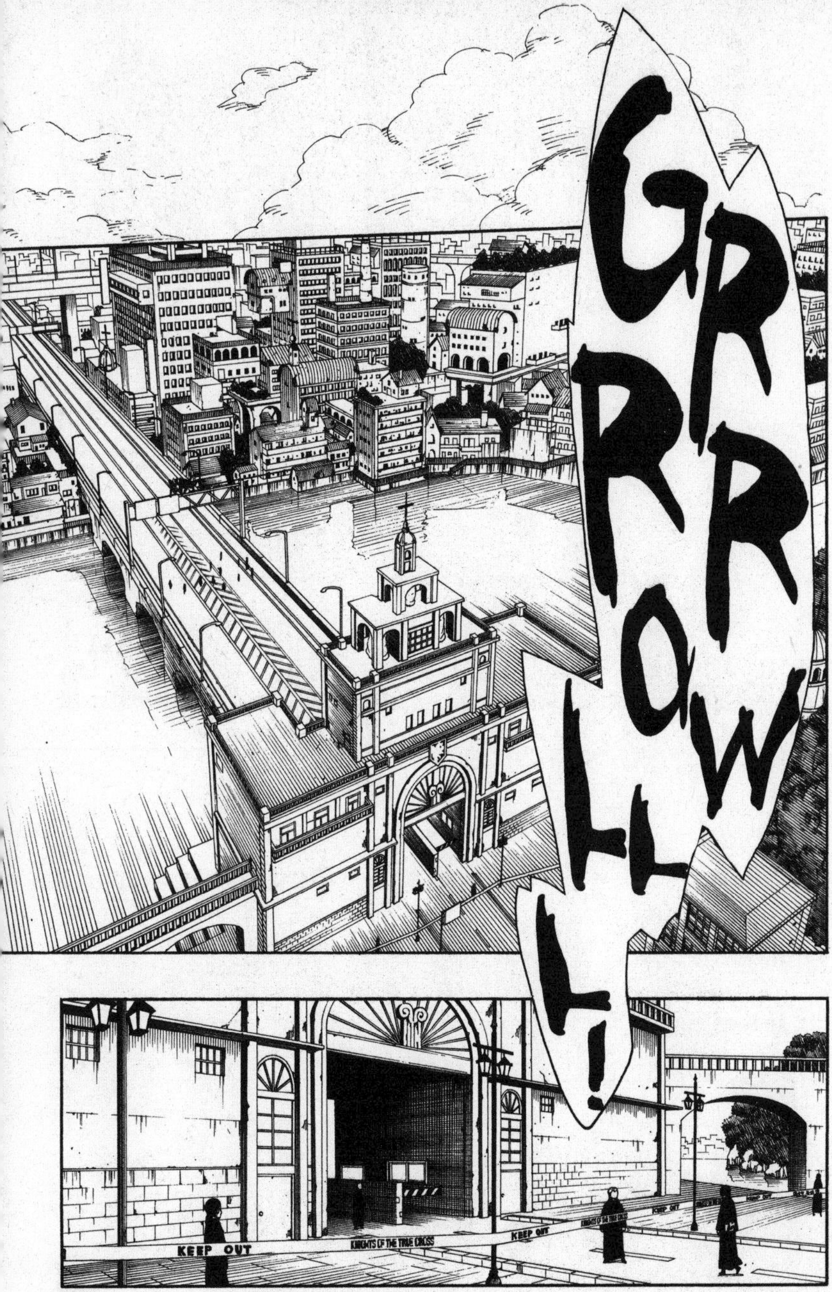
GRRRAWLLL!
KEEP OUT
KNIGHTS OF THE TRUE CROSS
KEEP OUT
KNIGHTS OF THE TRUE CROSS
KEEP OUT

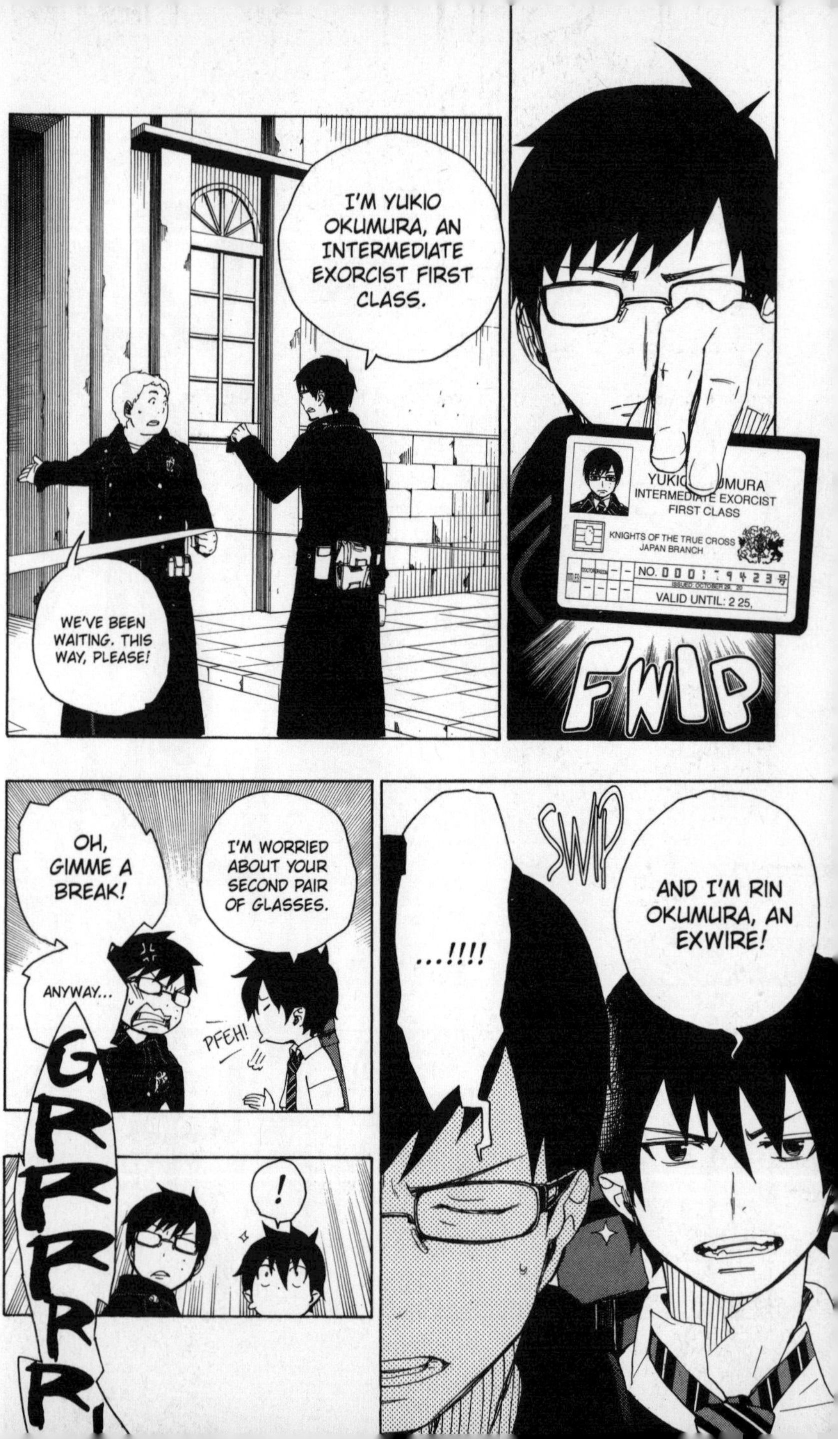
YUKIO
INTERMEDIATE EXORCIST
FIRST CLASS
KNIGHTS OF THE TRUE CROSS
JAPAN BRANCH
VALID UNTIL: 2 25,
FWIP
I'M YUKIO OKUMURA, AN INTERMEDIATE EXORCIST FIRST CLASS.
WE'VE BEEN WAITING. THIS WAY, PLEASE!
SWIP
AND I'M RIN OKUMURA, AN EXWIRE!
...!!!!
I'M WORRIED ABOUT YOUR SECOND PAIR OF GLASSES.
PFEH!
OH, GIMME A BREAK!
ANYWAY...
GRRRRRR
!

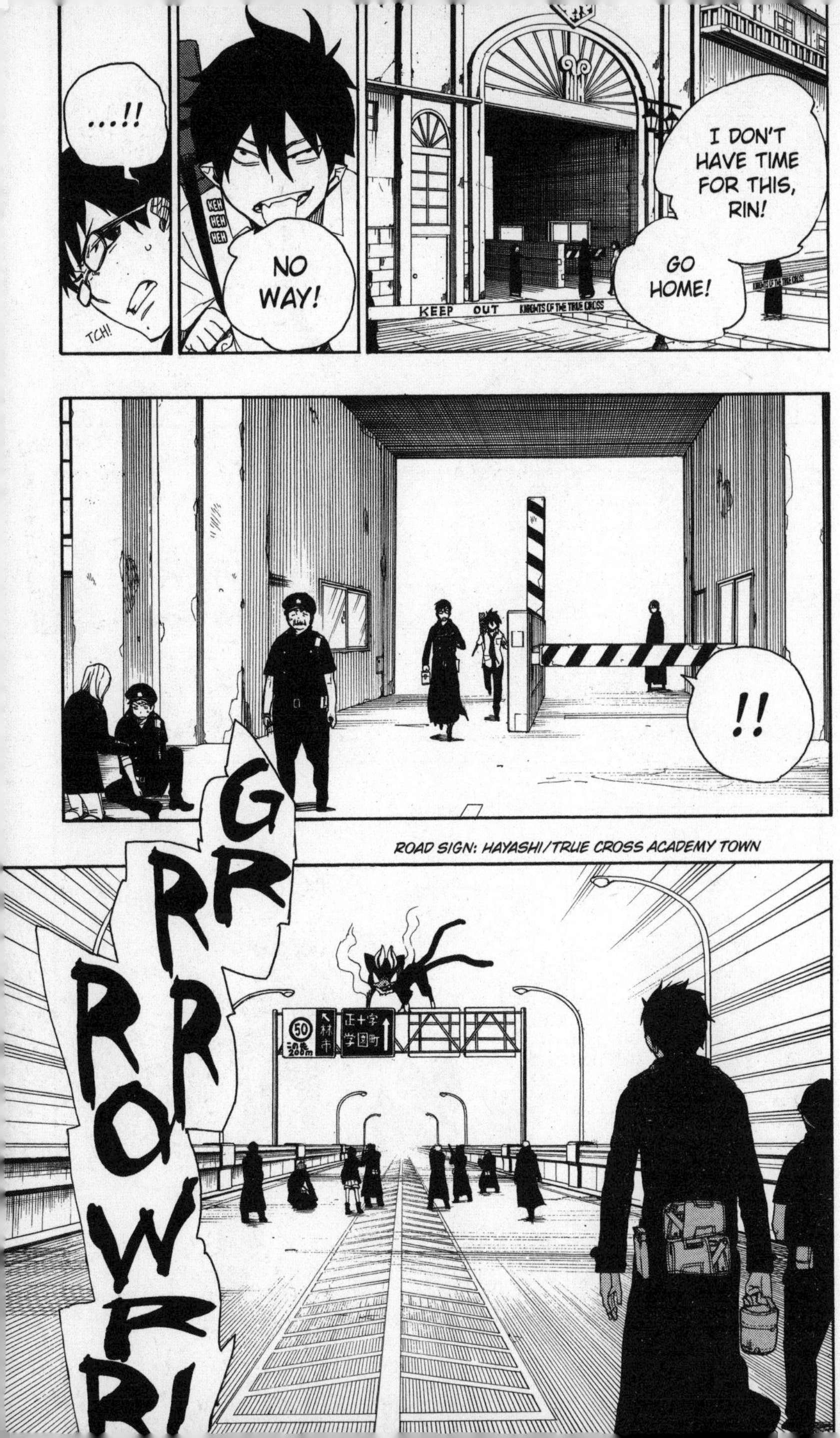

KEEP OUT
KNIGHTS OF THE TRUE CROSS
I DON'T HAVE TIME FOR THIS, RIN!
GO HOME!
KEH HEH HEH
NO WAY!
...!!
TCH!
!!
GRRRRROWRRI
ROAD SIGN: HAYASHI/TRUE CROSS ACADEMY TOWN
50
林市
正十字学園町

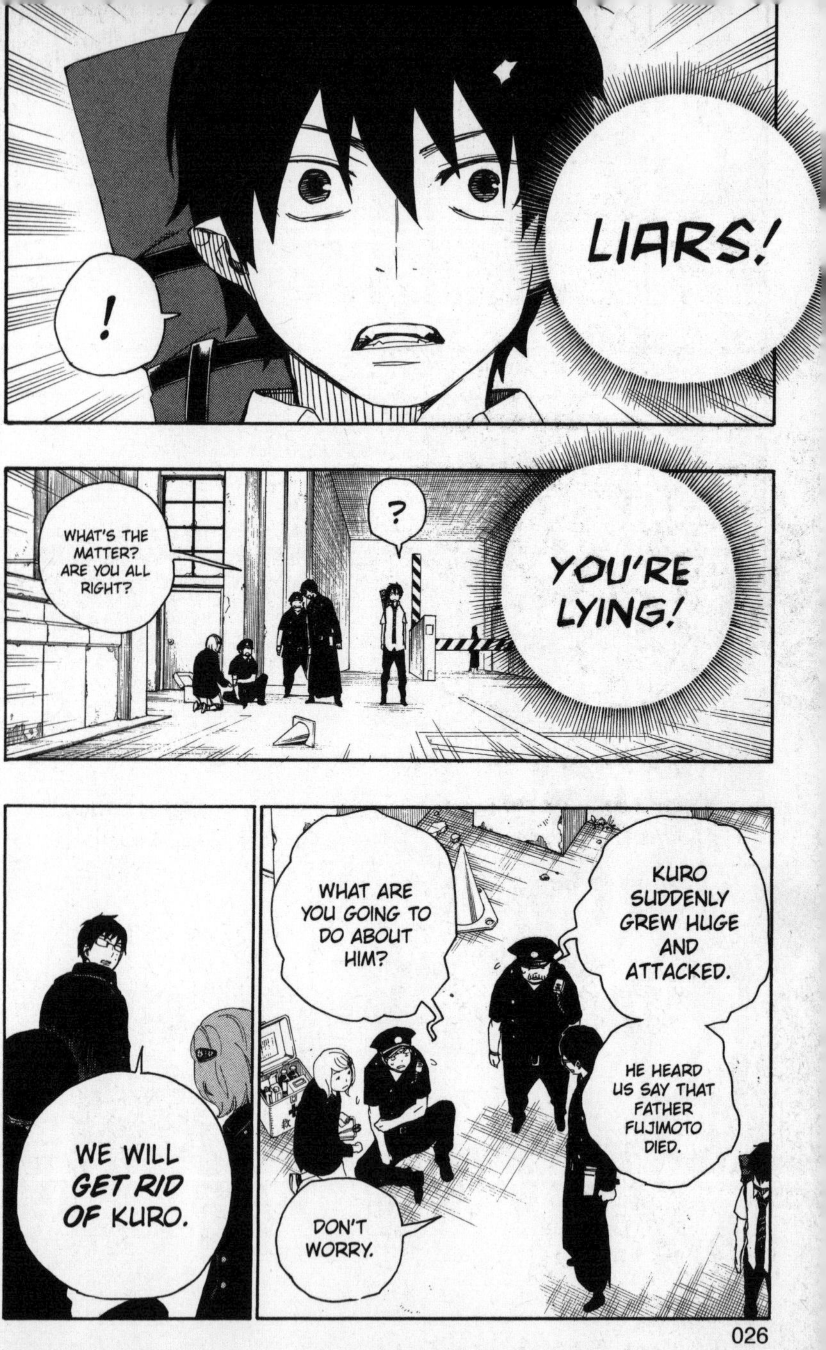

LIARS!
!
YOU'RE LYING!
?
WHAT'S THE MATTER? ARE YOU ALL RIGHT?
KURO SUDDENLY GREW HUGE AND ATTACKED.
HE HEARD US SAY THAT FATHER FUJIMOTO DIED.
WHAT ARE YOU GOING TO DO ABOUT HIM?
DON'T WORRY.
WE WILL *GET RID* OF KURO.

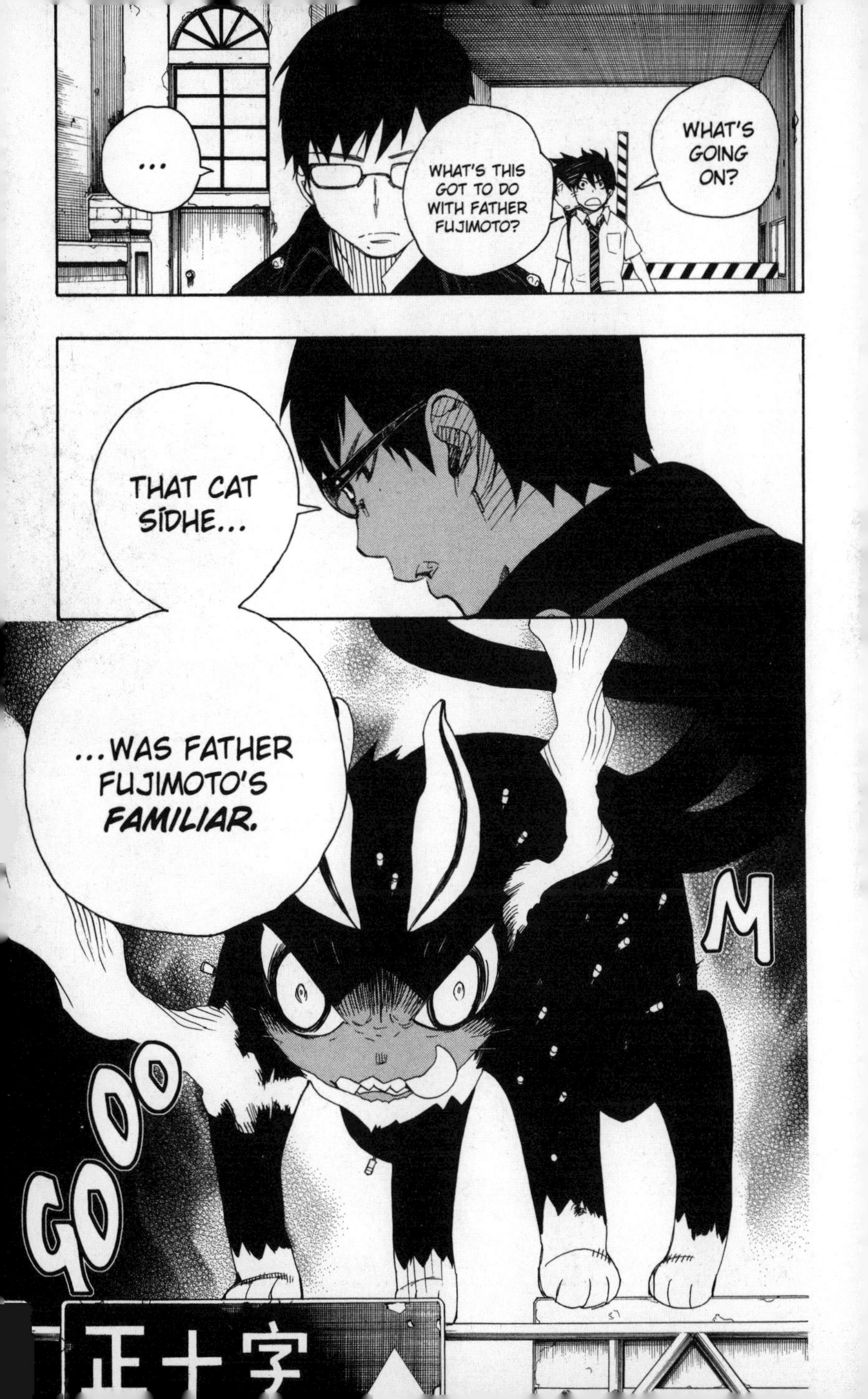
WHAT'S GOING ON?
WHAT'S THIS GOT TO DO WITH FATHER FUJIMOTO?
...
THAT CAT SIDHE...
...WAS FATHER FUJIMOTO'S *FAMILIAR.*
GOOO
M
正十字

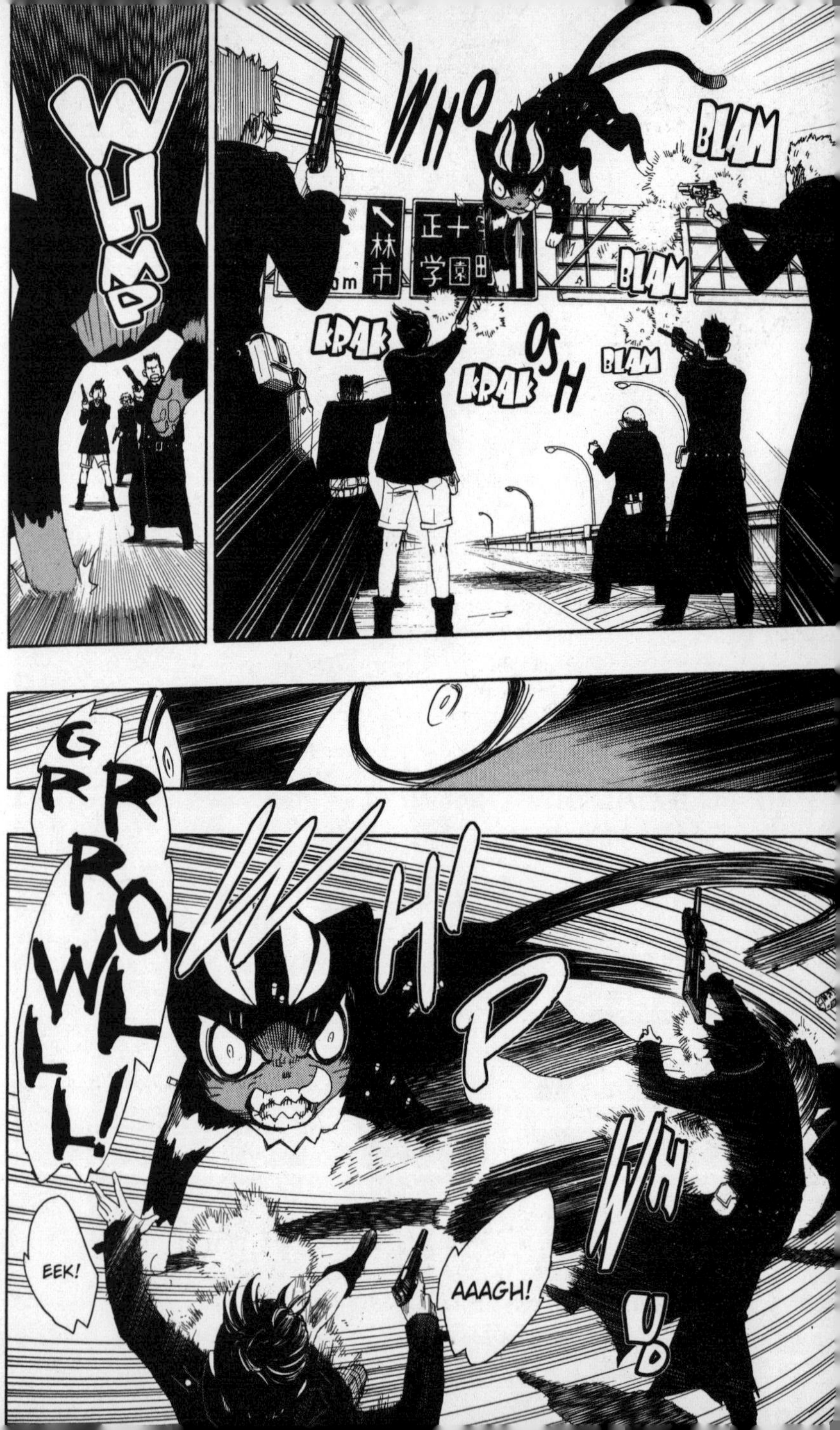

BLAM
WHO
OSH
BLAM
正十字学園町
林市
KRAK
KRAK
BLAM
WHUMP
GRROWLLL!
WHIP
WHUD
AAAGH!
EEK!

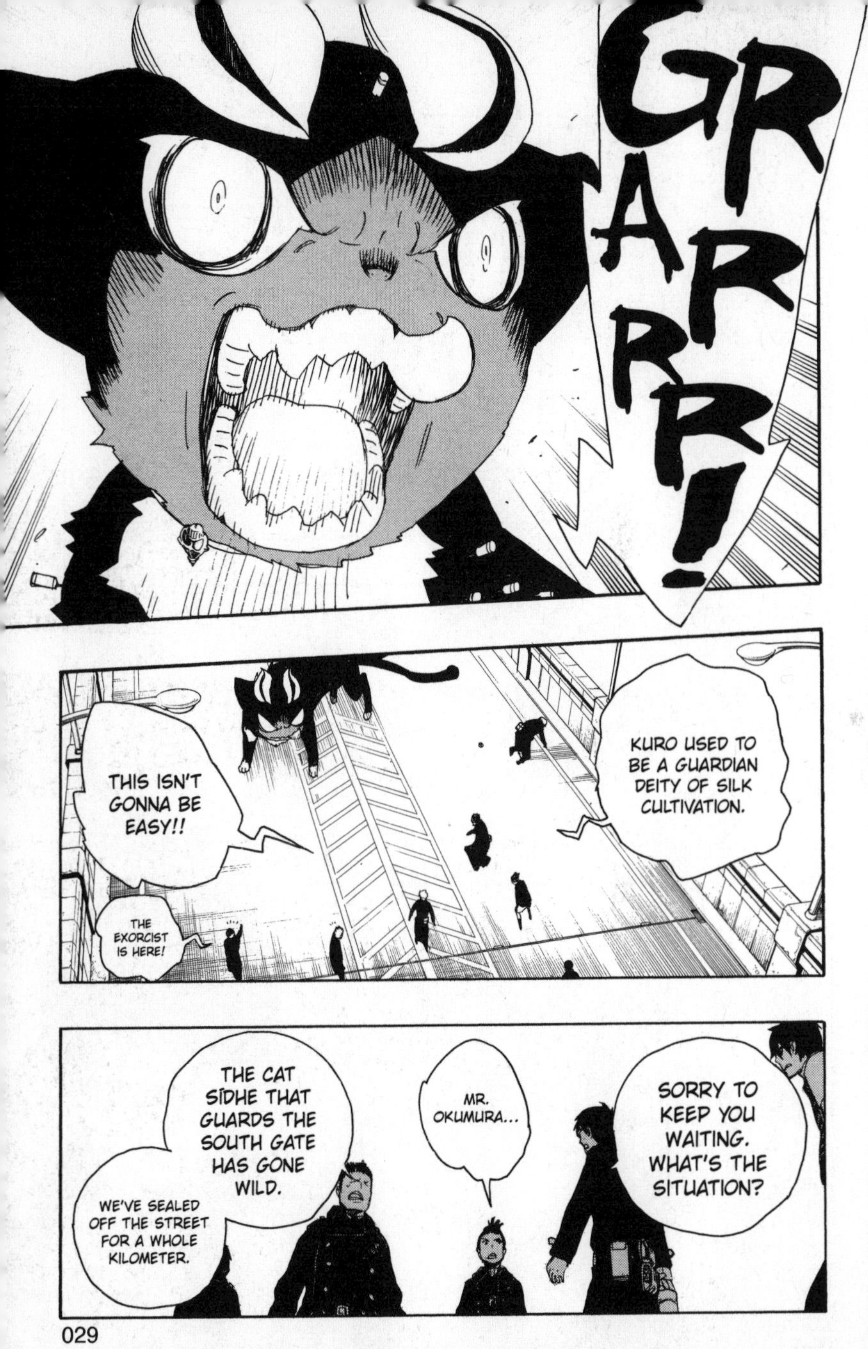
GRARRR!
KURO USED TO BE A GUARDIAN DEITY OF SILK CULTIVATION.
THIS ISN'T GONNA BE EASY!!
THE EXORCIST IS HERE!
SORRY TO KEEP YOU WAITING. WHAT'S THE SITUATION?
MR. OKUMURA...
THE CAT SÍDHE THAT GUARDS THE SOUTH GATE HAS GONE WILD.
WE'VE SEALED OFF THE STREET FOR A WHOLE KILOMETER.

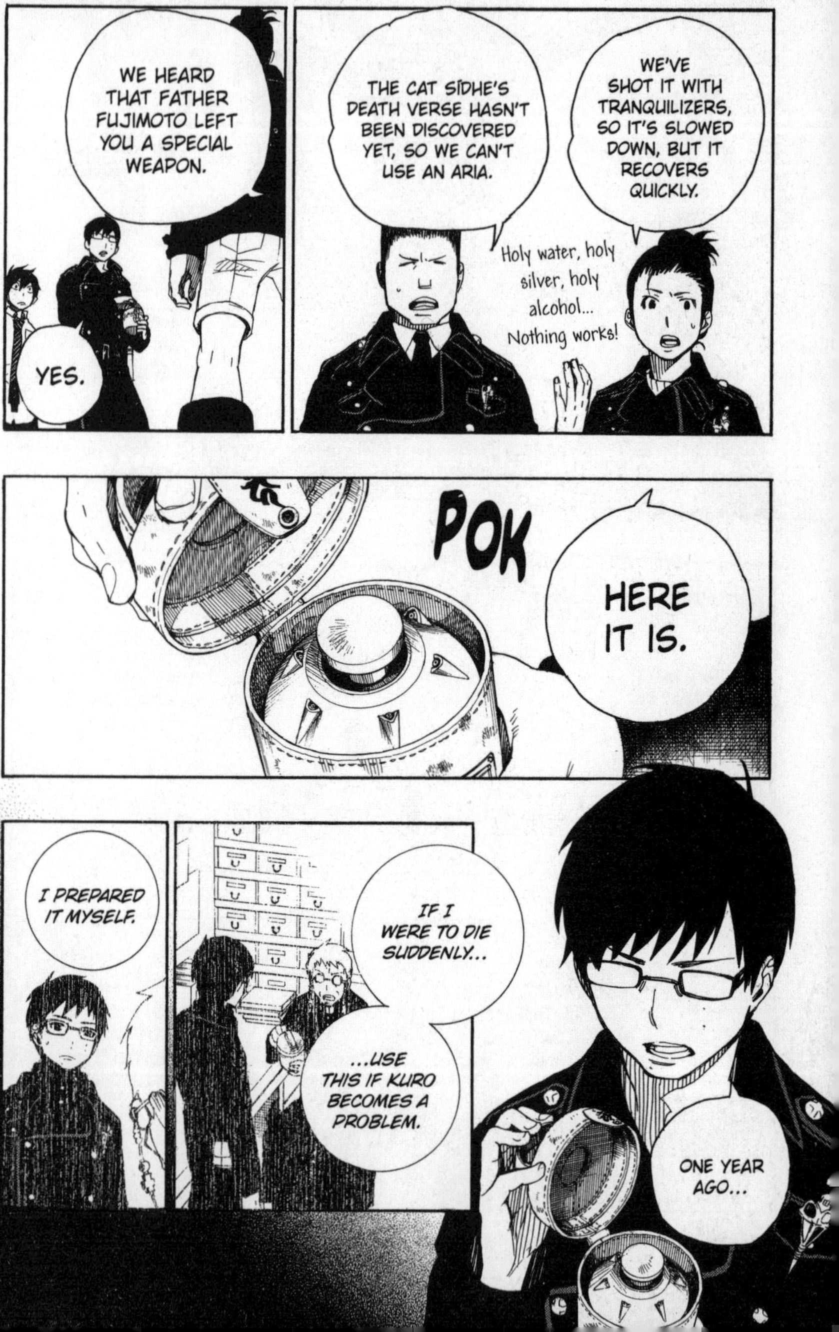

WE'VE SHOT IT WITH TRANQUILIZERS, SO IT'S SLOWED DOWN, BUT IT RECOVERS QUICKLY.
THE CAT SÍDHE'S DEATH VERSE HASN'T BEEN DISCOVERED YET, SO WE CAN'T USE AN ARIA.
Holy water, holy silver, holy alcohol... Nothing works!
WE HEARD THAT FATHER FUJIMOTO LEFT YOU A SPECIAL WEAPON.
YES.
POK
HERE IT IS.
ONE YEAR AGO...
IF I WERE TO DIE SUDDENLY...
...USE THIS IF KURO BECOMES A PROBLEM.
I PREPARED IT MYSELF.

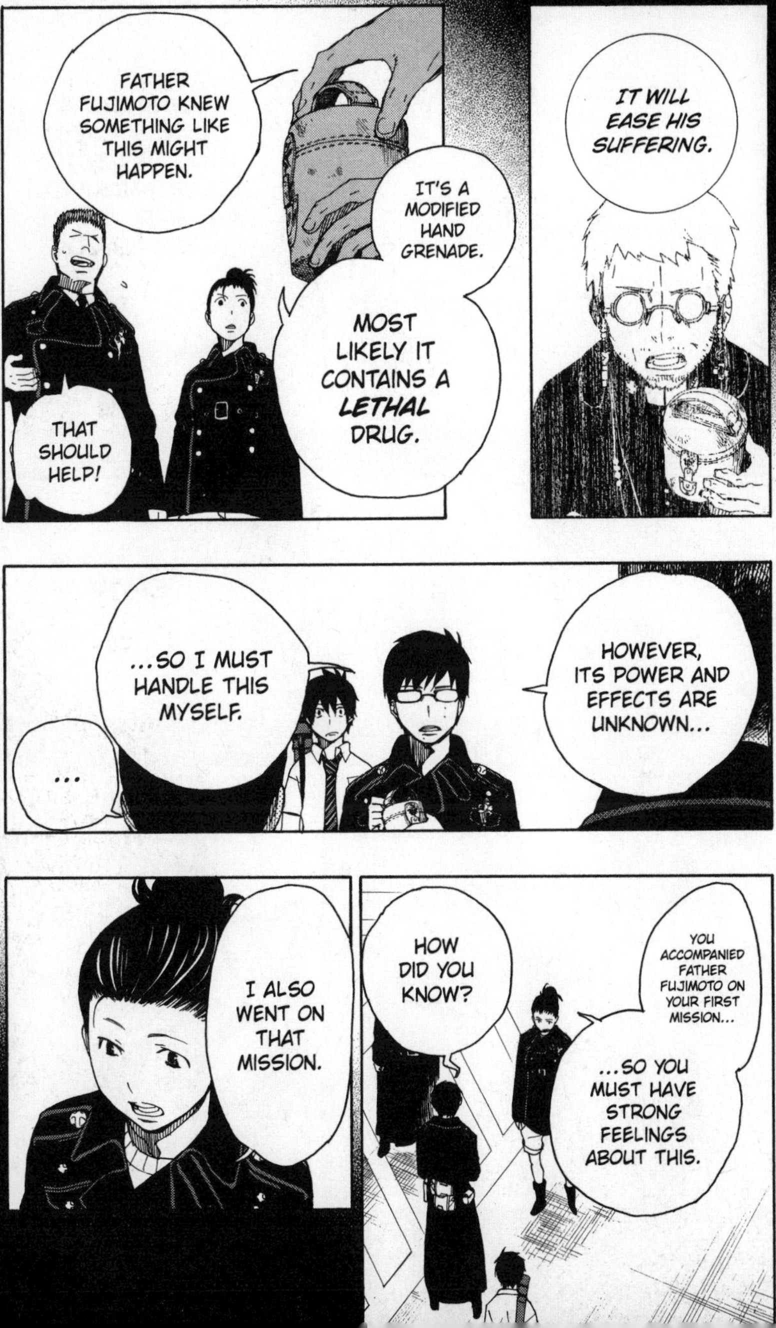
IT WILL EASE HIS SUFFERING.
FATHER FUJIMOTO KNEW SOMETHING LIKE THIS MIGHT HAPPEN.
THAT SHOULD HELP!
IT'S A MODIFIED HAND GRENADE.
MOST LIKELY IT CONTAINS A *LETHAL* DRUG.
HOWEVER, ITS POWER AND EFFECTS ARE UNKNOWN...
...SO I MUST HANDLE THIS MYSELF.
...
YOU ACCOMPANIED FATHER FUJIMOTO ON YOUR FIRST MISSION...
...SO YOU MUST HAVE STRONG FEELINGS ABOUT THIS.
HOW DID YOU KNOW?
I ALSO WENT ON THAT MISSION.

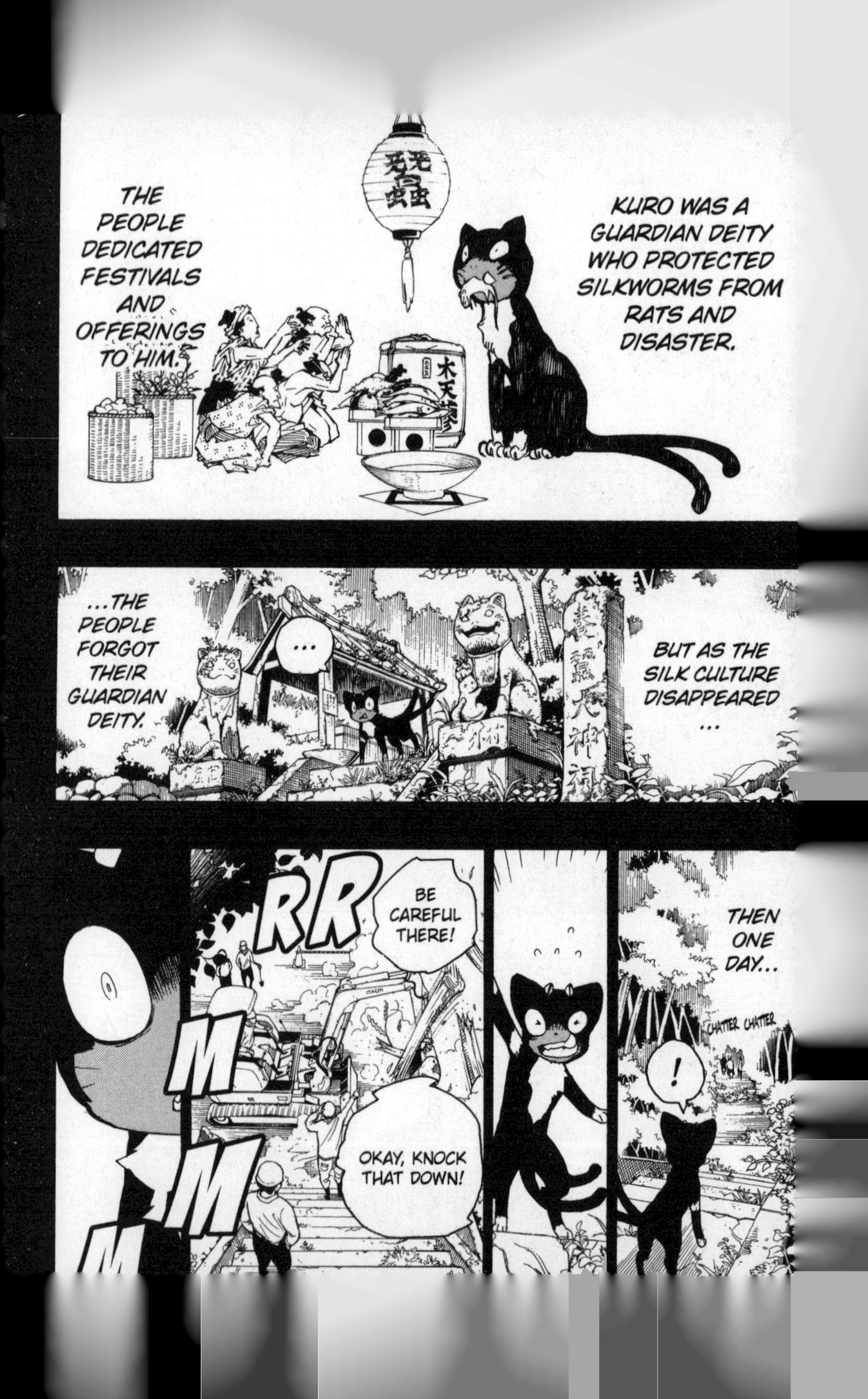
KURO WAS A GUARDIAN DEITY WHO PROTECTED SILKWORMS FROM RATS AND DISASTER.
THE PEOPLE DEDICATED FESTIVALS AND OFFERINGS TO HIM.
BUT AS THE SILK CULTURE DISAPPEARED ...
...
...THE PEOPLE FORGOT THEIR GUARDIAN DEITY.
THEN ONE DAY...
CHATTER CHATTER
!
BE CAREFUL THERE!
RR
ITACHI
OKAY, KNOCK THAT DOWN!
MMM

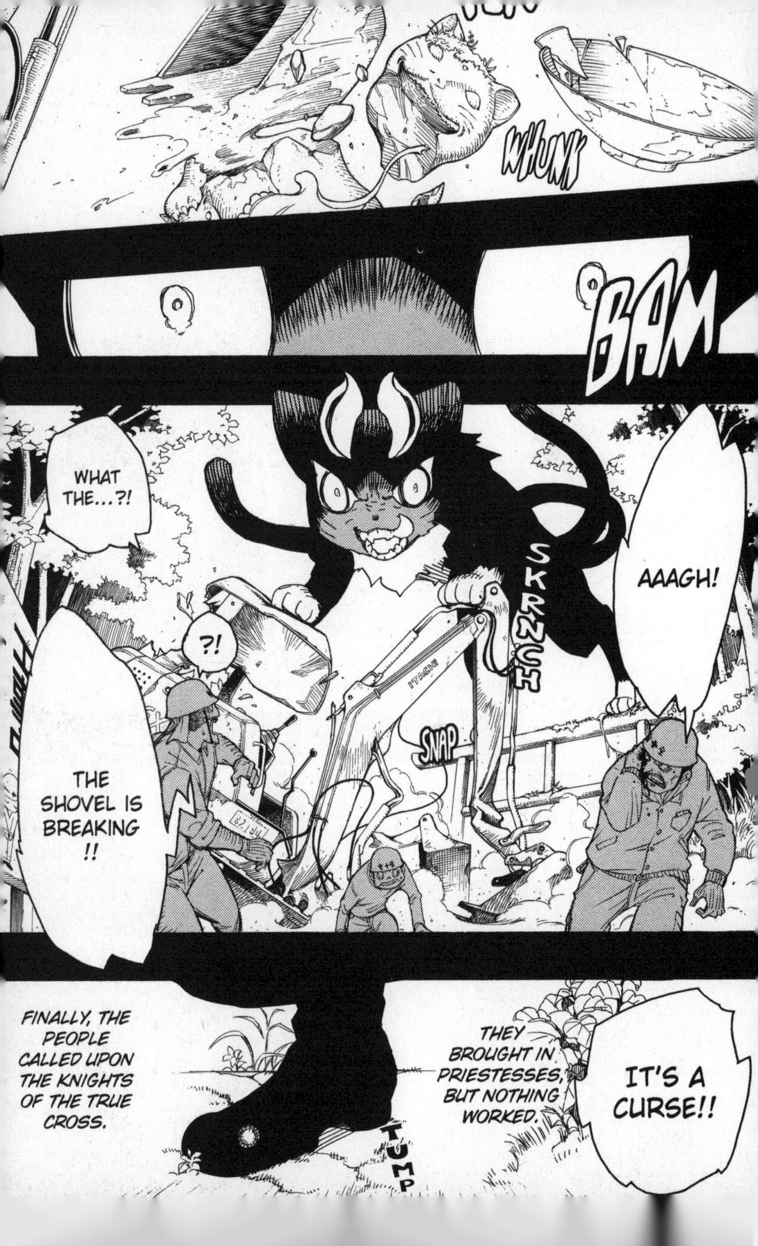
WHUNK
BAM
AAAGH!
SKRNCH
SNAP
?!
WHAT THE...?!
THE SHOVEL IS BREAKING!!
IT'S A CURSE!!
THEY BROUGHT IN PRIESTESSES, BUT NOTHING WORKED.
TUMP
FINALLY, THE PEOPLE CALLED UPON THE KNIGHTS OF THE TRUE CROSS.

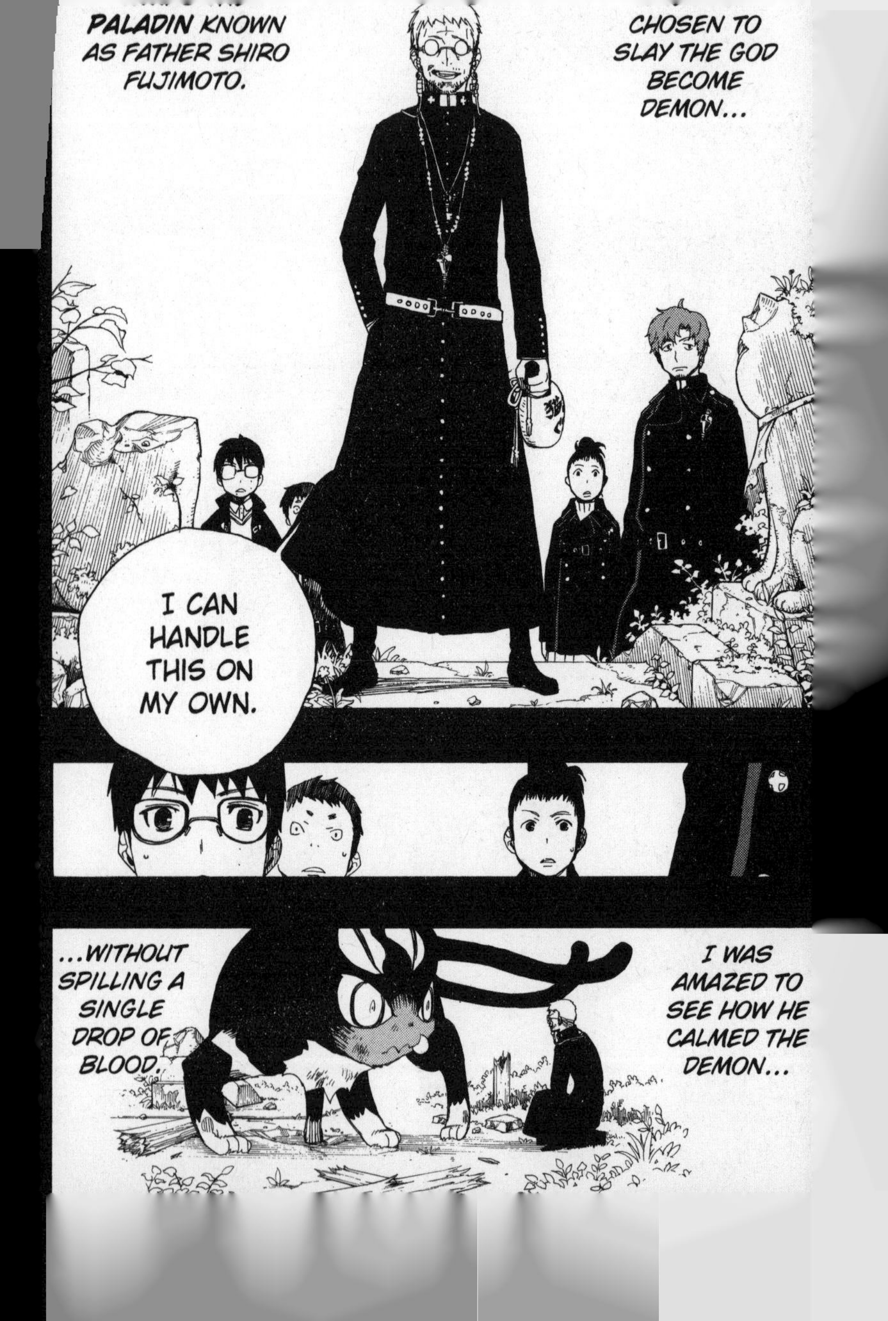
CHOSEN TO SLAY THE GOD BECOME DEMON...
PALADIN KNOWN AS FATHER SHIRO FUJIMOTO.
I CAN HANDLE THIS ON MY OWN.
I WAS AMAZED TO SEE HOW HE CALMED THE DEMON...
...WITHOUT SPILLING A SINGLE DROP OF BLOOD.

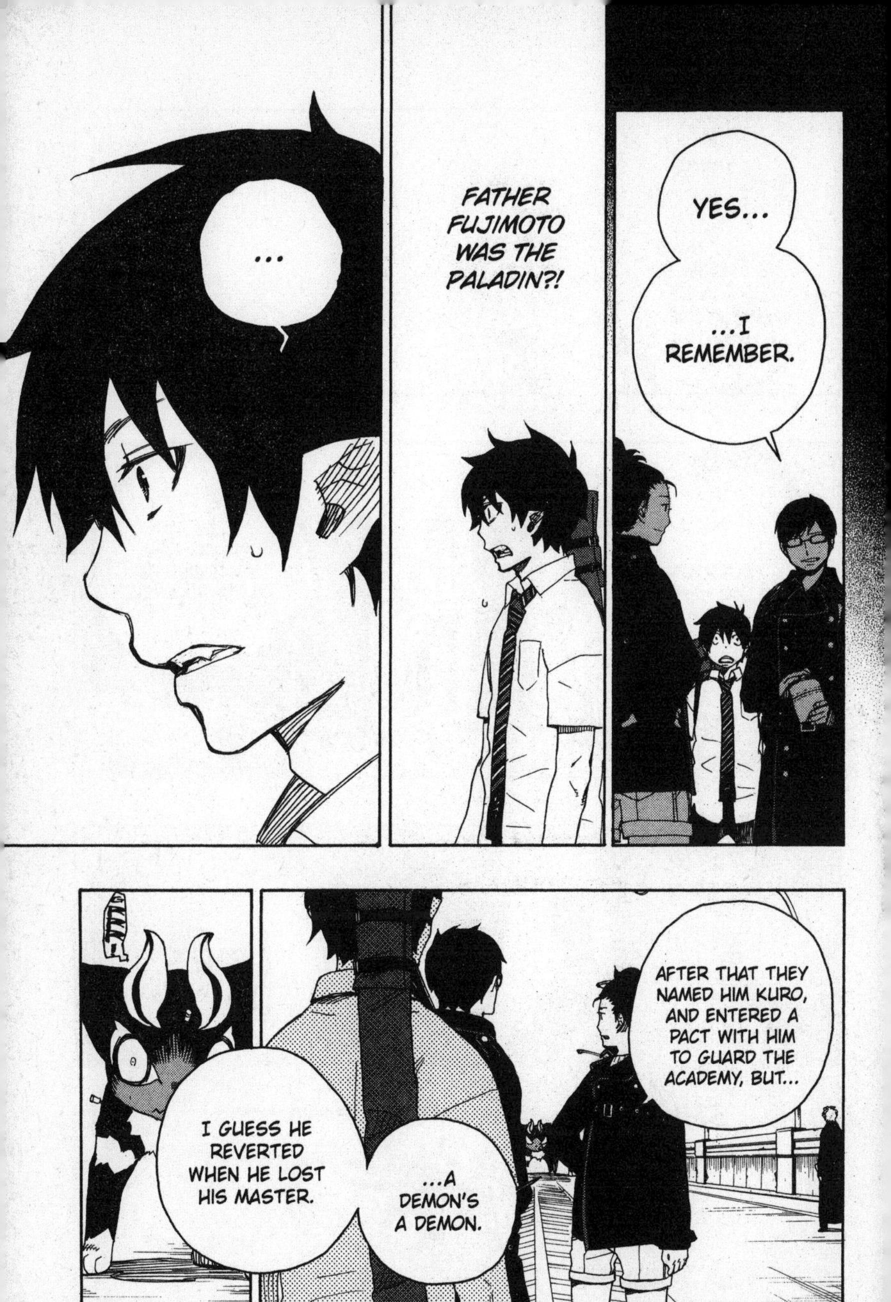
YES...
...I REMEMBER.
FATHER FUJIMOTO WAS THE PALADIN?!
...
AFTER THAT THEY NAMED HIM KURO, AND ENTERED A PACT WITH HIM TO GUARD THE ACADEMY, BUT...
I GUESS HE REVERTED WHEN HE LOST HIS MASTER.
...A DEMON'S A DEMON.

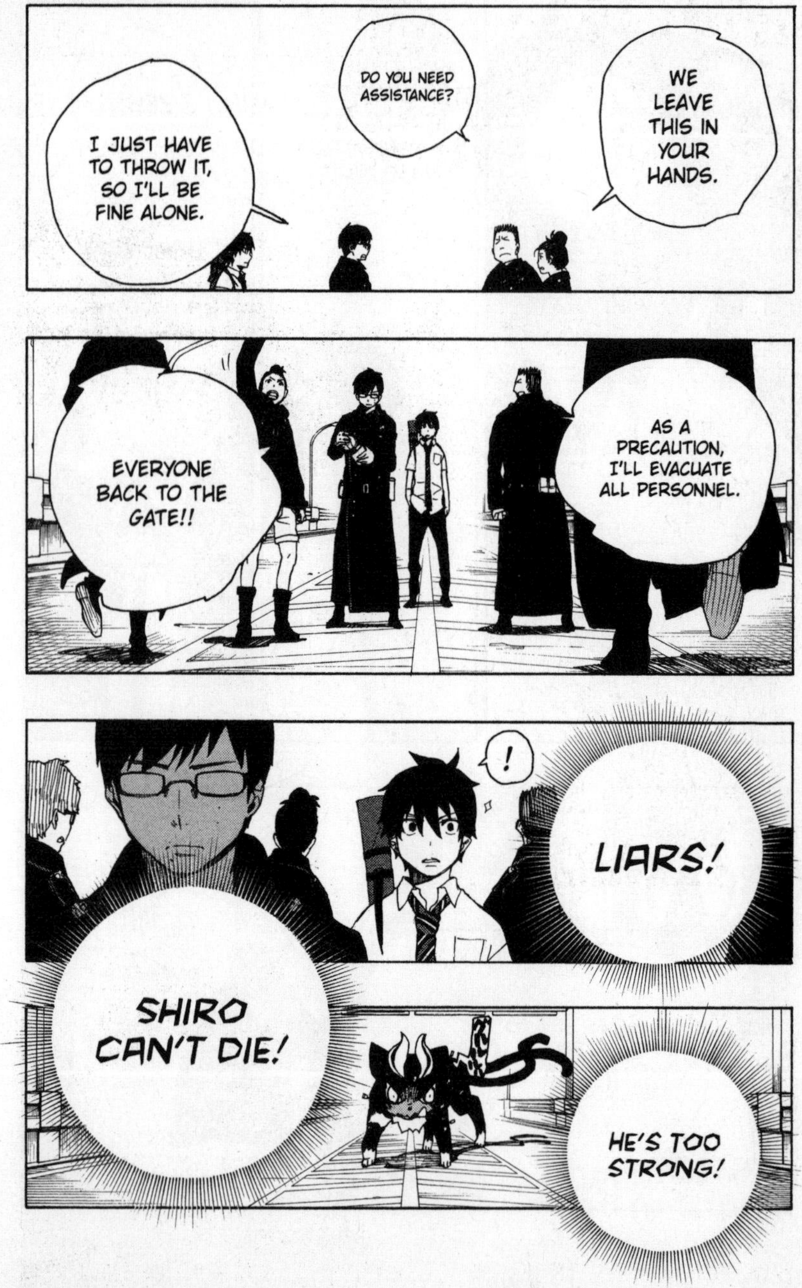
WE LEAVE THIS IN YOUR HANDS.
DO YOU NEED ASSISTANCE?
I JUST HAVE TO THROW IT, SO I'LL BE FINE ALONE.
AS A PRECAUTION, I'LL EVACUATE ALL PERSONNEL.
EVERYONE BACK TO THE GATE!!
!
LIARS!
SHIRO CAN'T DIE!
HE'S TOO STRONG!

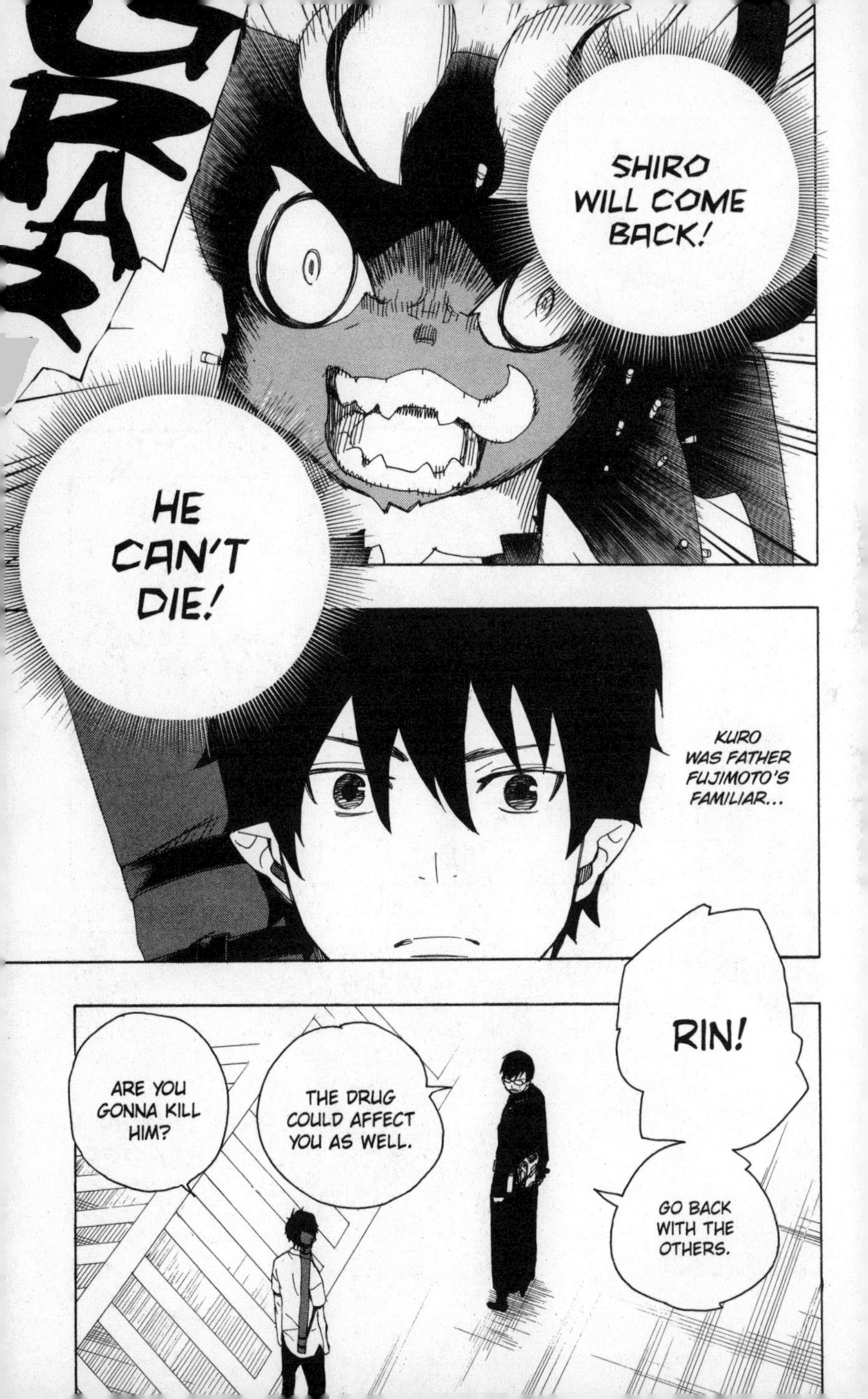
SHIRO WILL COME BACK!
HE CAN'T DIE!
KURO WAS FATHER FUJIMOTO'S FAMILIAR...
RIN!
GO BACK WITH THE OTHERS.
THE DRUG COULD AFFECT YOU AS WELL.
ARE YOU GONNA KILL HIM?

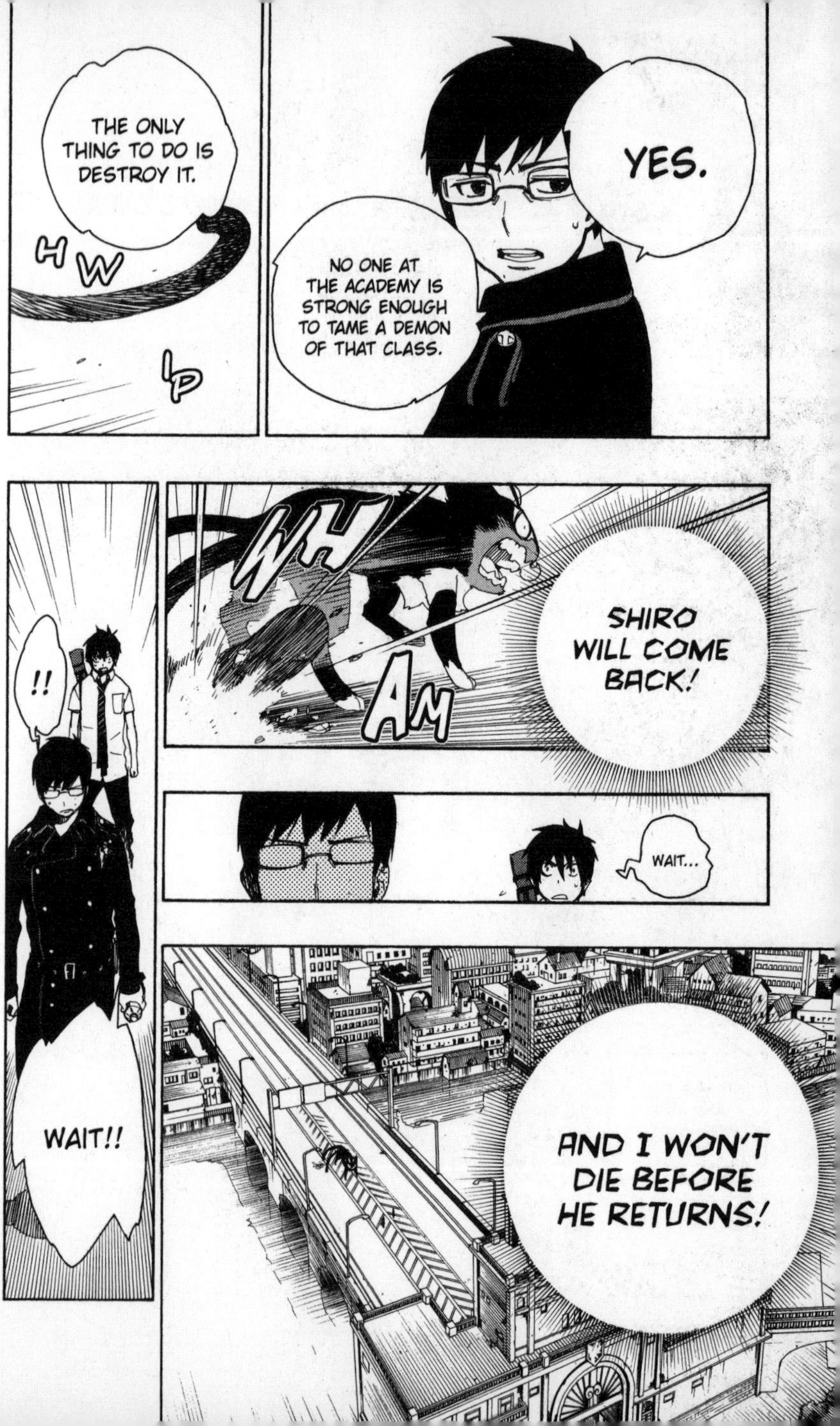
YES.
NO ONE AT THE ACADEMY IS STRONG ENOUGH TO TAME A DEMON OF THAT CLASS.
THE ONLY THING TO DO IS DESTROY IT.
HW
IP
WH
AM
SHIRO WILL COME BACK!
WAIT...
AND I WON'T DIE BEFORE HE RETURNS!
!!
WAIT!!

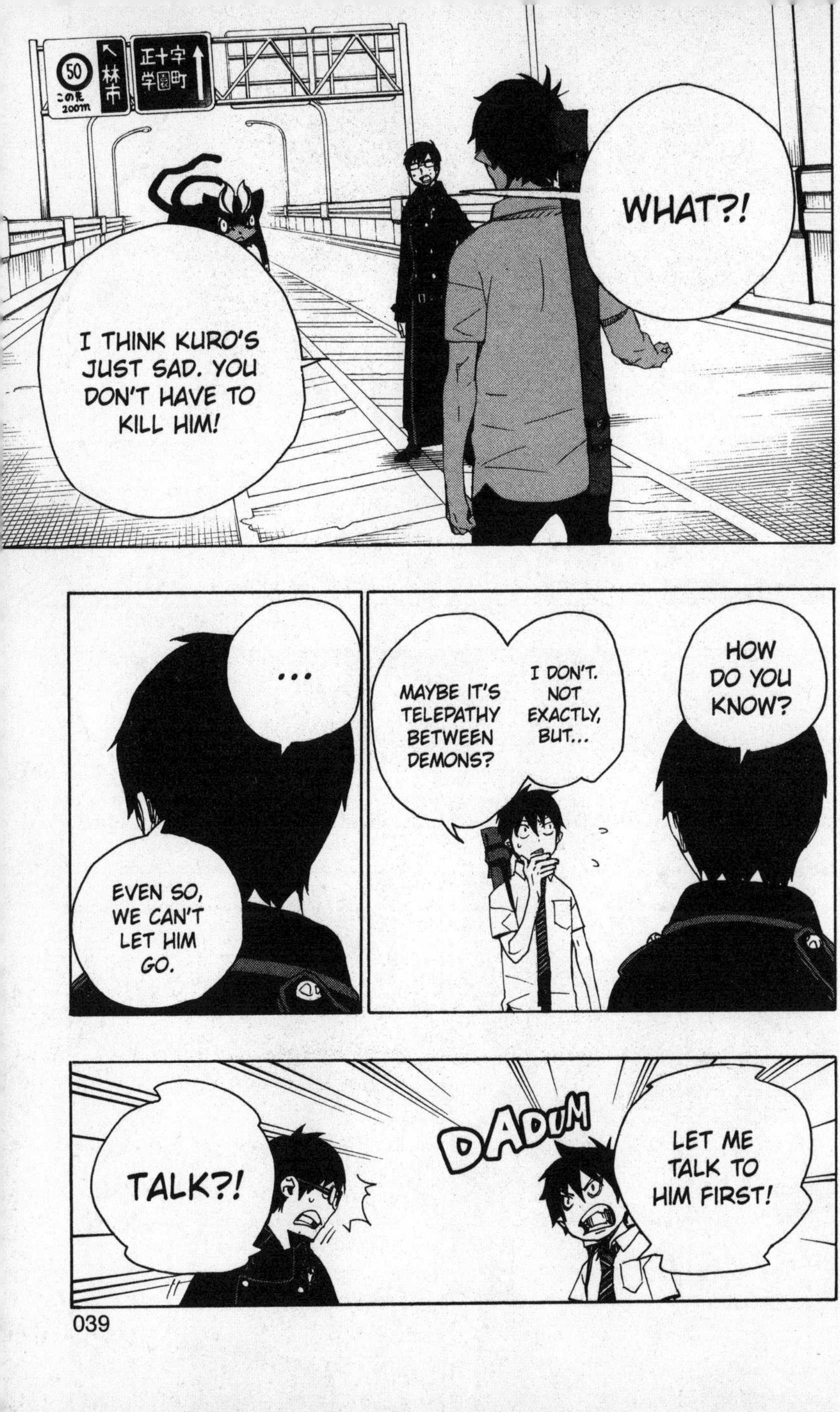
50
この先 200m
林市
正十字学園町
WHAT?!
I THINK KURO'S JUST SAD. YOU DON'T HAVE TO KILL HIM!
HOW DO YOU KNOW?
I DON'T. NOT EXACTLY, BUT...
MAYBE IT'S TELEPATHY BETWEEN DEMONS?
...
EVEN SO, WE CAN'T LET HIM GO.
LET ME TALK TO HIM FIRST!
DADUM
TALK?!

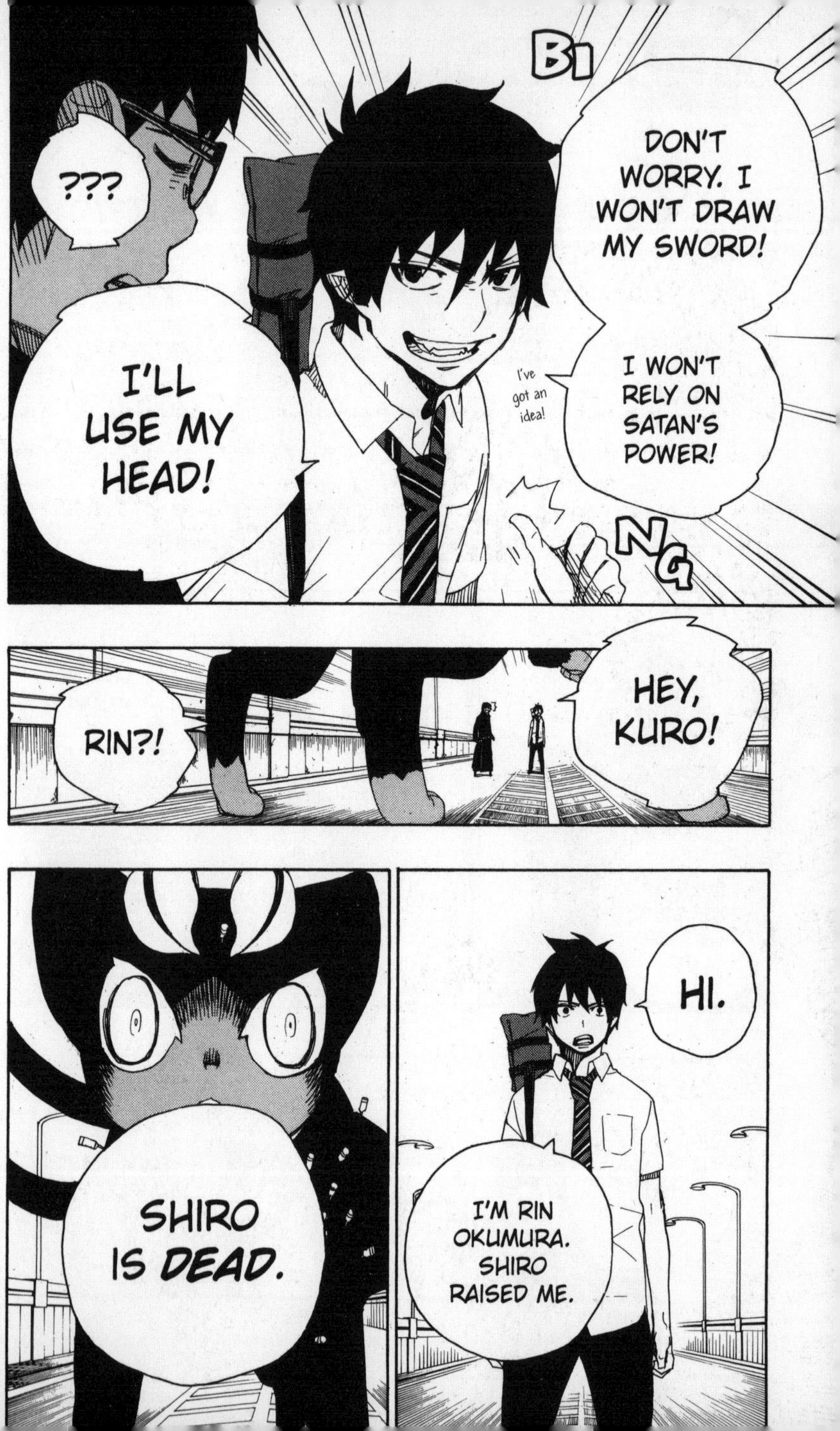
BI
DON'T WORRY. I WON'T DRAW MY SWORD!
I WON'T RELY ON SATAN'S POWER!
I've got an idea!
NG
???
I'LL USE MY HEAD!
HEY, KURO!
RIN?!
HI.
I'M RIN OKUMURA. SHIRO RAISED ME.
SHIRO IS DEAD.

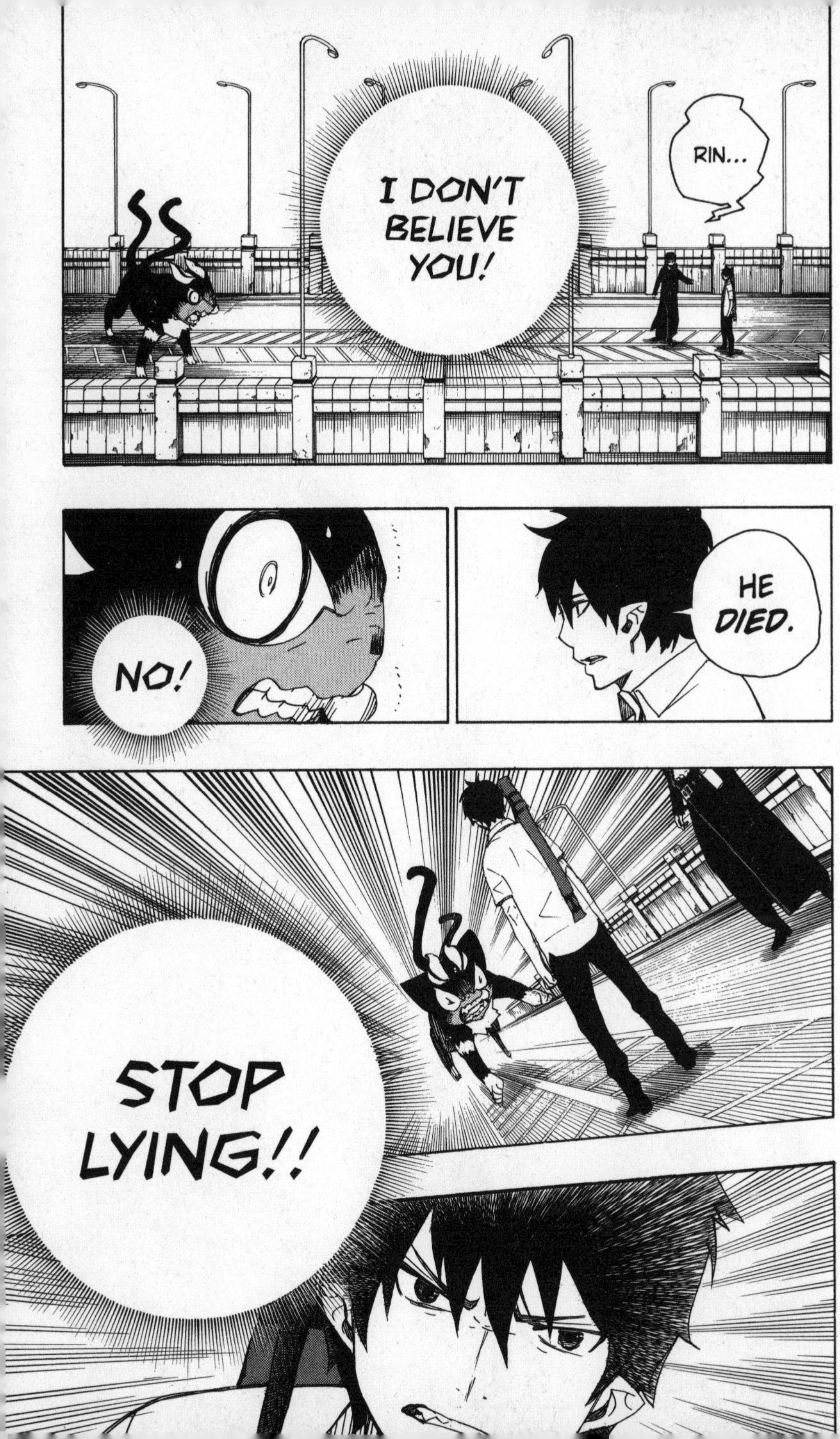
RIN...
I DON'T BELIEVE YOU!
HE DIED.
NO!
STOP LYING!!

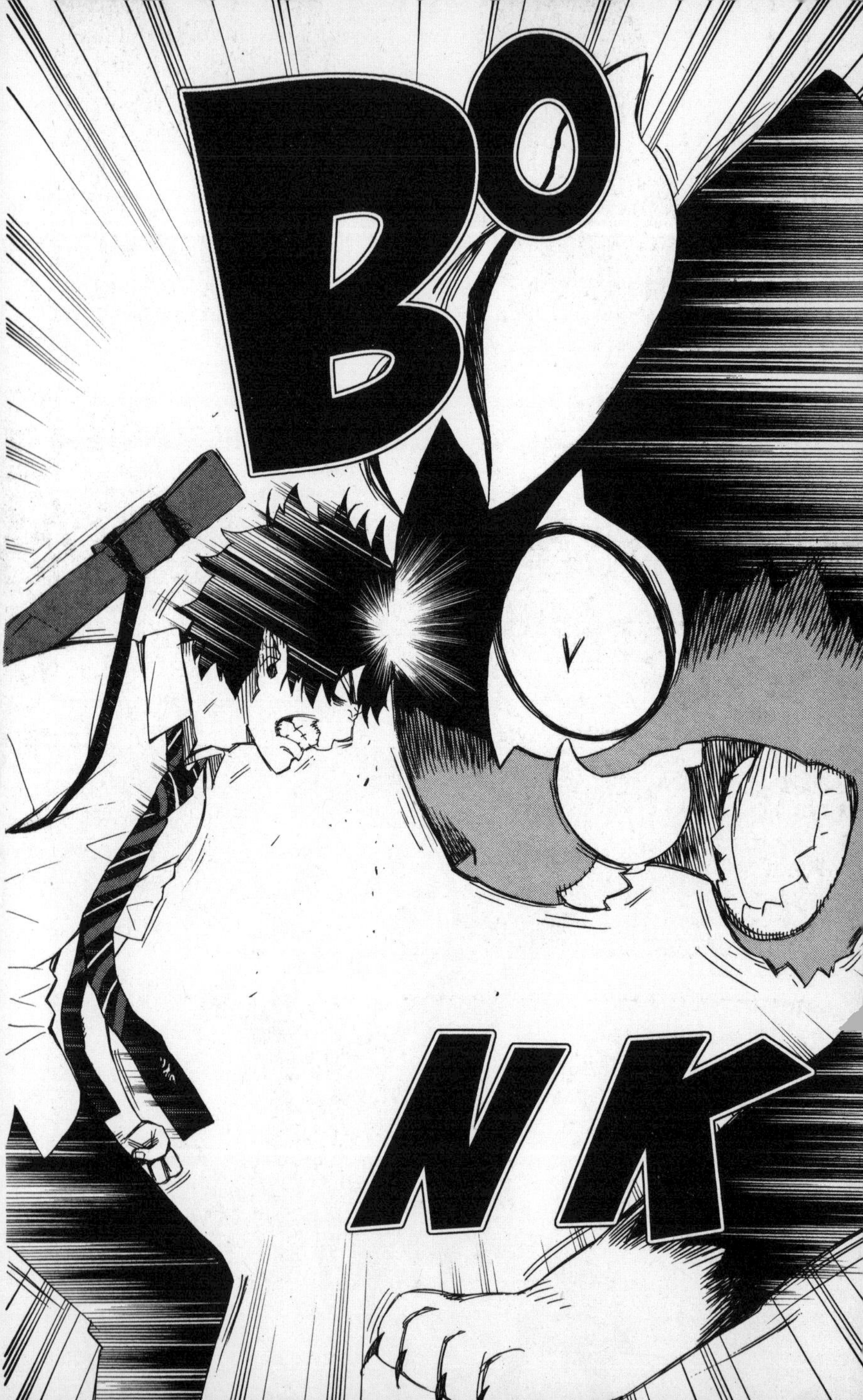
BOONK

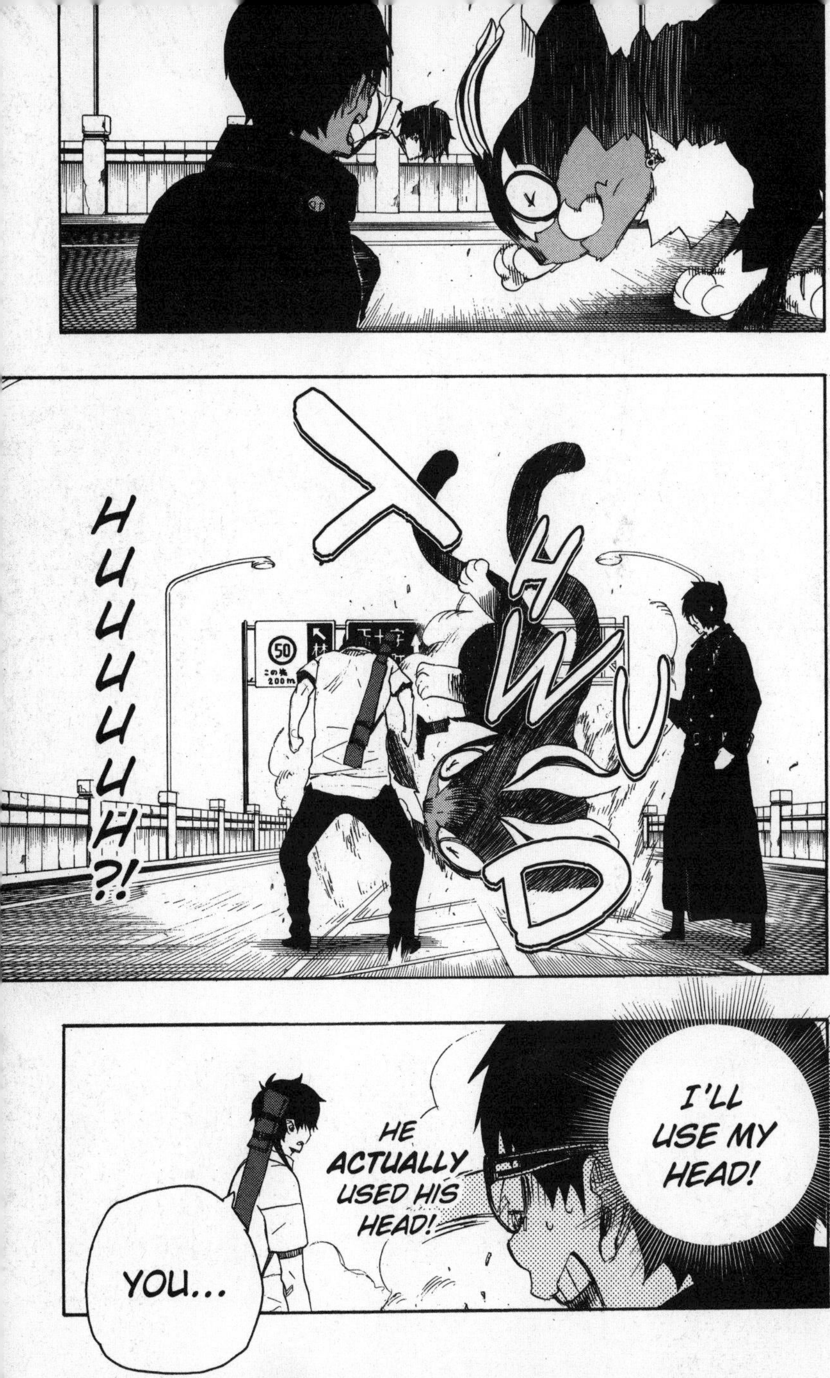
THWUD
HUUUUUUH?!
I'LL USE MY HEAD!
HE ACTUALLY USED HIS HEAD!
YOU...

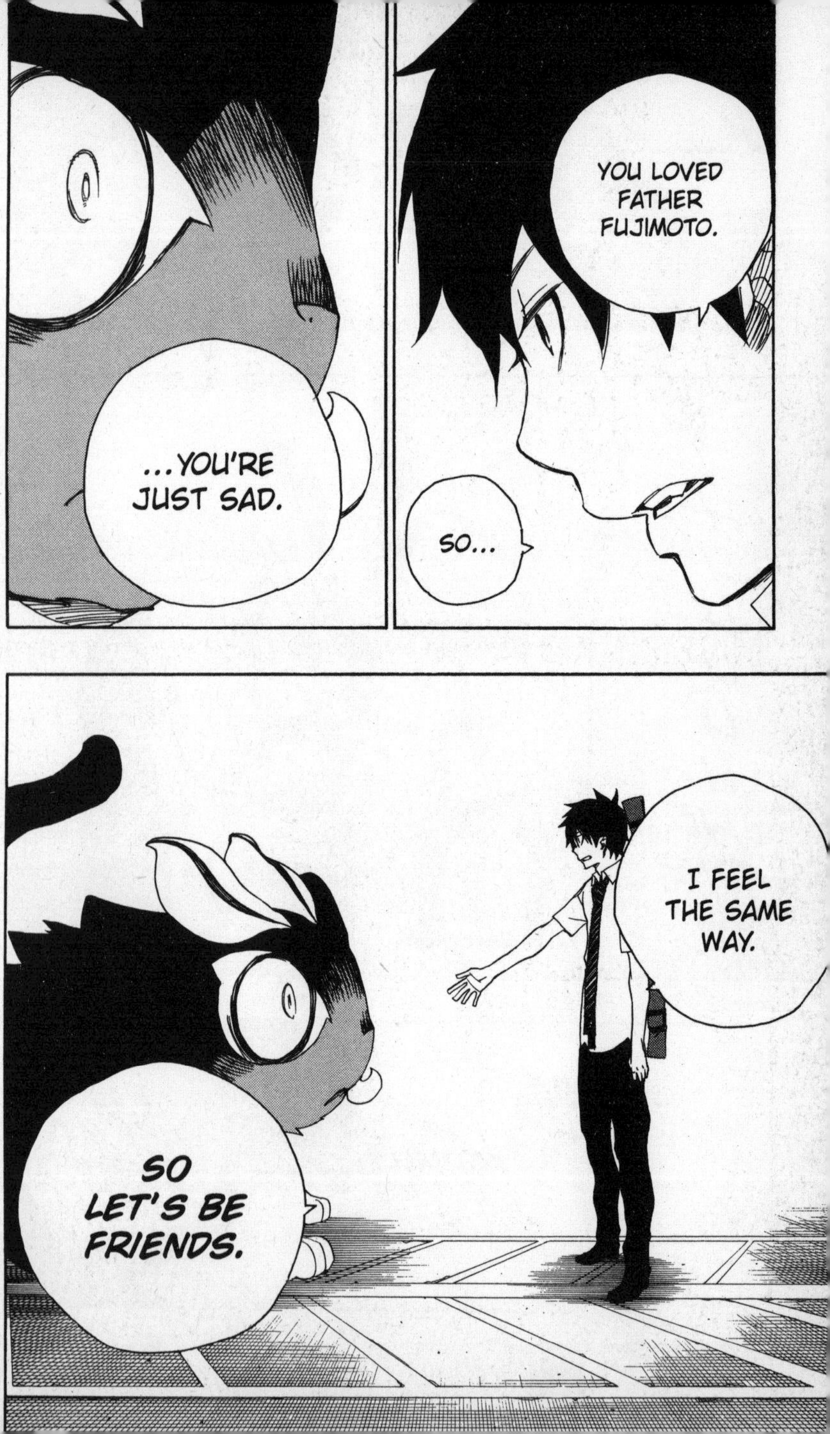
YOU LOVED FATHER FUJIMOTO.
SO...
...YOU'RE JUST SAD.
I FEEL THE SAME WAY.
SO LET'S BE FRIENDS.

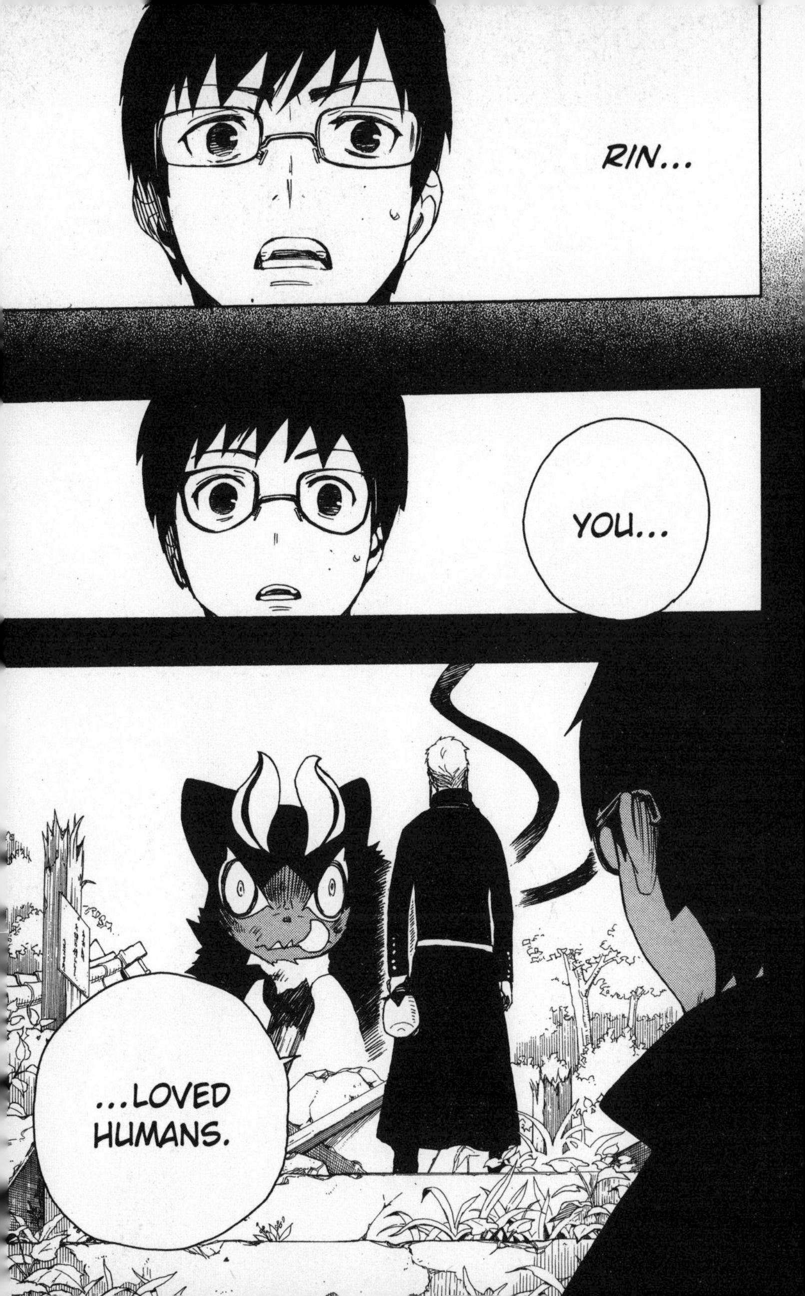
RIN...
YOU...
...LOVED HUMANS.

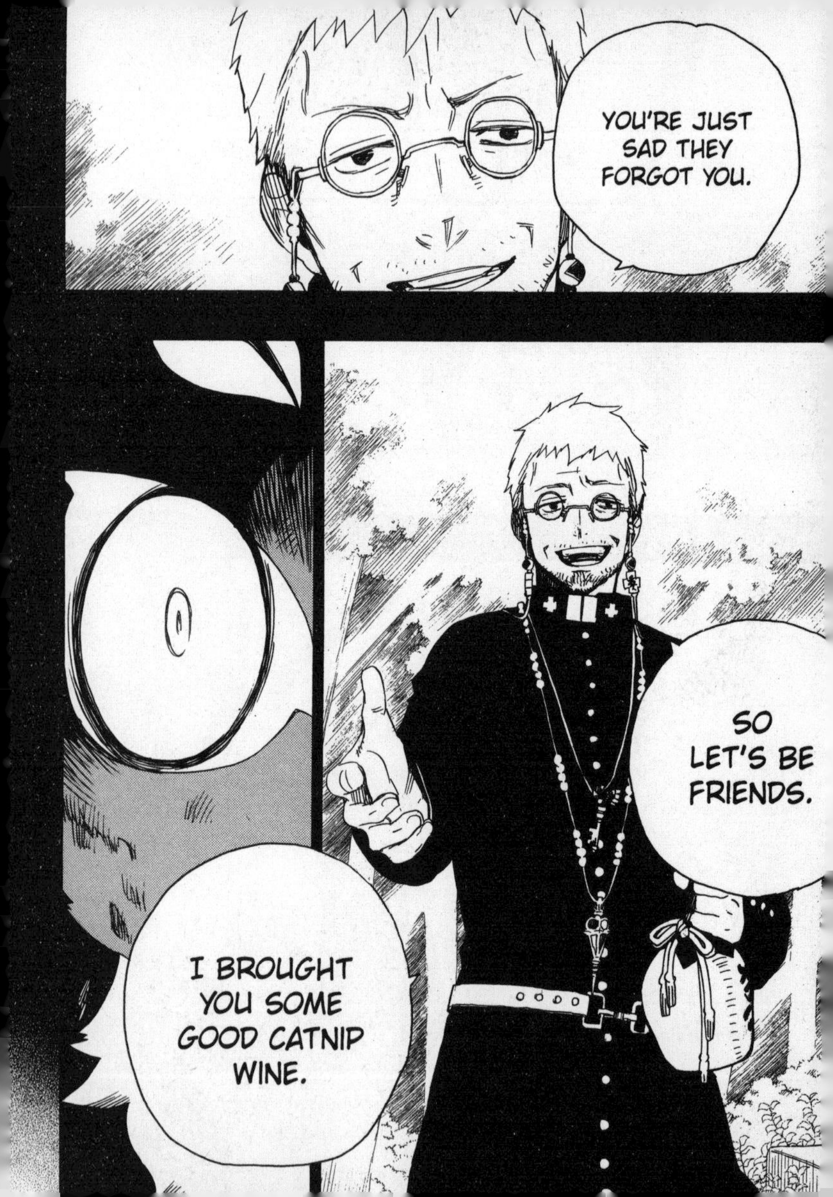
YOU'RE JUST SAD THEY FORGOT YOU.
SO LET'S BE FRIENDS.
I BROUGHT YOU SOME GOOD CATNIP WINE.

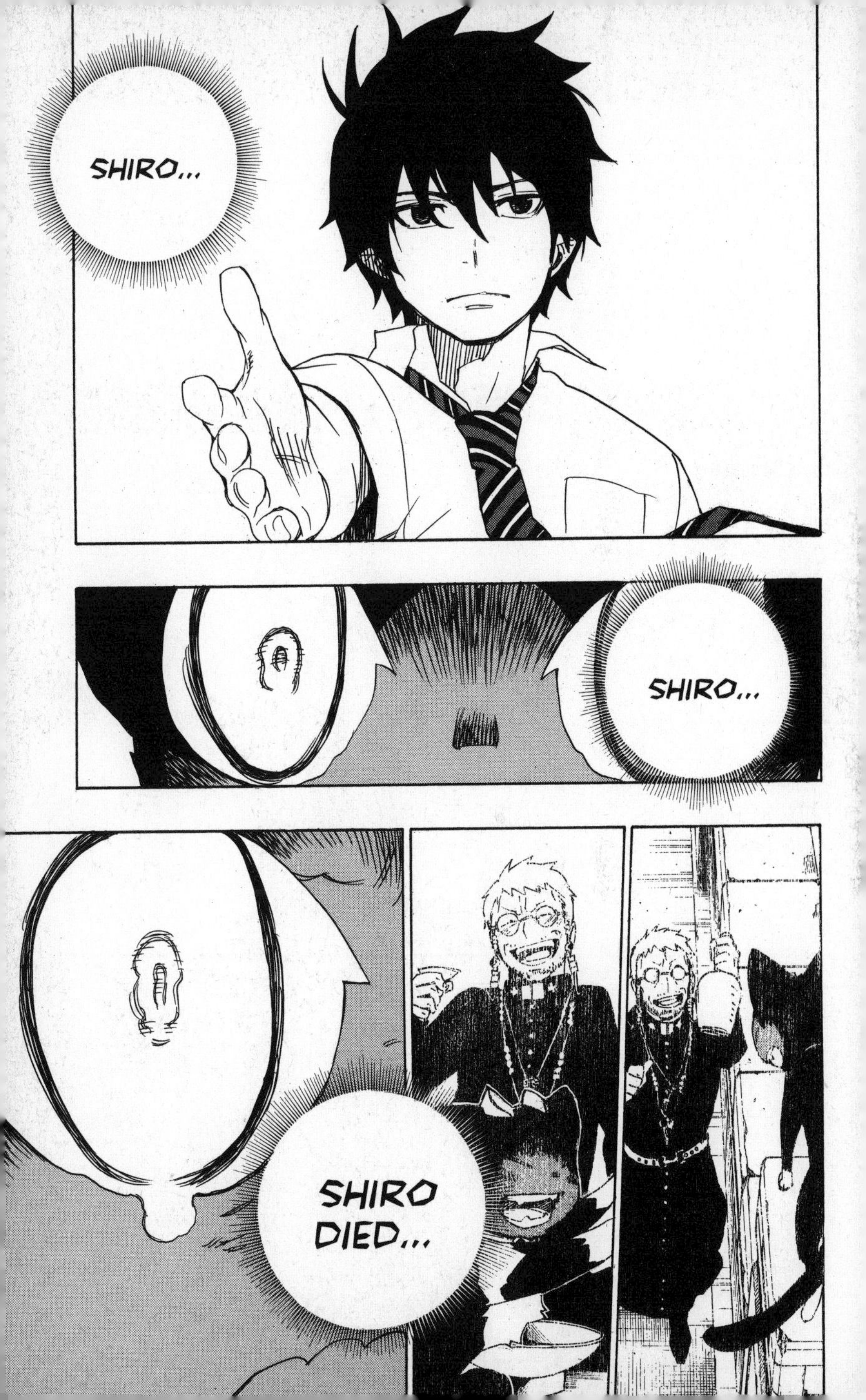
SHIRO...
SHIRO...
SHIRO DIED...

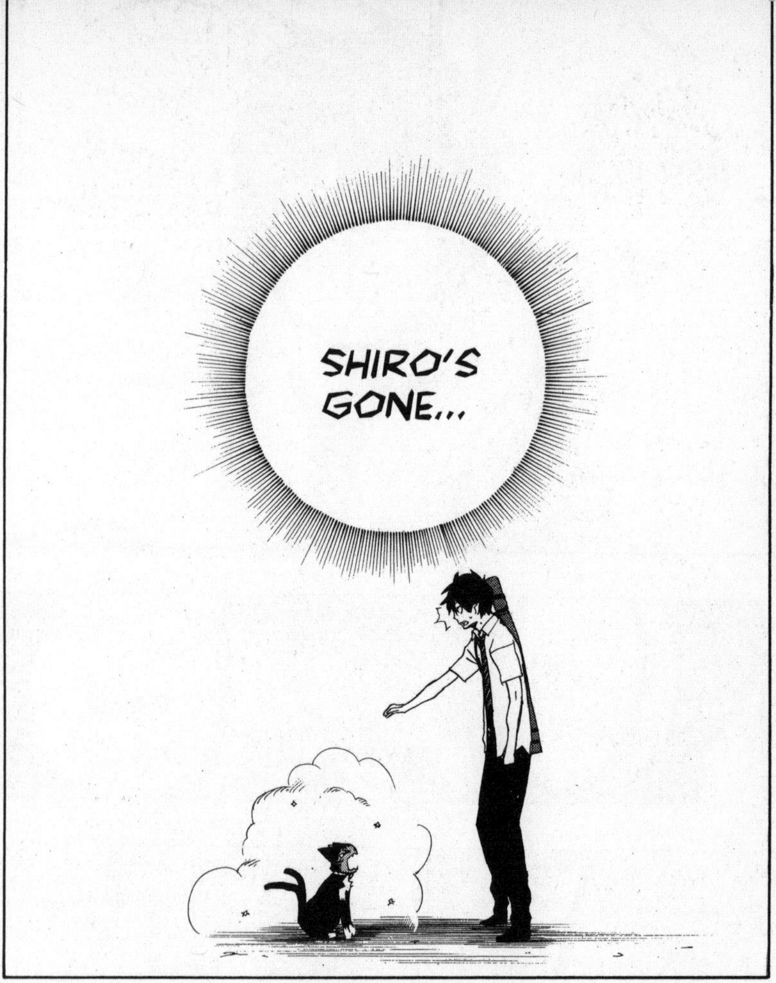
SHIRO'S
GONE...
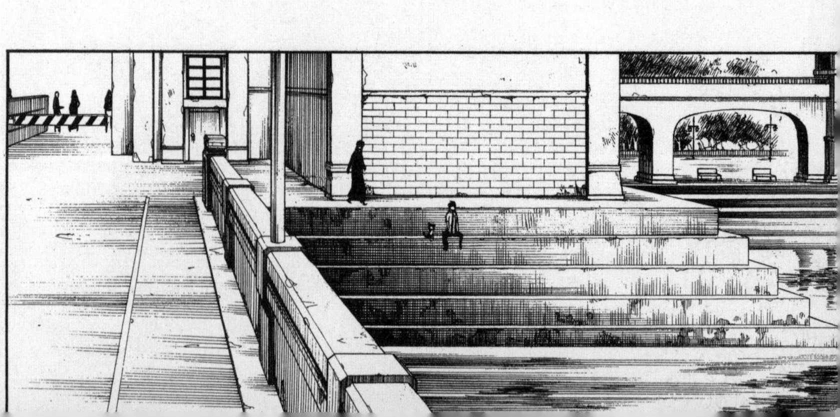

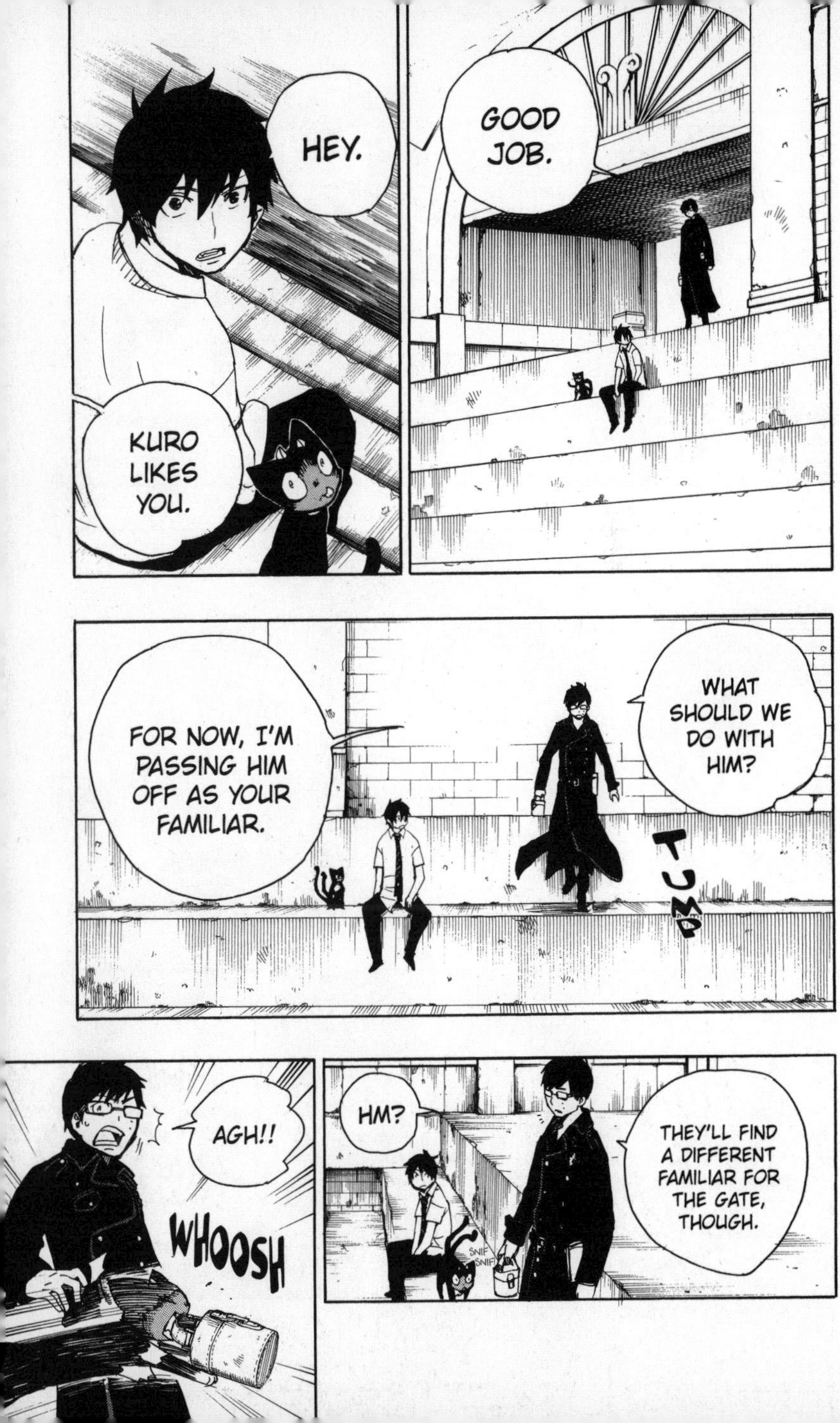
GOOD JOB.
HEY.
KURO LIKES YOU.
WHAT SHOULD WE DO WITH HIM?
TUMP
FOR NOW, I'M PASSING HIM OFF AS YOUR FAMILIAR.
THEY'LL FIND A DIFFERENT FAMILIAR FOR THE GATE, THOUGH.
SNIF SNIF
HM?
AGH!!
WHOOSH

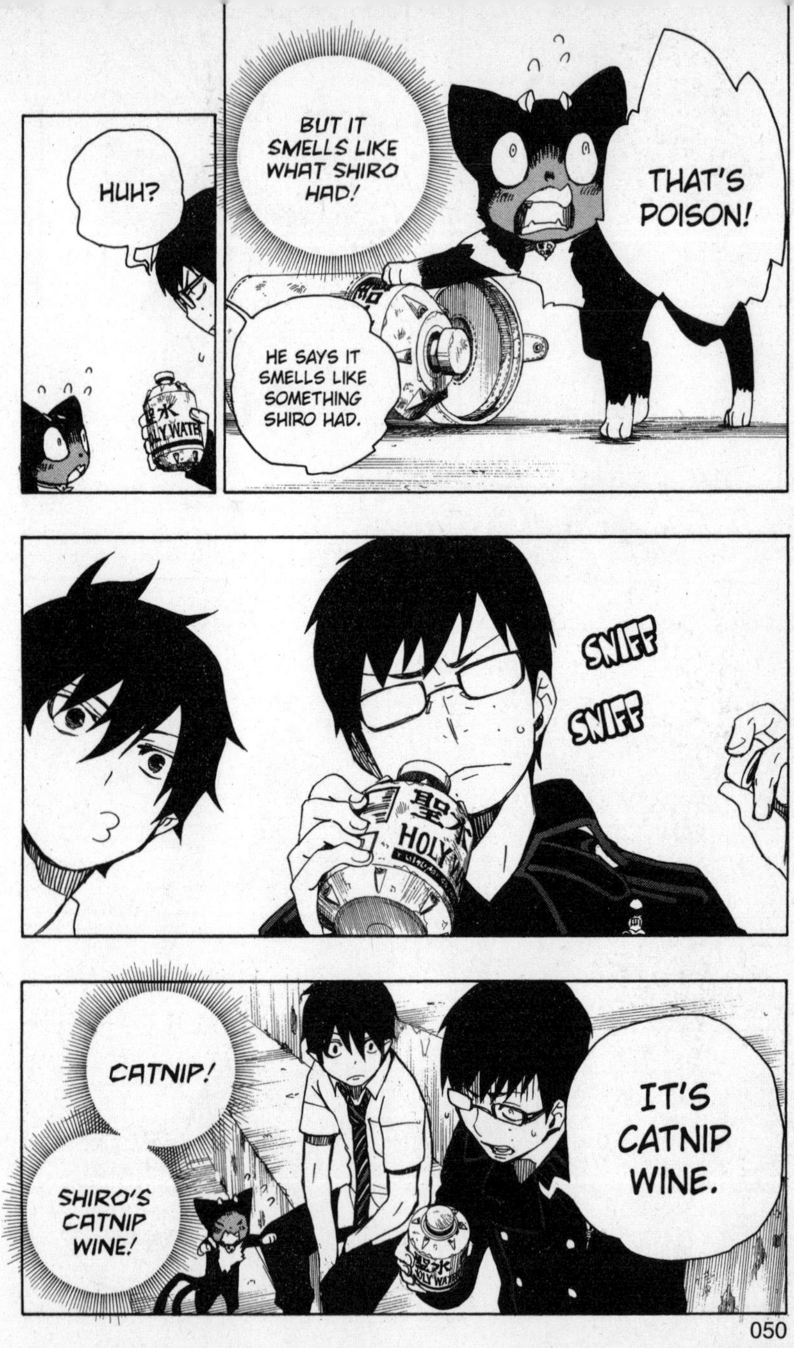
THAT'S POISON!
BUT IT SMELLS LIKE WHAT SHIRO HAD!
HE SAYS IT SMELLS LIKE SOMETHING SHIRO HAD.
HUH?
SNIFF
SNIFF
IT'S CATNIP WINE.
CATNIP!
SHIRO'S CATNIP WINE!

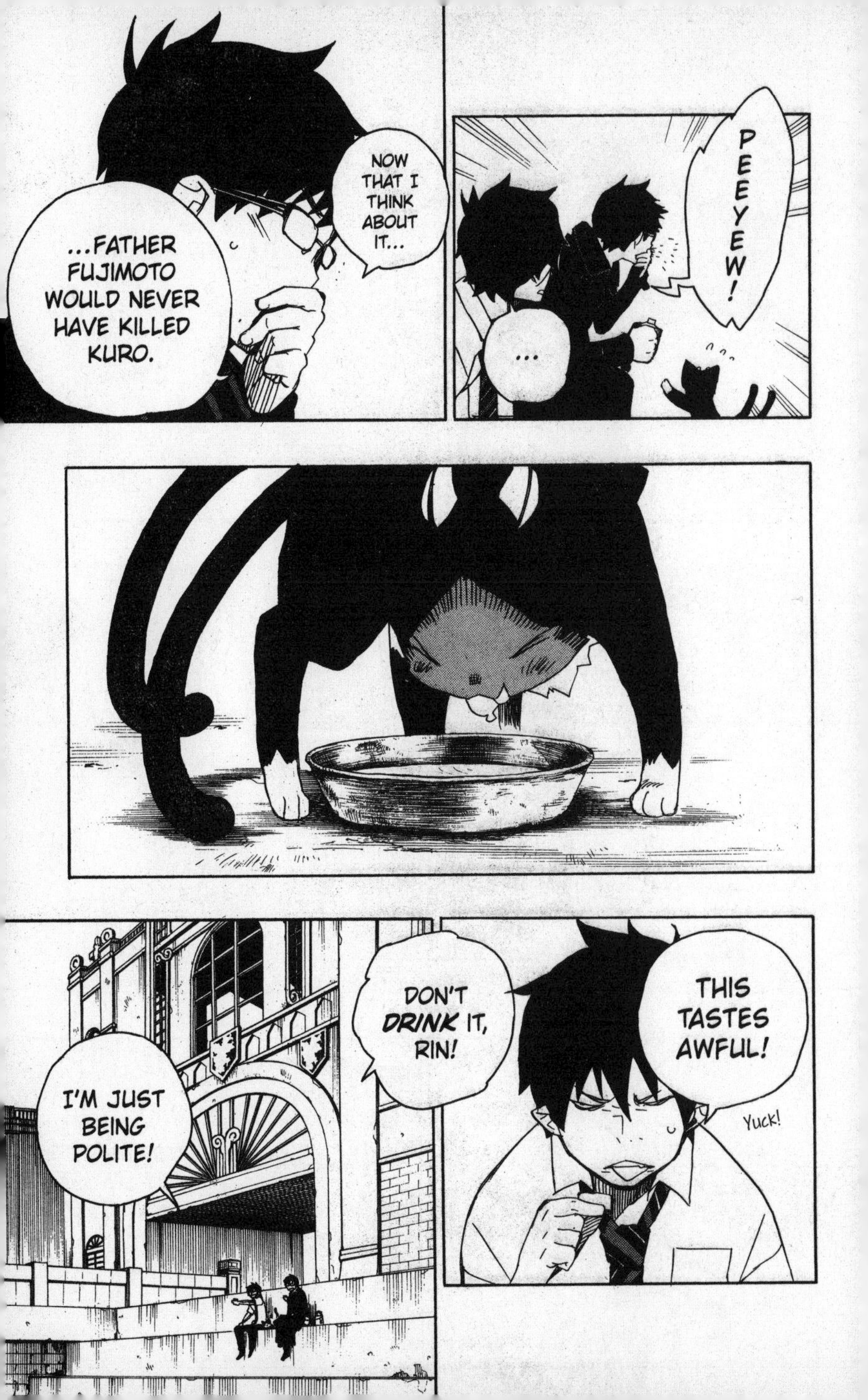
PEEYEW!
...
NOW THAT I THINK ABOUT IT...
...FATHER FUJIMOTO WOULD NEVER HAVE KILLED KURO.
THIS TASTES AWFUL!
Yuck!
DON'T *DRINK* IT, RIN!
I'M JUST BEING POLITE!

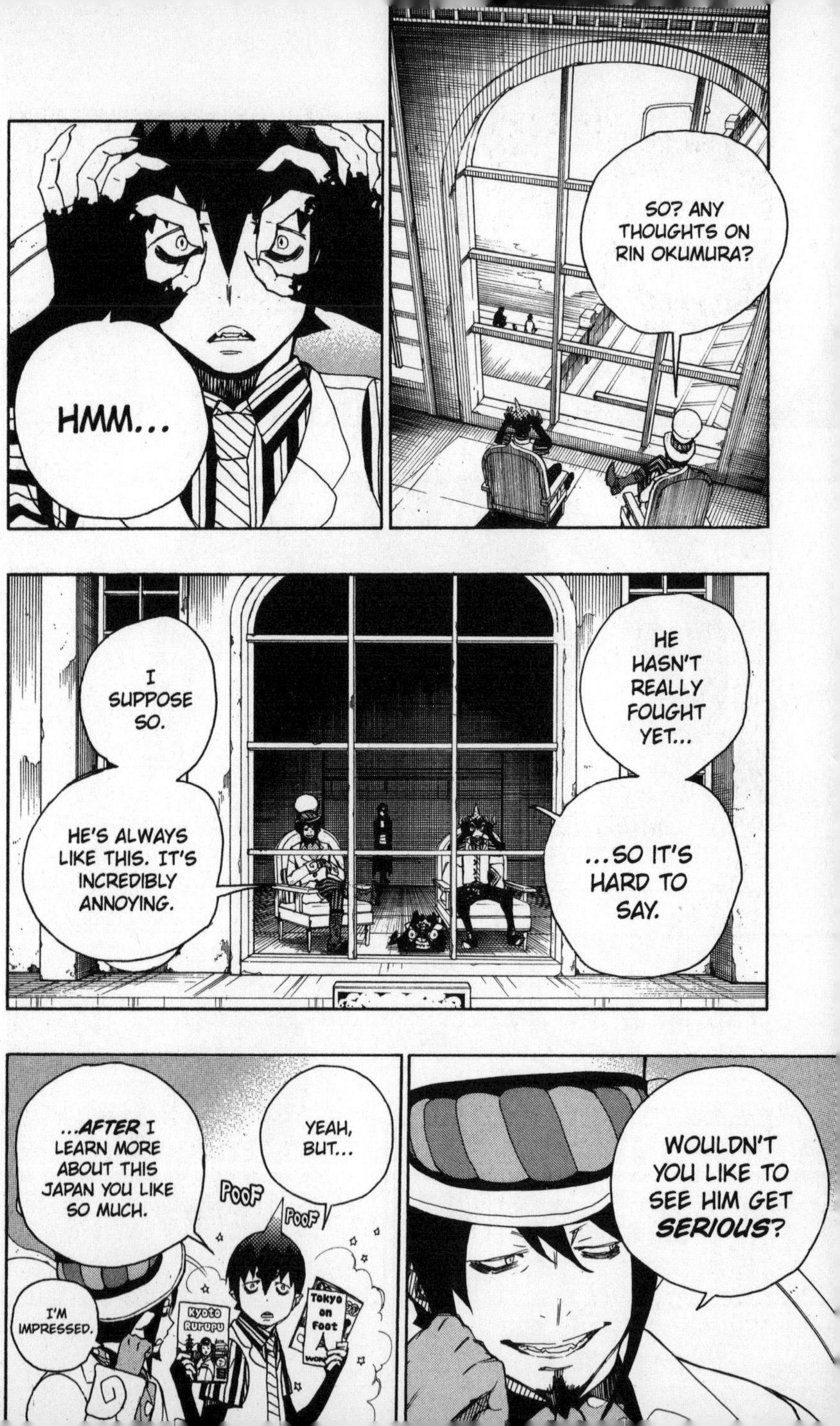
SO? ANY THOUGHTS ON RIN OKUMURA?
HMM...
HE HASN'T REALLY FOUGHT YET...
...SO IT'S HARD TO SAY.
I SUPPOSE SO.
HE'S ALWAYS LIKE THIS. IT'S INCREDIBLY ANNOYING.
WOULDN'T YOU LIKE TO SEE HIM GET *SERIOUS*?
YEAH, BUT...
POOF
POOF
...*AFTER* I LEARN MORE ABOUT THIS JAPAN YOU LIKE SO MUCH.
Tokyo on Foot
Kyoto Rurupu
I'M IMPRESSED.

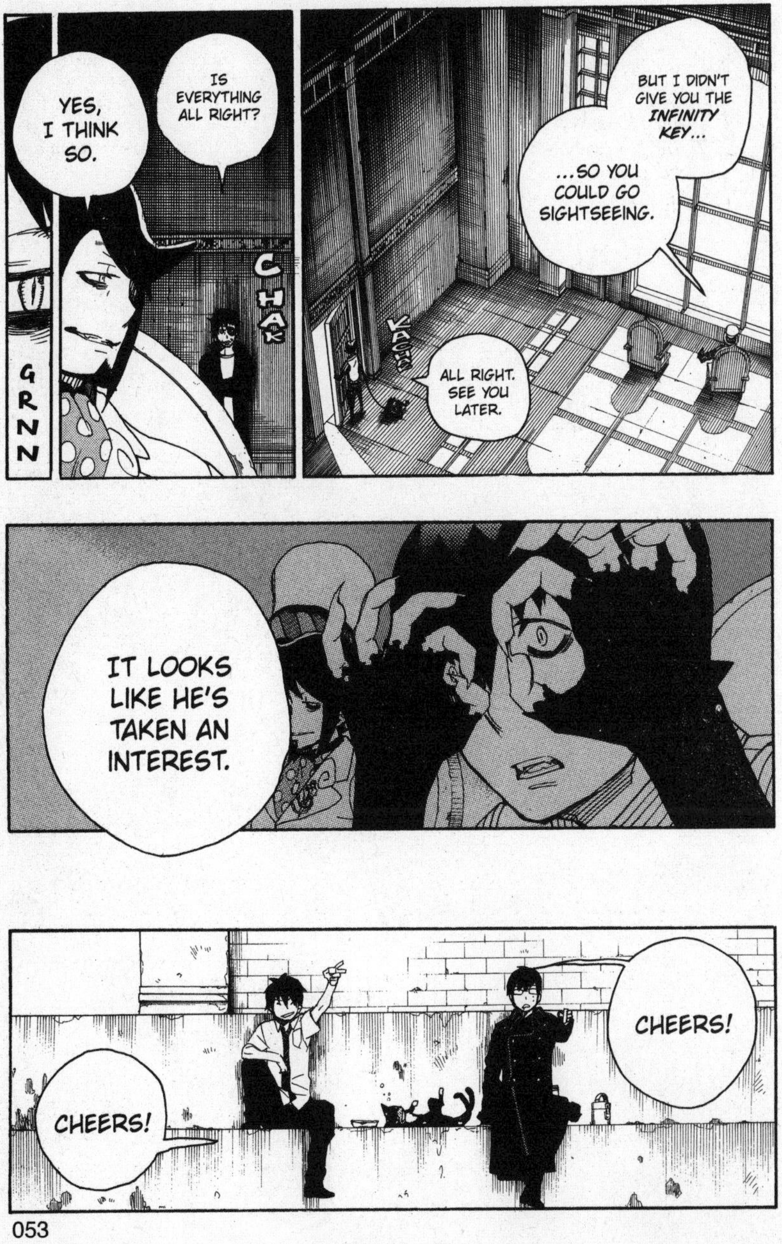
BUT I DIDN'T GIVE YOU THE *INFINITY KEY*...
...SO YOU COULD GO SIGHTSEEING.
KACHA
ALL RIGHT. SEE YOU LATER.
IS EVERYTHING ALL RIGHT?
CHAK
YES, I THINK SO.
GRNN
IT LOOKS LIKE HE'S TAKEN AN INTEREST.
CHEERS!
CHEERS!

Blue Exorcist Chapter 8 Black Cat

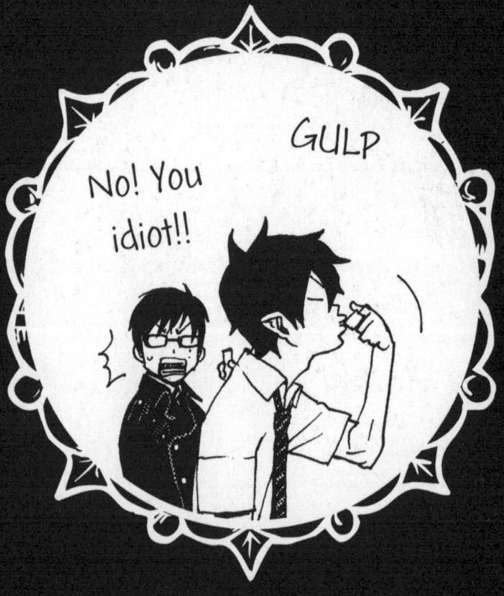
GULP
No! You idiot!!

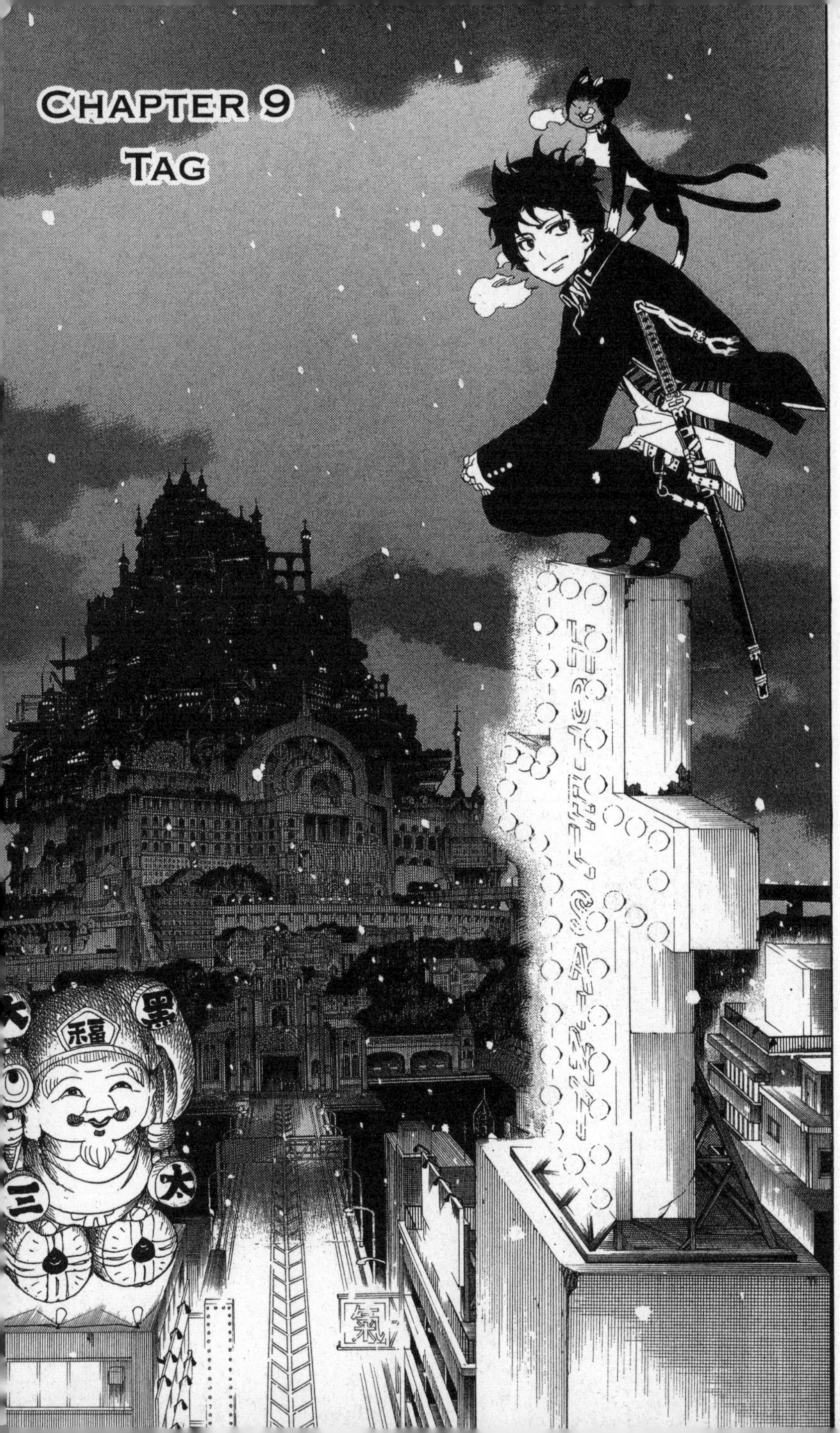
CHAPTER 9
TAG

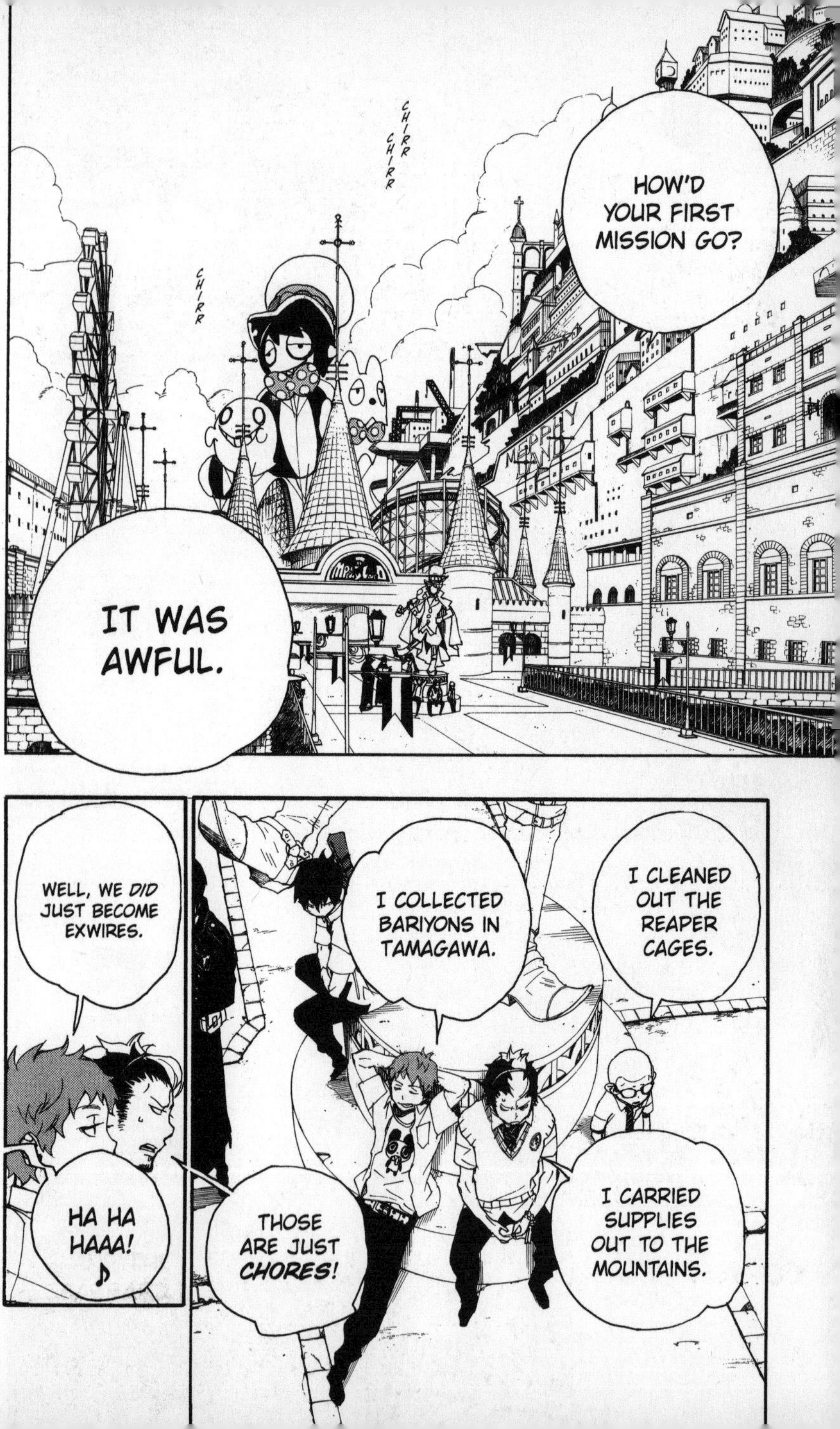
CHIRR CHIRR
CHIRR
HOW'D YOUR FIRST MISSION GO?
IT WAS AWFUL.
I CLEANED OUT THE REAPER CAGES.
I COLLECTED BARIYONS IN TAMAGAWA.
I CARRIED SUPPLIES OUT TO THE MOUNTAINS.
THOSE ARE JUST *CHORES!*
WELL, WE *DID* JUST BECOME EXWIRES.
HA HA HAAA! ♪

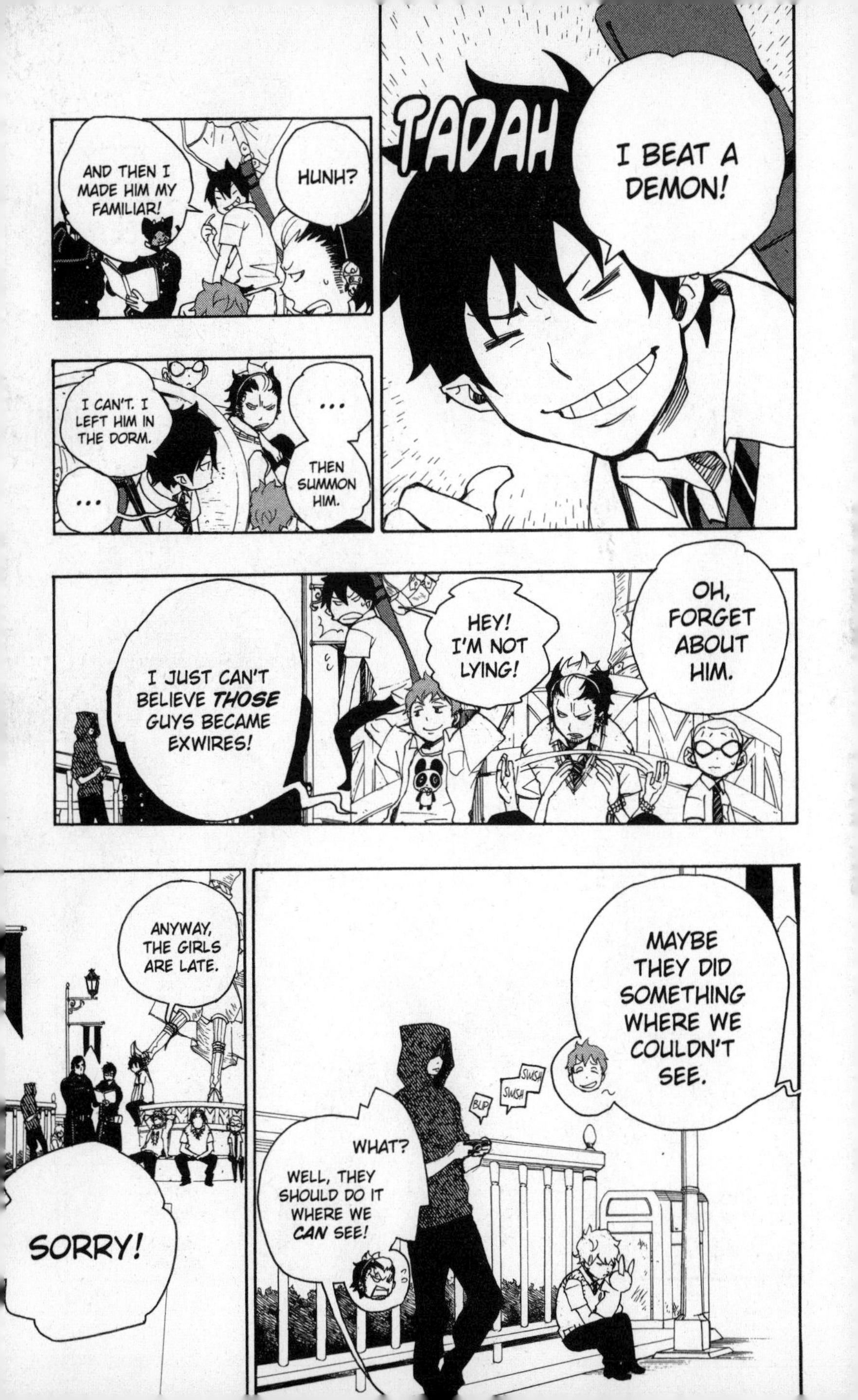
TADAH
I BEAT A DEMON!
HUNH?
AND THEN I MADE HIM MY FAMILIAR!
...
THEN SUMMON HIM.
I CAN'T. I LEFT HIM IN THE DORM.
...
OH, FORGET ABOUT HIM.
HEY! I'M NOT LYING!
I JUST CAN'T BELIEVE *THOSE* GUYS BECAME EXWIRES!
MAYBE THEY DID SOMETHING WHERE WE COULDN'T SEE.
SWISH
SWISH
BLIP
WHAT?
WELL, THEY SHOULD DO IT WHERE WE *CAN* SEE!
ANYWAY, THE GIRLS ARE LATE.
SORRY!

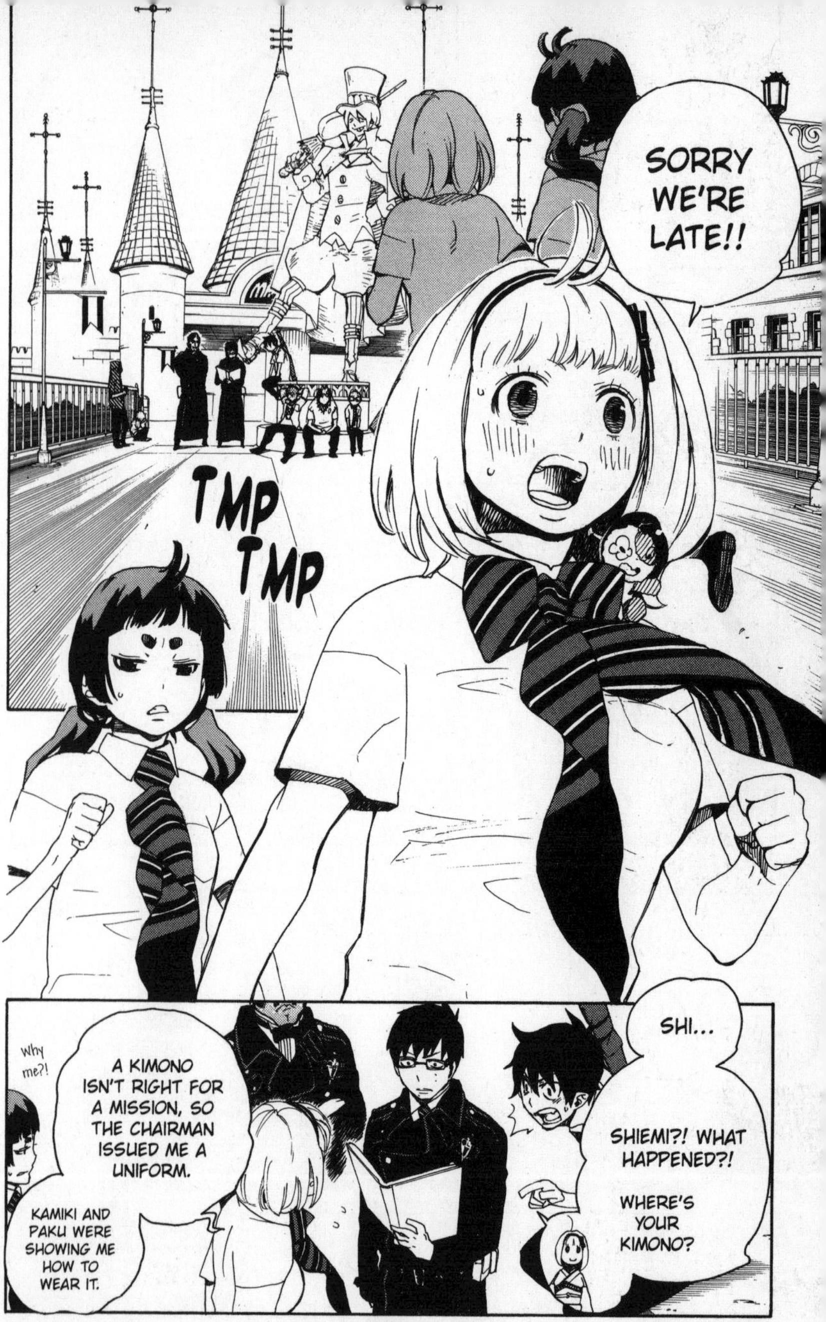
SORRY WE'RE LATE!!
TMP TMP
SHI...
SHIEMI?! WHAT HAPPENED?!
WHERE'S YOUR KIMONO?
A KIMONO ISN'T RIGHT FOR A MISSION, SO THE CHAIRMAN ISSUED ME A UNIFORM.
KAMIKI AND PAKU WERE SHOWING ME HOW TO WEAR IT.
Why me?!

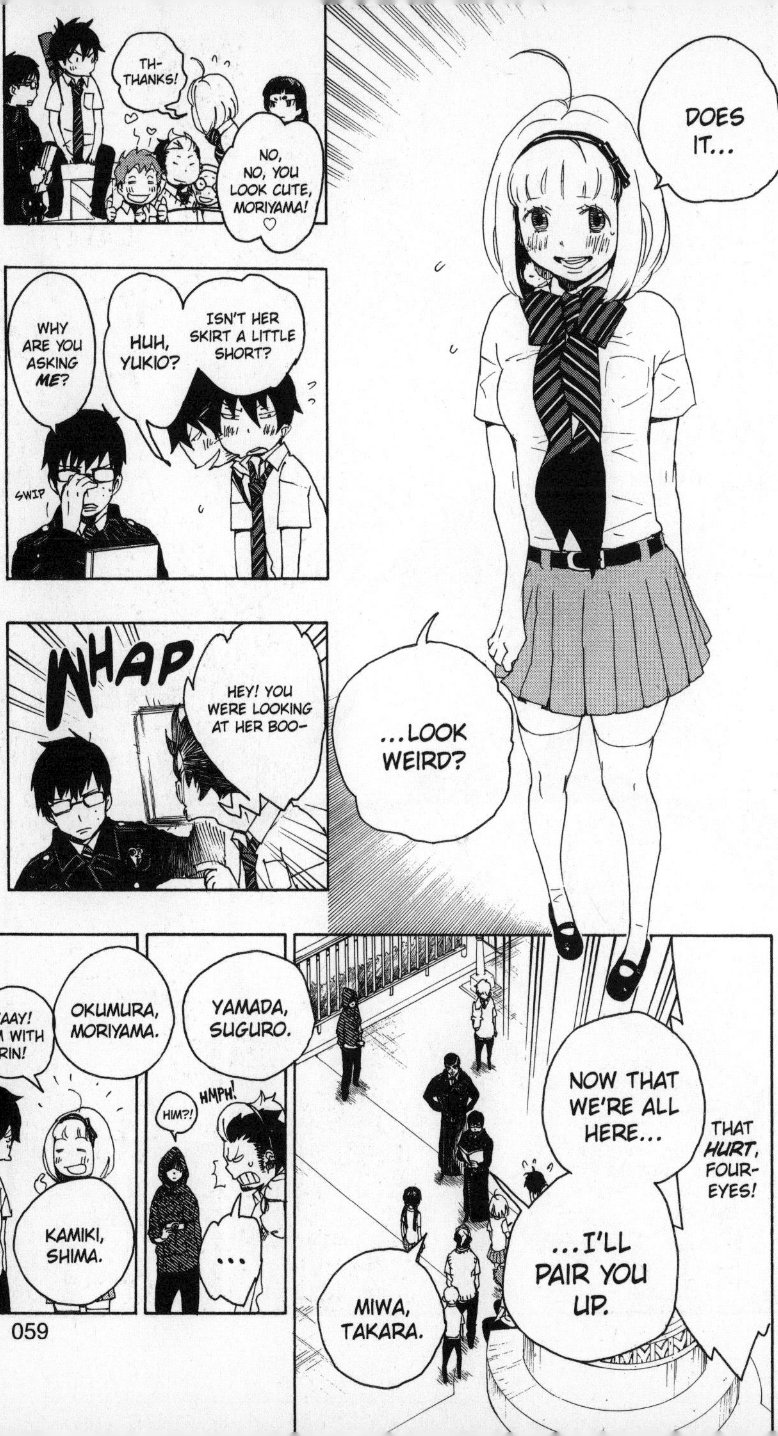
DOES IT...
...LOOK WEIRD?
NO, NO, YOU LOOK CUTE, MORIYAMA! ♡
TH-THANKS!
ISN'T HER SKIRT A LITTLE SHORT?
HUH, YUKIO?
WHY ARE YOU ASKING *ME*?
SWIP
HEY! YOU WERE LOOKING AT HER BOO-
WHAP
NOW THAT WE'RE ALL HERE...
...I'LL PAIR YOU UP.
THAT *HURT*, FOUR-EYES!
MIWA, TAKARA.
YAMADA, SUGURO.
HMPH!
HIM?!
...
OKUMURA, MORIYAMA.
YAAY! I'M WITH RIN!
KAMIKI, SHIMA.

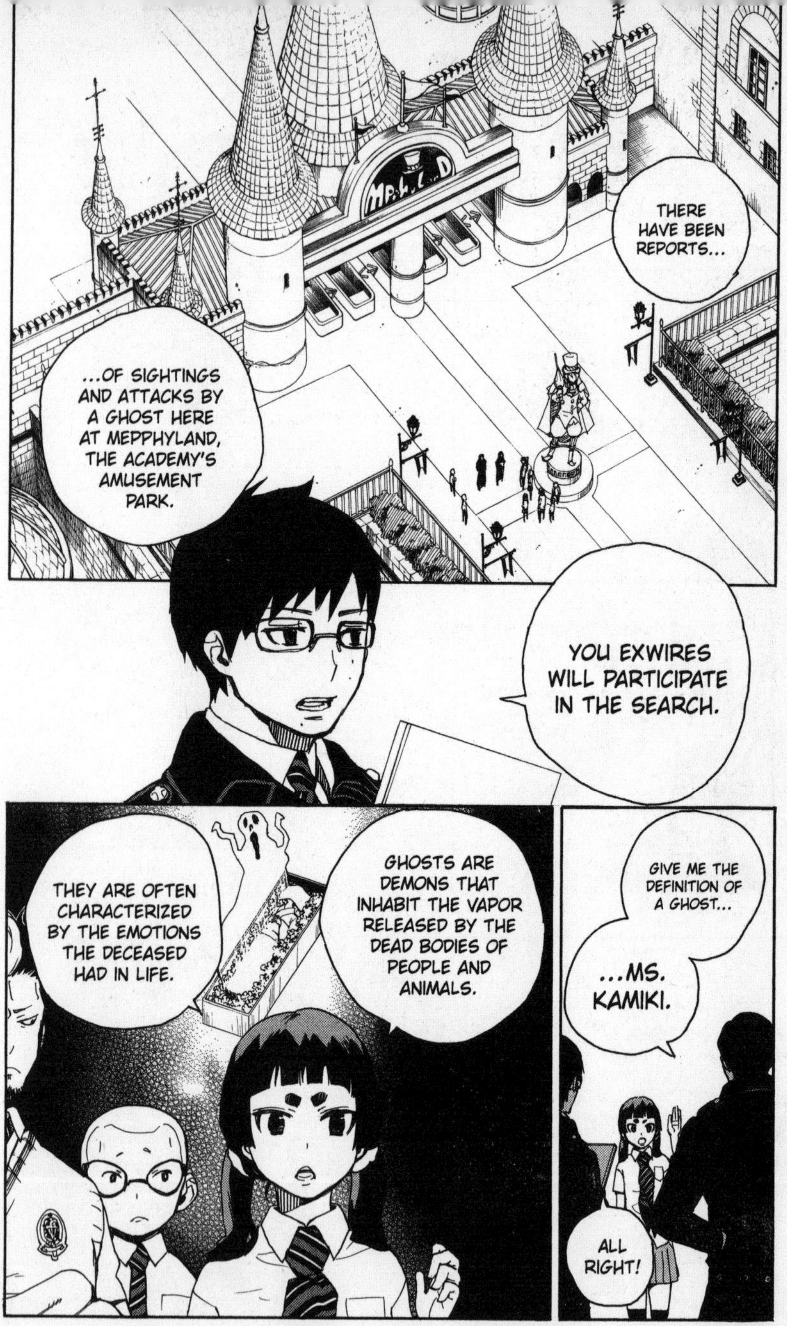
THERE HAVE BEEN REPORTS...
...OF SIGHTINGS AND ATTACKS BY A GHOST HERE AT MEPPHYLAND, THE ACADEMY'S AMUSEMENT PARK.
YOU EXWIRES WILL PARTICIPATE IN THE SEARCH.
GIVE ME THE DEFINITION OF A GHOST...
...MS. KAMIKI.
ALL RIGHT!
GHOSTS ARE DEMONS THAT INHABIT THE VAPOR RELEASED BY THE DEAD BODIES OF PEOPLE AND ANIMALS.
THEY ARE OFTEN CHARACTERIZED BY THE EMOTIONS THE DECEASED HAD IN LIFE.

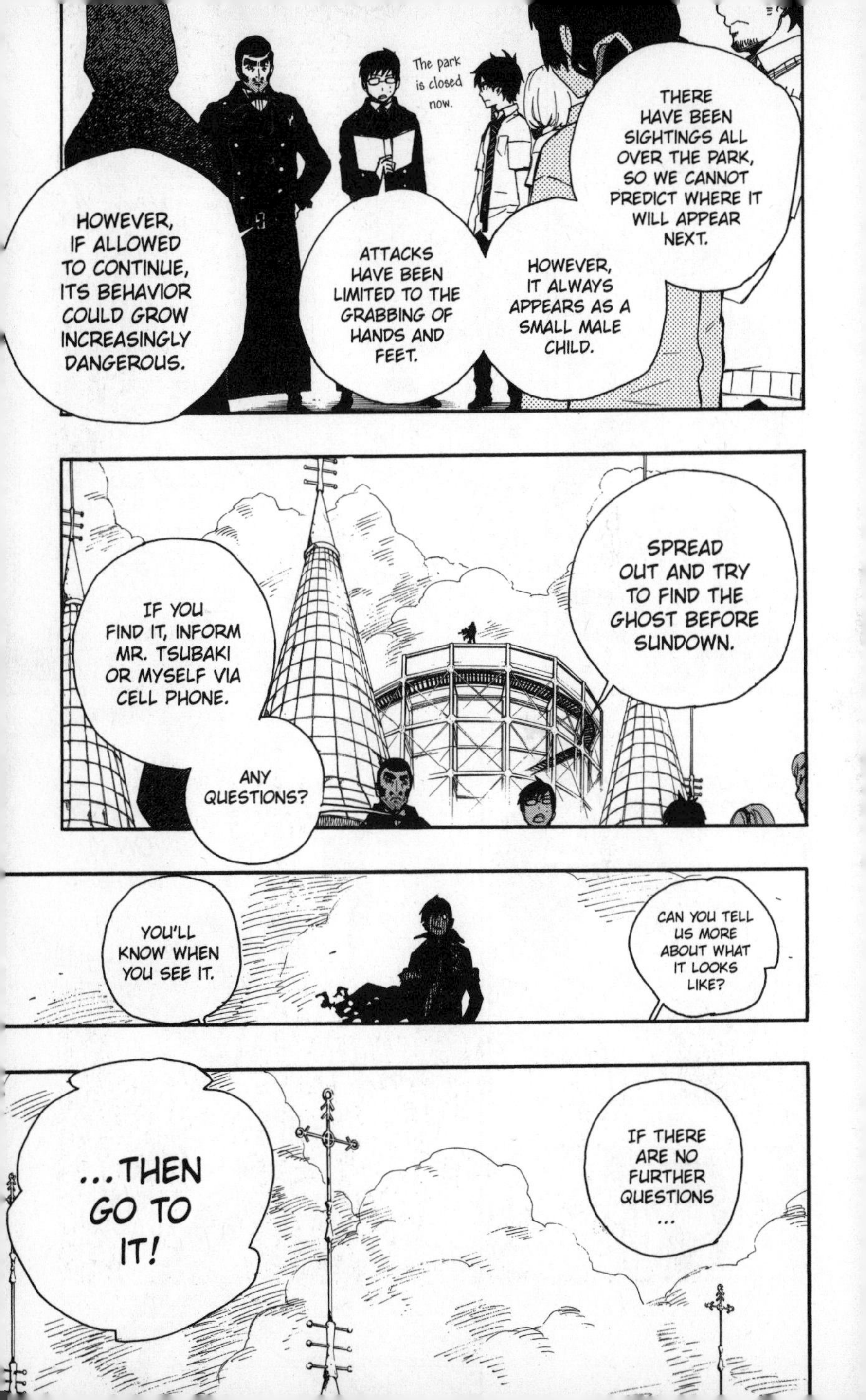
THERE HAVE BEEN SIGHTINGS ALL OVER THE PARK, SO WE CANNOT PREDICT WHERE IT WILL APPEAR NEXT.
The park is closed now.
HOWEVER, IT ALWAYS APPEARS AS A SMALL MALE CHILD.
ATTACKS HAVE BEEN LIMITED TO THE GRABBING OF HANDS AND FEET.
HOWEVER, IF ALLOWED TO CONTINUE, ITS BEHAVIOR COULD GROW INCREASINGLY DANGEROUS.
SPREAD OUT AND TRY TO FIND THE GHOST BEFORE SUNDOWN.
IF YOU FIND IT, INFORM MR. TSUBAKI OR MYSELF VIA CELL PHONE.
ANY QUESTIONS?
CAN YOU TELL US MORE ABOUT WHAT IT LOOKS LIKE?
YOU'LL KNOW WHEN YOU SEE IT.
IF THERE ARE NO FURTHER QUESTIONS ...
...THEN GO TO IT!

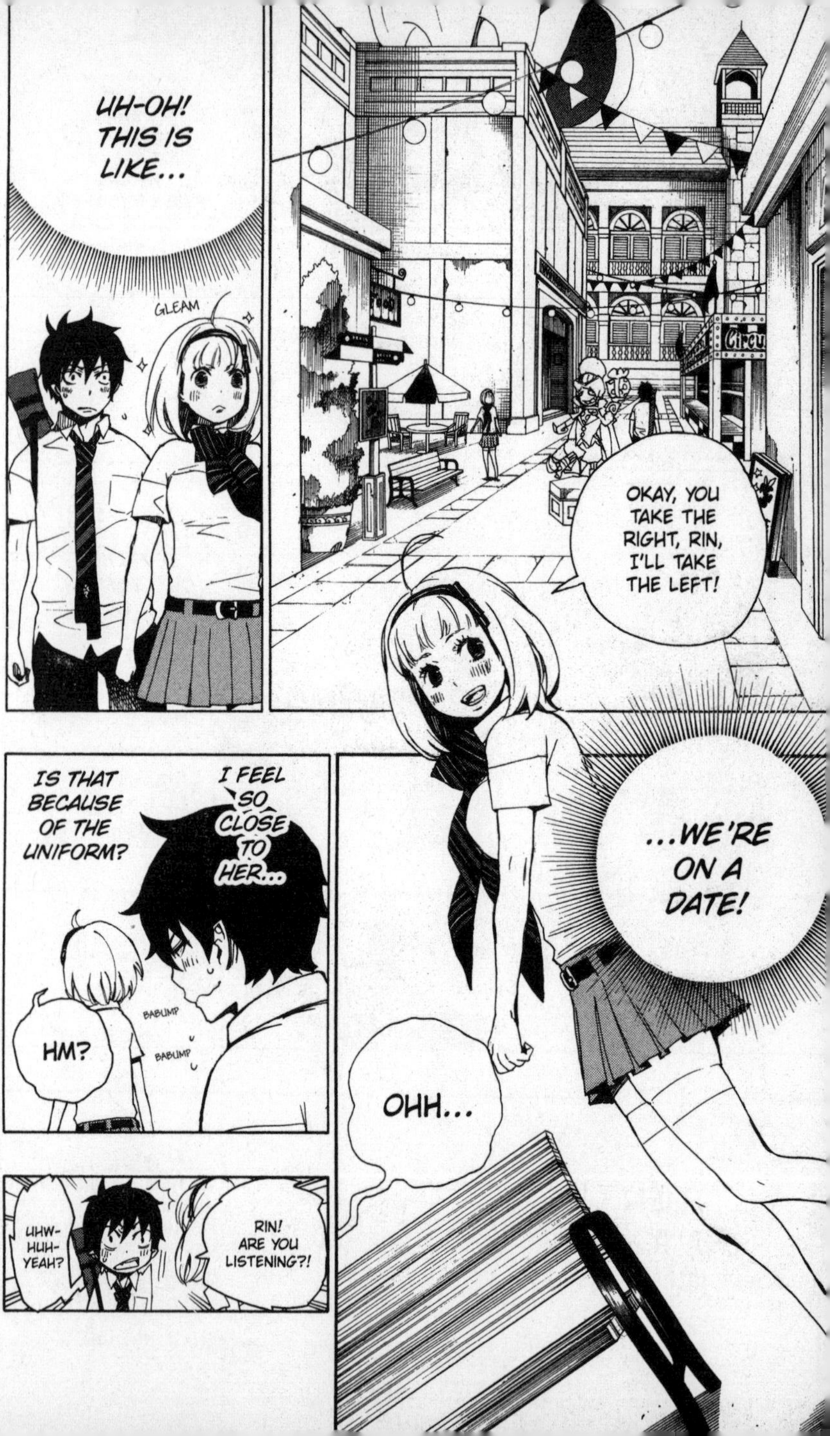
OKAY, YOU TAKE THE RIGHT, RIN, I'LL TAKE THE LEFT!
GLEAM
UH-OH! THIS IS LIKE...
...WE'RE ON A DATE!
OHH...
I FEEL SO CLOSE TO HER...
IS THAT BECAUSE OF THE UNIFORM?
BABUMP
BABUMP
HM?
RIN! ARE YOU LISTENING?!
UHW-HUH-YEAH?

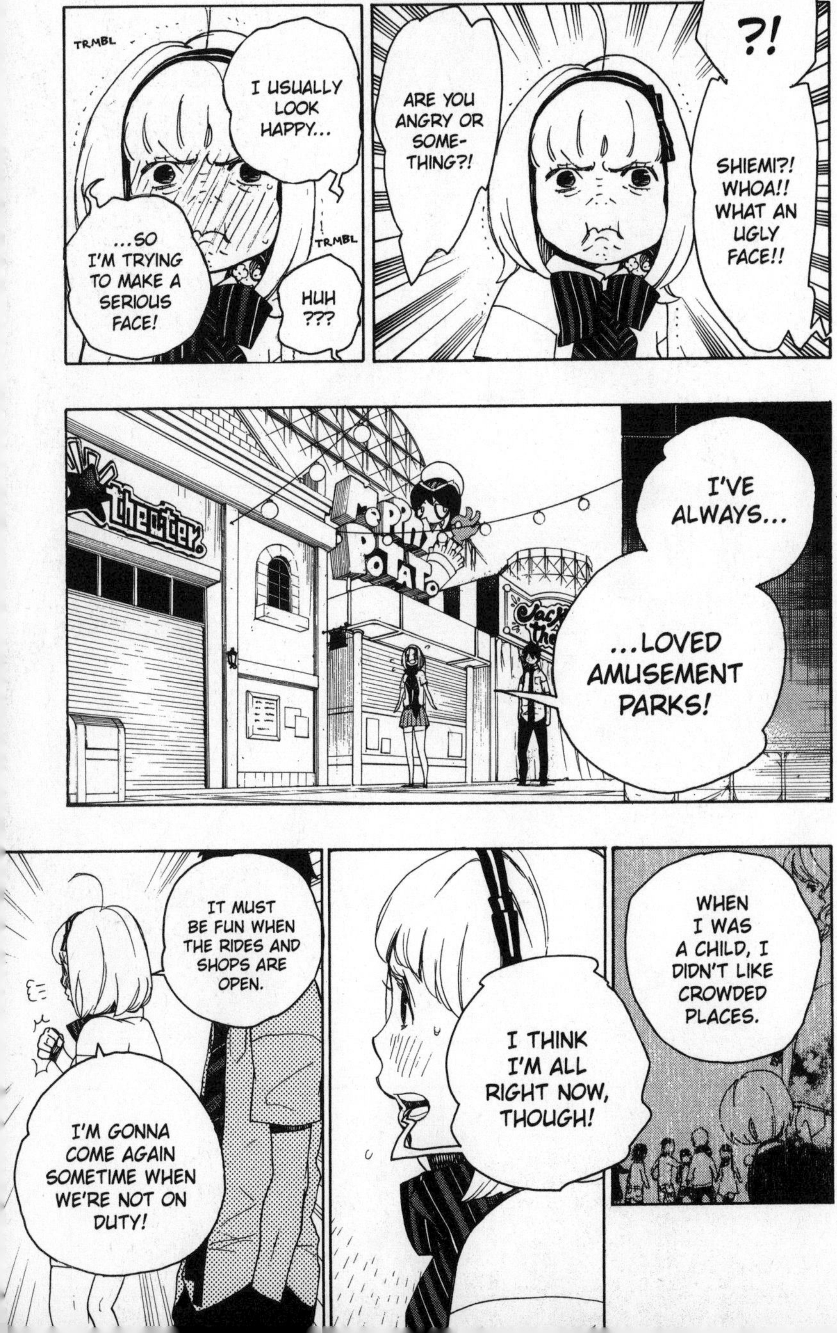

?!
SHIEMI?! WHOA!! WHAT AN UGLY FACE!!
ARE YOU ANGRY OR SOME-THING?!
I USUALLY LOOK HAPPY...
TRMBL
...SO I'M TRYING TO MAKE A SERIOUS FACE!
TRMBL
HUH ???
I'VE ALWAYS...
...LOVED AMUSEMENT PARKS!
WHEN I WAS A CHILD, I DIDN'T LIKE CROWDED PLACES.
I THINK I'M ALL RIGHT NOW, THOUGH!
IT MUST BE FUN WHEN THE RIDES AND SHOPS ARE OPEN.
I'M GONNA COME AGAIN SOMETIME WHEN WE'RE NOT ON DUTY!

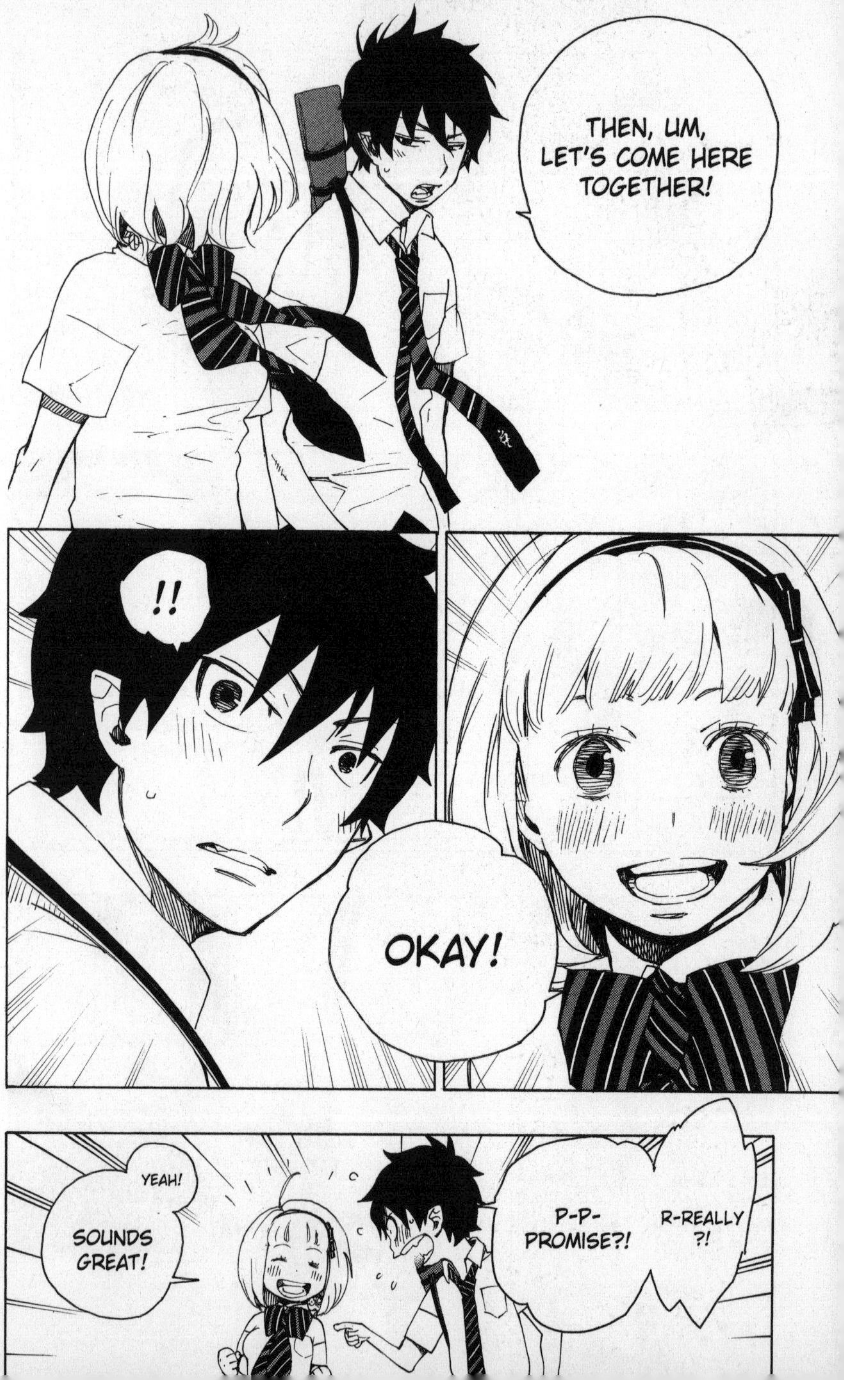
THEN, UM, LET'S COME HERE TOGETHER!
OKAY!
!!
R-REALLY ?!
P-P-PROMISE?!
YEAH!
SOUNDS GREAT!

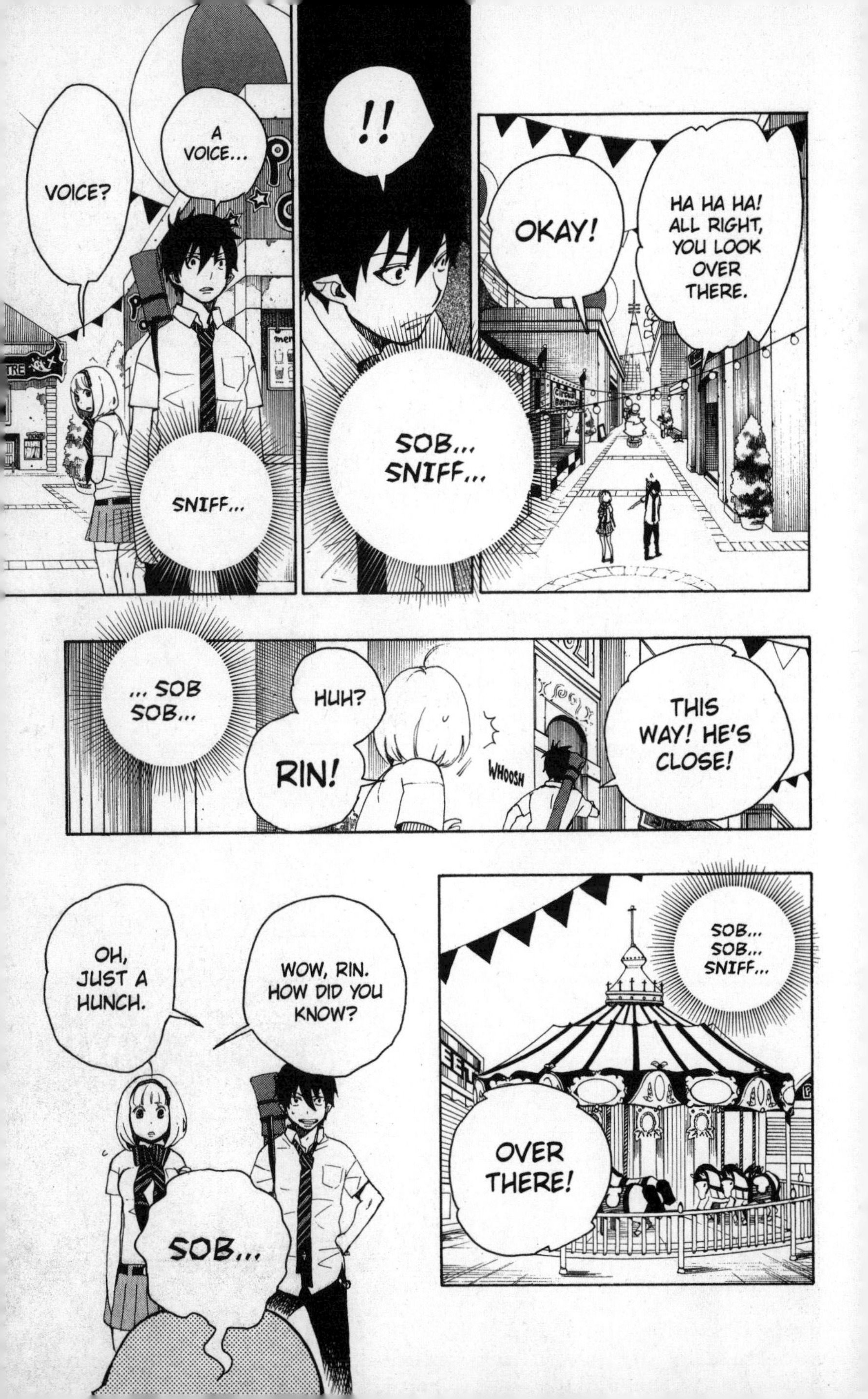
HA HA HA! ALL RIGHT, YOU LOOK OVER THERE.
OKAY!
!!
SOB... SNIFF...
A VOICE...
VOICE?
SNIFF...
THIS WAY! HE'S CLOSE!
WHOOSH
HUH?
RIN!
... SOB SOB...
SOB... SOB... SNIFF...
OVER THERE!
WOW, RIN. HOW DID YOU KNOW?
OH, JUST A HUNCH.
SOB...

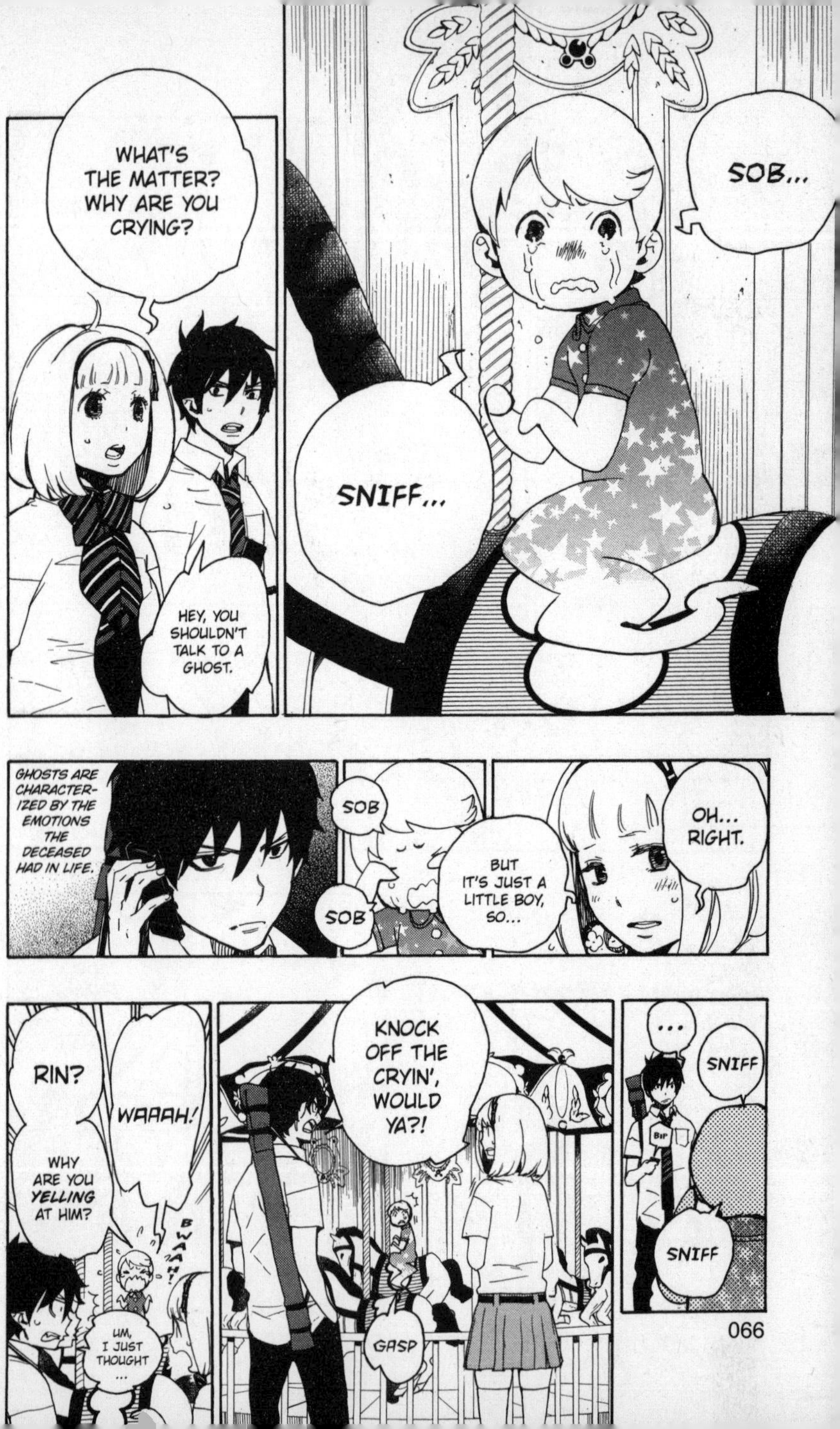
SOB...
SNIFF...
WHAT'S THE MATTER? WHY ARE YOU CRYING?
HEY, YOU SHOULDN'T TALK TO A GHOST.
OH... RIGHT.
BUT IT'S JUST A LITTLE BOY, SO...
SOB
SOB
GHOSTS ARE CHARACTER-IZED BY THE EMOTIONS THE DECEASED HAD IN LIFE.
...
SNIFF
BIP
SNIFF
KNOCK OFF THE CRYIN', WOULD YA?!
GASP
WAAAH!
RIN?
WHY ARE YOU *YELLING* AT HIM?
BWAAAH!
UM, I JUST THOUGHT ...

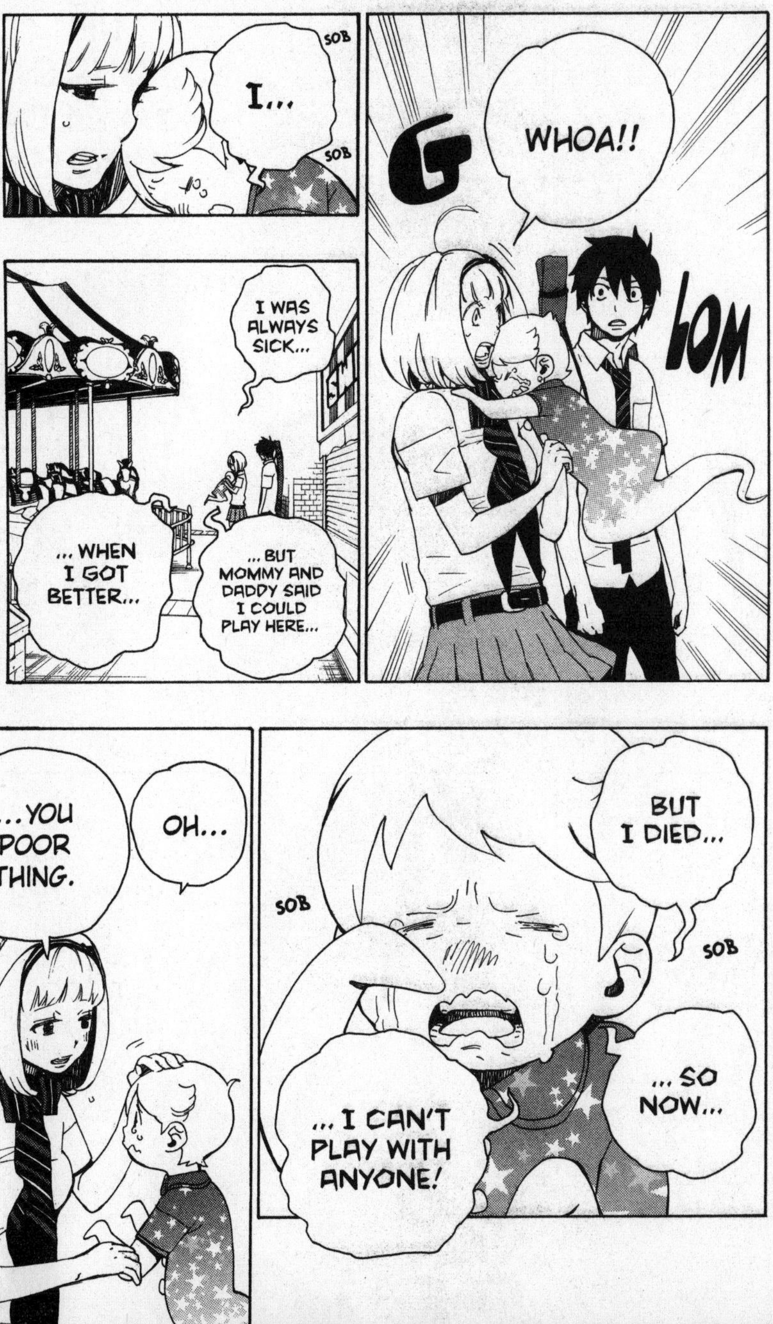
WHOA!!
G
BOM
SOB
I...
SOB
I WAS ALWAYS SICK...
... BUT MOMMY AND DADDY SAID I COULD PLAY HERE...
... WHEN I GOT BETTER...
BUT I DIED...
SOB
SOB
... SO NOW...
... I CAN'T PLAY WITH ANYONE!
OH...
... YOU POOR THING.

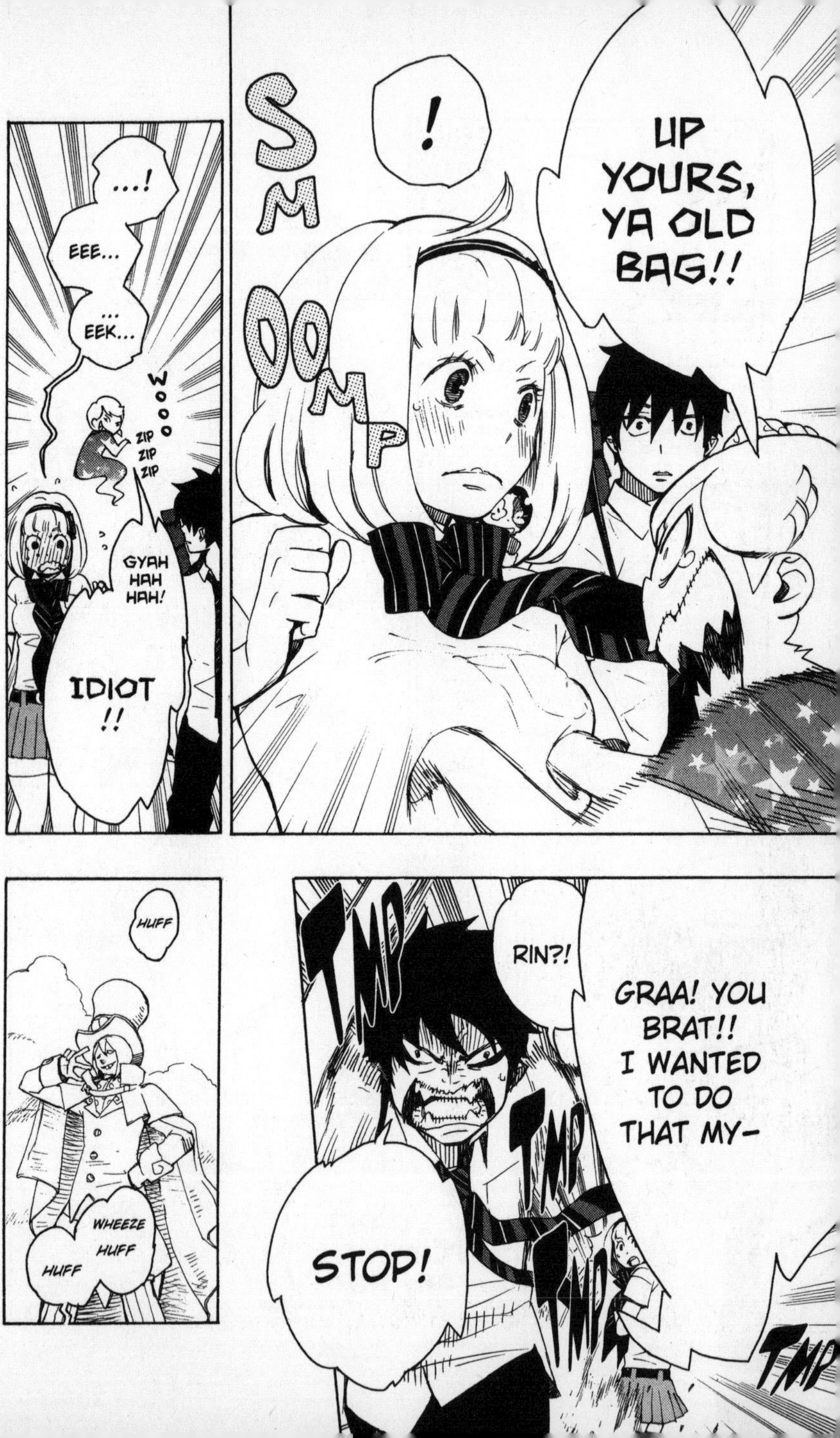
UP YOURS, YA OLD BAG!!
!
SMOOMP
...!
EEE...
...EEK...
WOOO
ZIP ZIP ZIP
GYAH HAH HAH!
IDIOT!!
GRAA! YOU BRAT!! I WANTED TO DO THAT MY-
RIN?!
TMP TMP TMP TMP TMP
STOP!
HUFF
WHEEZE HUFF
HUFF

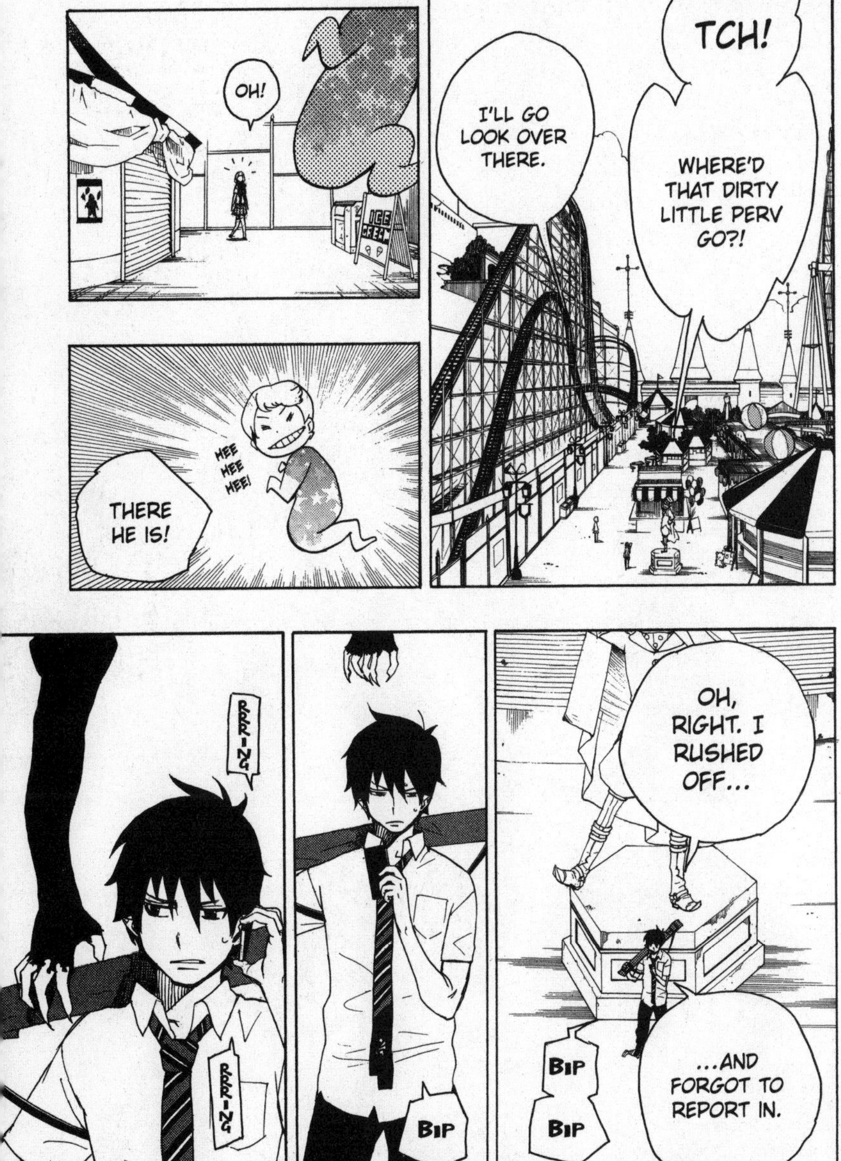
TCH!
WHERE'D THAT DIRTY LITTLE PERV GO?!
I'LL GO LOOK OVER THERE.
OH!
ICE CREAM
HEE HEE HEE!
THERE HE IS!
OH, RIGHT. I RUSHED OFF...
...AND FORGOT TO REPORT IN.
BIP
BIP
BIP
RRRING
RRRING

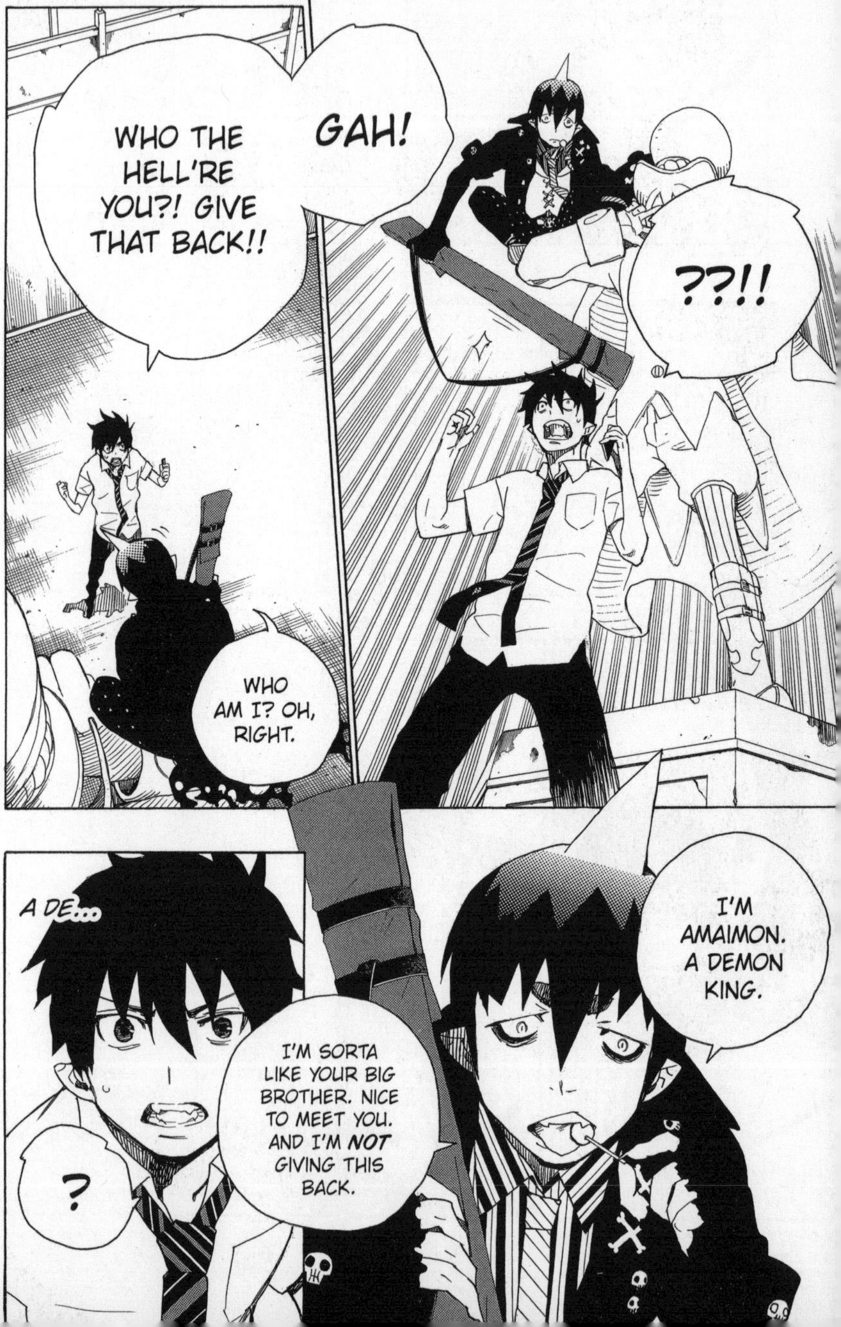
??!!
GAH!
WHO THE HELL'RE YOU?! GIVE THAT BACK!!
WHO AM I? OH, RIGHT.
I'M AMAIMON. A DEMON KING.
I'M SORTA LIKE YOUR BIG BROTHER. NICE TO MEET YOU. AND I'M *NOT* GIVING THIS BACK.
A DE...
?

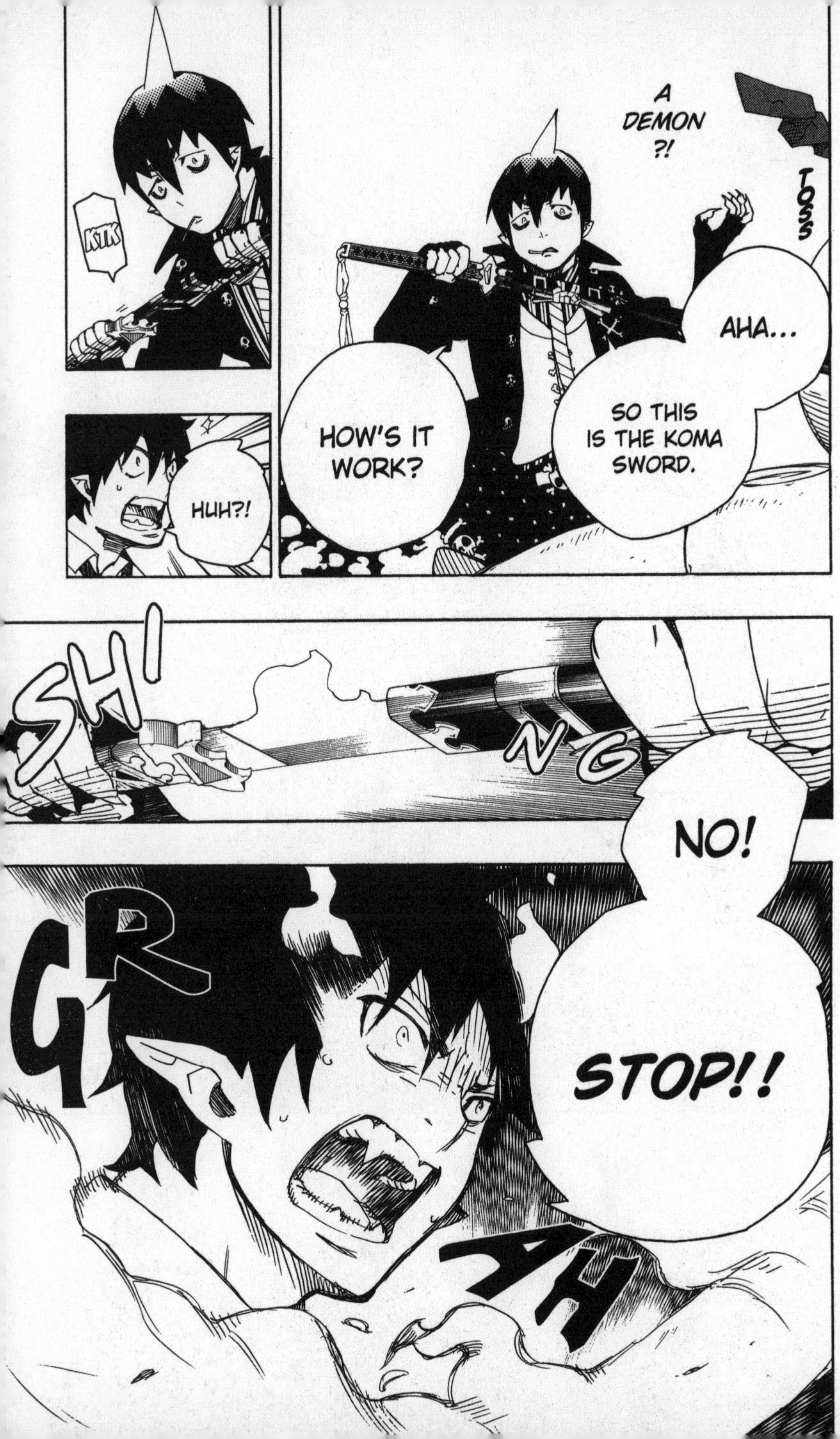
TOSS
A DEMON ?!
AHA...
SO THIS IS THE KOMA SWORD.
HOW'S IT WORK?
KTK
HUH?!
SHING
NO!
STOP!!
GR
AH

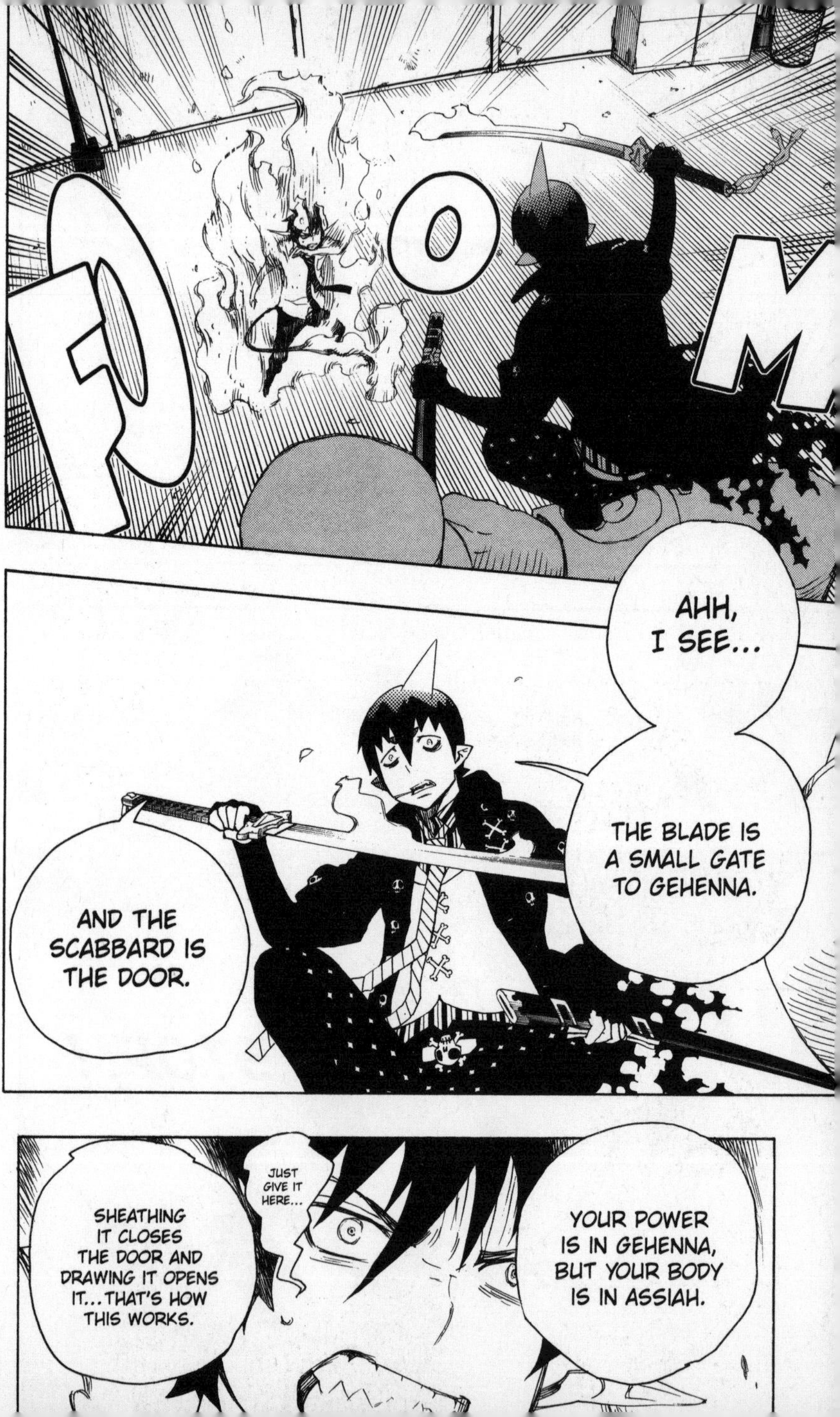
FOOM
AHH, I SEE...
THE BLADE IS A SMALL GATE TO GEHENNA.
AND THE SCABBARD IS THE DOOR.
YOUR POWER IS IN GEHENNA, BUT YOUR BODY IS IN ASSIAH.
JUST GIVE IT HERE...
SHEATHING IT CLOSES THE DOOR AND DRAWING IT OPENS IT...THAT'S HOW THIS WORKS.

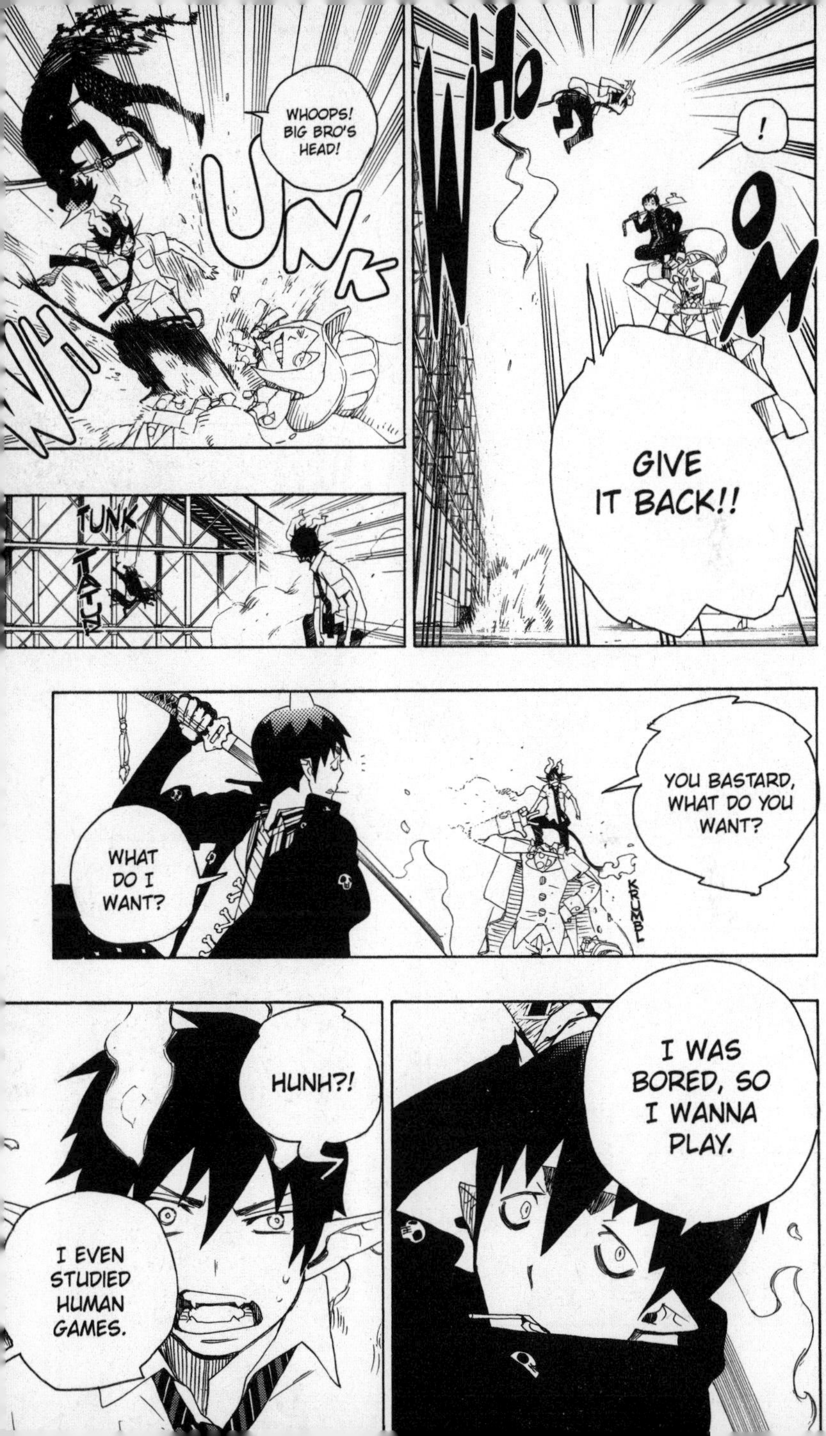
WHOOM
!
GIVE IT BACK!!
WHOOPS! BIG BRO'S HEAD!
WHUNK
TUNK
YOU BASTARD, WHAT DO YOU WANT?
KRUMBL
WHAT DO I WANT?
I WAS BORED, SO I WANNA PLAY.
HUNH?!
I EVEN STUDIED HUMAN GAMES.

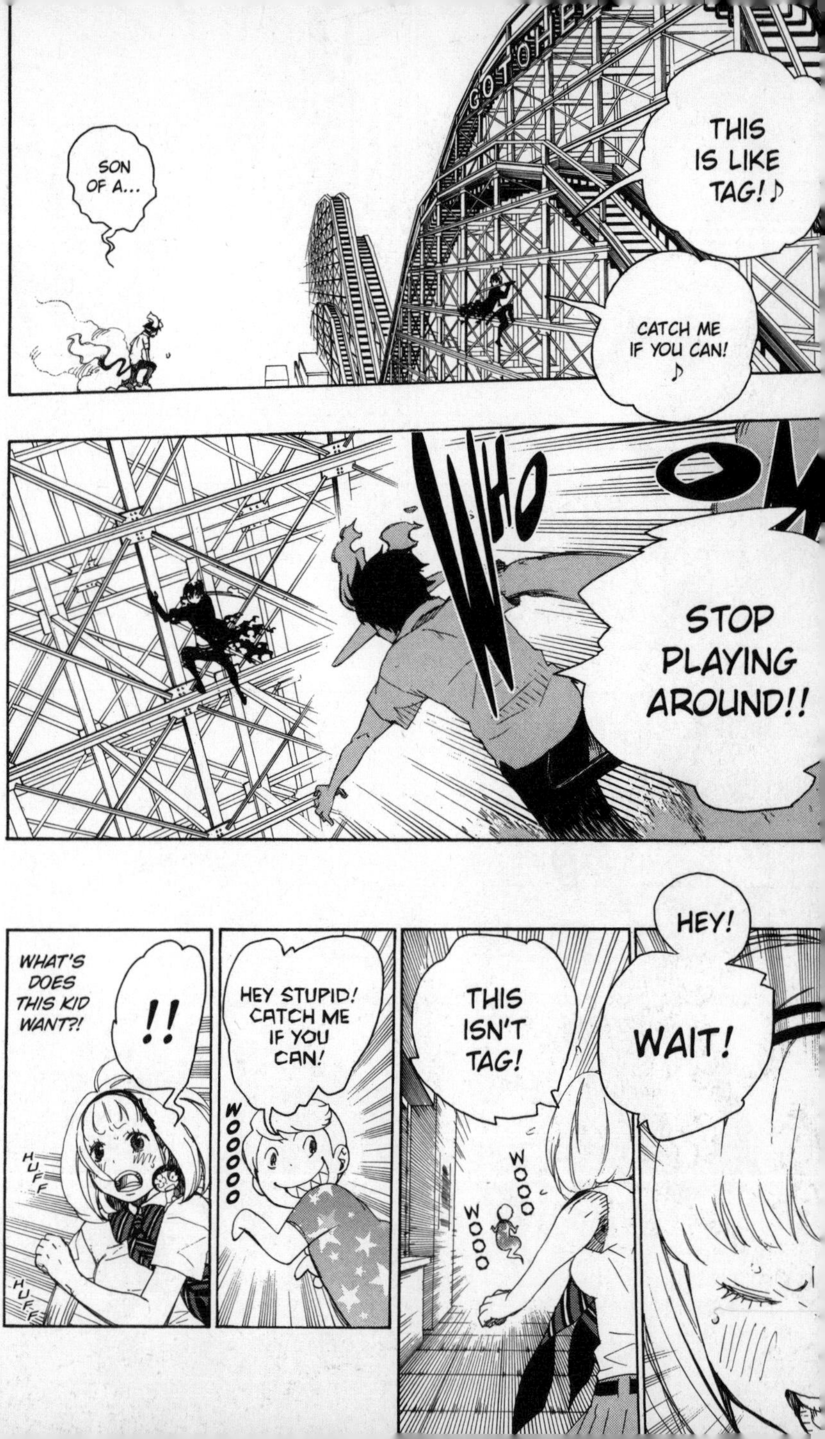
THIS IS LIKE TAG!♪
CATCH ME IF YOU CAN! ♪
SON OF A...
WHOOM
STOP PLAYING AROUND!!
HEY!
WAIT!
THIS ISN'T TAG!
WOOO
WOOO
HEY STUPID! CATCH ME IF YOU CAN!
WOOOOO
!!
WHAT'S DOES THIS KID WANT?!
HUFF
HUFF

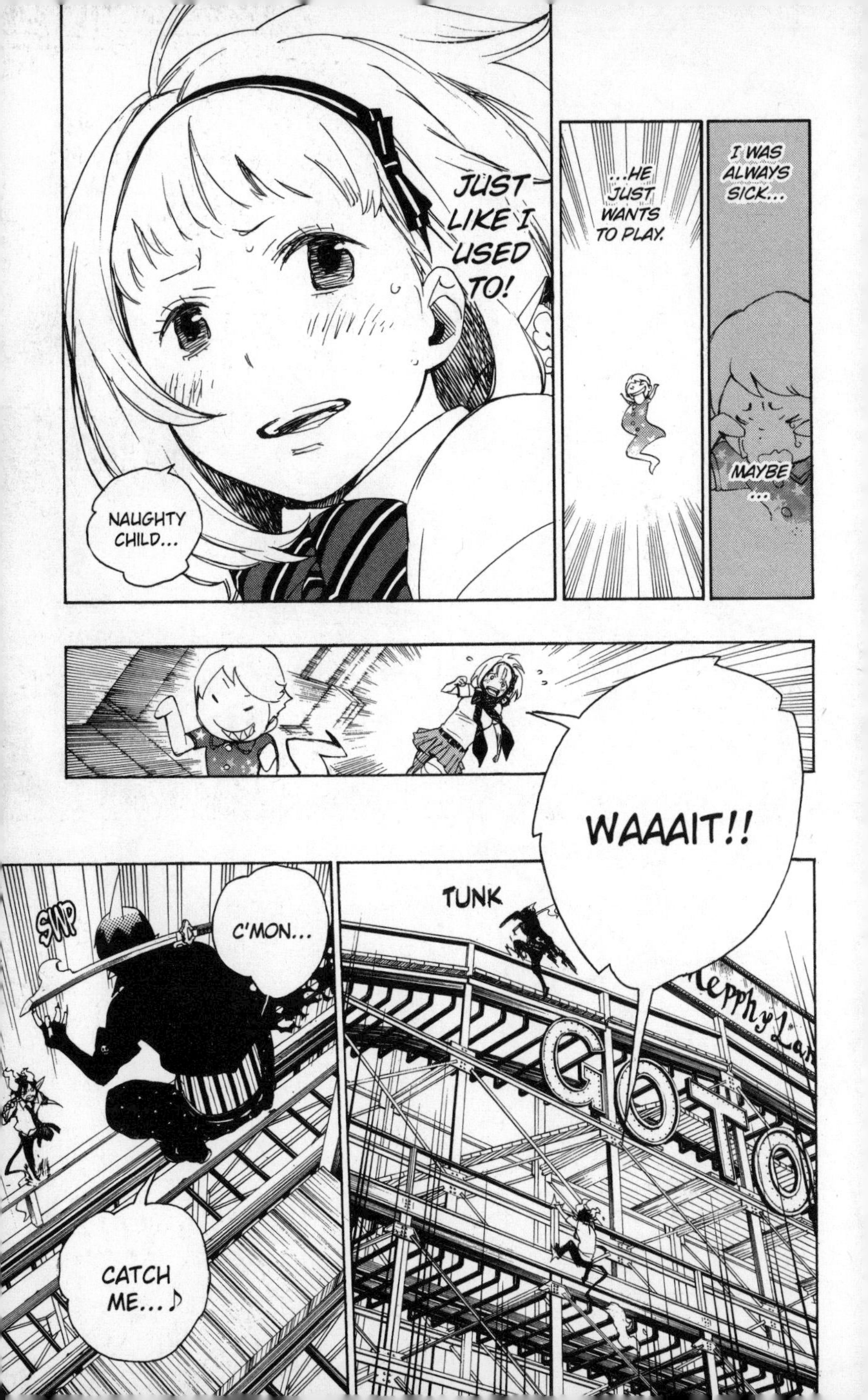
I WAS ALWAYS SICK...
MAYBE...
...HE JUST WANTS TO PLAY.
JUST LIKE I USED TO!
NAUGHTY CHILD...
WAAAIT!!
TUNK
GOTO
SWP
C'MON...
CATCH ME...♪

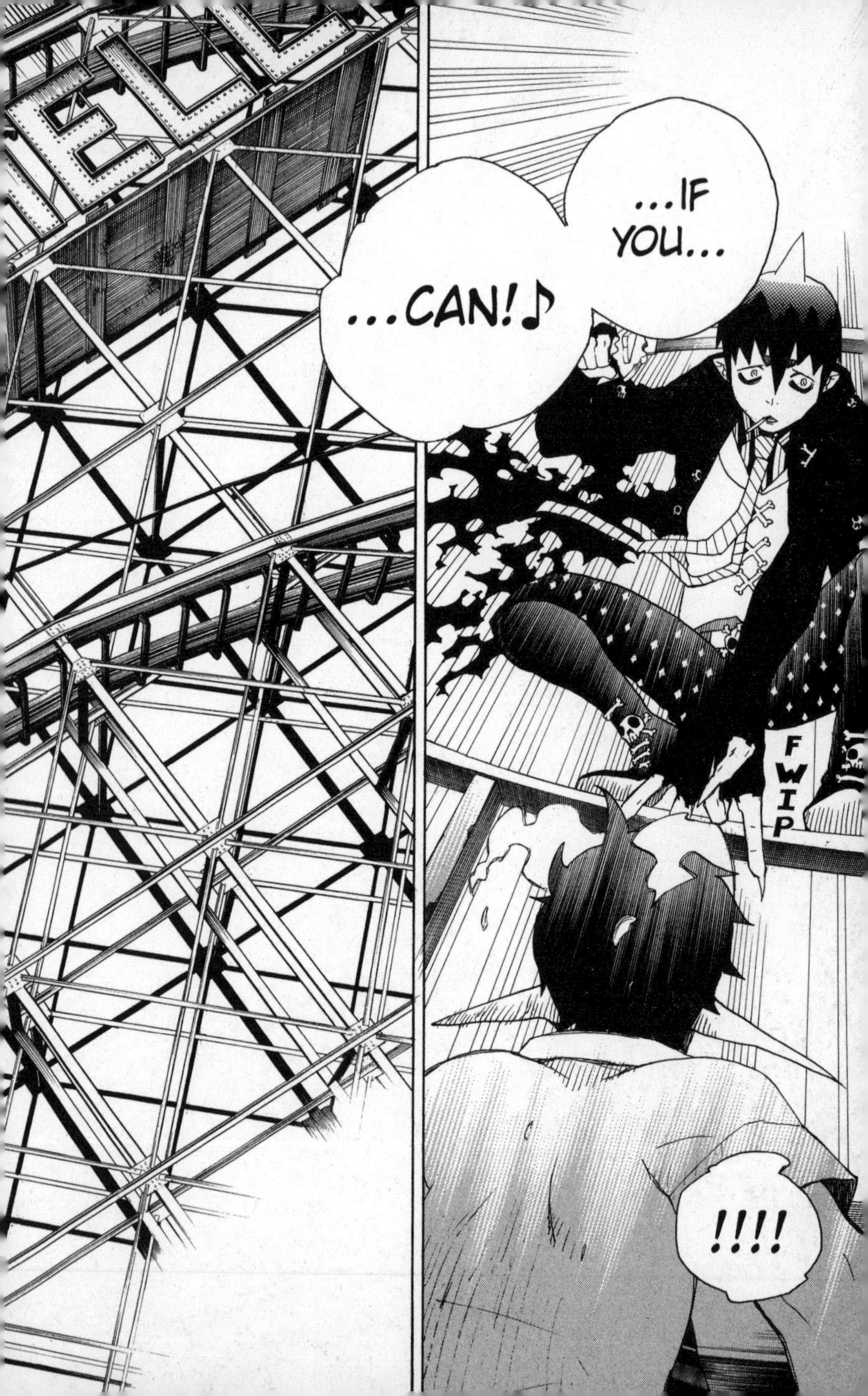
...IF YOU...
...CAN!♪
FWIP
!!!!

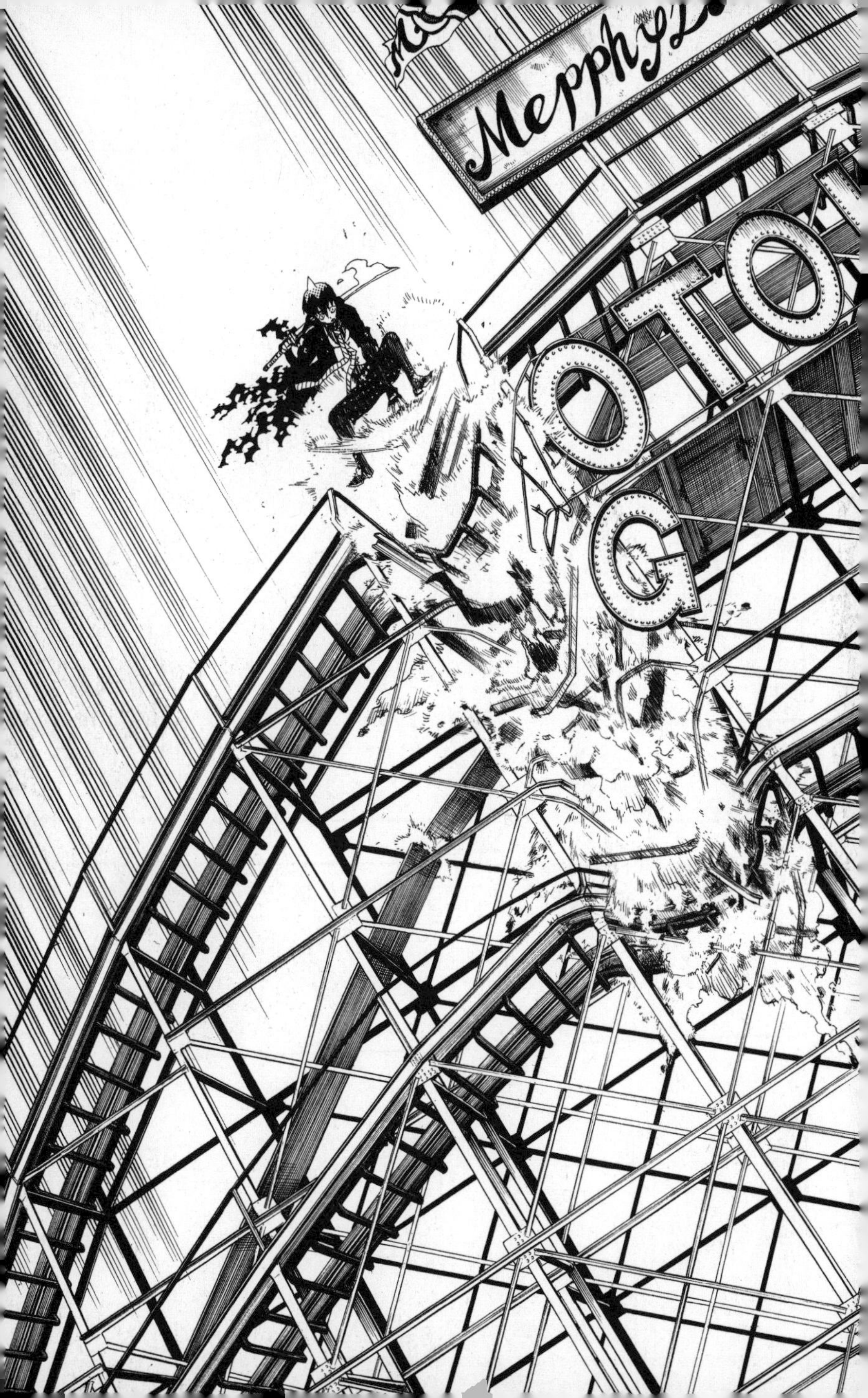
Mepph's

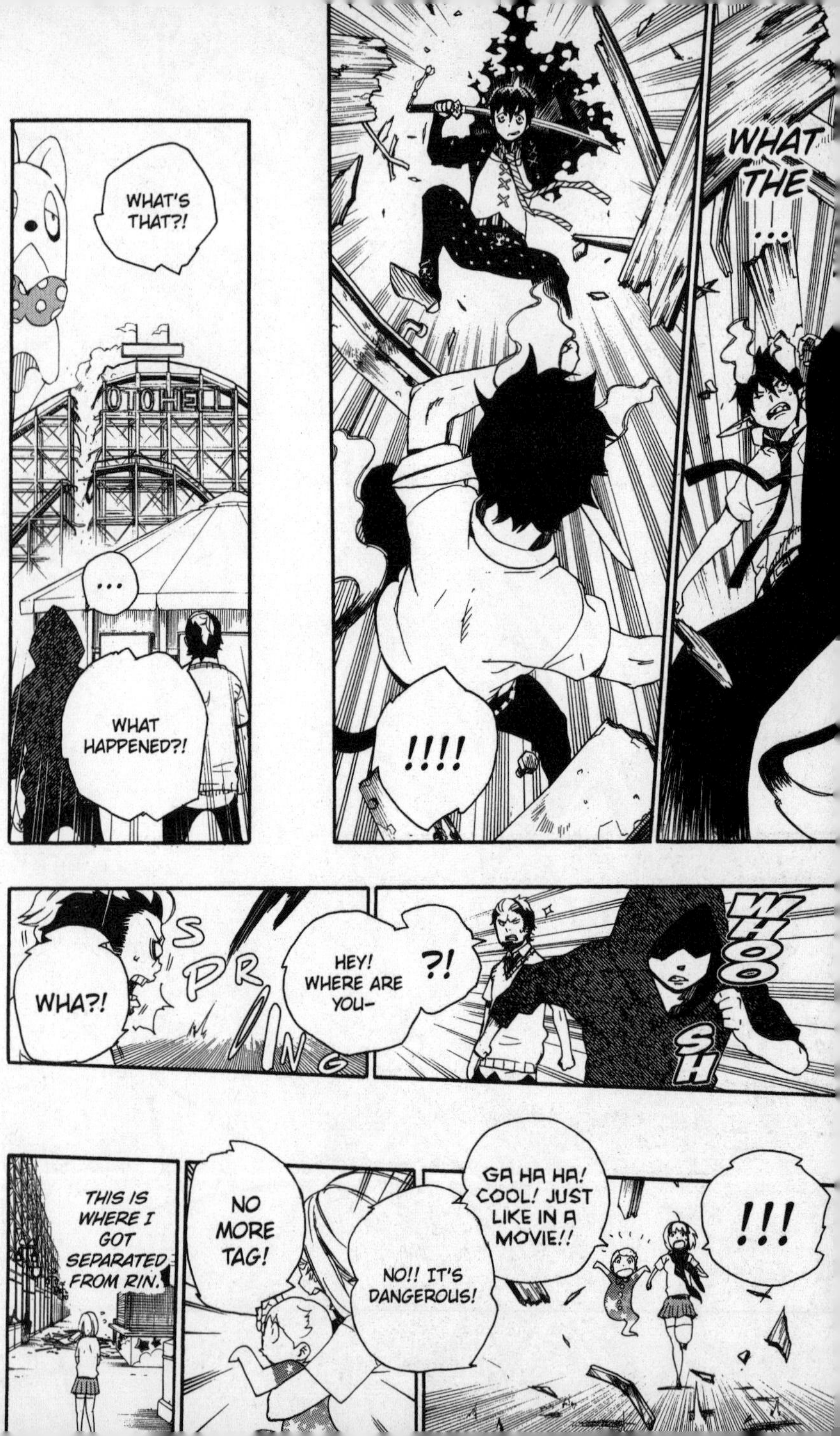
WHAT THE ...
!!!!
WHAT'S THAT?!
...
WHAT HAPPENED?!
WHOOSH
?!
HEY! WHERE ARE YOU-
SPRING
WHA?!
!!!
GA HA HA! COOL! JUST LIKE IN A MOVIE!!
NO!! IT'S DANGEROUS!
NO MORE TAG!
THIS IS WHERE I GOT SEPARATED FROM RIN.

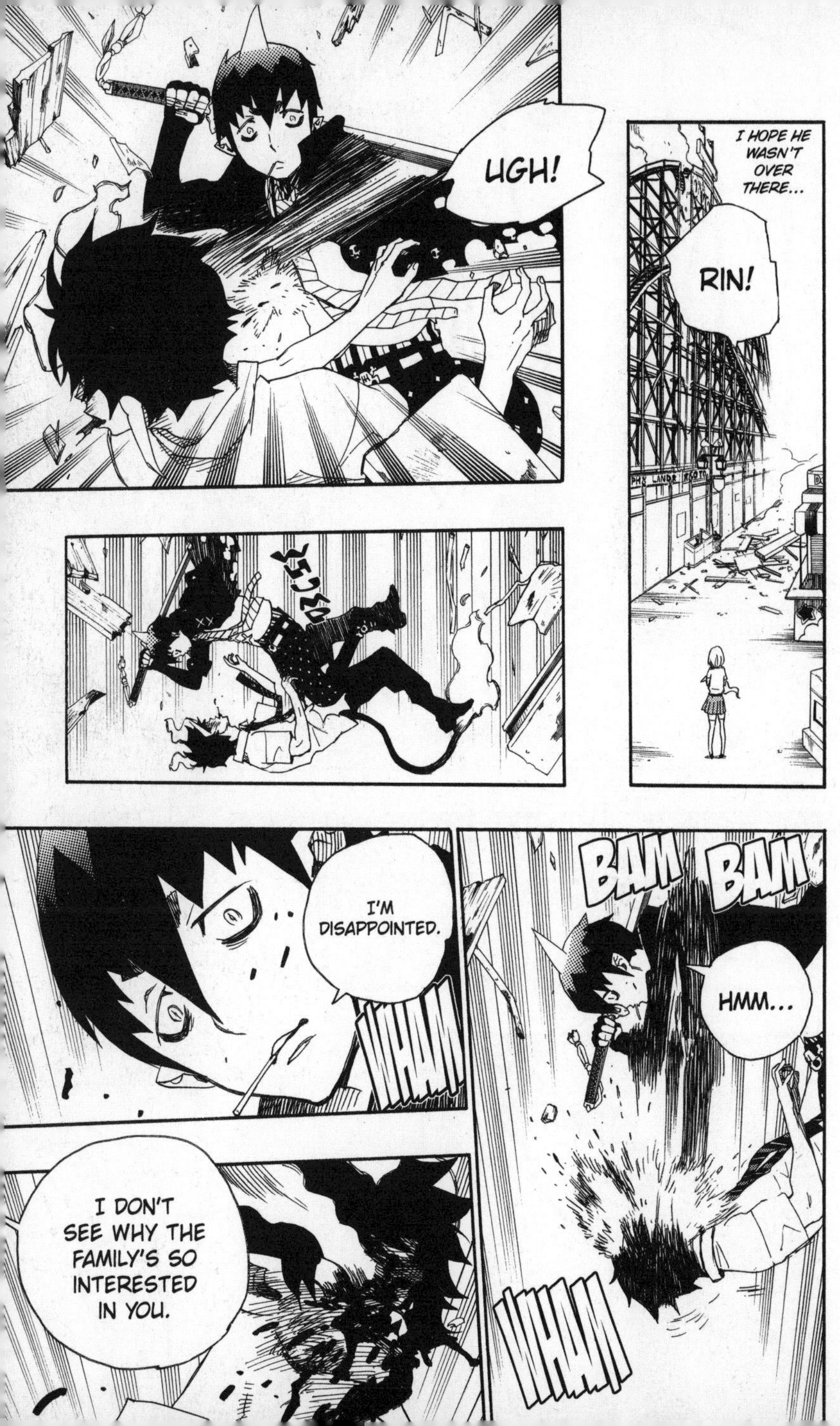
I HOPE HE WASN'T OVER THERE...
RIN!
UGH!
BAM BAM
HMM...
WHAM
I'M DISAPPOINTED.
WHAM
I DON'T SEE WHY THE FAMILY'S SO INTERESTED IN YOU.

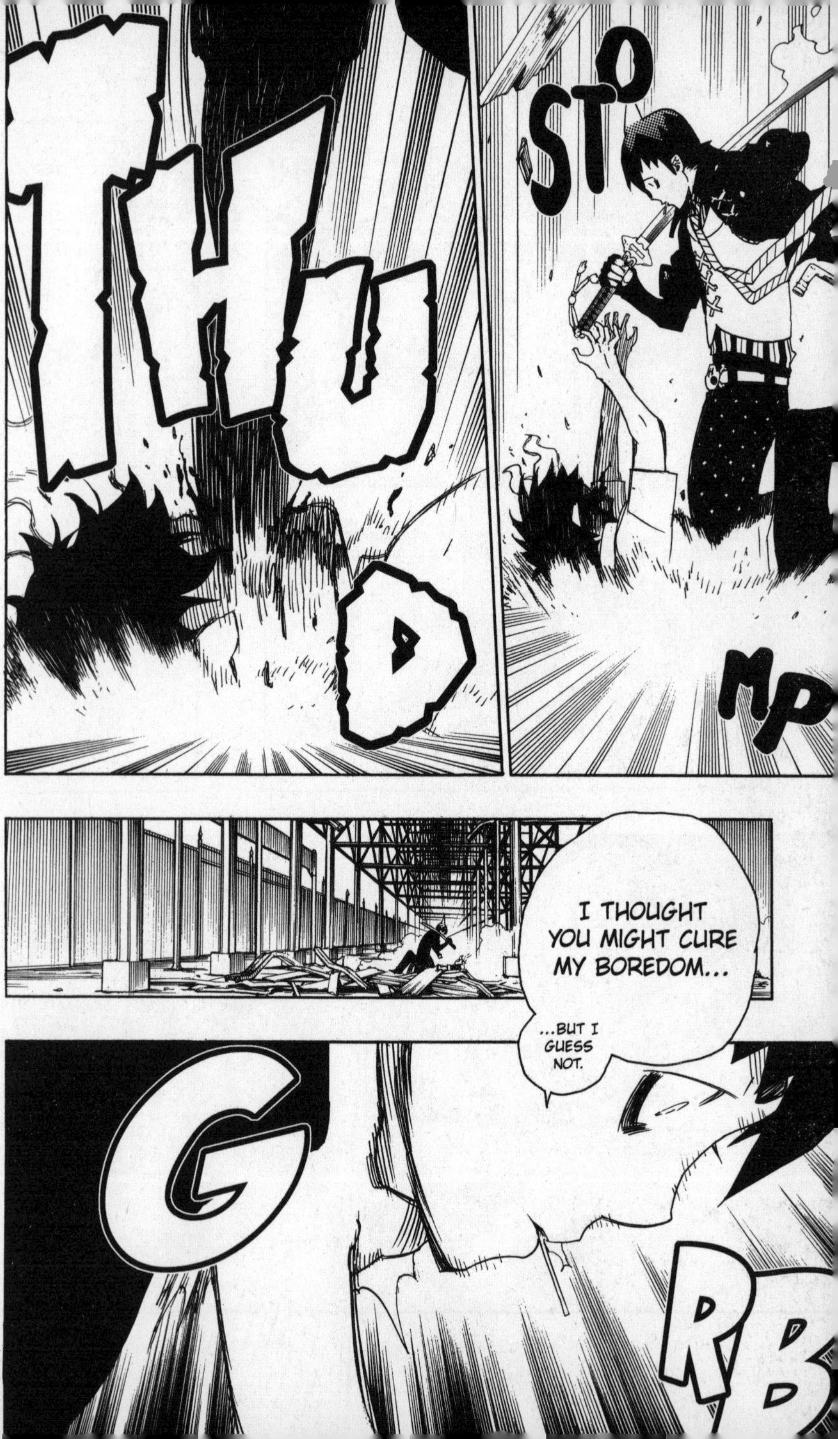
STO
MP
THU
D
I THOUGHT YOU MIGHT CURE MY BOREDOM...
...BUT I GUESS NOT.
G
RB

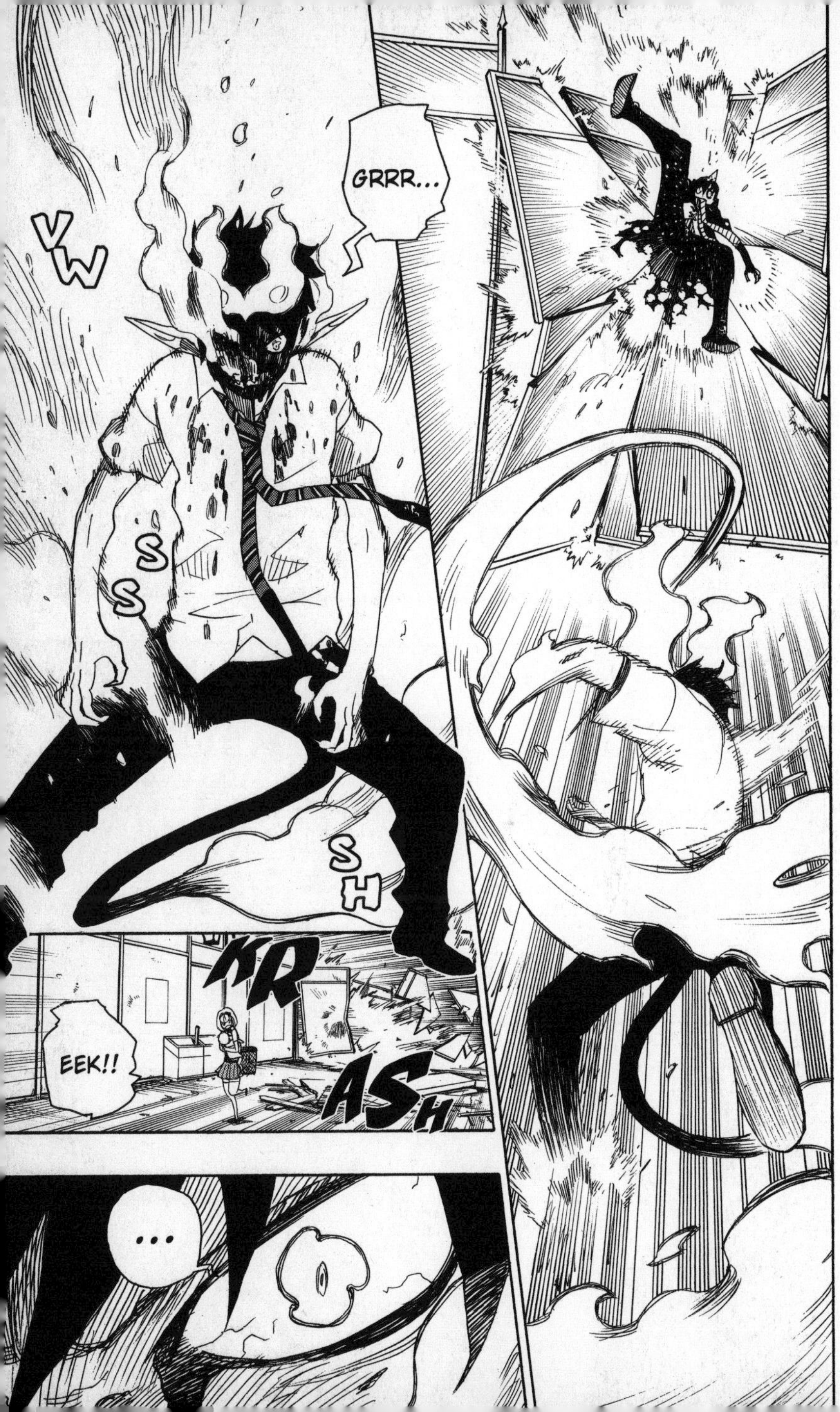
GRRR...
VW
SS
SH
KRASH
EEK!!
...

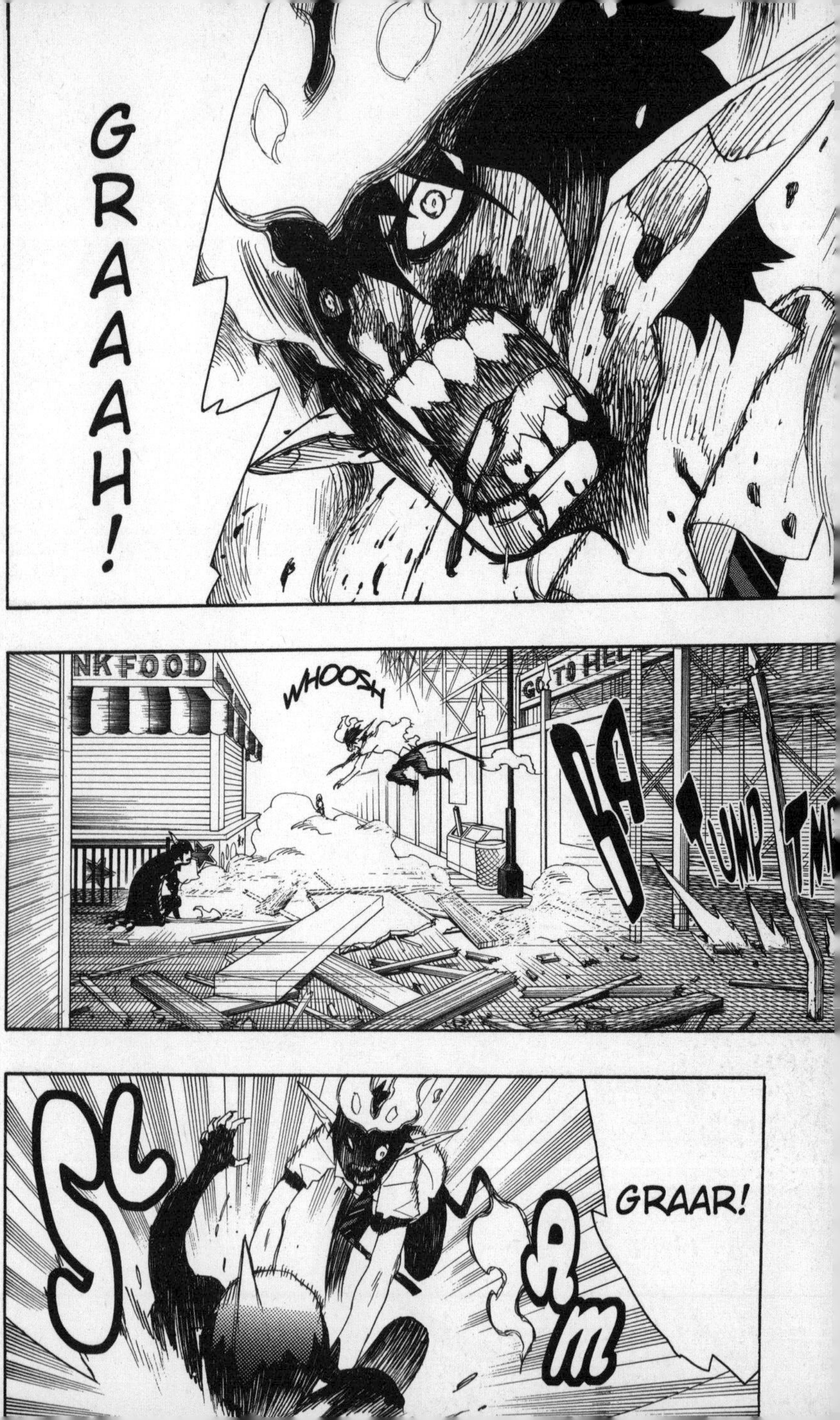
GRAAAH!
NKFOOD
WHOOSH
GRAAR!

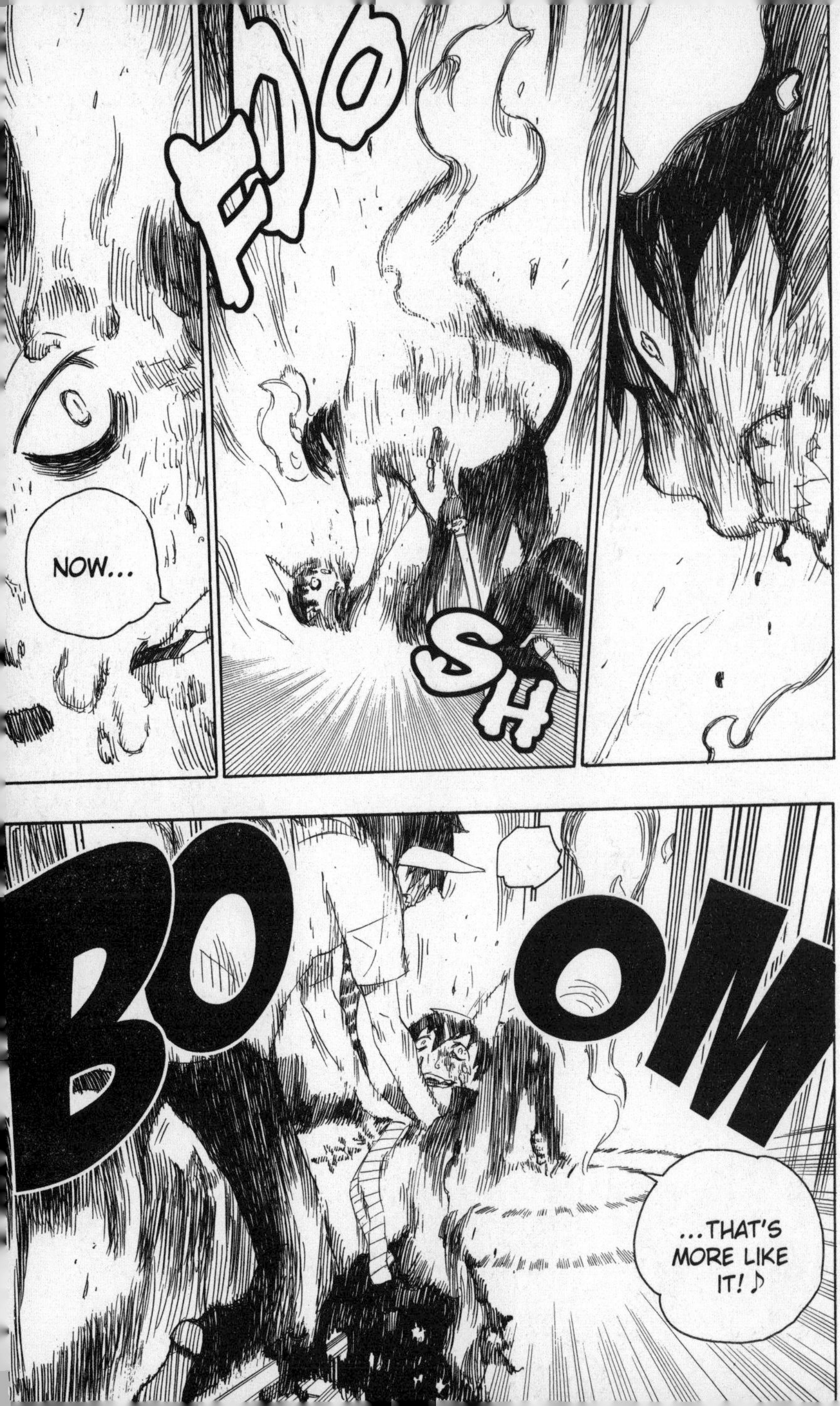
SH
NOW...
BOOM
...THAT'S MORE LIKE IT!♪

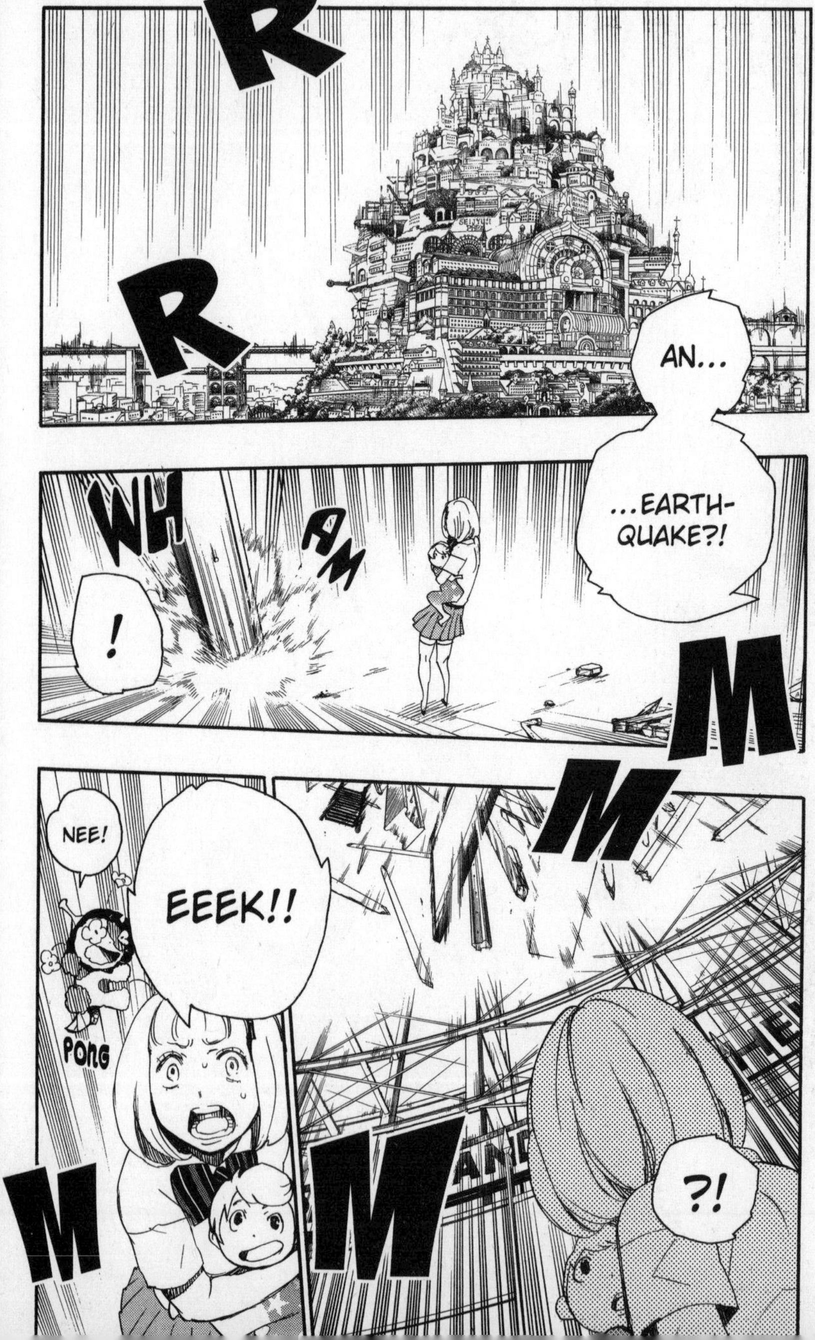

R
R
AN...
...EARTH-QUAKE?!
WH
AM
!
M
M
?!
M
NEE!
EEEK!!
PONG
M

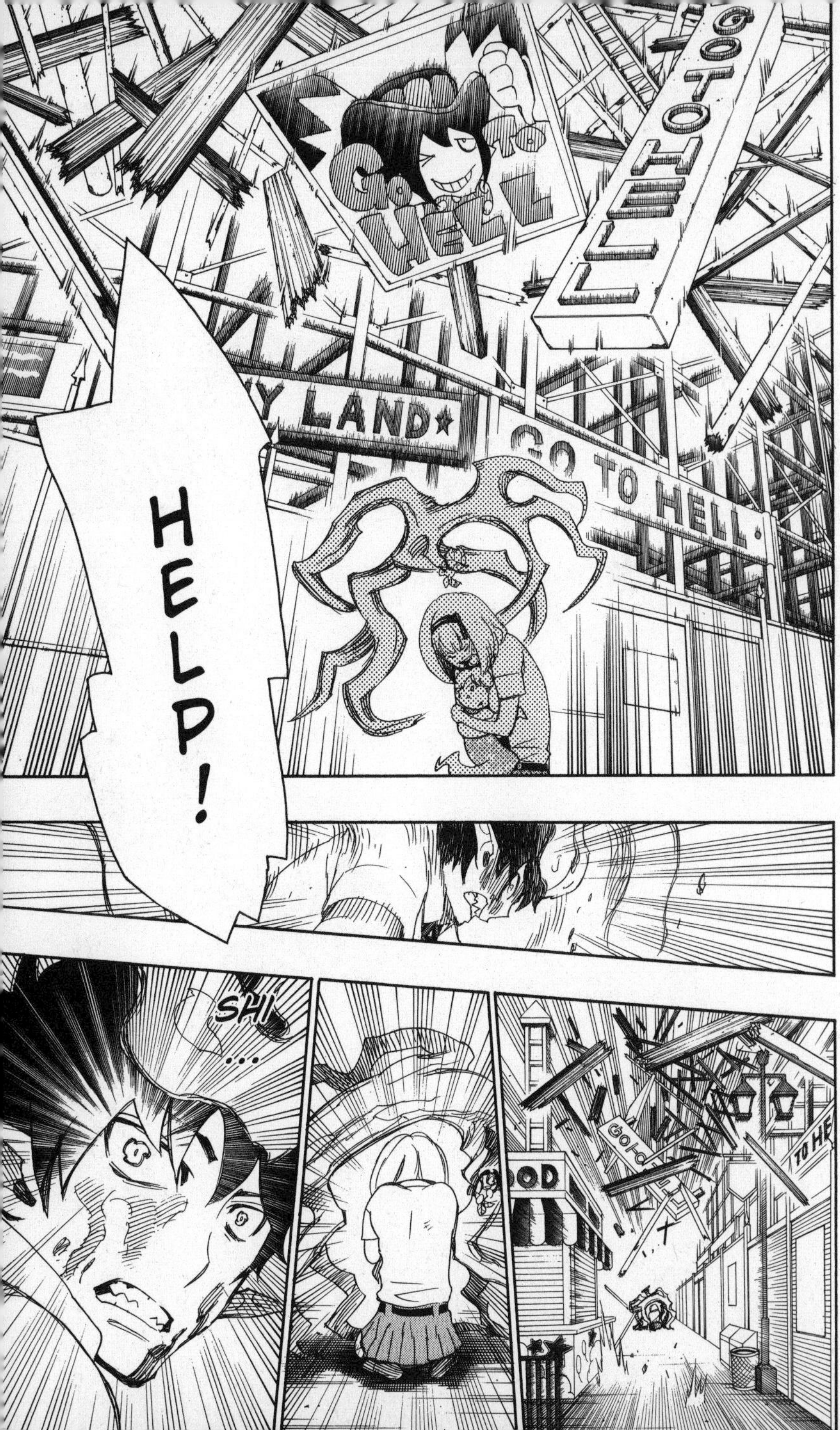
GO TO HELL
GO TO HELL
LAND
GO TO HELL
HELP!
SHI
...
OD
GO TO
TO HE

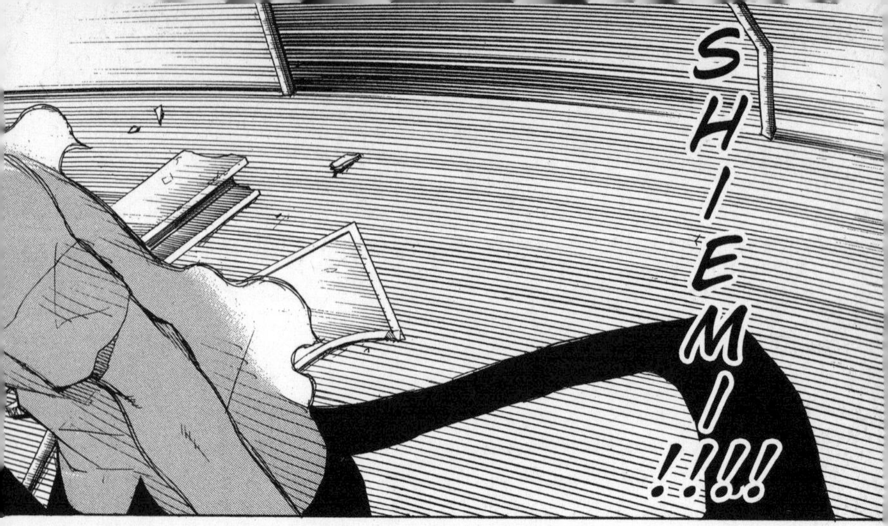
SHIEMI!!!!!
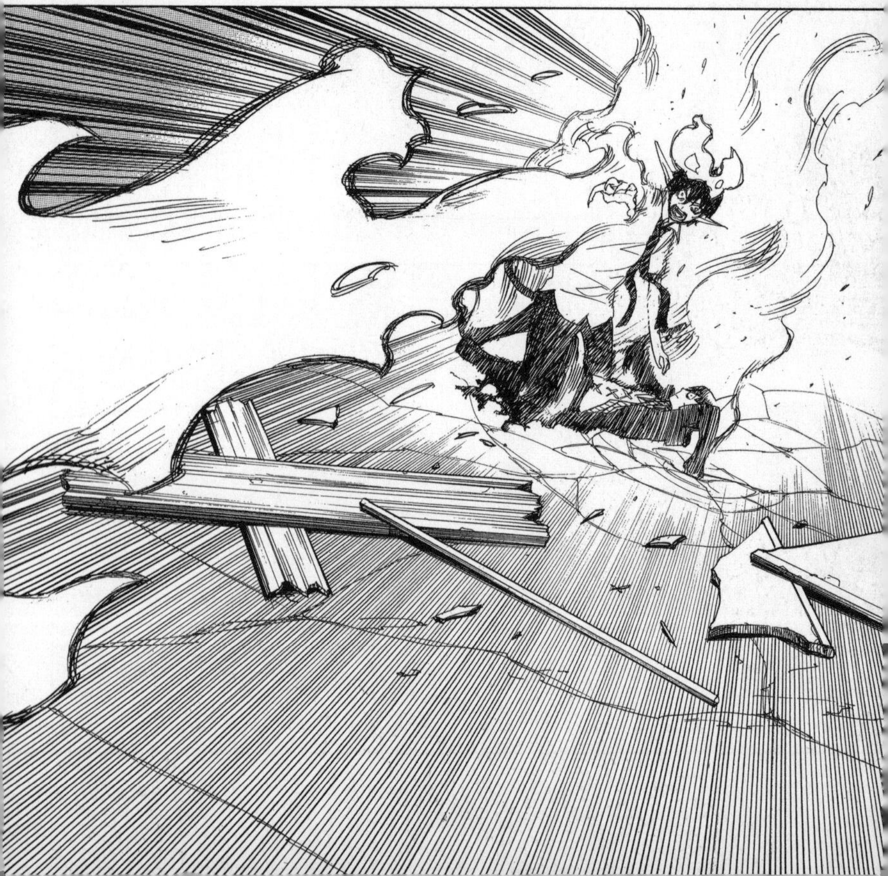

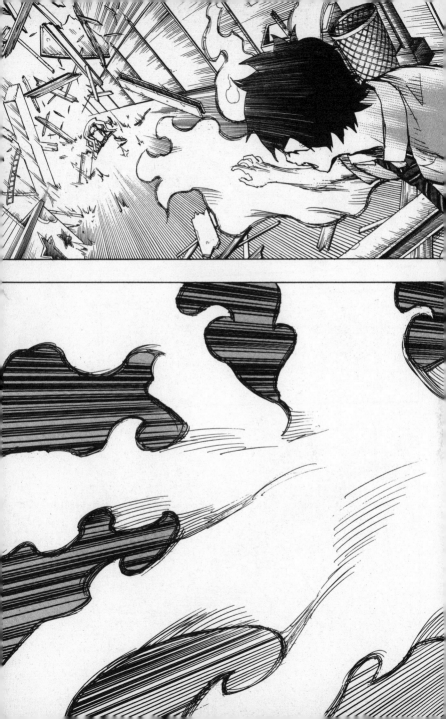

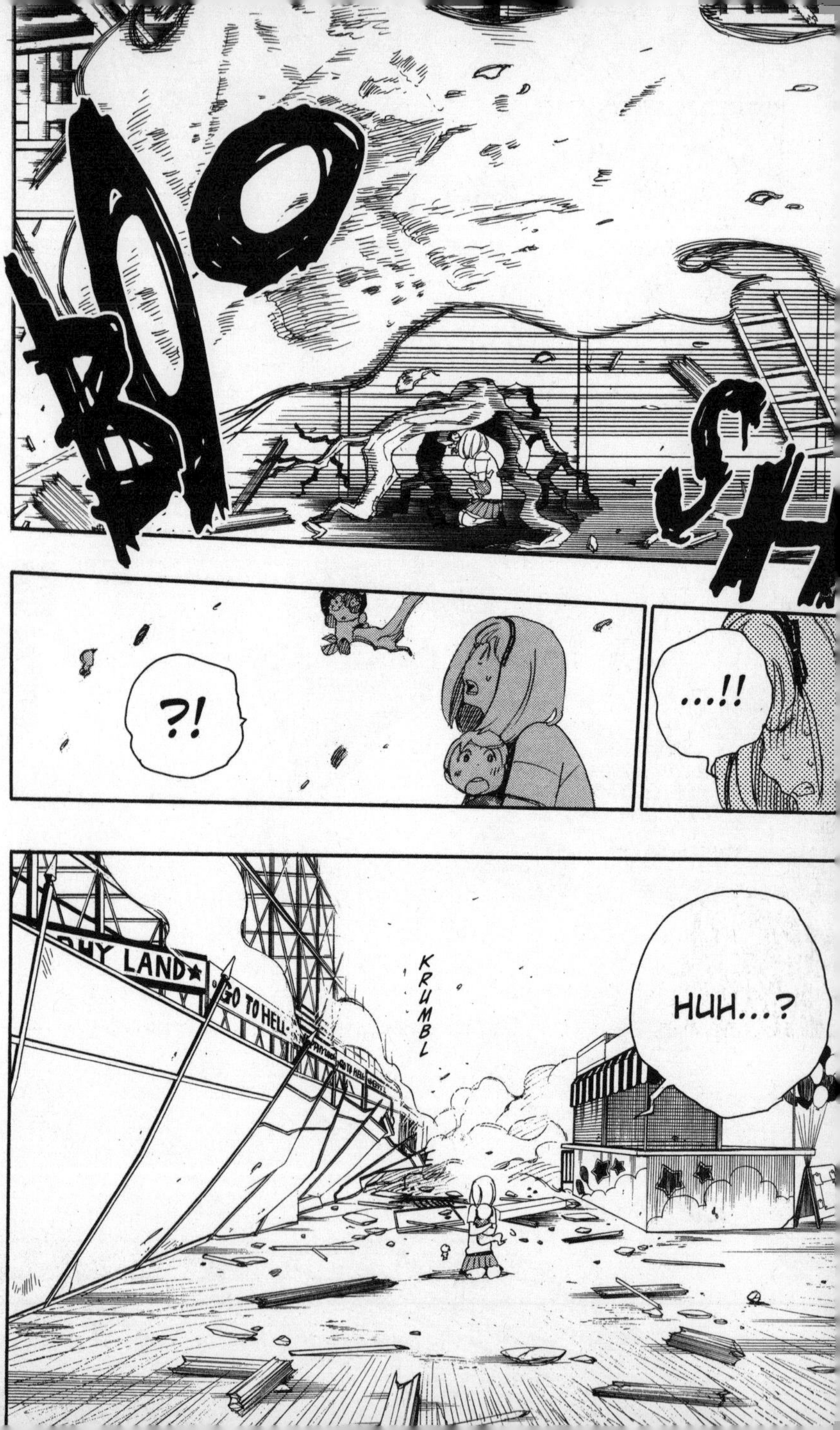
...!!
?!
HUH...?
KRUMBL
GO TO HELL

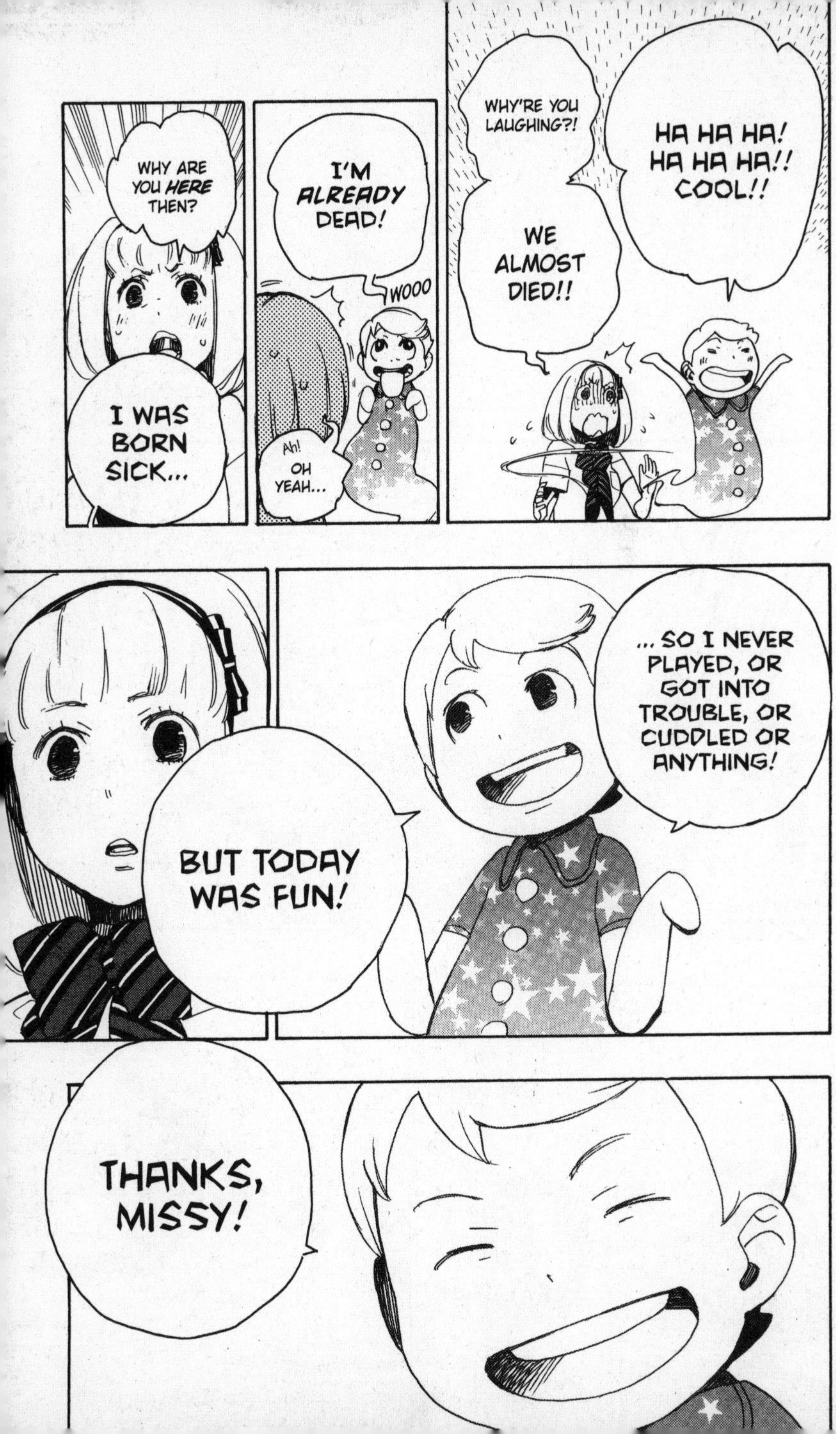
HA HA HA! HA HA HA!! COOL!!
WHY'RE YOU LAUGHING?!
WE ALMOST DIED!!
I'M *ALREADY* DEAD!
WOOO
Ah! OH YEAH...
WHY ARE YOU *HERE* THEN?
I WAS BORN SICK...
...SO I NEVER PLAYED, OR GOT INTO TROUBLE, OR CUDDLED OR ANYTHING!
BUT TODAY WAS FUN!
THANKS, MISSY!

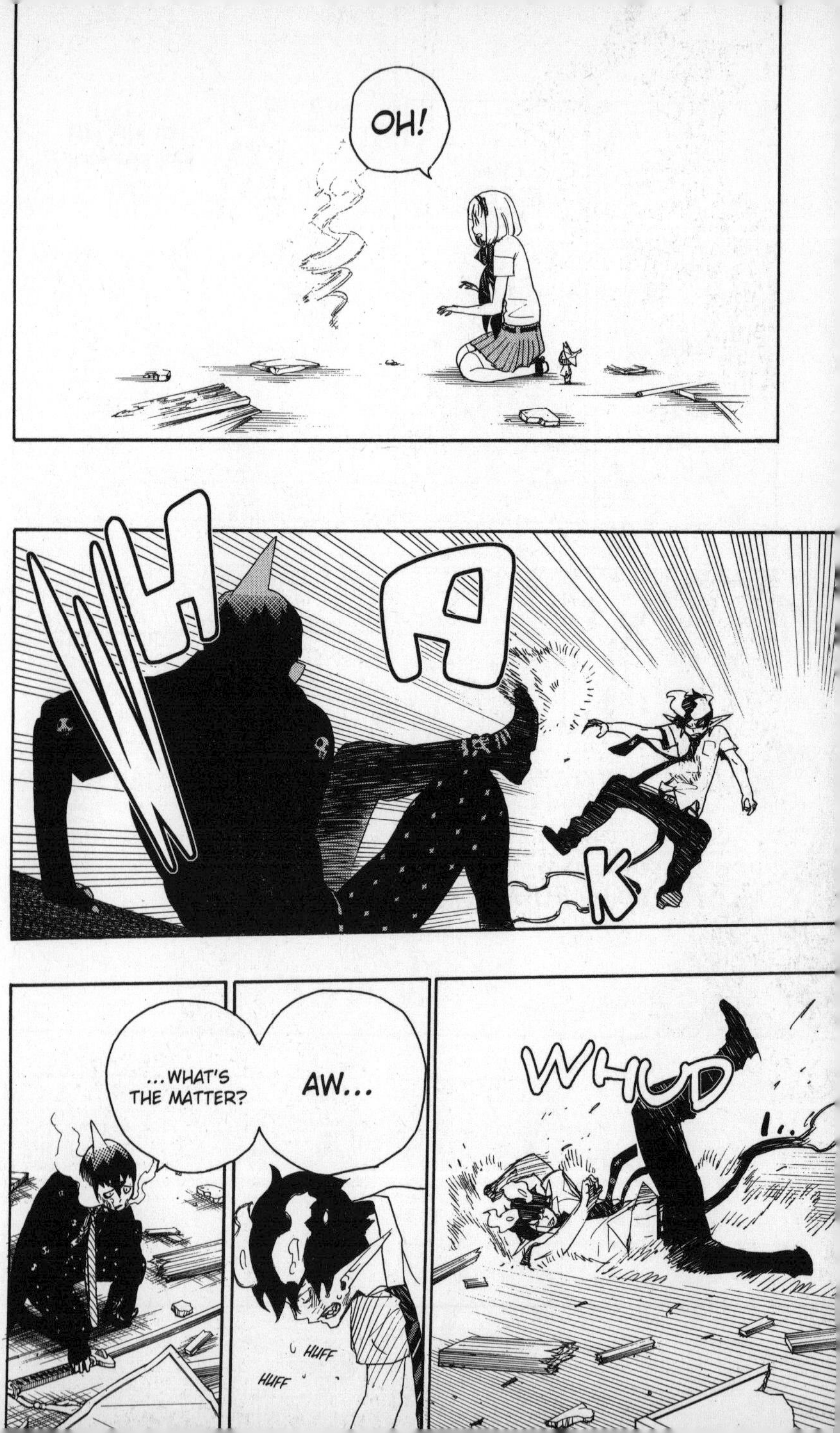
OH!
WHAK
WHUD
AW...
HUFF
HUFF
...WHAT'S THE MATTER?

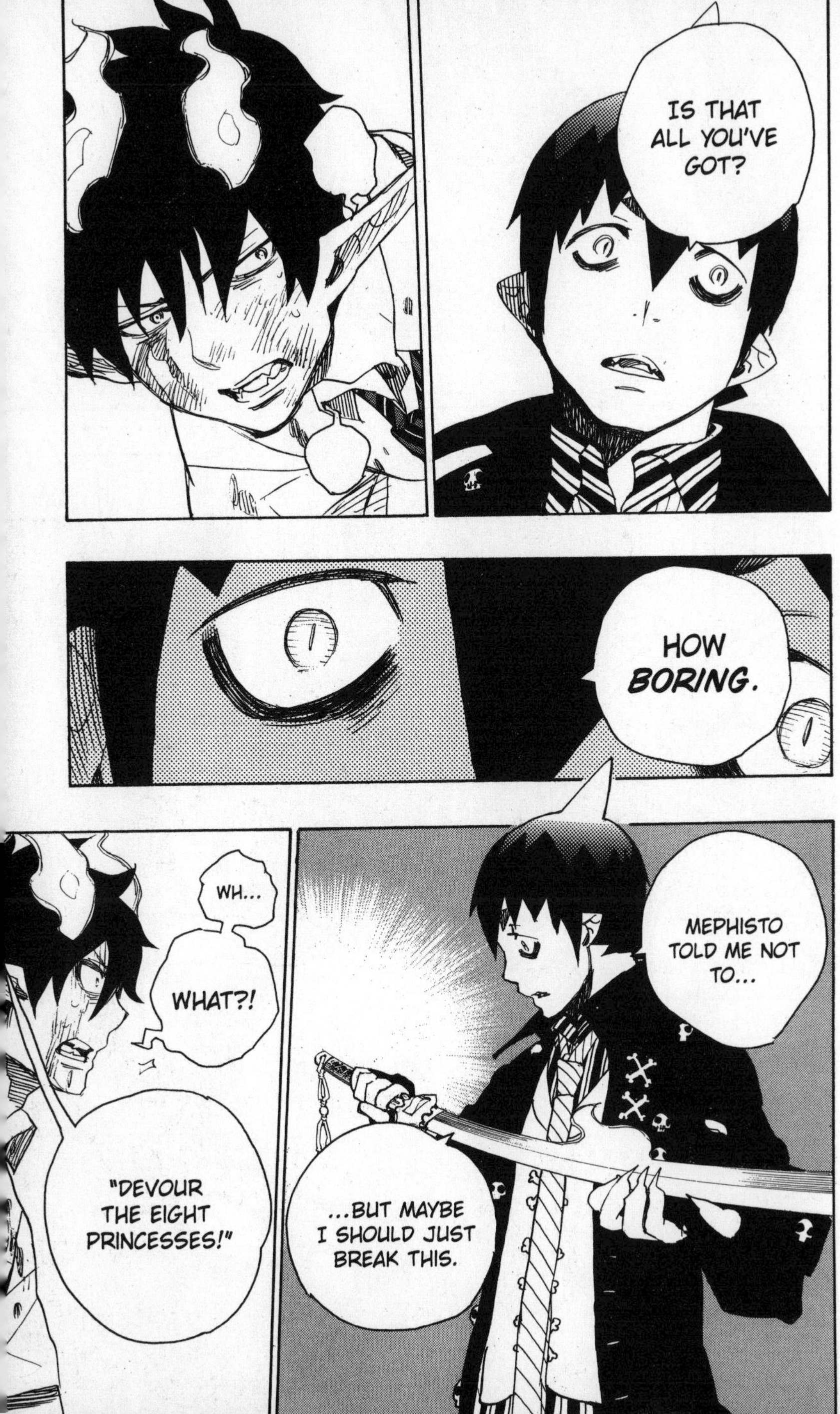
IS THAT ALL YOU'VE GOT?
HOW BORING.
MEPHISTO TOLD ME NOT TO...
...BUT MAYBE I SHOULD JUST BREAK THIS.
WH...
WHAT?!
"DEVOUR THE EIGHT PRINCESSES!"

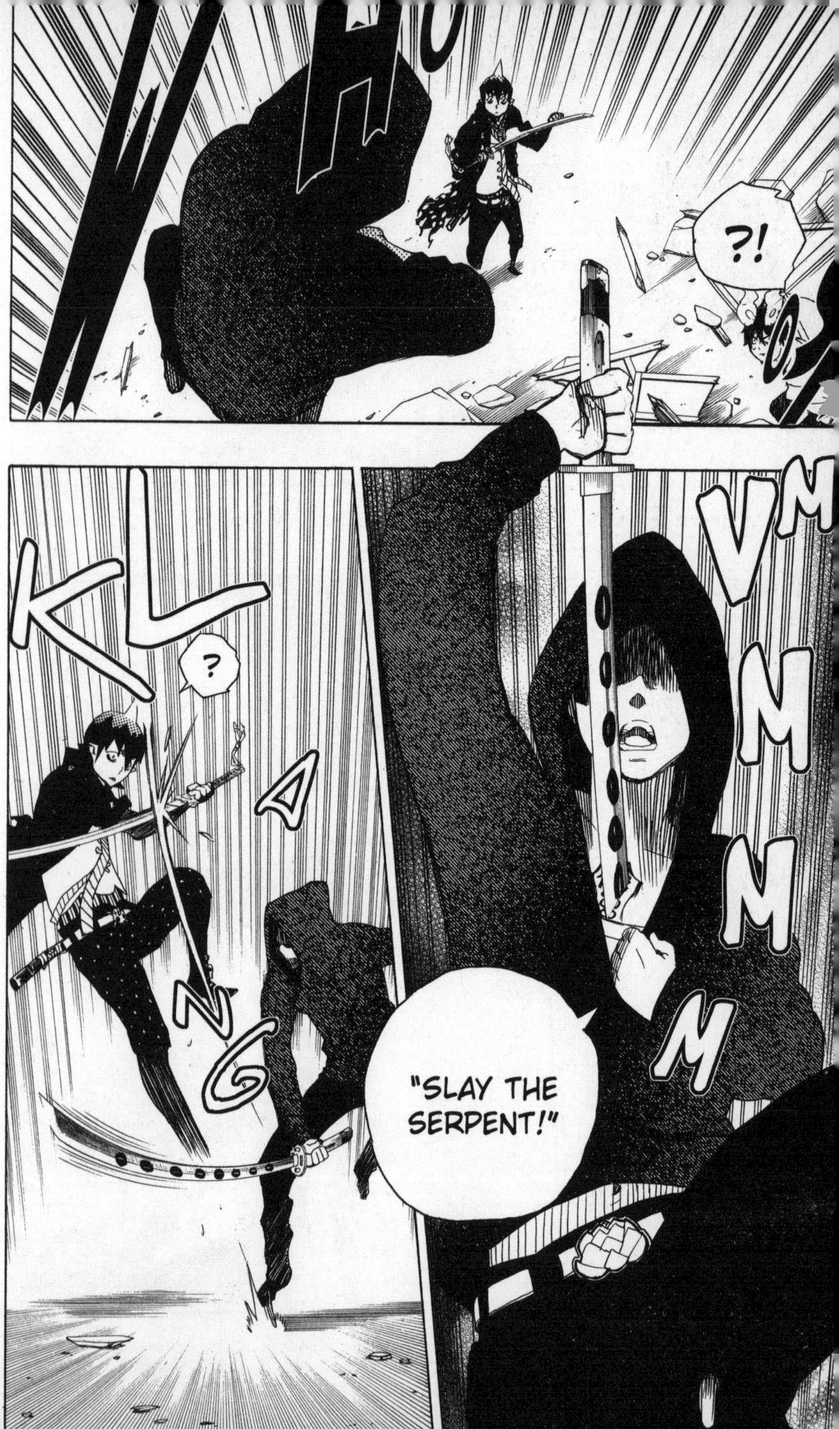
WHU
?!
VMVMMMM
"SLAY THE SERPENT!"
KLANG
?

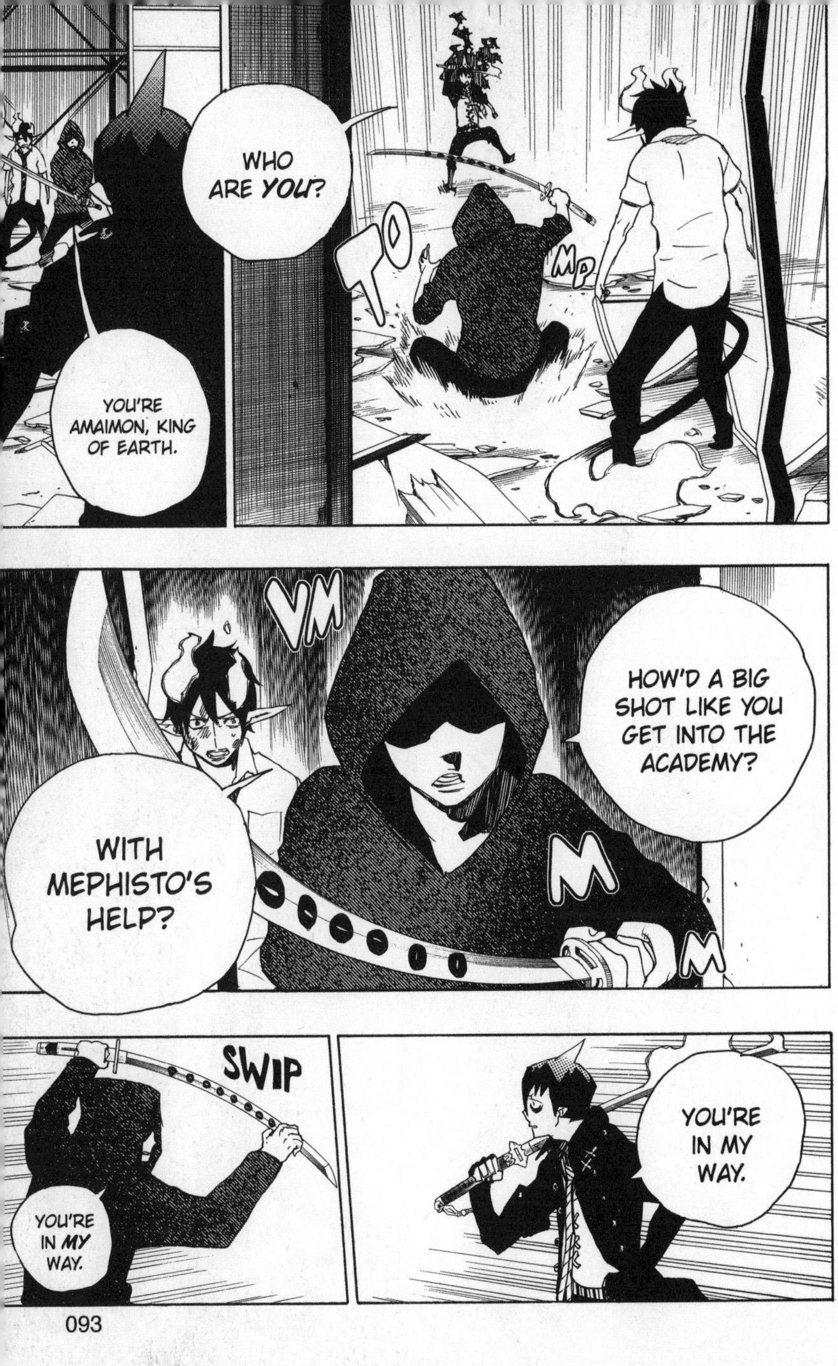
TO
MP
WHO ARE YOU?
YOU'RE AMAIMON, KING OF EARTH.
VM
HOW'D A BIG SHOT LIKE YOU GET INTO THE ACADEMY?
M
M
WITH MEPHISTO'S HELP?
YOU'RE IN MY WAY.
SWIP
YOU'RE IN *MY* WAY.

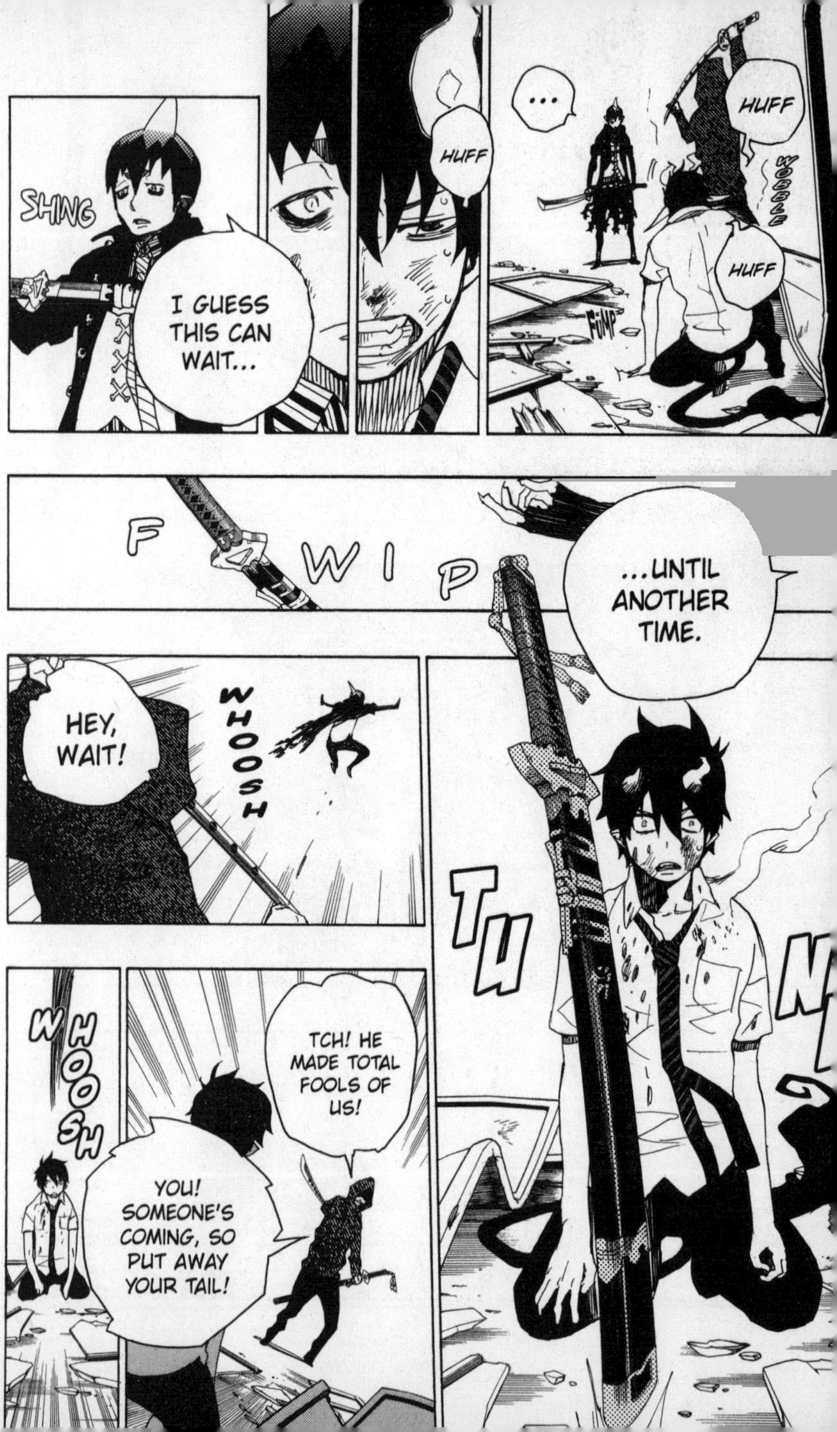
...
HUFF
WOBBLE
HUFF
FUMP
HUFF
SHING
I GUESS THIS CAN WAIT...
F W I P
...UNTIL ANOTHER TIME.
TUN
HEY, WAIT!
WHOOSH
TCH! HE MADE TOTAL FOOLS OF US!
YOU! SOMEONE'S COMING, SO PUT AWAY YOUR TAIL!
WHOOSH

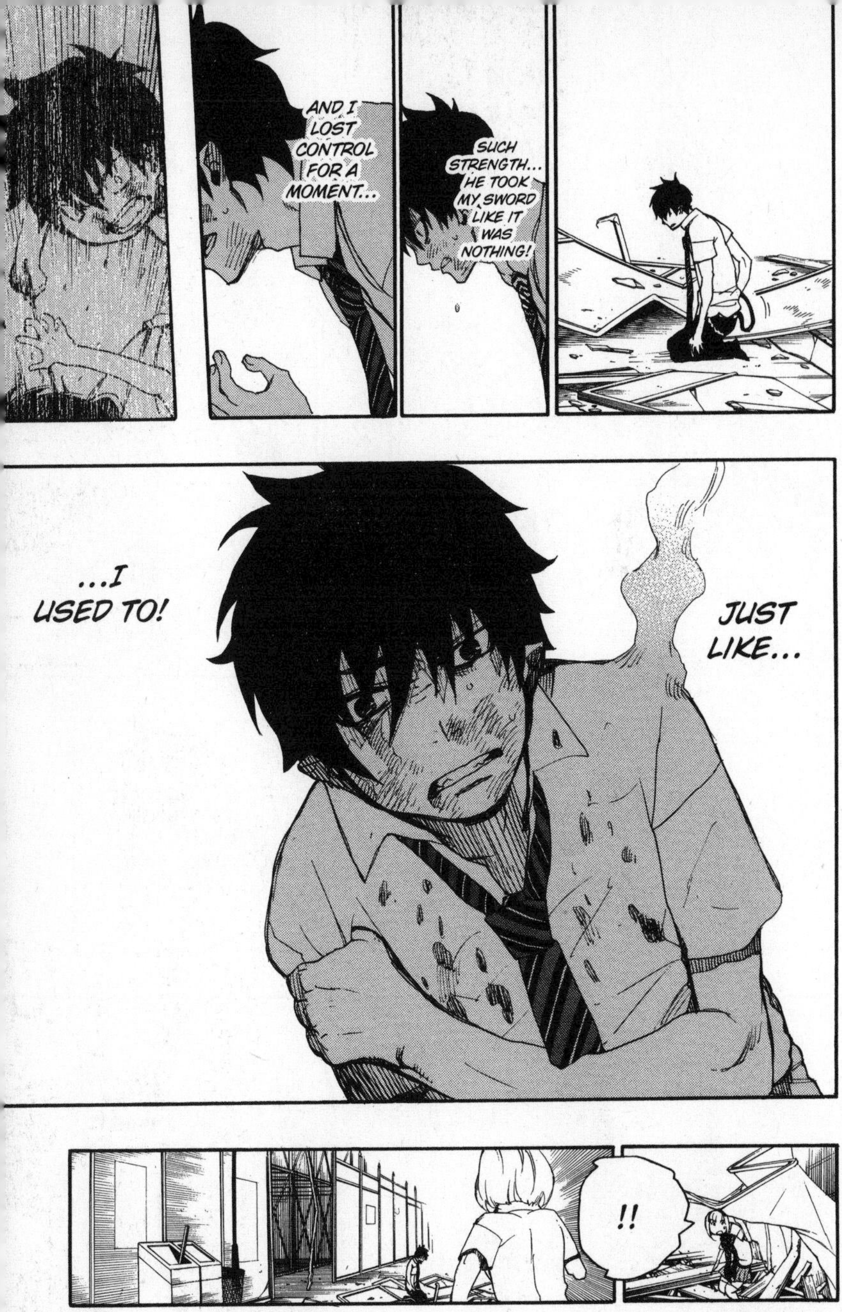
SUCH STRENGTH... HE TOOK MY SWORD LIKE IT WAS NOTHING!
AND I LOST CONTROL FOR A MOMENT...
JUST LIKE...
...I USED TO!
!!

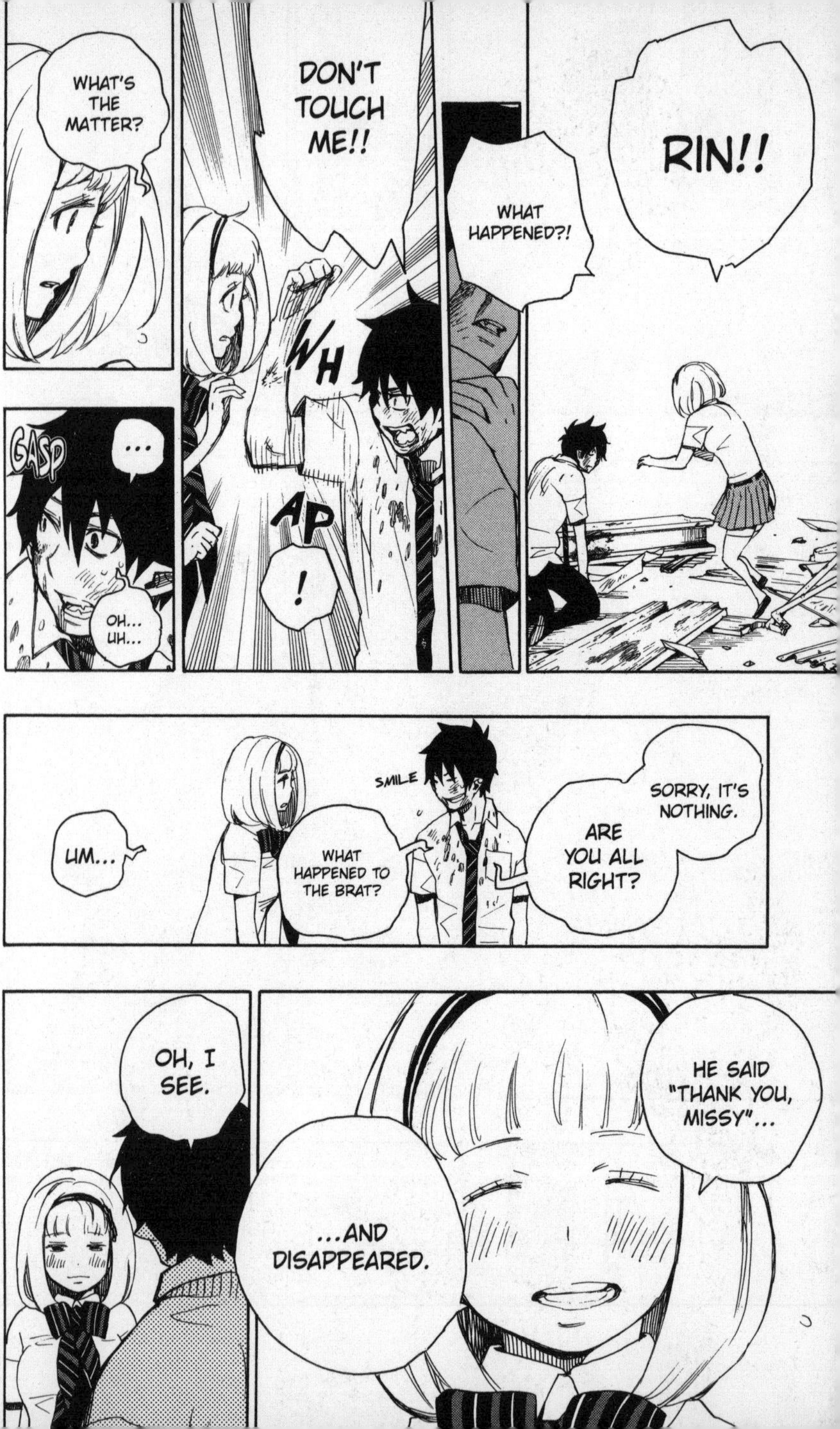
RIN!!
WHAT HAPPENED?!
DON'T TOUCH ME!!
WHAP
!
WHAT'S THE MATTER?
GASP
...
OH... UH...
SORRY, IT'S NOTHING.
ARE YOU ALL RIGHT?
SMILE
WHAT HAPPENED TO THE BRAT?
UM...
HE SAID "THANK YOU, MISSY"...
...AND DISAPPEARED.
OH, I SEE.

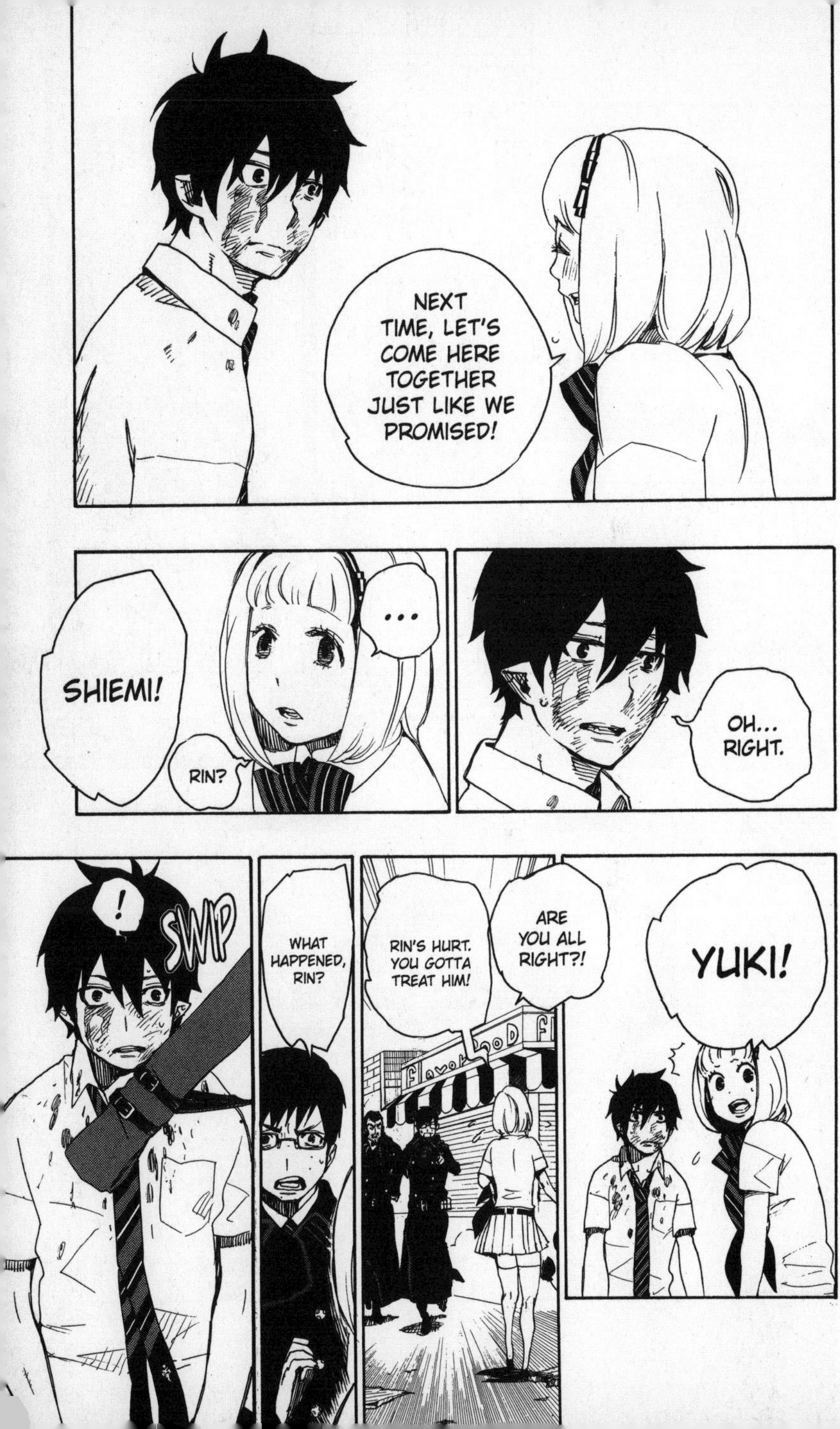
NEXT TIME, LET'S COME HERE TOGETHER JUST LIKE WE PROMISED!
OH... RIGHT.
...
SHIEMI!
RIN?
YUKI!
ARE YOU ALL RIGHT?!
RIN'S HURT. YOU GOTTA TREAT HIM!
WHAT HAPPENED, RIN?
!
SWIP

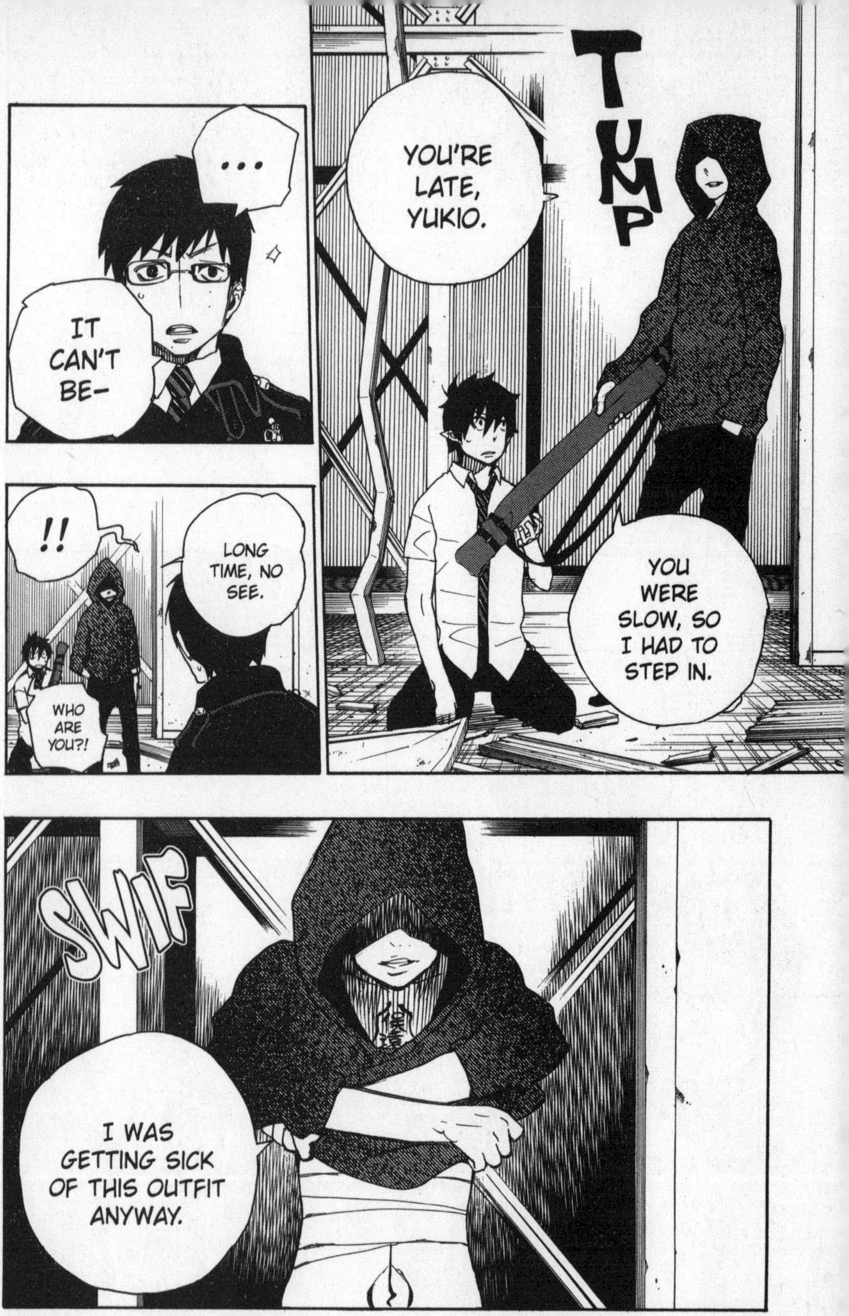
TUMP
YOU'RE LATE, YUKIO.
YOU WERE SLOW, SO I HAD TO STEP IN.
...
IT CAN'T BE-
LONG TIME, NO SEE.
!!
WHO ARE YOU?!
SWIF
I WAS GETTING SICK OF THIS OUTFIT ANYWAY.

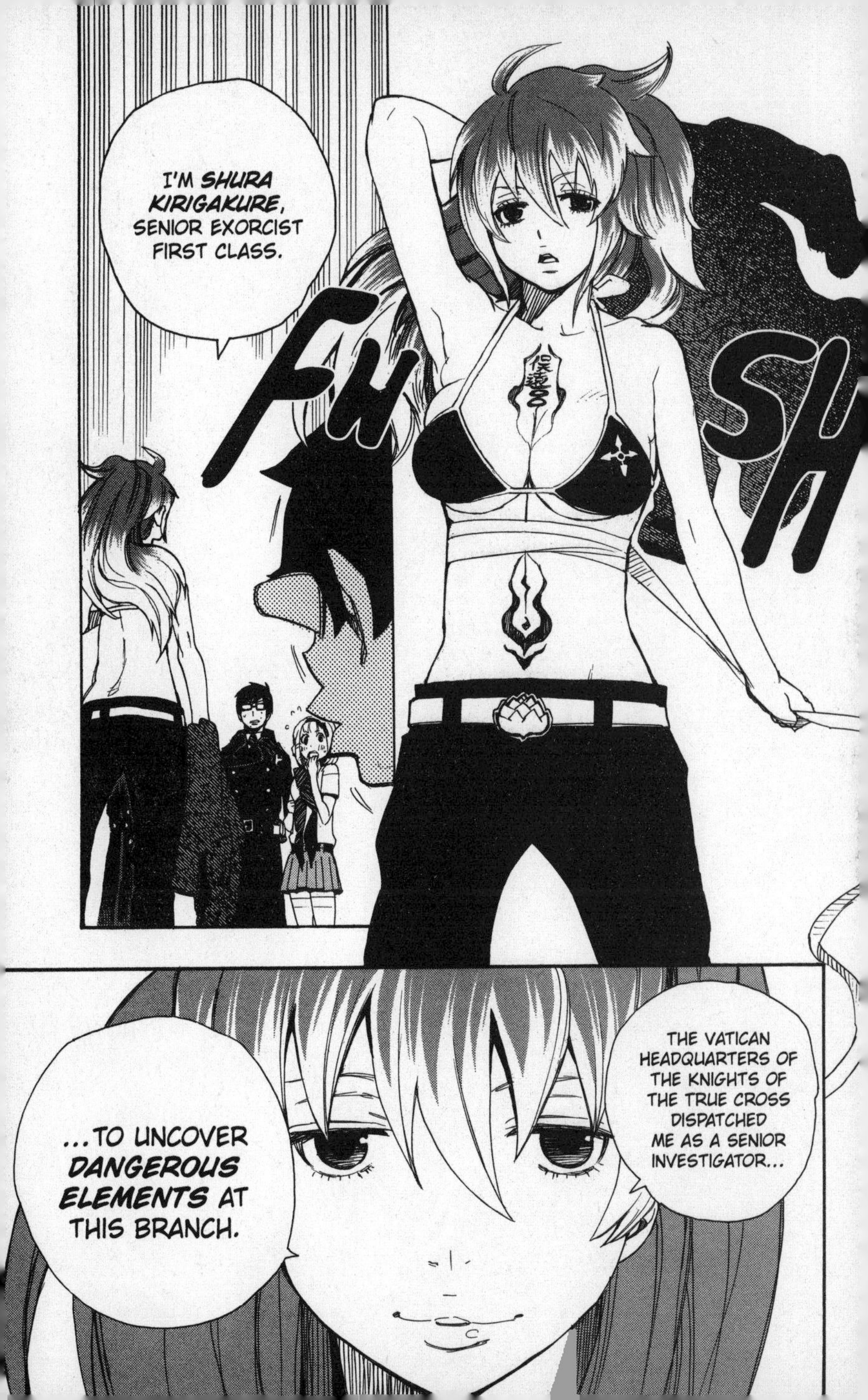
I'M SHURA KIRIGAKURE, SENIOR EXORCIST FIRST CLASS.
FWSH
THE VATICAN HEADQUARTERS OF THE KNIGHTS OF THE TRUE CROSS DISPATCHED ME AS A SENIOR INVESTIGATOR...
...TO UNCOVER DANGEROUS ELEMENTS AT THIS BRANCH.

Blue Exorcist Chapter 9 Tag

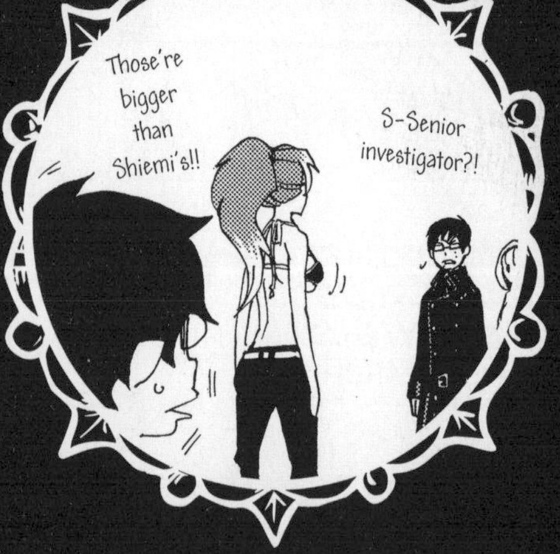
S-Senior investigator?!
Those're bigger than Shiemi's!!

Chapter 10 Proof

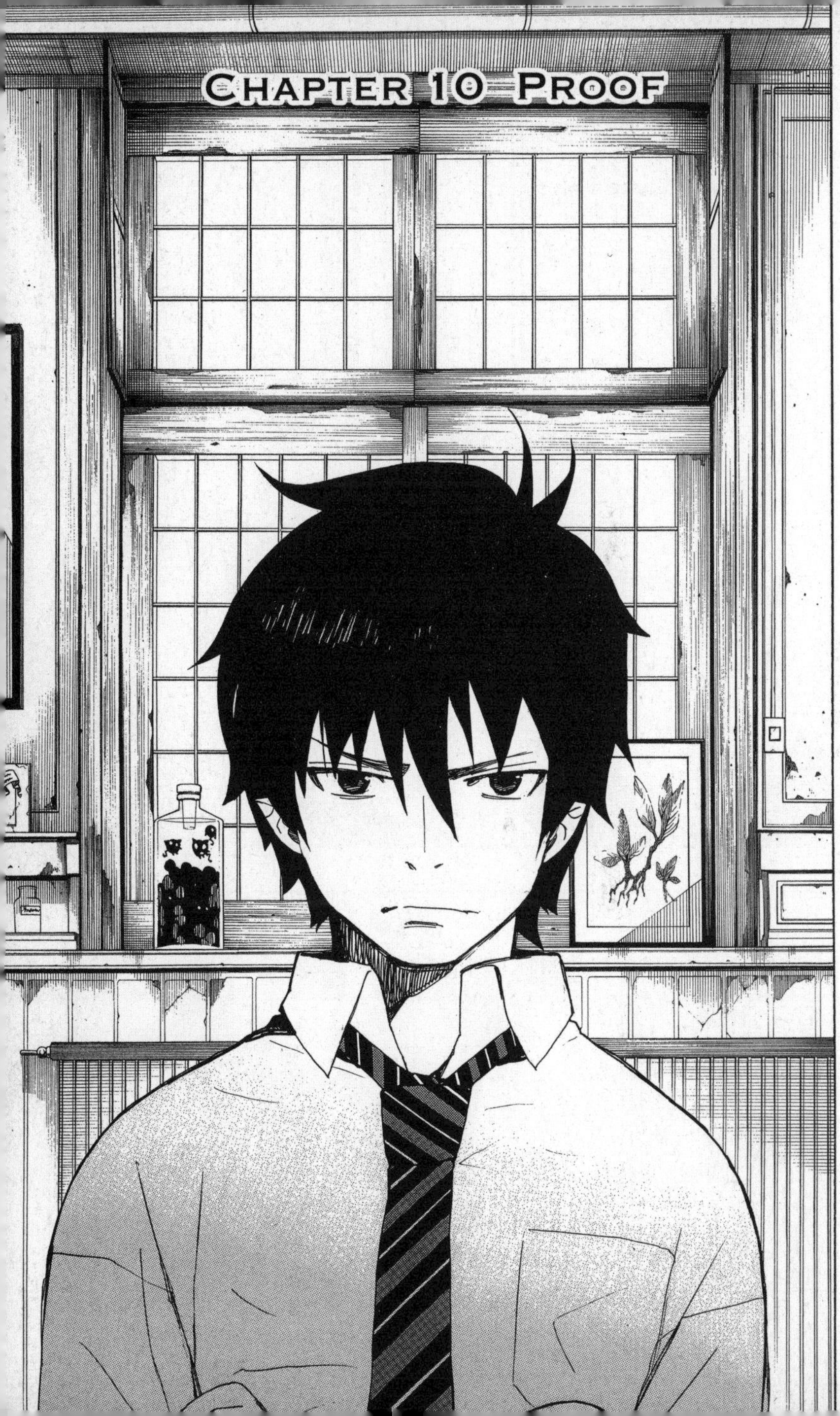

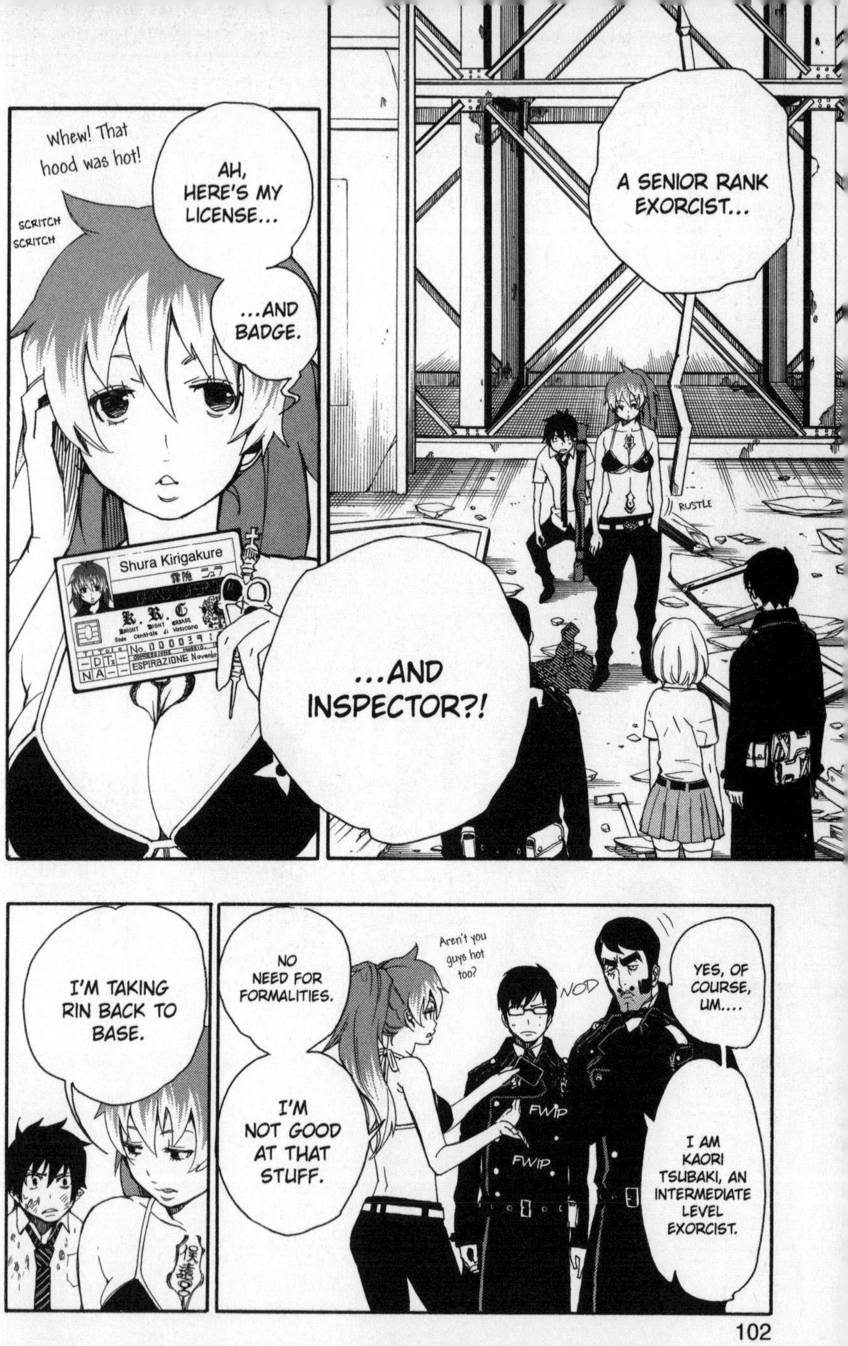
A SENIOR RANK EXORCIST...
RUSTLE
...AND INSPECTOR?!
AH, HERE'S MY LICENSE...
Whew! That hood was hot!
SCRITCH SCRITCH
...AND BADGE.
Shura Kirigakure
霧隠 シュラ
K. R. C
ESPIRAZIONE
YES, OF COURSE, UM....
I AM KAORI TSUBAKI, AN INTERMEDIATE LEVEL EXORCIST.
NOD
Aren't you guys hot too?
NO NEED FOR FORMALITIES.
FWIP
FWIP
I'M NOT GOOD AT THAT STUFF.
I'M TAKING RIN BACK TO BASE.

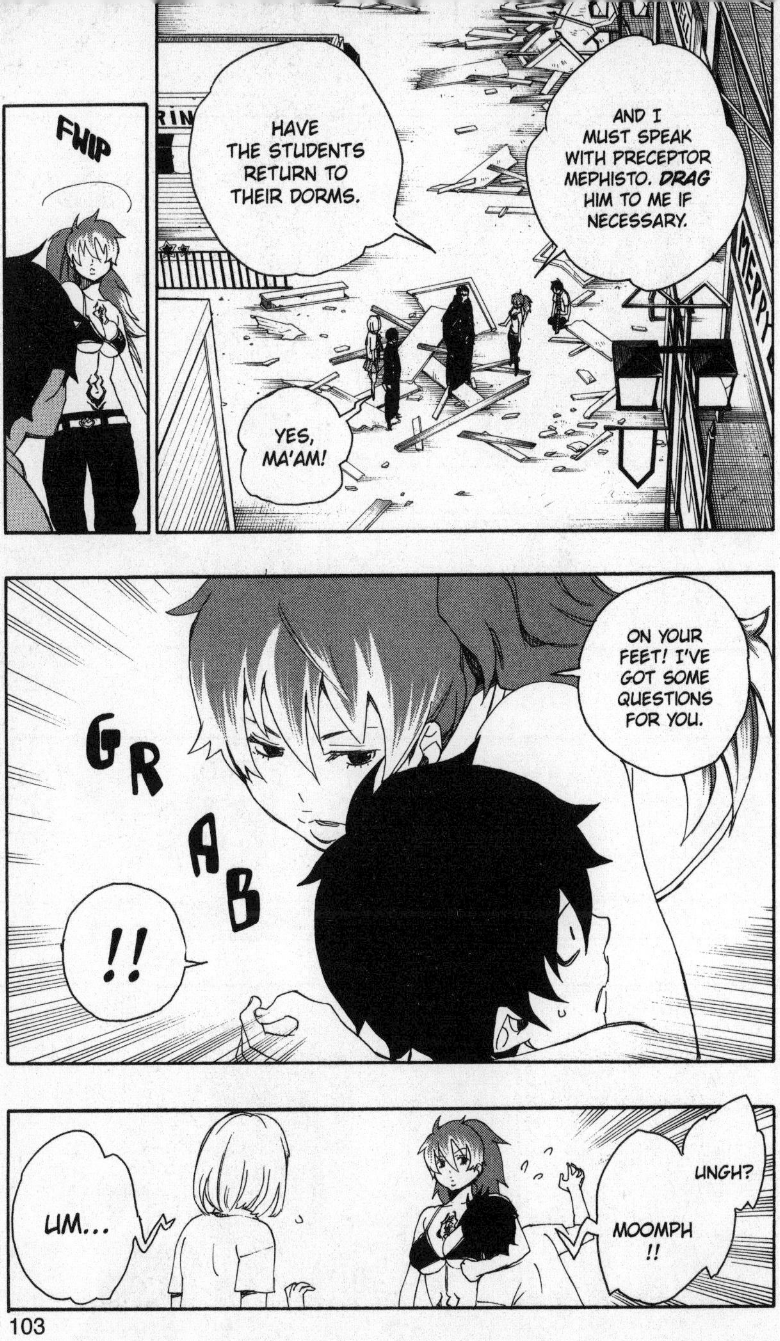
AND I MUST SPEAK WITH PRECEPTOR MEPHISTO. *DRAG* HIM TO ME IF NECESSARY.
HAVE THE STUDENTS RETURN TO THEIR DORMS.
YES, MA'AM!
FWIP
ON YOUR FEET! I'VE GOT SOME QUESTIONS FOR YOU.
GRAB
!!
UNGH?
MOOMPH !!
UM...

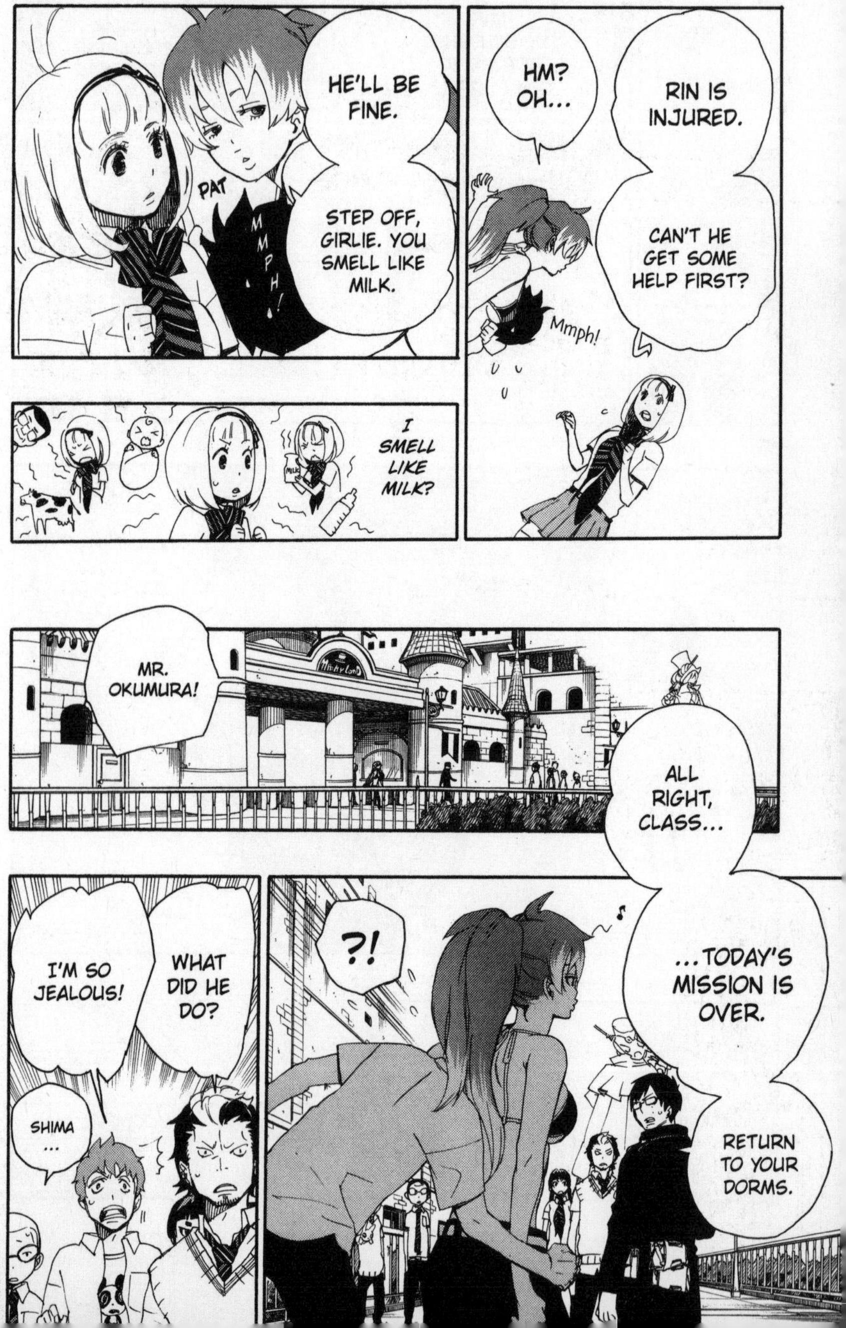
RIN IS INJURED.
HM? OH...
CAN'T HE GET SOME HELP FIRST?
Mmph!
HE'LL BE FINE.
STEP OFF, GIRLIE. YOU SMELL LIKE MILK.
MMPH!
PAT
I SMELL LIKE MILK?
MILK
MR. OKUMURA!
ALL RIGHT, CLASS...
...TODAY'S MISSION IS OVER.
RETURN TO YOUR DORMS.
?!
WHAT DID HE DO?
I'M SO JEALOUS!
SHIMA ...

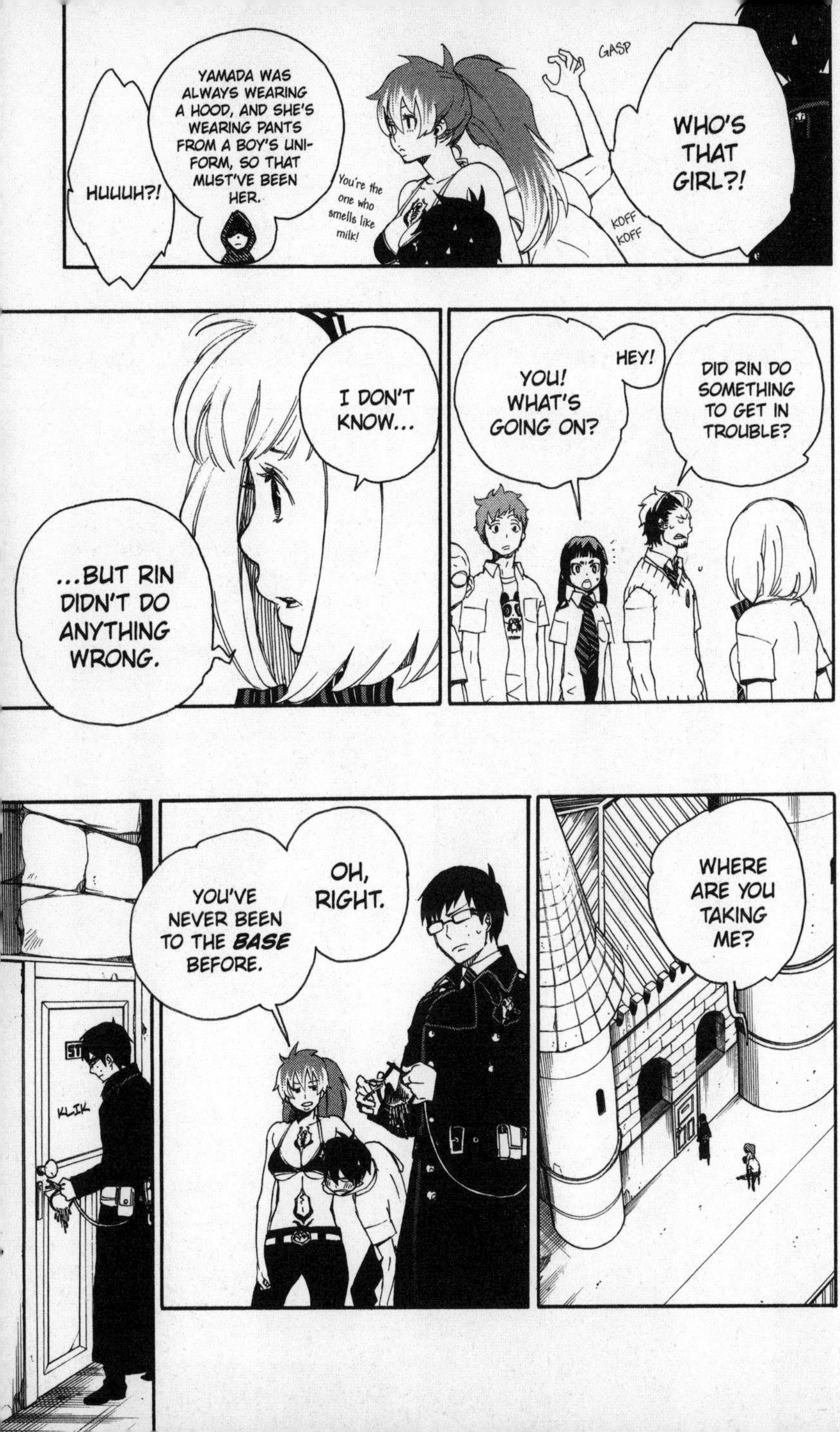
WHO'S THAT GIRL?!
GASP
KOFF KOFF
You're the one who smells like milk!
YAMADA WAS ALWAYS WEARING A HOOD, AND SHE'S WEARING PANTS FROM A BOY'S UNI-FORM, SO THAT MUST'VE BEEN HER.
HUUUH?!
DID RIN DO SOMETHING TO GET IN TROUBLE?
HEY!
YOU! WHAT'S GOING ON?
I DON'T KNOW...
...BUT RIN DIDN'T DO ANYTHING WRONG.
WHERE ARE YOU TAKING ME?
OH, RIGHT.
YOU'VE NEVER BEEN TO THE *BASE* BEFORE.
KLIK

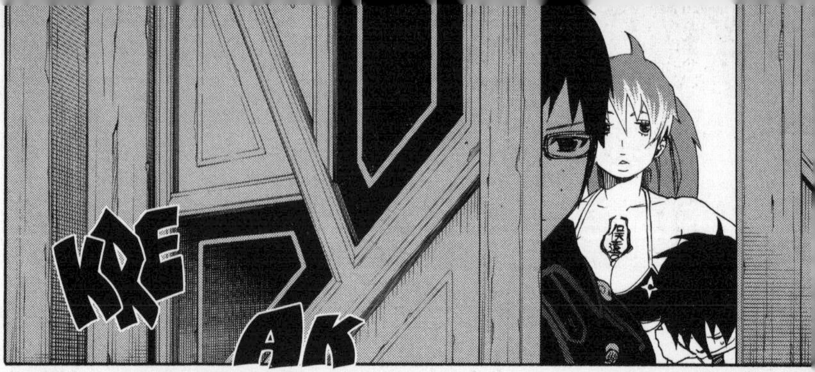
KREAK
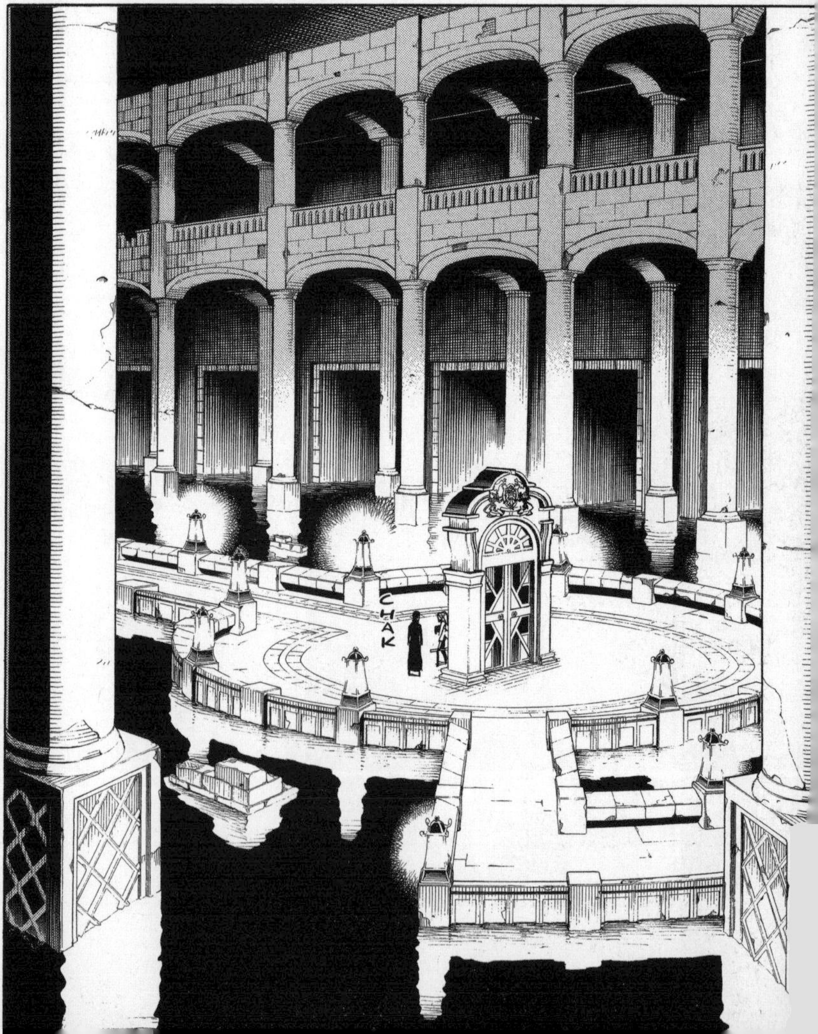
CHAK

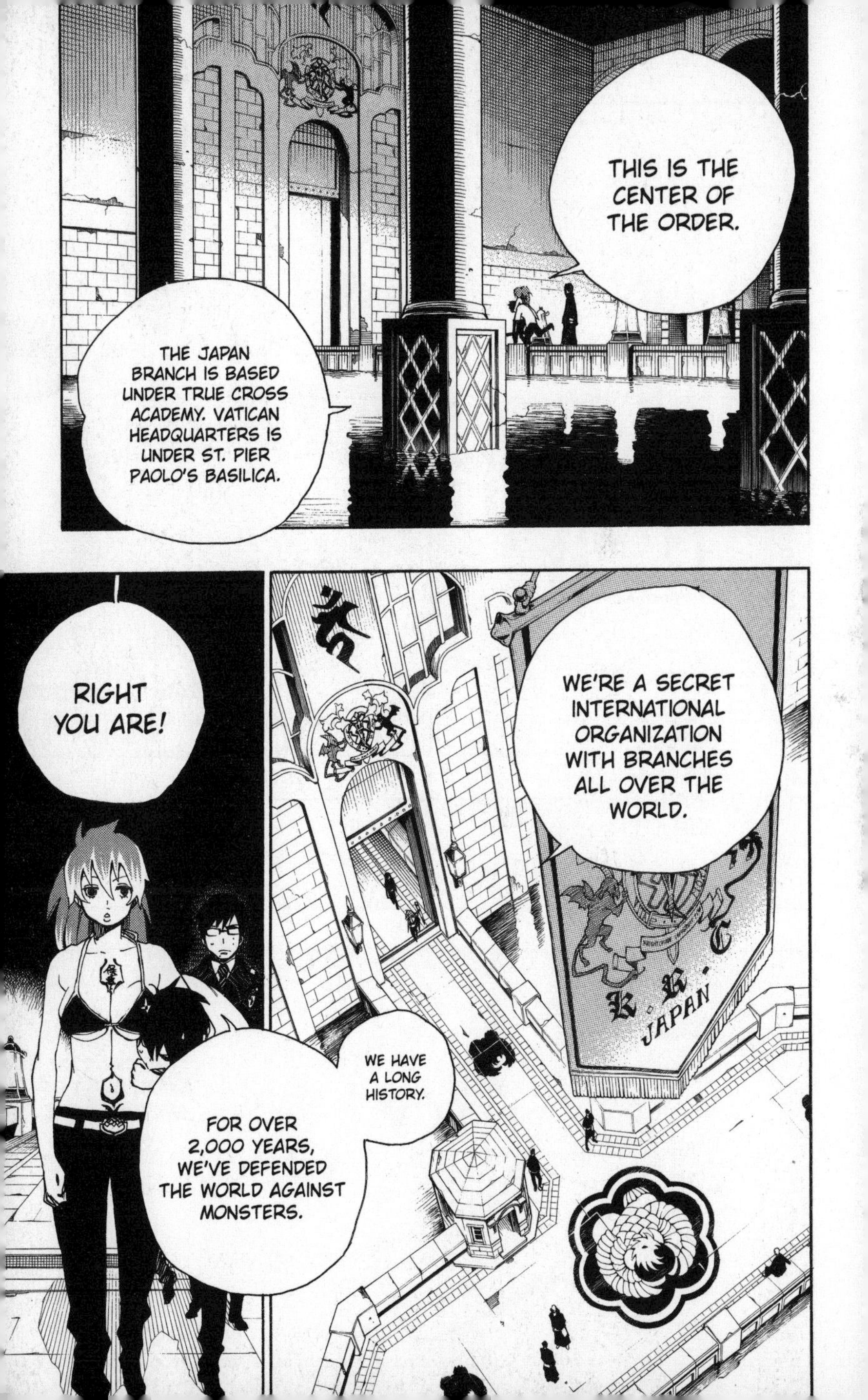
THIS IS THE CENTER OF THE ORDER.
THE JAPAN BRANCH IS BASED UNDER TRUE CROSS ACADEMY. VATICAN HEADQUARTERS IS UNDER ST. PIER PAOLO'S BASILICA.
WE'RE A SECRET INTERNATIONAL ORGANIZATION WITH BRANCHES ALL OVER THE WORLD.
JAPAN
WE HAVE A LONG HISTORY.
FOR OVER 2,000 YEARS, WE'VE DEFENDED THE WORLD AGAINST MONSTERS.
RIGHT YOU ARE!

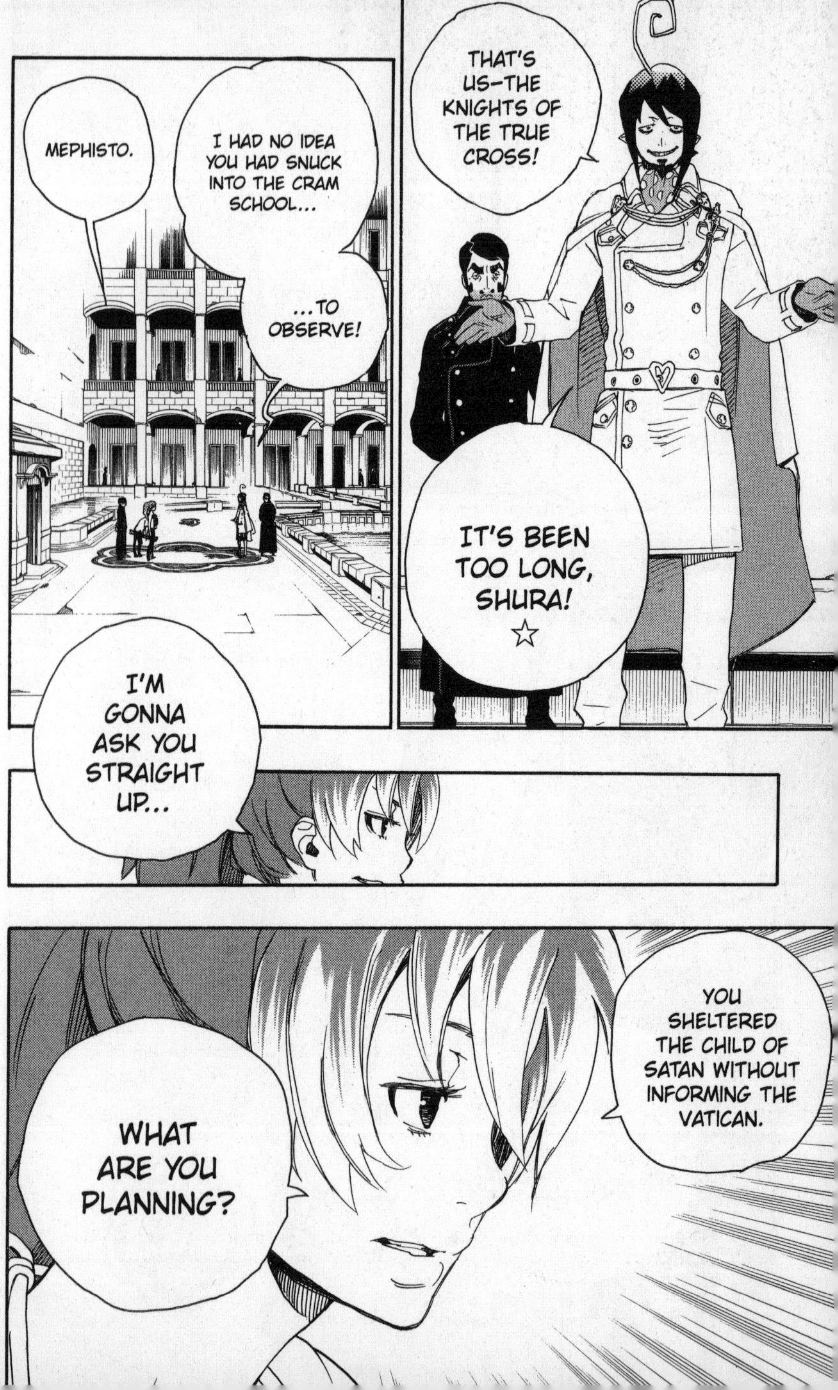
THAT'S US—THE KNIGHTS OF THE TRUE CROSS!
IT'S BEEN TOO LONG, SHURA! ☆
I HAD NO IDEA YOU HAD SNUCK INTO THE CRAM SCHOOL...
...TO OBSERVE!
MEPHISTO.
I'M GONNA ASK YOU STRAIGHT UP...
YOU SHELTERED THE CHILD OF SATAN WITHOUT INFORMING THE VATICAN.
WHAT ARE YOU PLANNING?

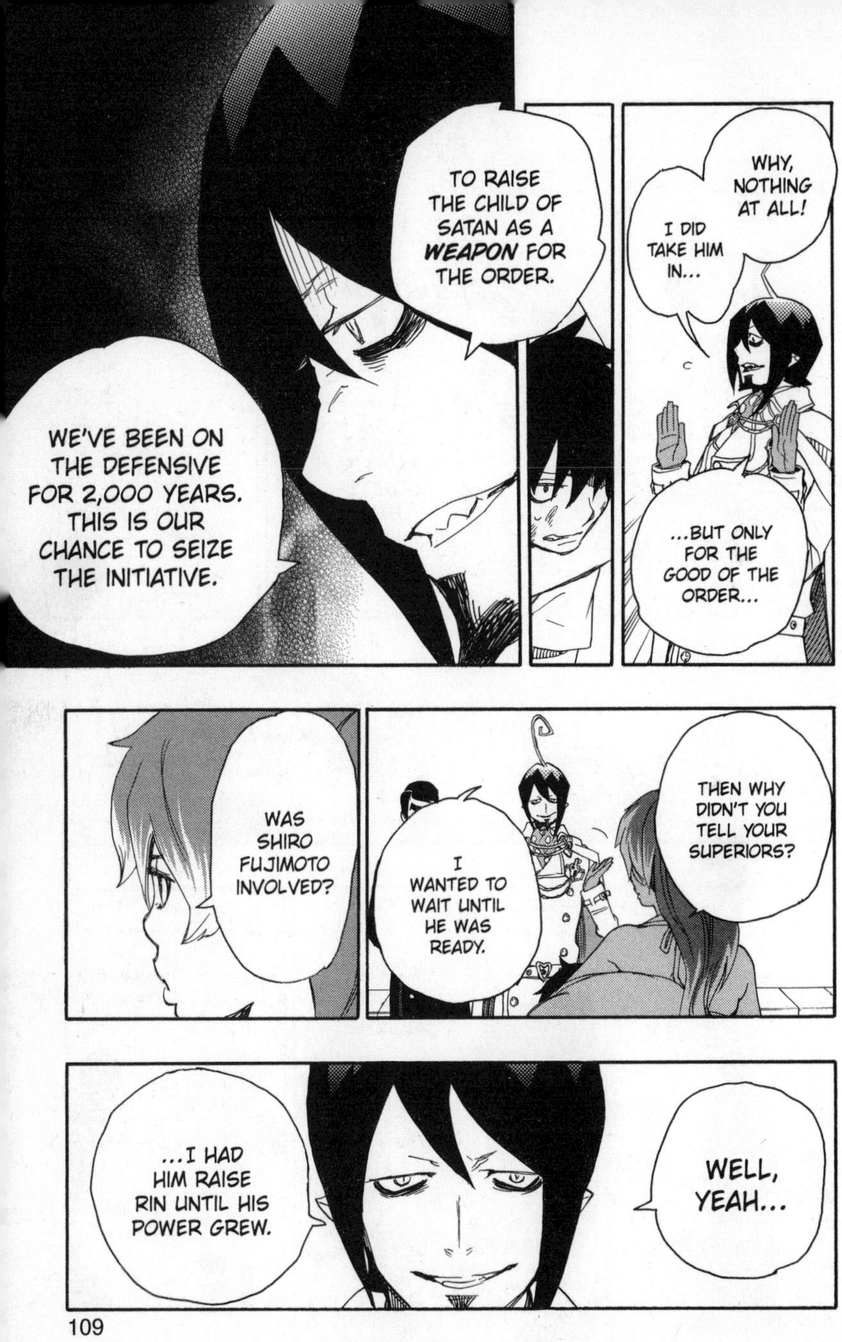
WHY, NOTHING AT ALL!
I DID TAKE HIM IN...
...BUT ONLY FOR THE GOOD OF THE ORDER...
TO RAISE THE CHILD OF SATAN AS A ***WEAPON*** FOR THE ORDER.
WE'VE BEEN ON THE DEFENSIVE FOR 2,000 YEARS. THIS IS OUR CHANCE TO SEIZE THE INITIATIVE.
THEN WHY DIDN'T YOU TELL YOUR SUPERIORS?
I WANTED TO WAIT UNTIL HE WAS READY.
WAS SHIRO FUJIMOTO INVOLVED?
WELL, YEAH...
...I HAD HIM RAISE RIN UNTIL HIS POWER GREW.

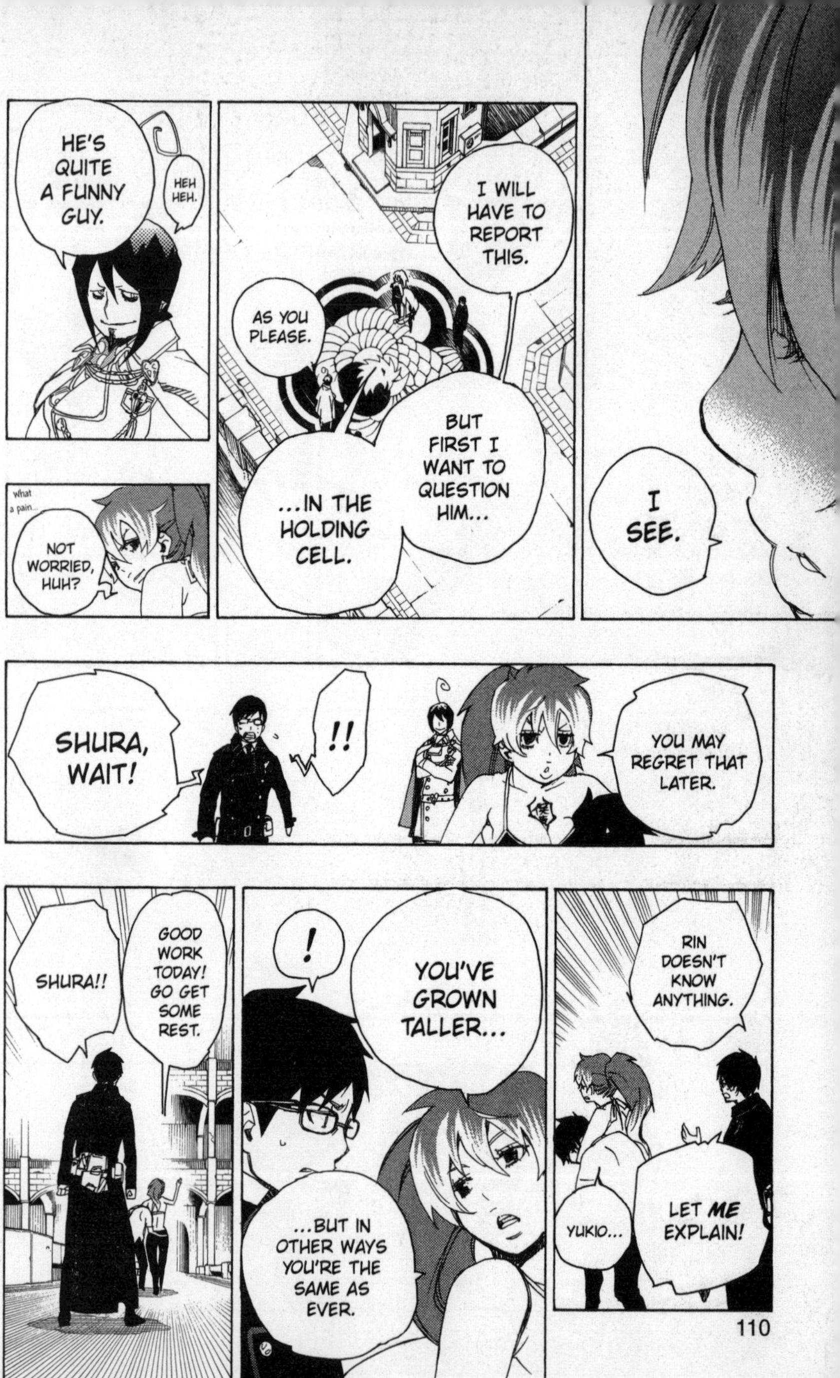
I SEE.
I WILL HAVE TO REPORT THIS.
AS YOU PLEASE.
BUT FIRST I WANT TO QUESTION HIM...
...IN THE HOLDING CELL.
HE'S QUITE A FUNNY GUY.
HEH HEH.
What a pain...
NOT WORRIED, HUH?
YOU MAY REGRET THAT LATER.
!!
SHURA, WAIT!
RIN DOESN'T KNOW ANYTHING.
LET *ME* EXPLAIN!
YUKIO...
YOU'VE GROWN TALLER...
!
...BUT IN OTHER WAYS YOU'RE THE SAME AS EVER.
GOOD WORK TODAY! GO GET SOME REST.
SHURA!!

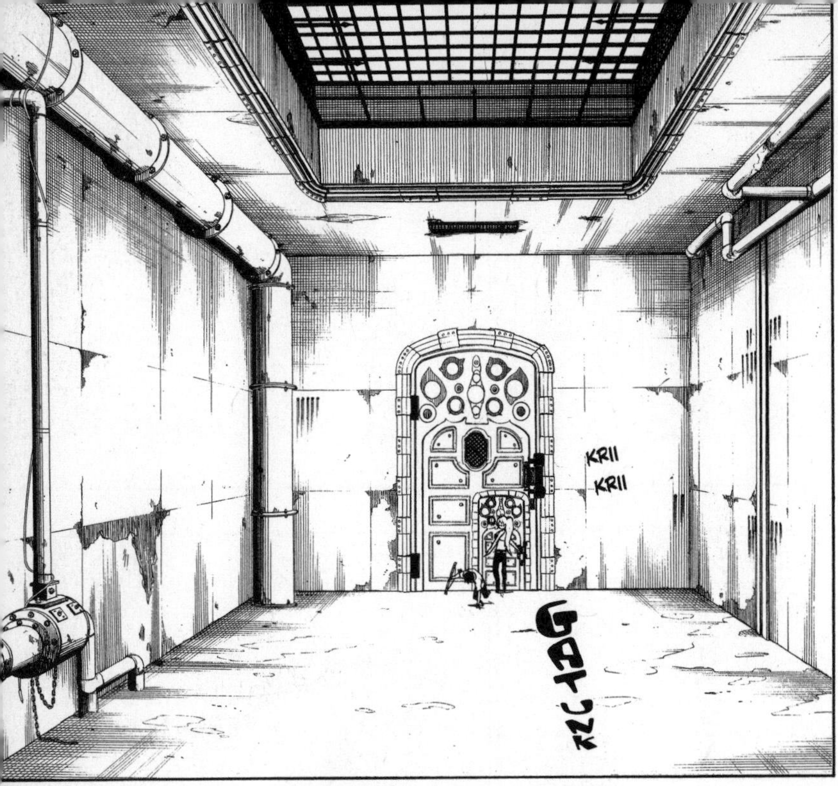
KRII
KRII
GATJNK

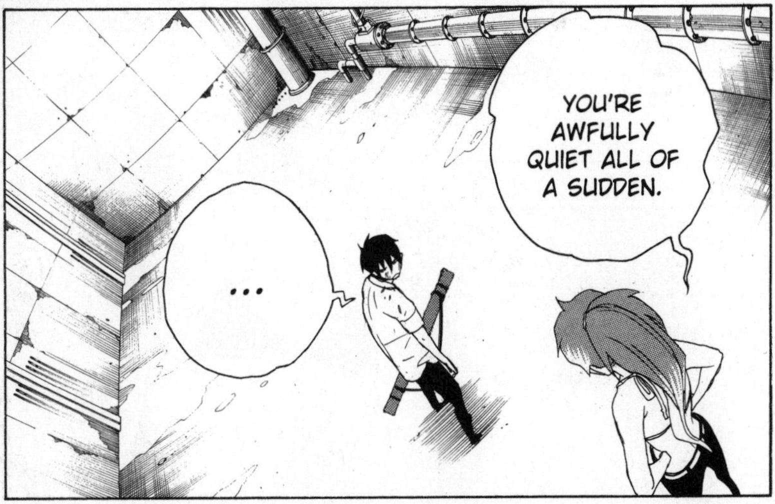
YOU'RE AWFULLY QUIET ALL OF A SUDDEN.
...

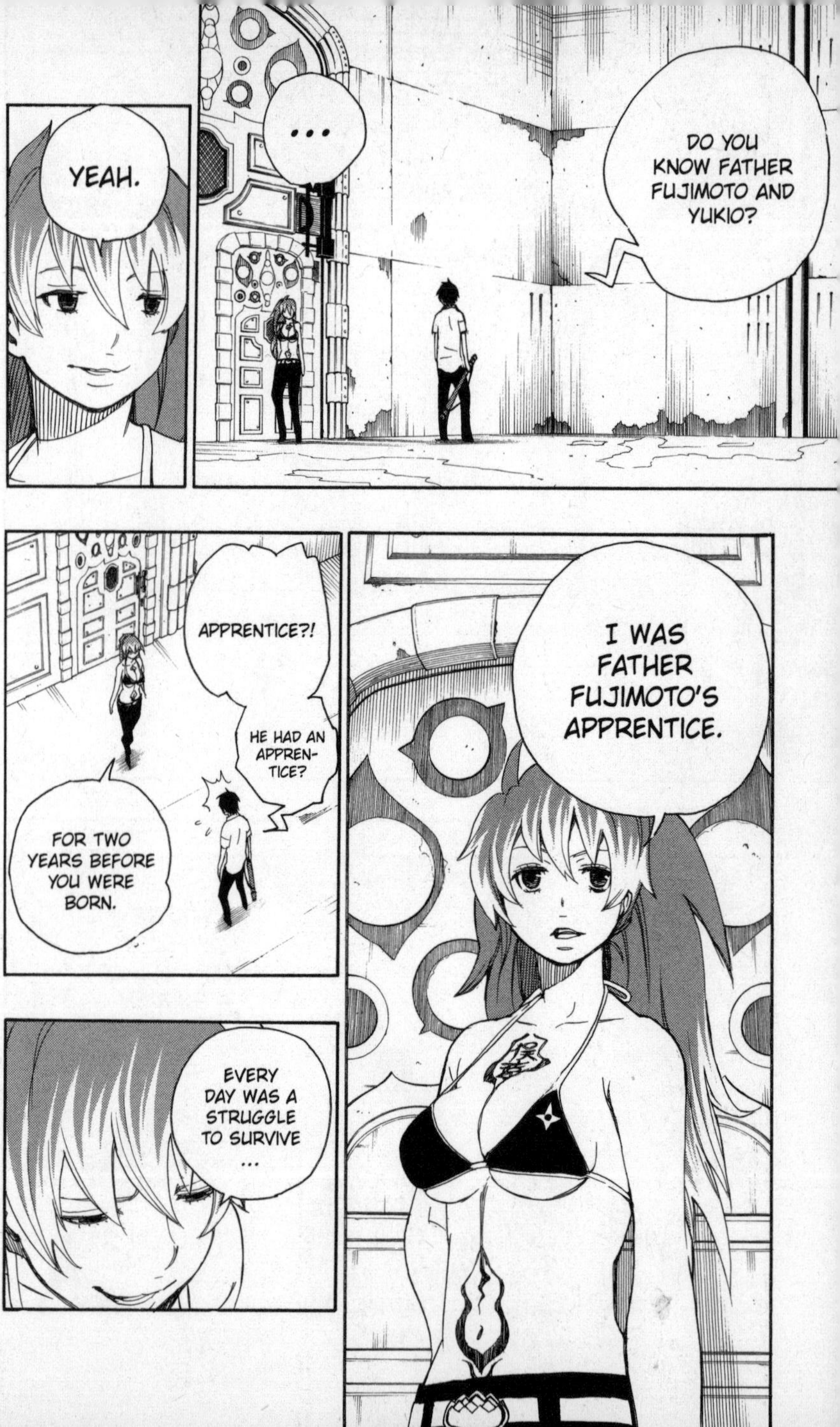
DO YOU KNOW FATHER FUJIMOTO AND YUKIO?
...
YEAH.
I WAS FATHER FUJIMOTO'S APPRENTICE.
APPRENTICE?!
HE HAD AN APPREN-TICE?
FOR TWO YEARS BEFORE YOU WERE BORN.
EVERY DAY WAS A STRUGGLE TO SURVIVE ...

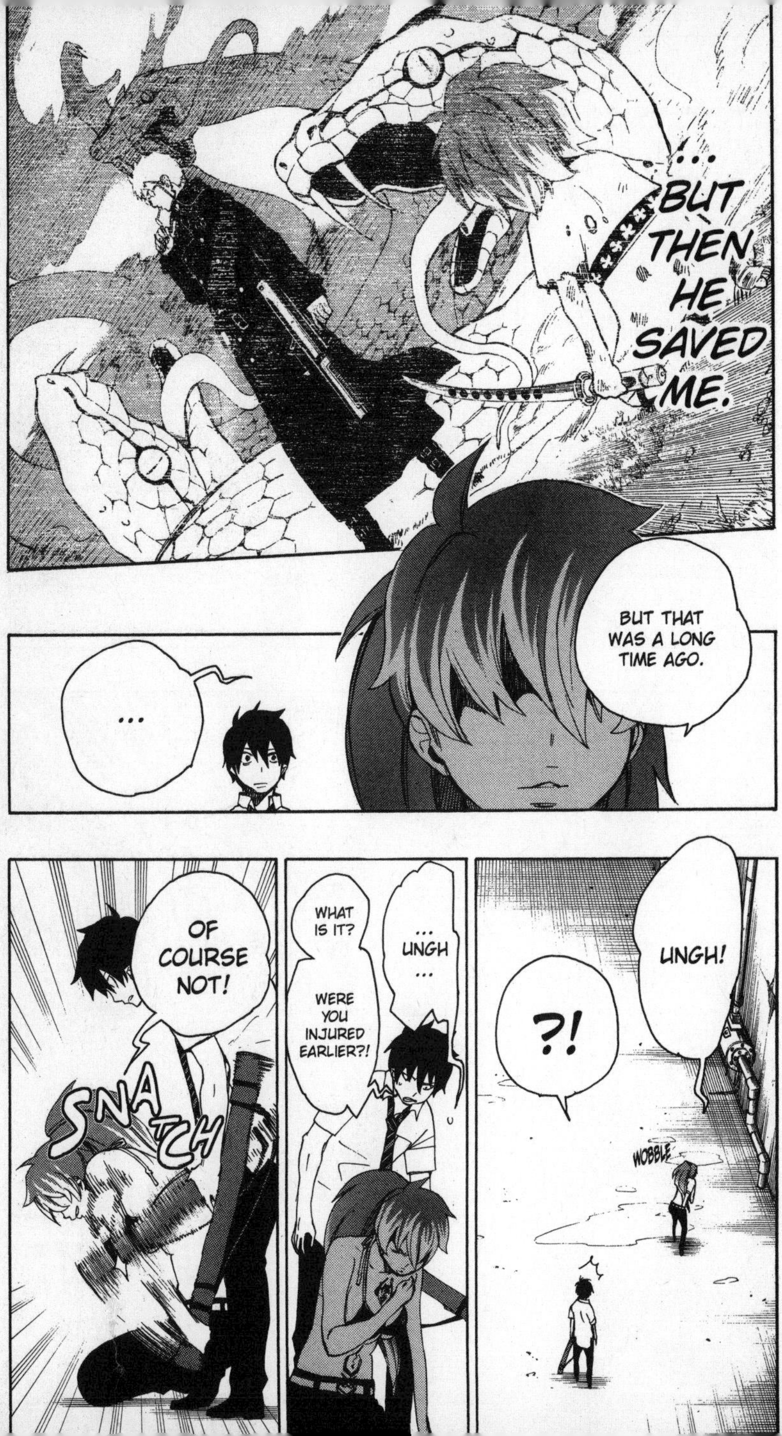
...BUT THEN HE SAVED ME.
BUT THAT WAS A LONG TIME AGO.
...
UNGH!
?!
WOBBLE
... UNGH ...
WHAT IS IT?
WERE YOU INJURED EARLIER?!
OF COURSE NOT!
SNATCH

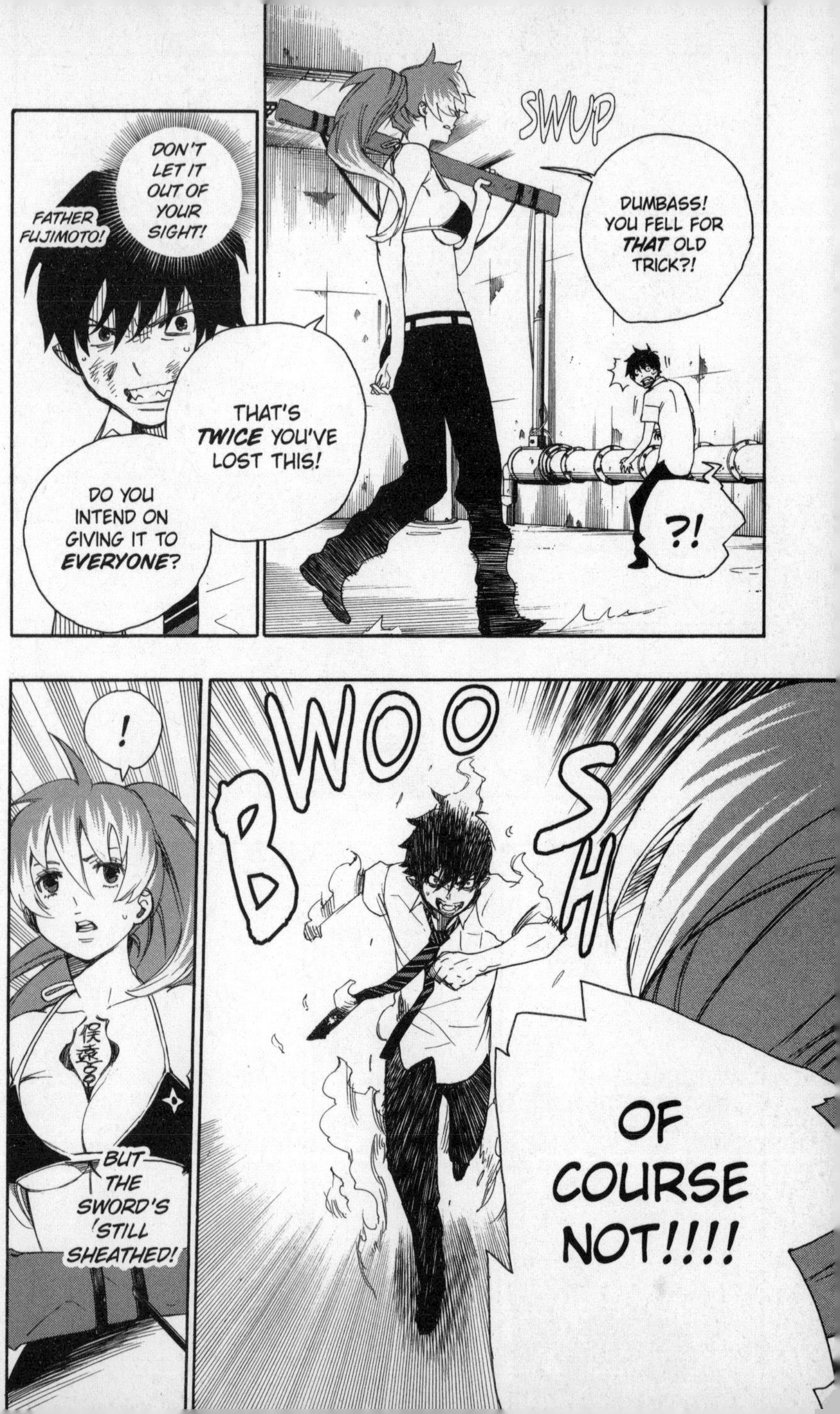
SWUP
DUMBASS! YOU FELL FOR THAT OLD TRICK?!
?!
DON'T LET IT OUT OF YOUR SIGHT!
FATHER FUJIMOTO!
THAT'S TWICE YOU'VE LOST THIS!
DO YOU INTEND ON GIVING IT TO EVERYONE?
BWOOSH
OF COURSE NOT!!!!
!
BUT THE SWORD'S STILL SHEATHED!

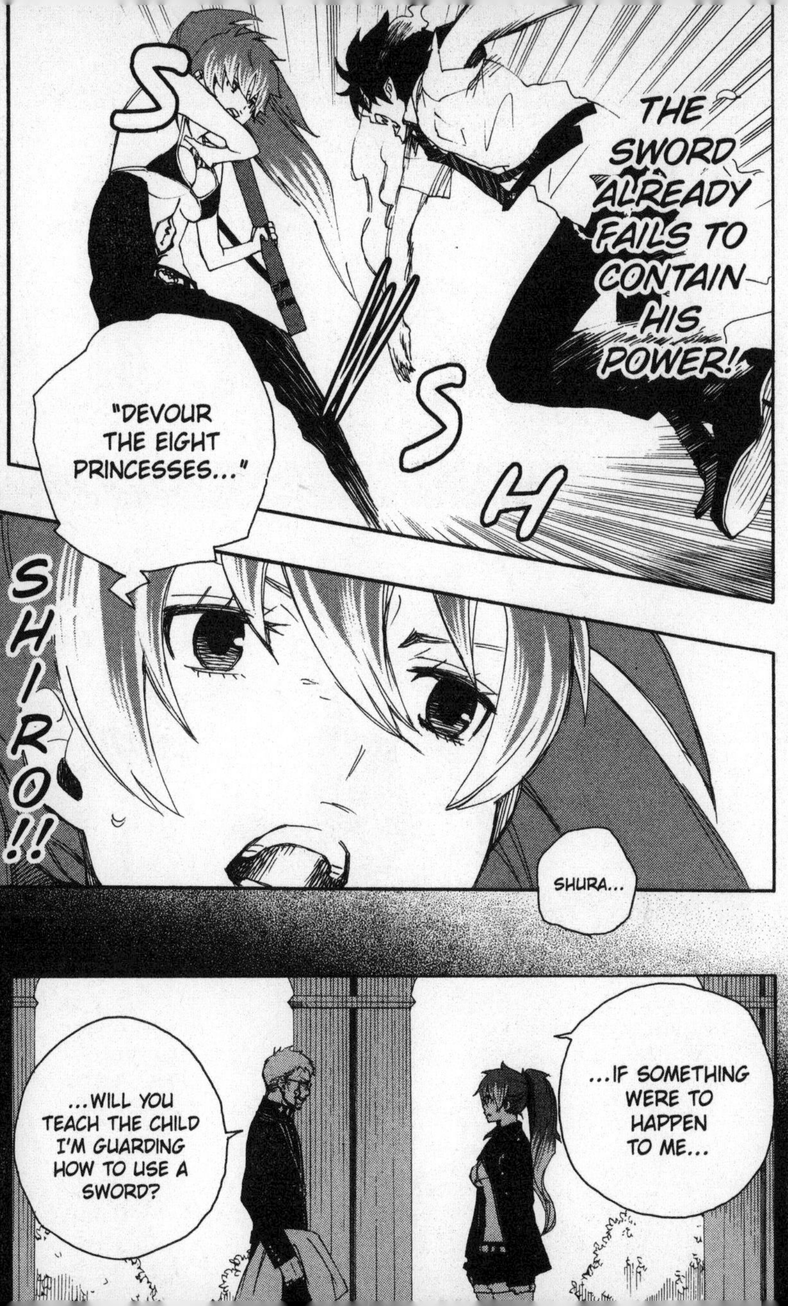
THE SWORD ALREADY FAILS TO CONTAIN HIS POWER!
S S H
"DEVOUR THE EIGHT PRINCESSES..."
SHIRO!!
SHURA...
...IF SOMETHING WERE TO HAPPEN TO ME...
...WILL YOU TEACH THE CHILD I'M GUARDING HOW TO USE A SWORD?

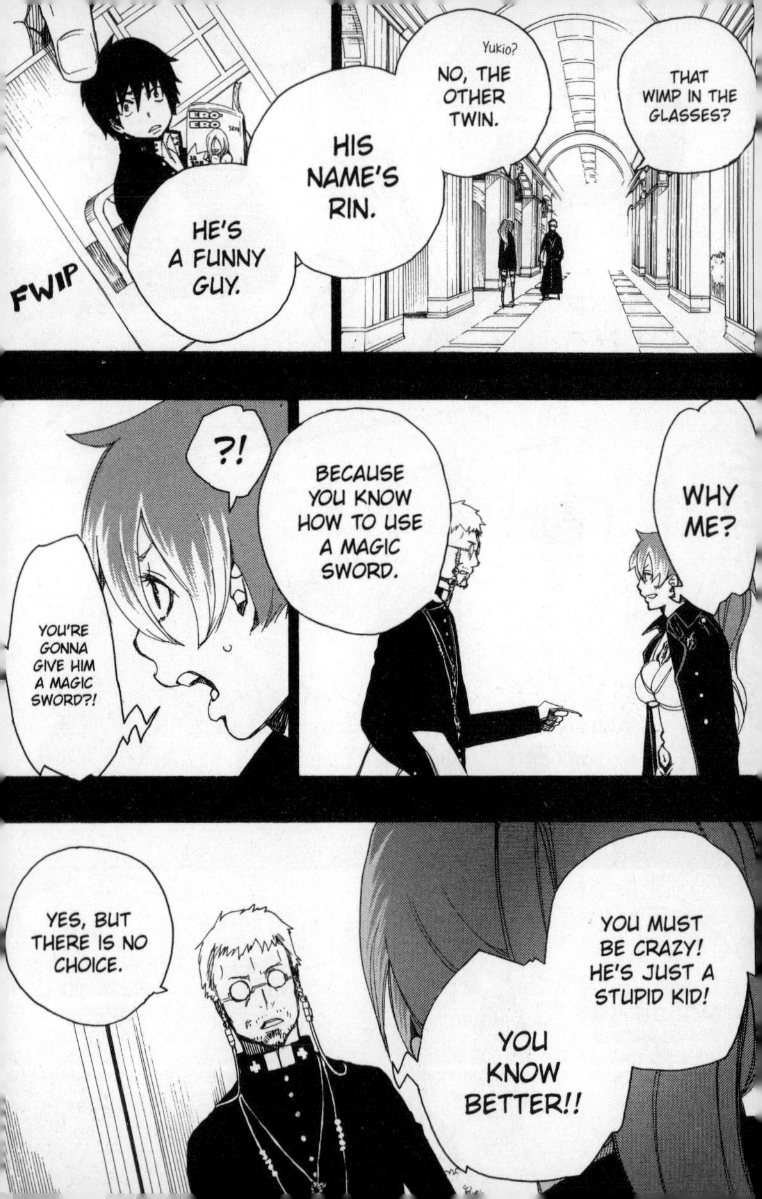
THAT WIMP IN THE GLASSES?
Yukio?
NO, THE OTHER TWIN.
HIS NAME'S RIN.
HE'S A FUNNY GUY.
ERO-ERO
FWIP
WHY ME?
BECAUSE YOU KNOW HOW TO USE A MAGIC SWORD.
?!
YOU'RE GONNA GIVE HIM A MAGIC SWORD?!
YOU MUST BE CRAZY! HE'S JUST A STUPID KID!
YOU KNOW BETTER!!
YES, BUT THERE IS NO CHOICE.

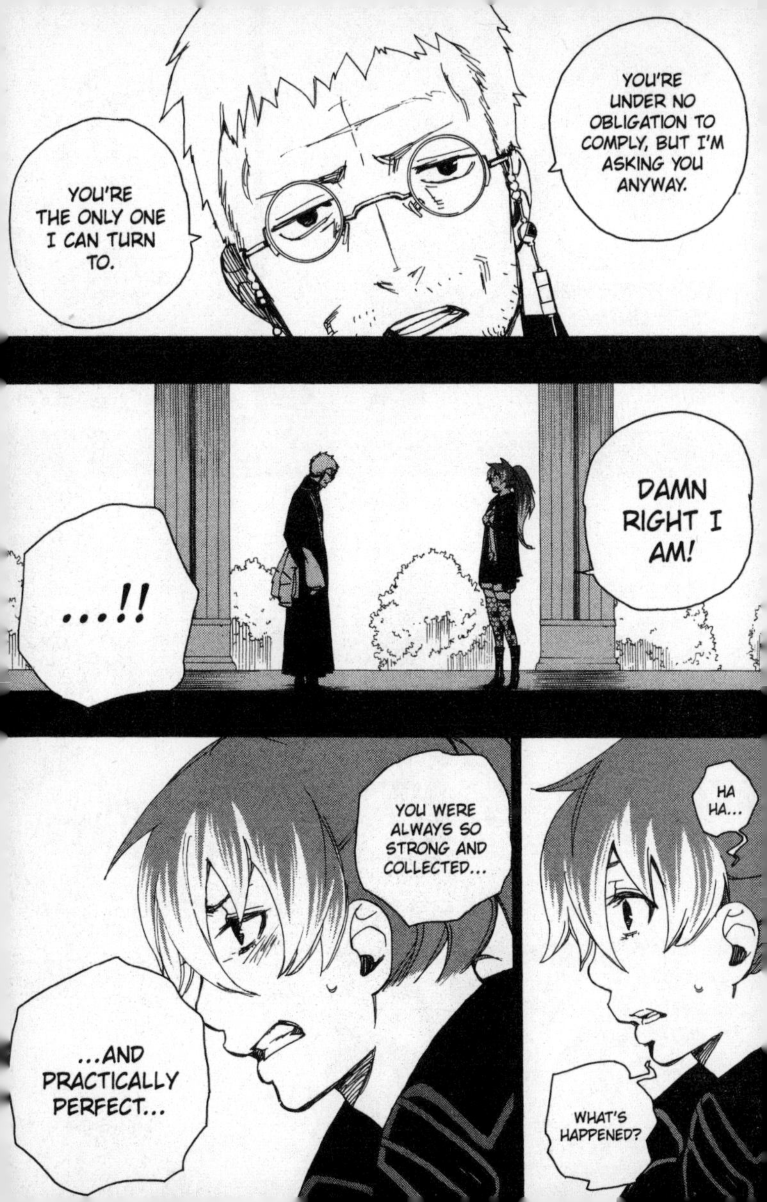
YOU'RE UNDER NO OBLIGATION TO COMPLY, BUT I'M ASKING YOU ANYWAY.
YOU'RE THE ONLY ONE I CAN TURN TO.
DAMN RIGHT I AM!
...!!
HA HA...
WHAT'S HAPPENED?
YOU WERE ALWAYS SO STRONG AND COLLECTED...
...AND PRACTICALLY PERFECT...

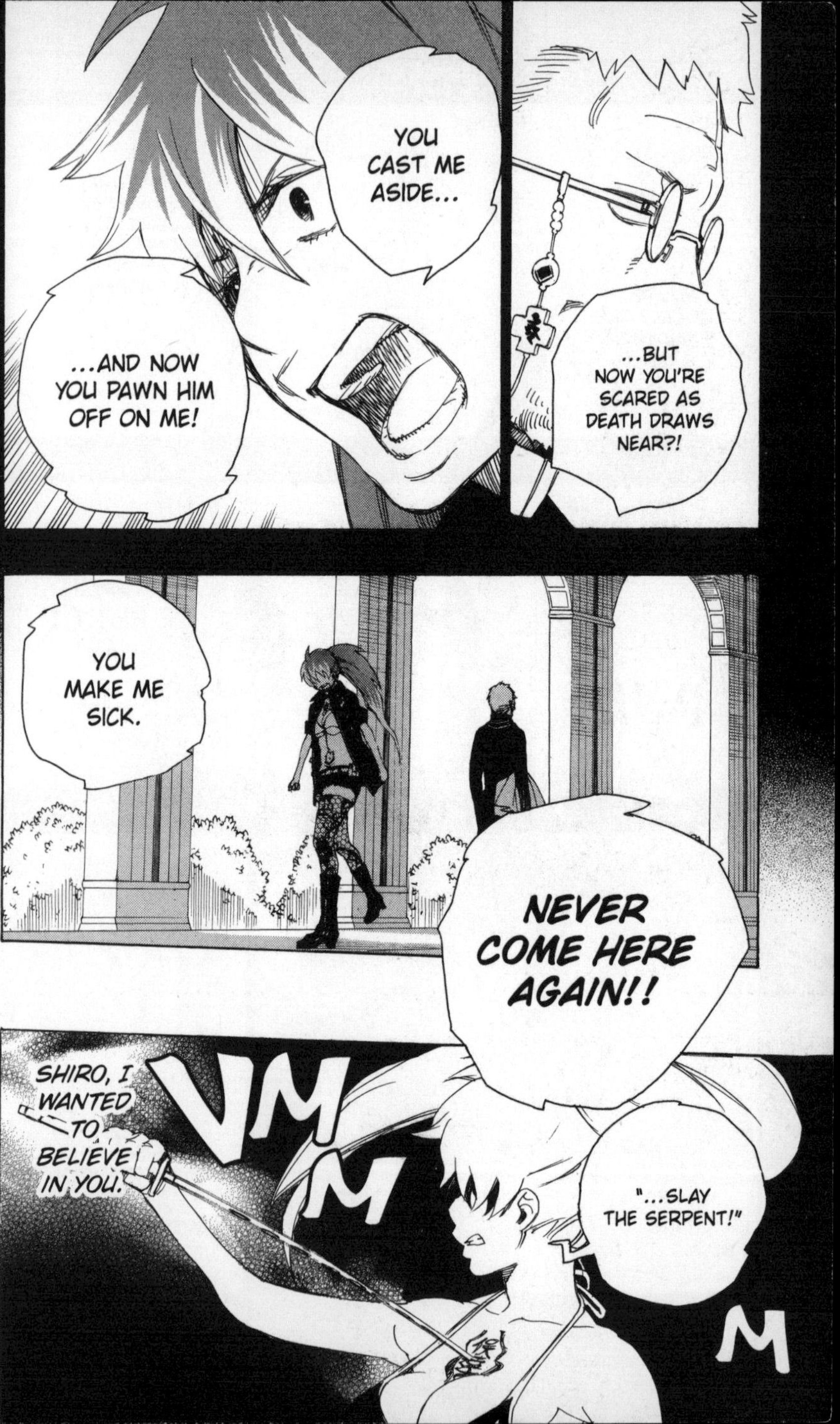
...BUT NOW YOU'RE SCARED AS DEATH DRAWS NEAR?!
YOU CAST ME ASIDE...
...AND NOW YOU PAWN HIM OFF ON ME!
YOU MAKE ME SICK.
NEVER COME HERE AGAIN!!
"...SLAY THE SERPENT!"
VMMM
SHIRO, I WANTED TO BELIEVE IN YOU.

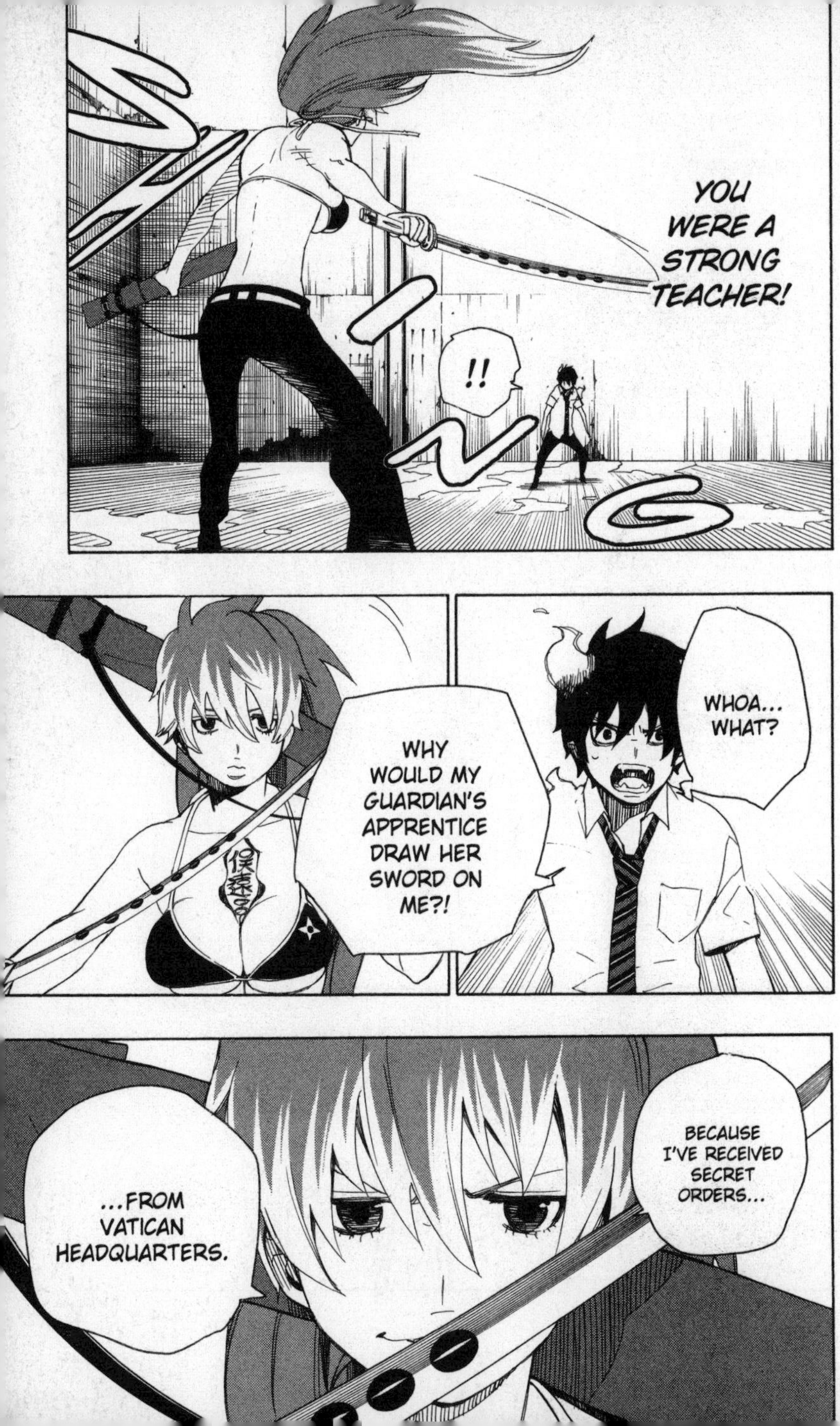
YOU WERE A STRONG TEACHER!
SHING
!!
WHOA... WHAT?
WHY WOULD MY GUARDIAN'S APPRENTICE DRAW HER SWORD ON ME?!
BECAUSE I'VE RECEIVED SECRET ORDERS...
...FROM VATICAN HEADQUARTERS.

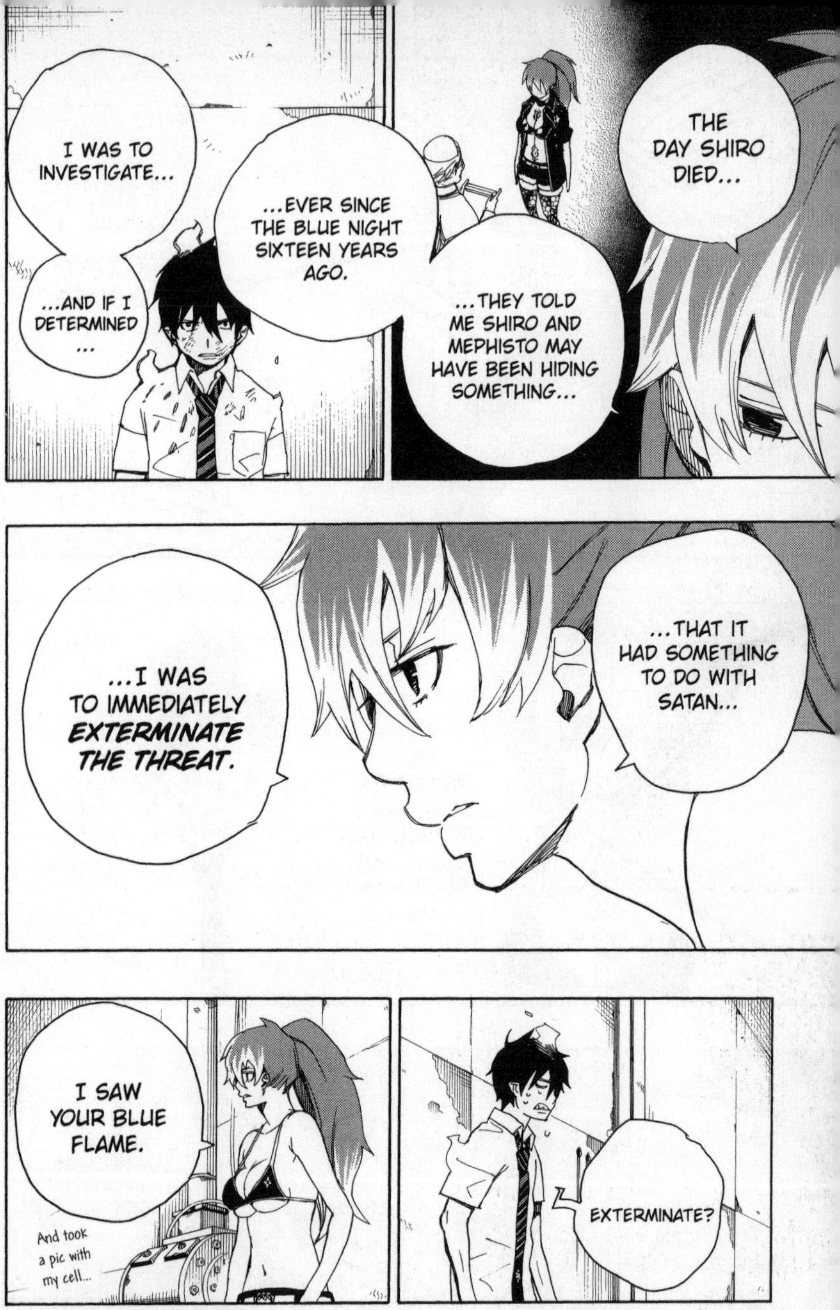
THE DAY SHIRO DIED...
...THEY TOLD ME SHIRO AND MEPHISTO MAY HAVE BEEN HIDING SOMETHING...
I WAS TO INVESTIGATE...
...EVER SINCE THE BLUE NIGHT SIXTEEN YEARS AGO.
...AND IF I DETERMINED...
...THAT IT HAD SOMETHING TO DO WITH SATAN...
...I WAS TO IMMEDIATELY *EXTERMINATE THE THREAT.*
EXTERMINATE?
I SAW YOUR BLUE FLAME.
And took a pic with my cell...

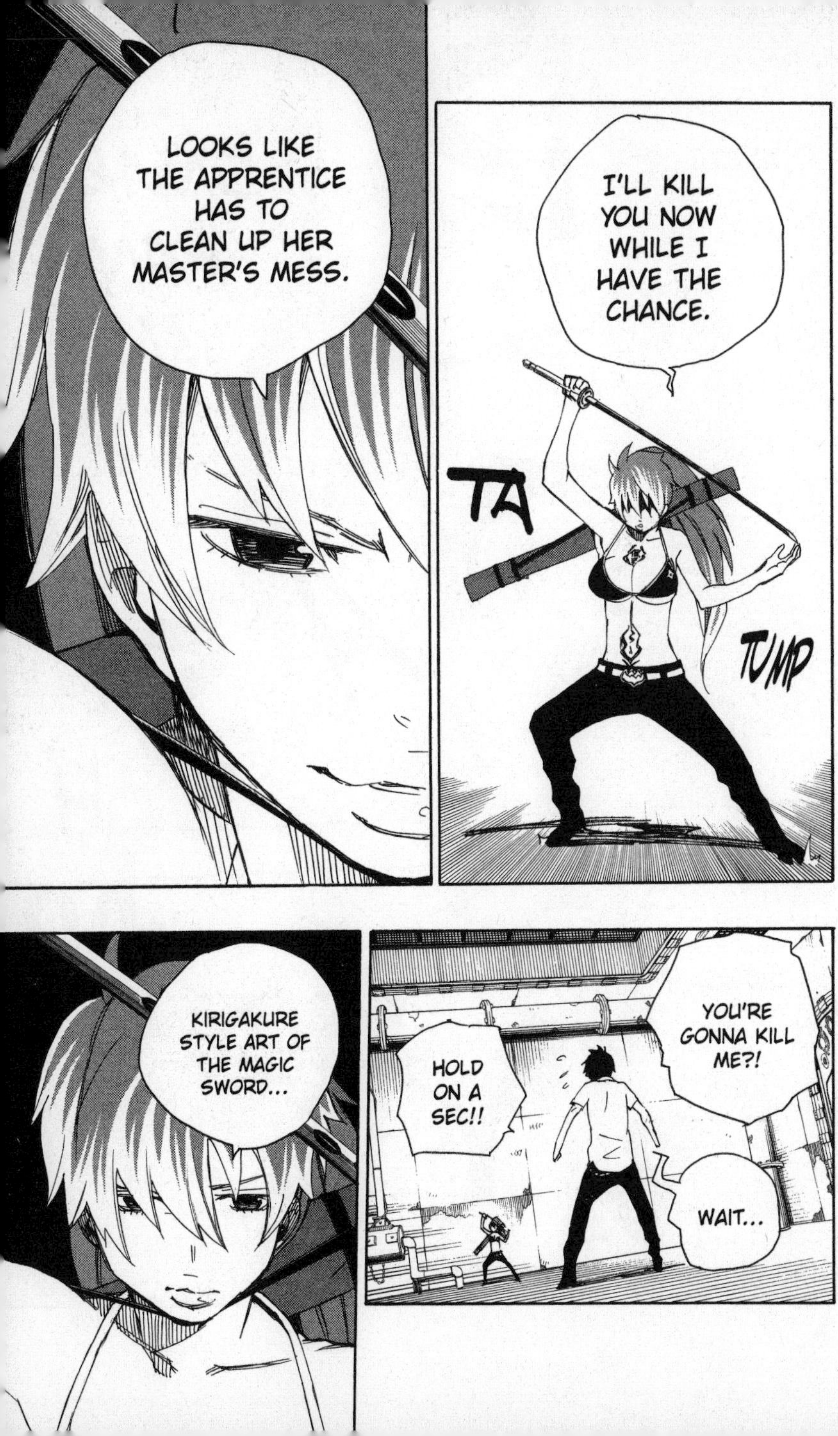
I'LL KILL YOU NOW WHILE I HAVE THE CHANCE.
TA
TUMP
LOOKS LIKE THE APPRENTICE HAS TO CLEAN UP HER MASTER'S MESS.
YOU'RE GONNA KILL ME?!
HOLD ON A SEC!!
WAIT...
KIRIGAKURE STYLE ART OF THE MAGIC SWORD...

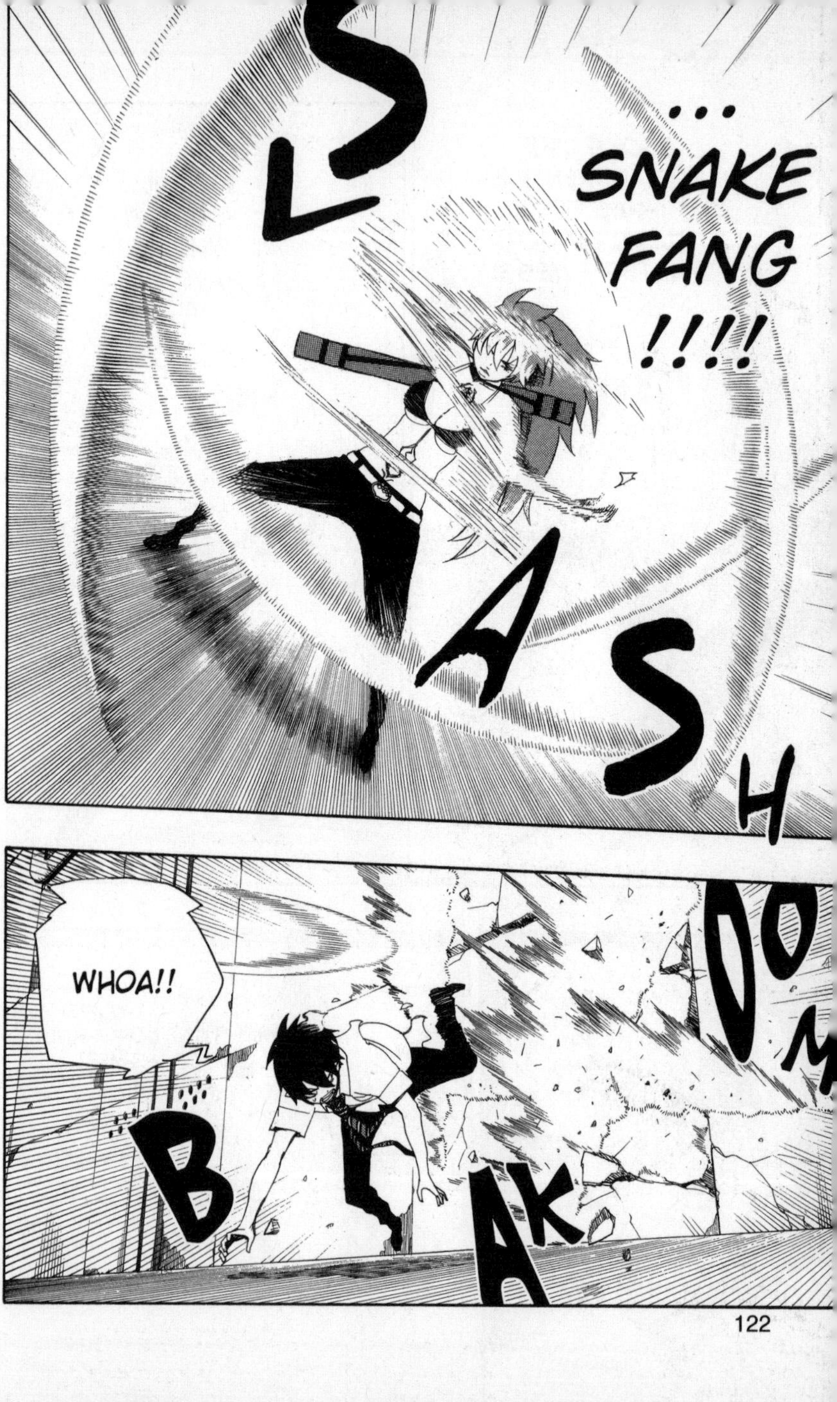
...SNAKE FANG!!!!
SLASH
WHOA!!
OOM
BAK

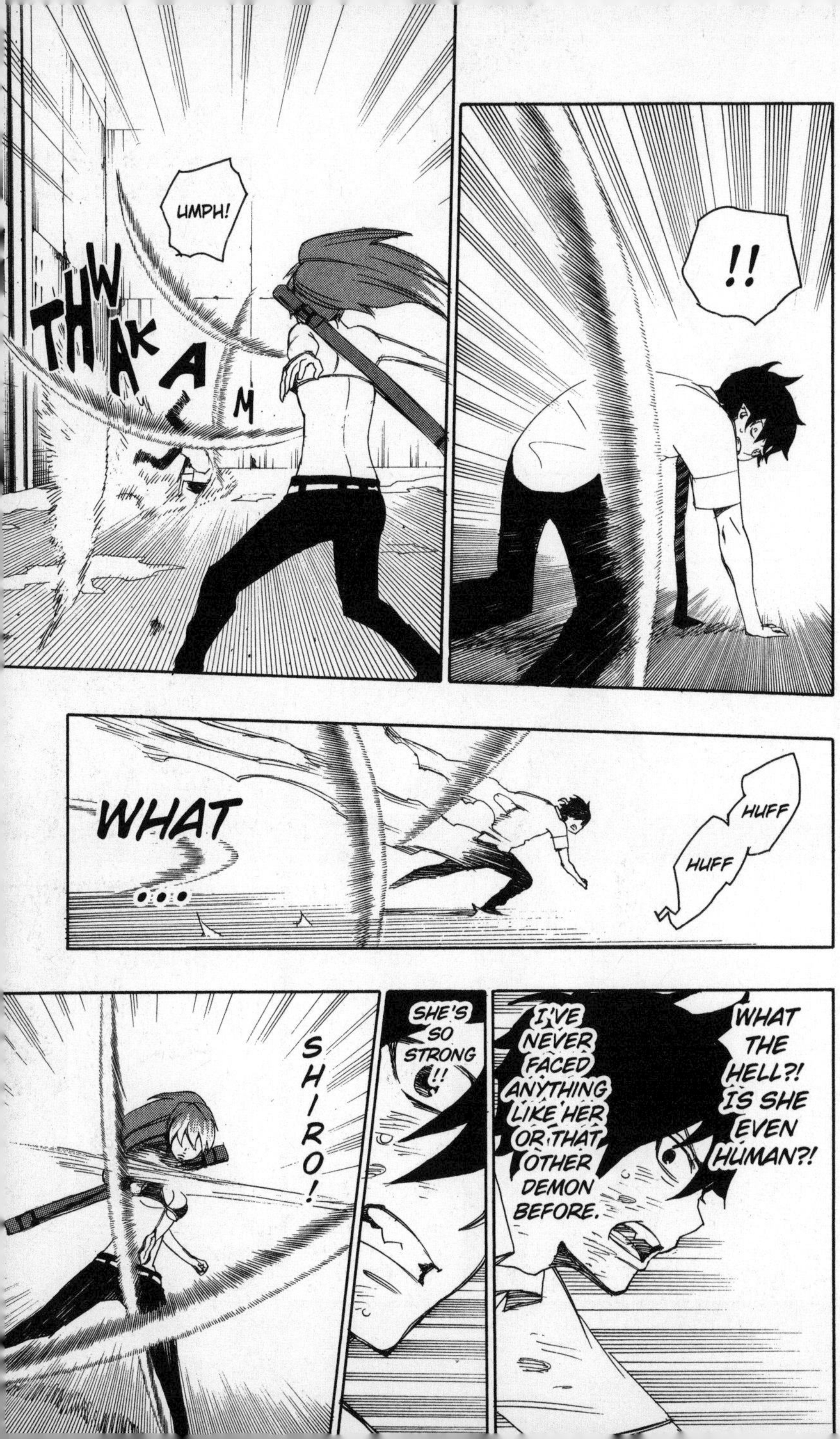
!!
UMPH!
THWAKAM
HUFF
HUFF
WHAT...
WHAT THE HELL?! IS SHE EVEN HUMAN?!
I'VE NEVER FACED ANYTHING LIKE HER OR THAT OTHER DEMON BEFORE.
SHE'S SO STRONG!!
SHIRO!

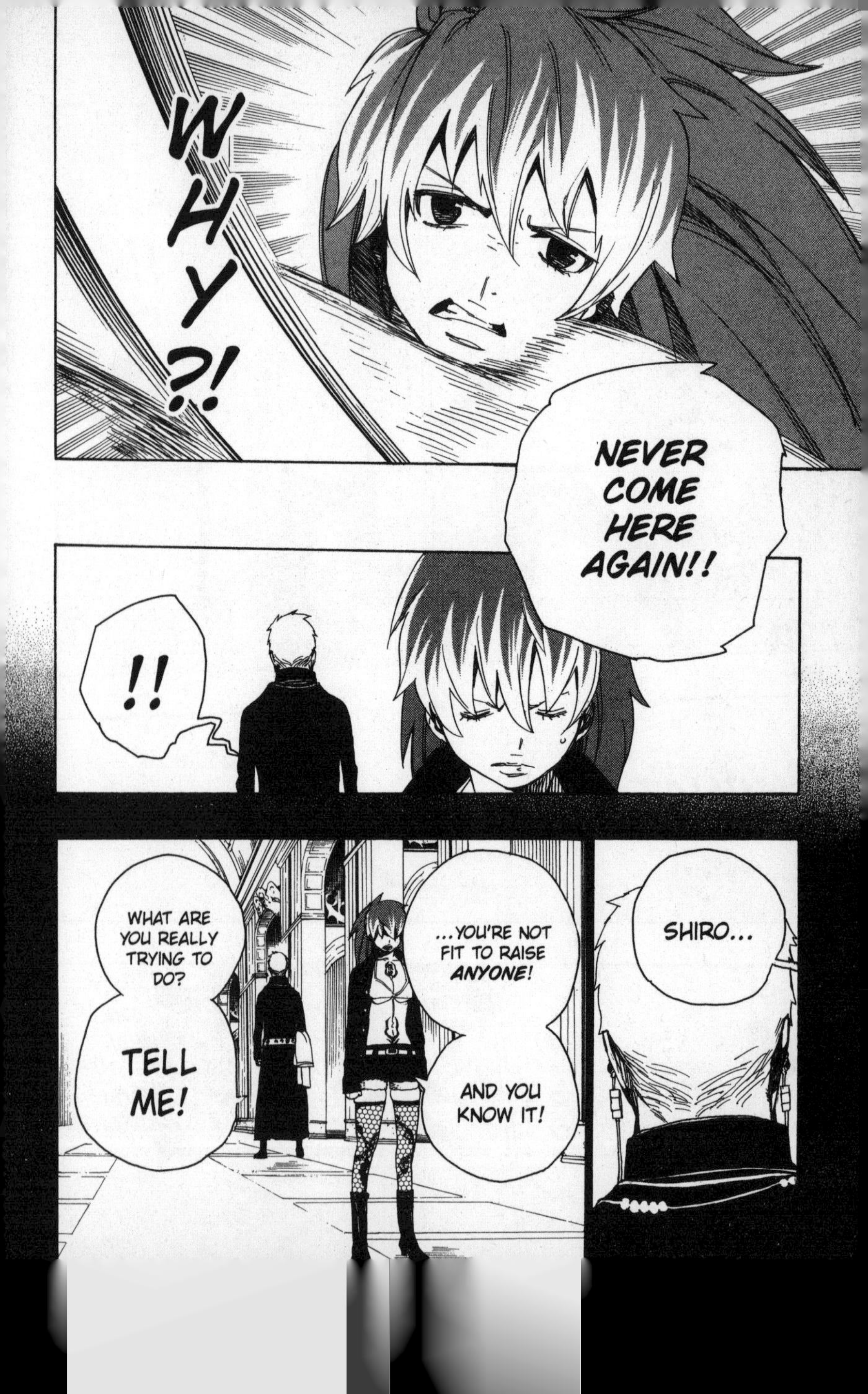
WHY?!
NEVER COME HERE AGAIN!!
!!
SHIRO...
...YOU'RE NOT FIT TO RAISE ANYONE!
AND YOU KNOW IT!
WHAT ARE YOU REALLY TRYING TO DO?
TELL ME!

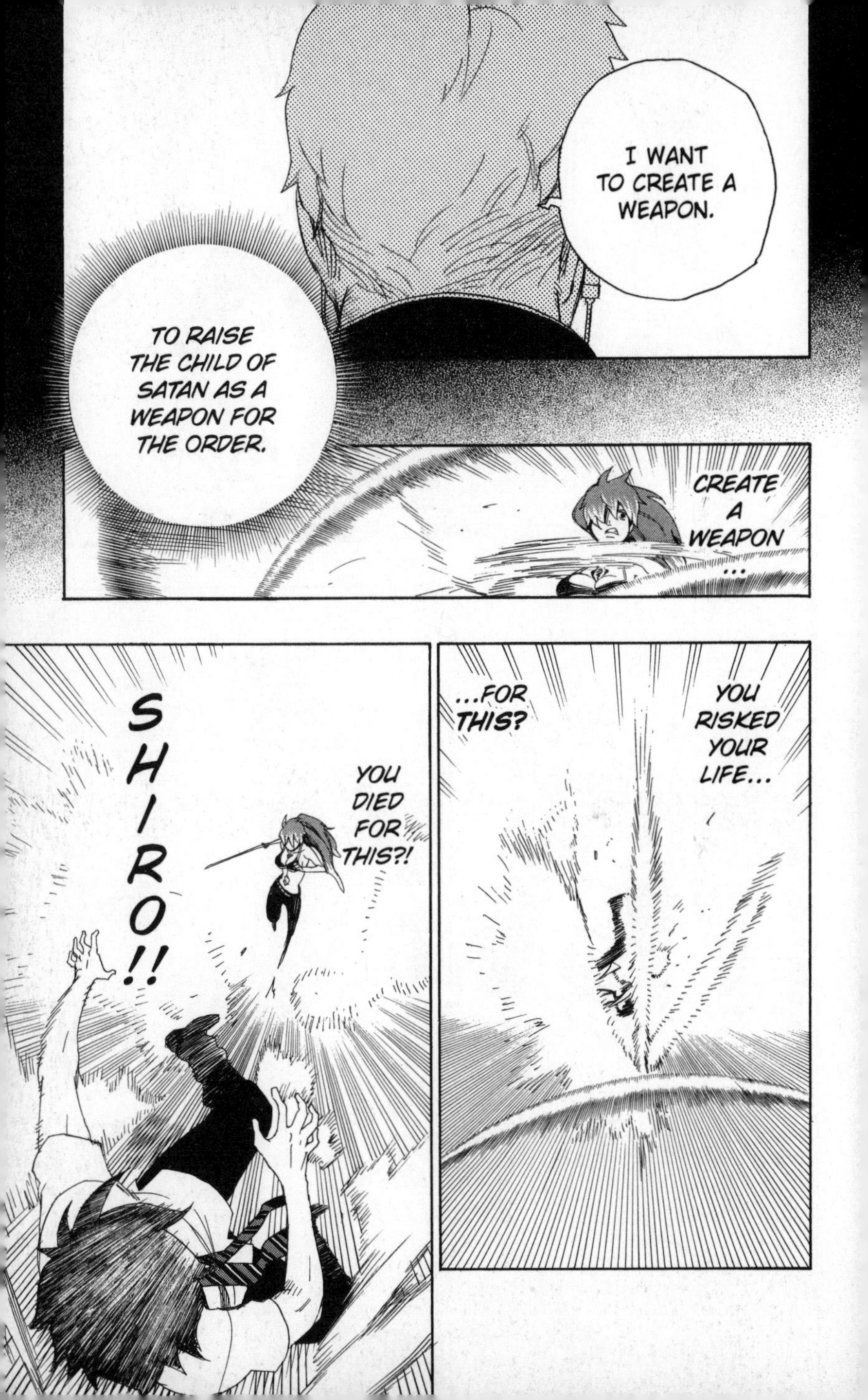
I WANT TO CREATE A WEAPON.
TO RAISE THE CHILD OF SATAN AS A WEAPON FOR THE ORDER.
CREATE A WEAPON ...
YOU RISKED YOUR LIFE...
...FOR THIS?
YOU DIED FOR THIS?!
SHIRO!!

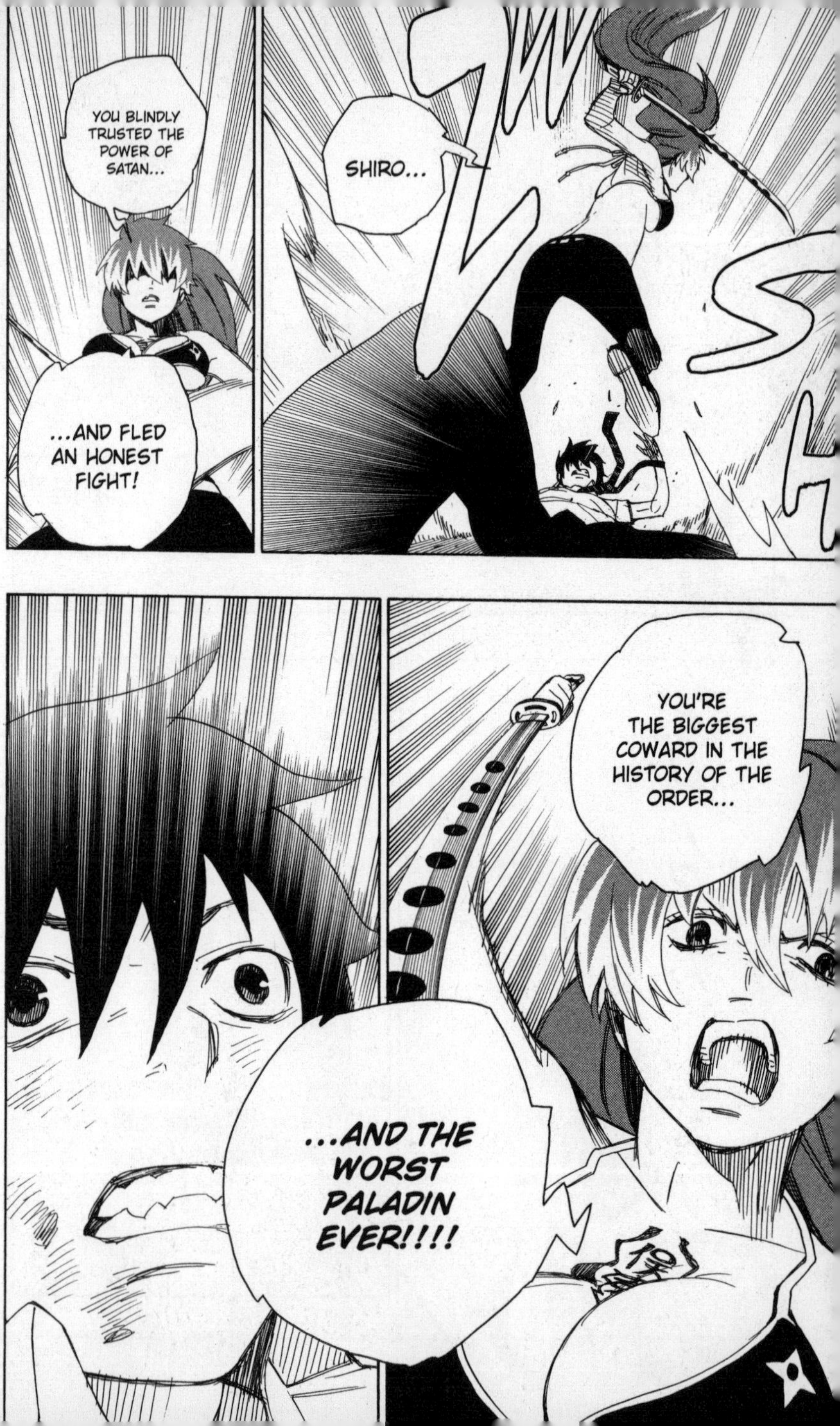
SHIRO...
YOU BLINDLY TRUSTED THE POWER OF SATAN...
...AND FLED AN HONEST FIGHT!
YOU'RE THE BIGGEST COWARD IN THE HISTORY OF THE ORDER...
...AND THE WORST PALADIN EVER!!!!

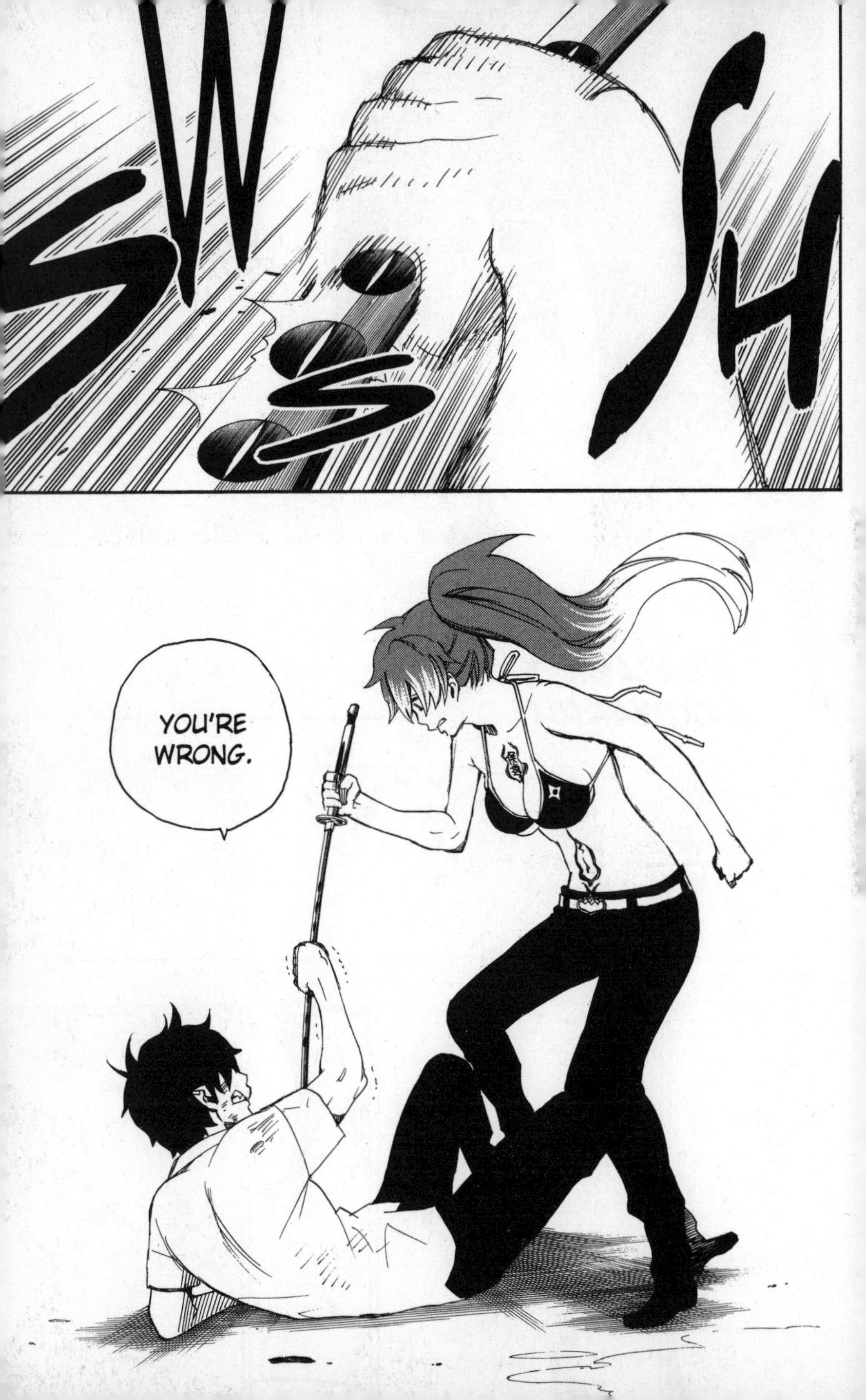
SWISH
YOU'RE WRONG.

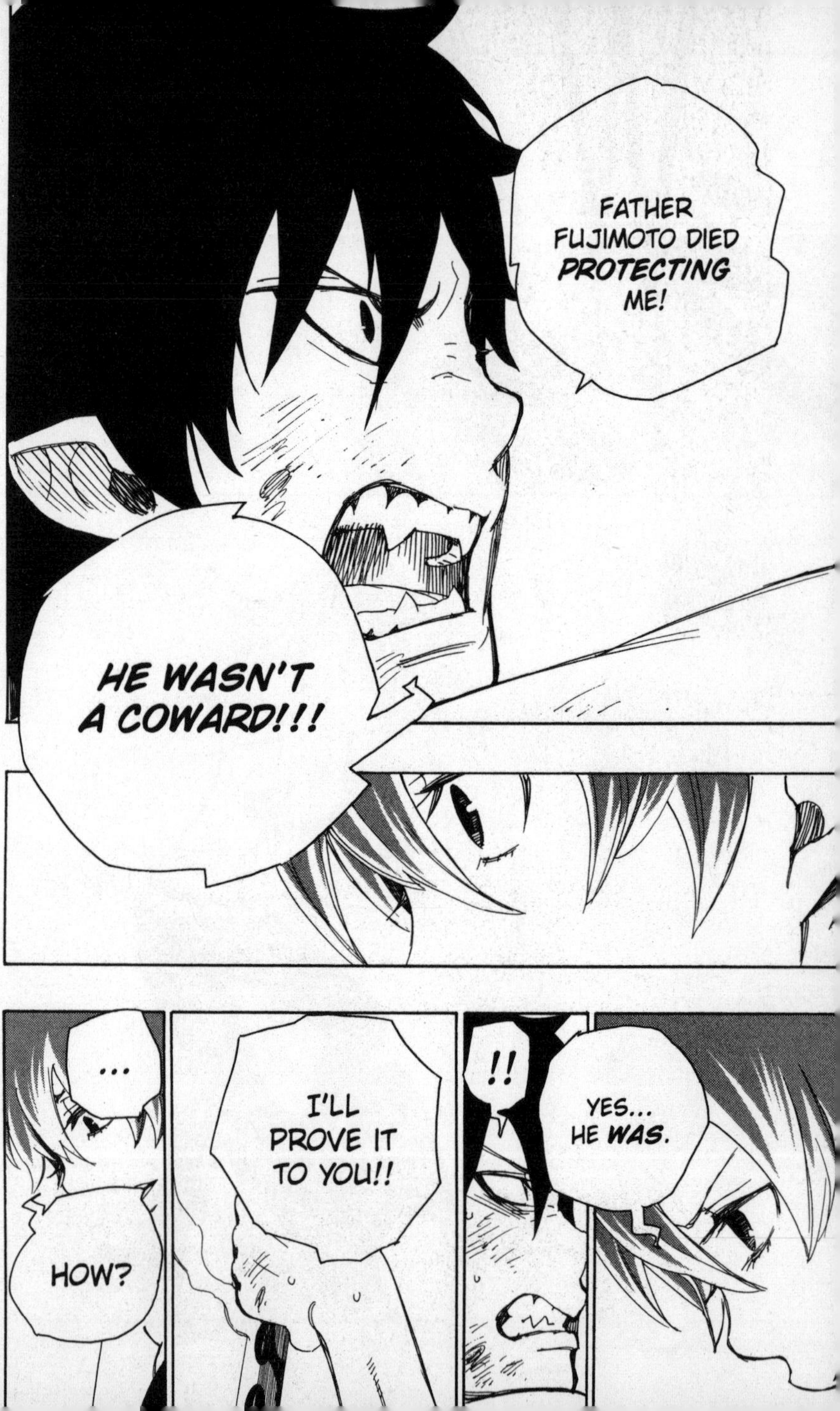
FATHER FUJIMOTO DIED PROTECTING ME!
HE WASN'T A COWARD!!!
YES... HE WAS.
!!
I'LL PROVE IT TO YOU!!
...
HOW?

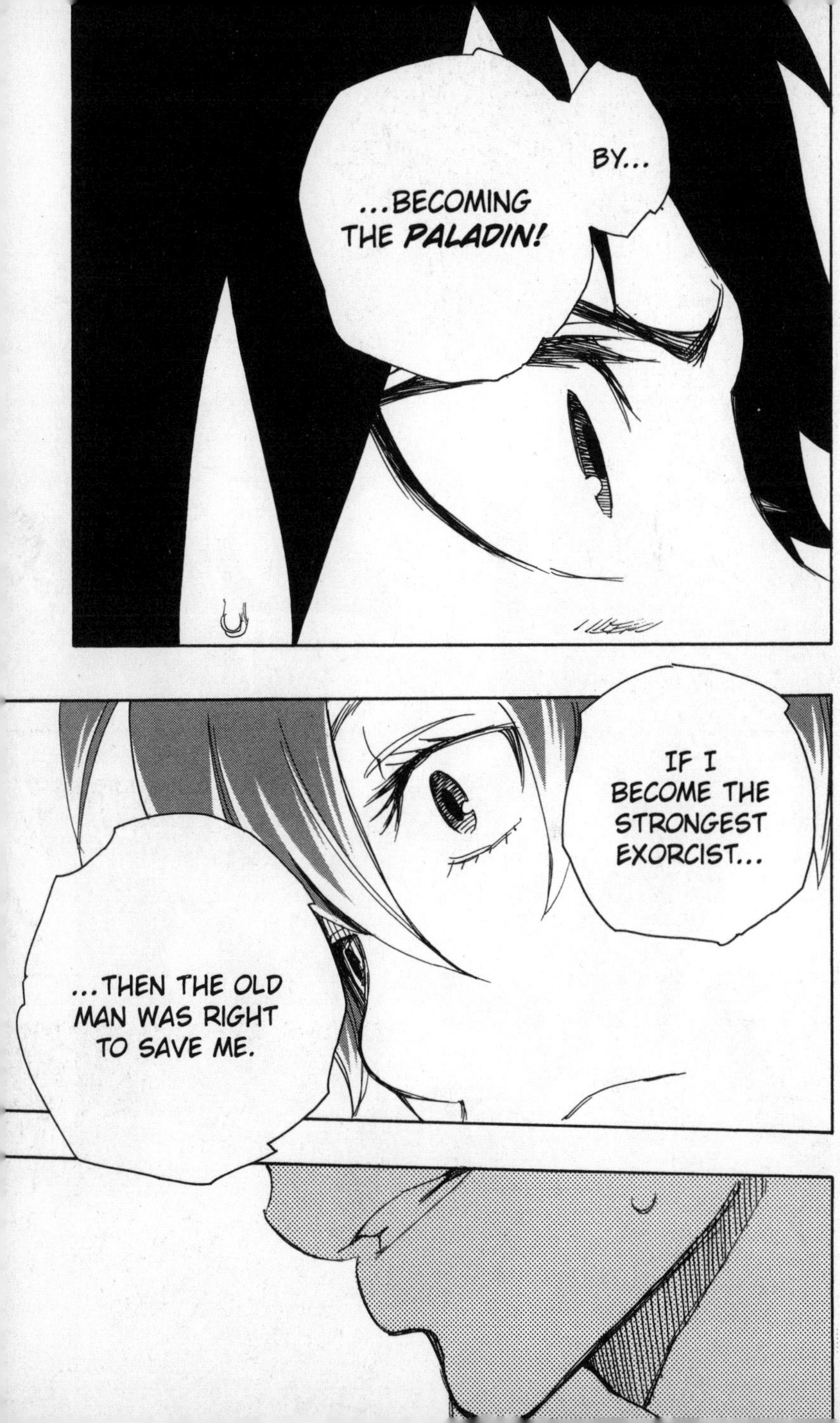
BY...
...BECOMING THE PALADIN!
IF I BECOME THE STRONGEST EXORCIST...
...THEN THE OLD MAN WAS RIGHT TO SAVE ME.

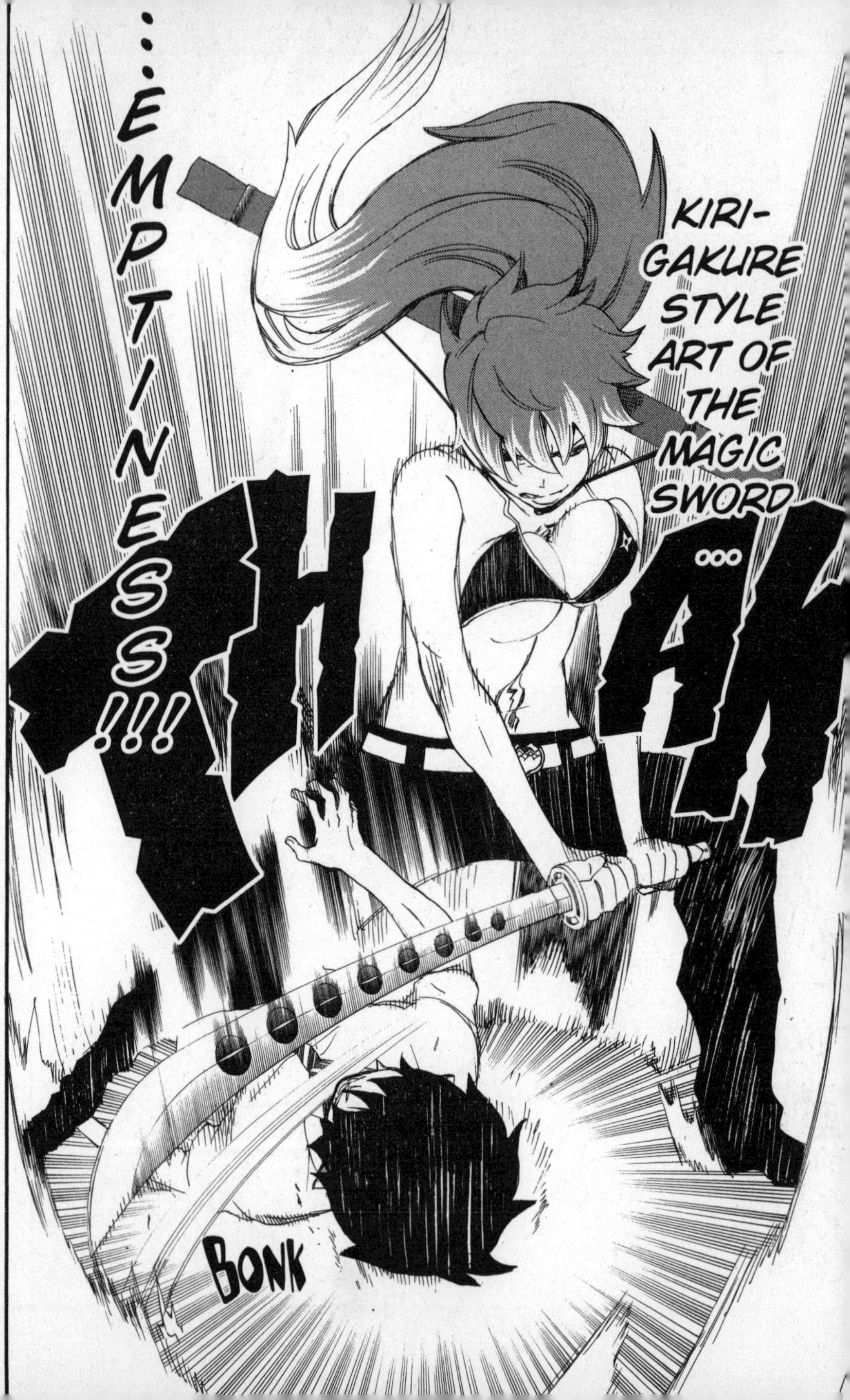
KIRI-GAKURE STYLE ART OF THE MAGIC SWORD...
...EMPTINESS!!!
BONK

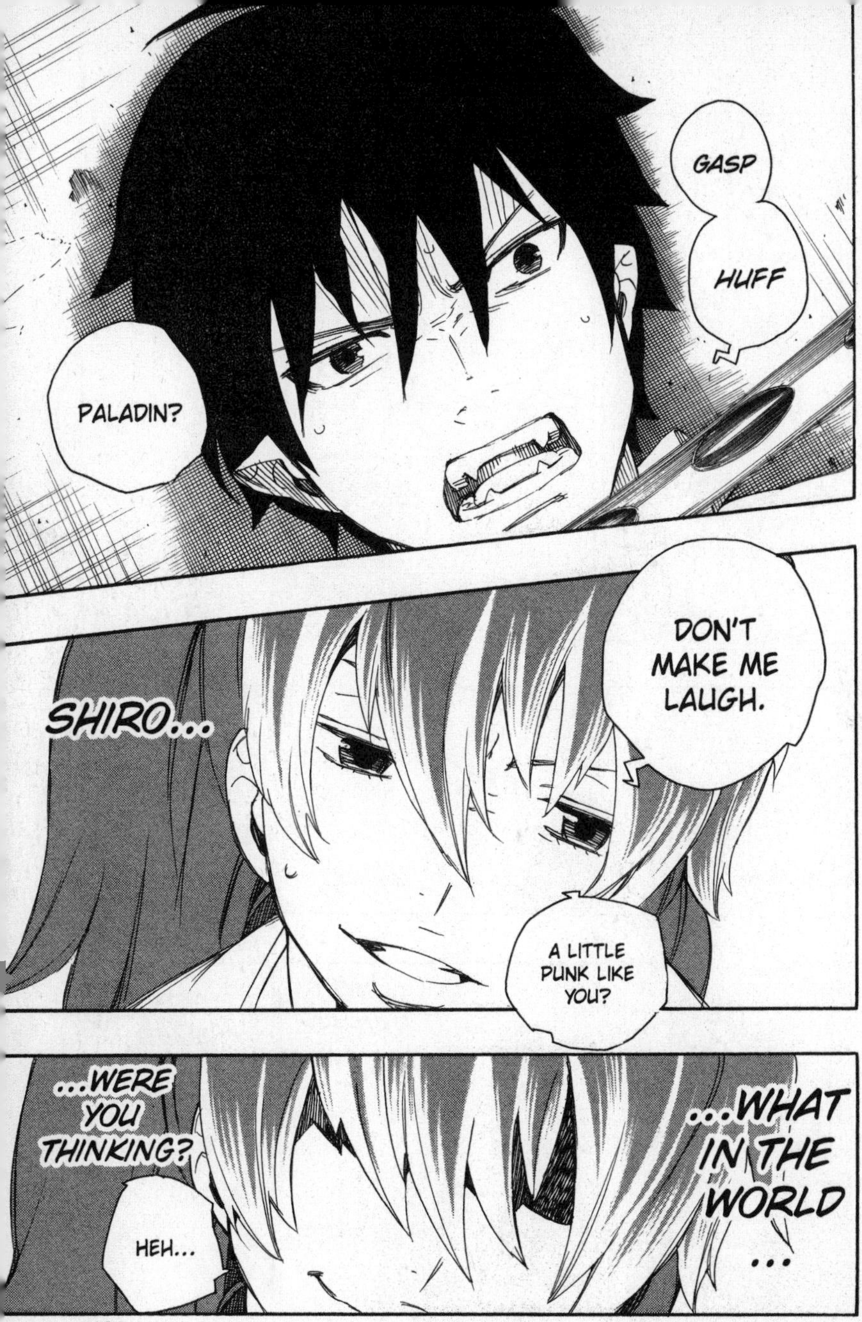
GASP
HUFF
PALADIN?
DON'T MAKE ME LAUGH.
SHIRO...
A LITTLE PUNK LIKE YOU?
...WHAT IN THE WORLD ...
...WERE YOU THINKING?
HEH...

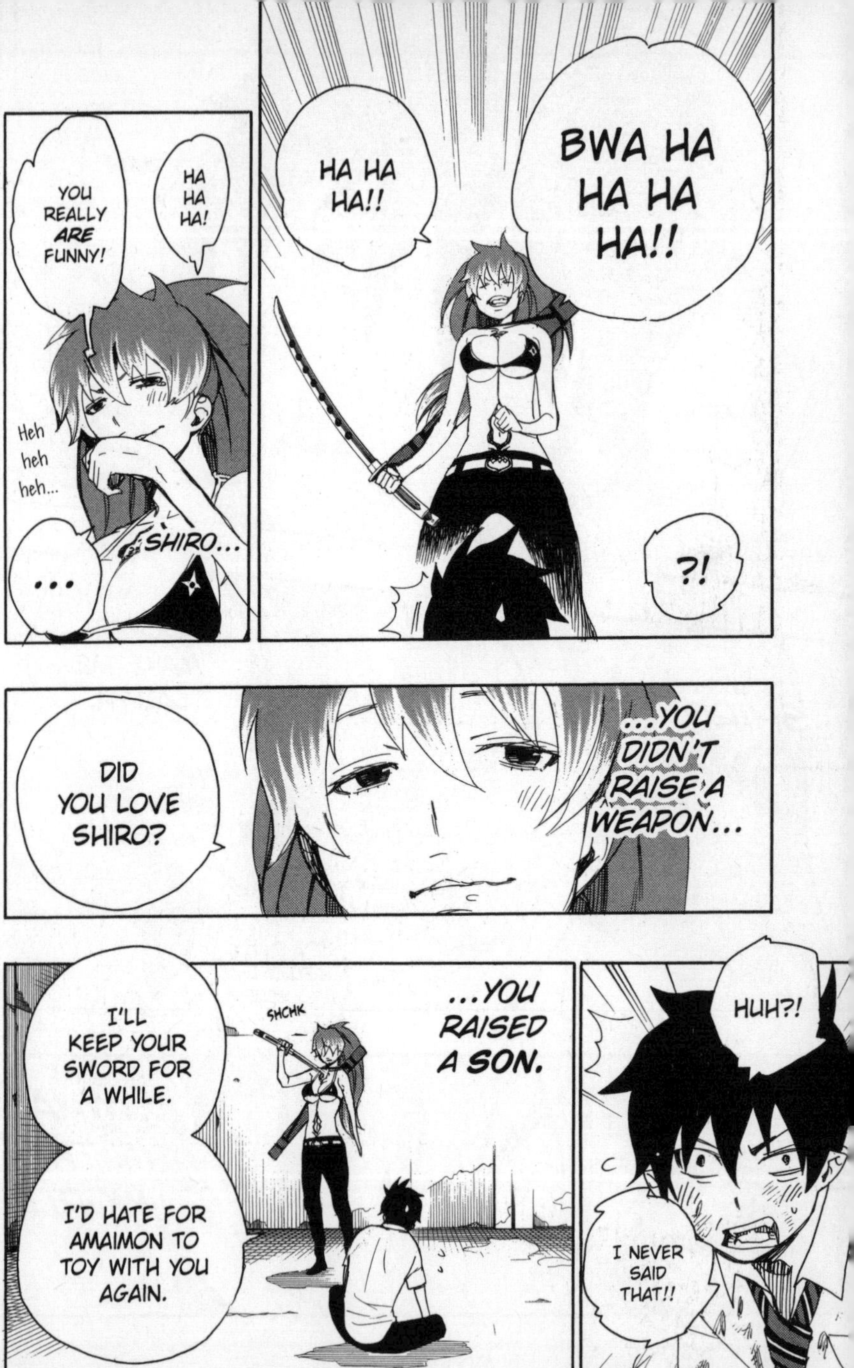
BWA HA HA HA HA HA!!
HA HA HA!!
?!
HA HA HA!
YOU REALLY ARE FUNNY!
Heh heh heh...
SHIRO...
...
...YOU DIDN'T RAISE A WEAPON...
DID YOU LOVE SHIRO?
HUH?!
I NEVER SAID THAT!!
...YOU RAISED A SON.
SHCHK
I'LL KEEP YOUR SWORD FOR A WHILE.
I'D HATE FOR AMAIMON TO TOY WITH YOU AGAIN.

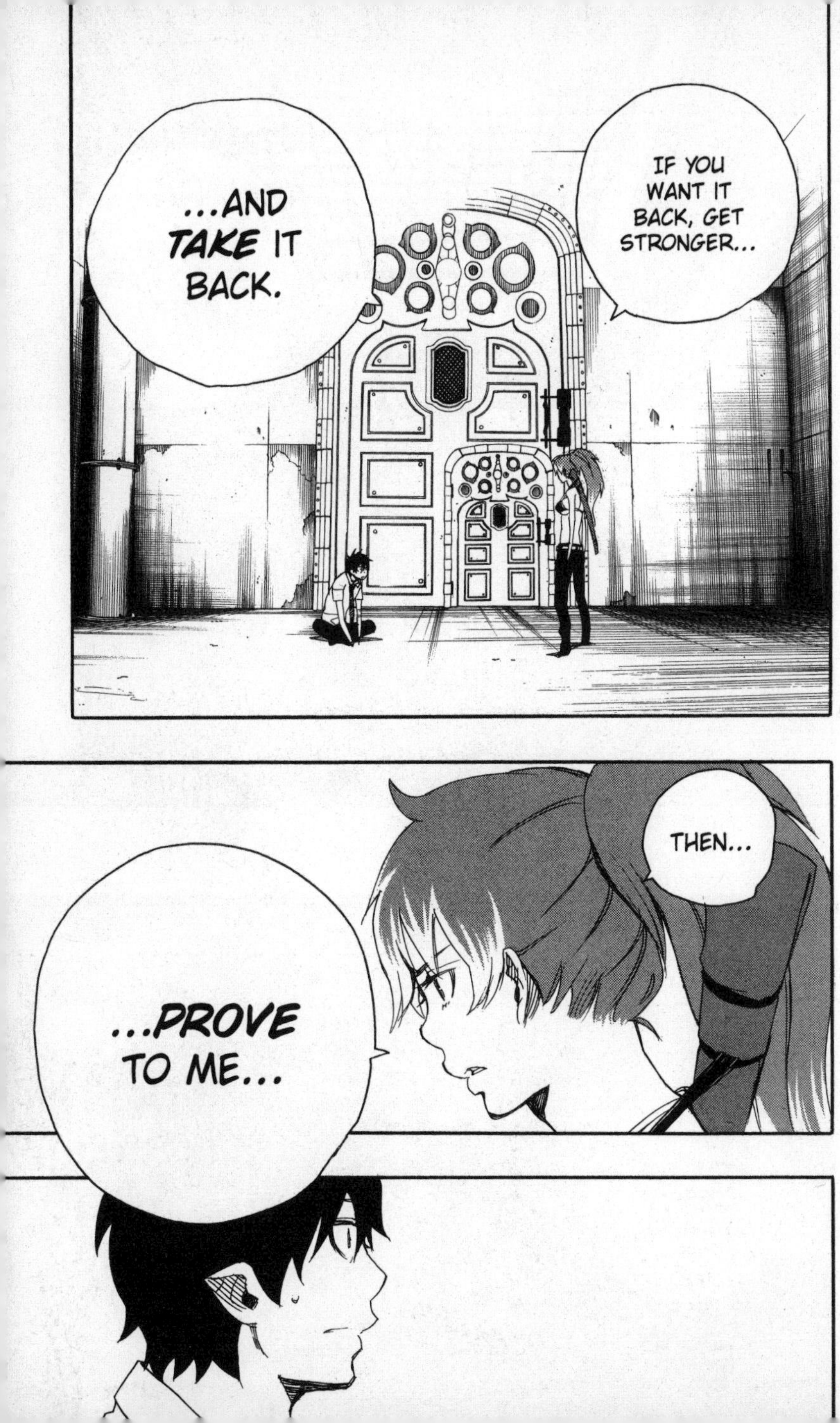
IF YOU WANT IT BACK, GET STRONGER...
...AND *TAKE* IT BACK.
THEN...
...*PROVE* TO ME...

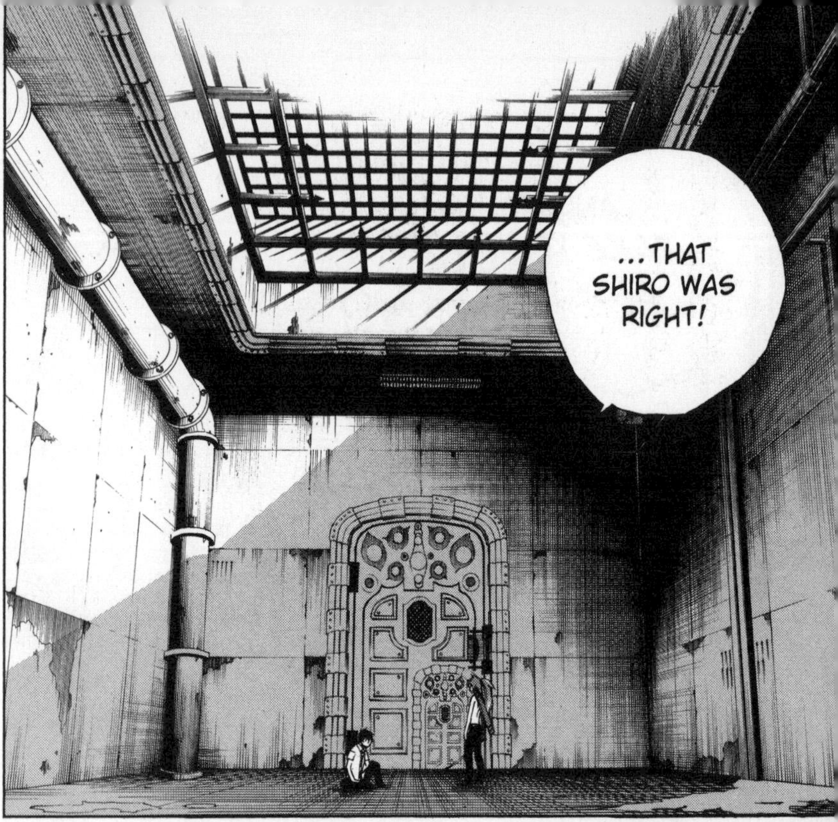
...THAT SHIRO WAS RIGHT!

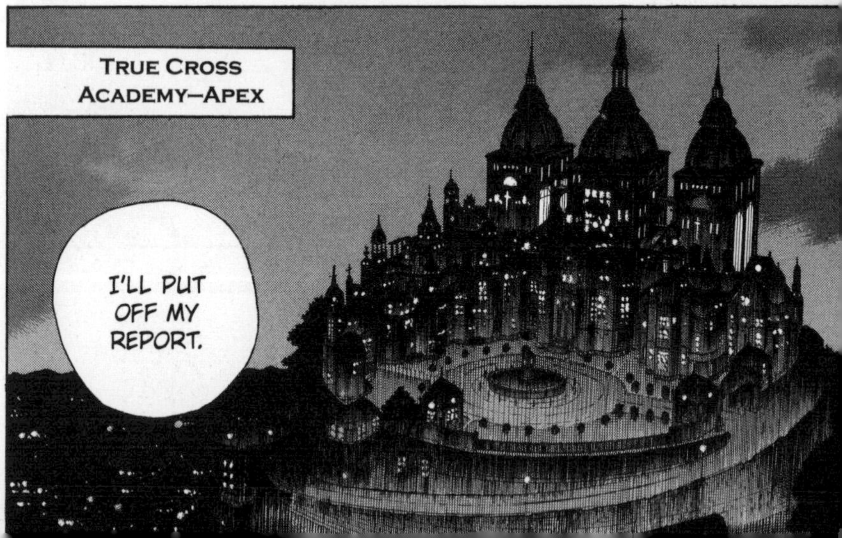
TRUE CROSS ACADEMY—APEX
I'LL PUT OFF MY REPORT.

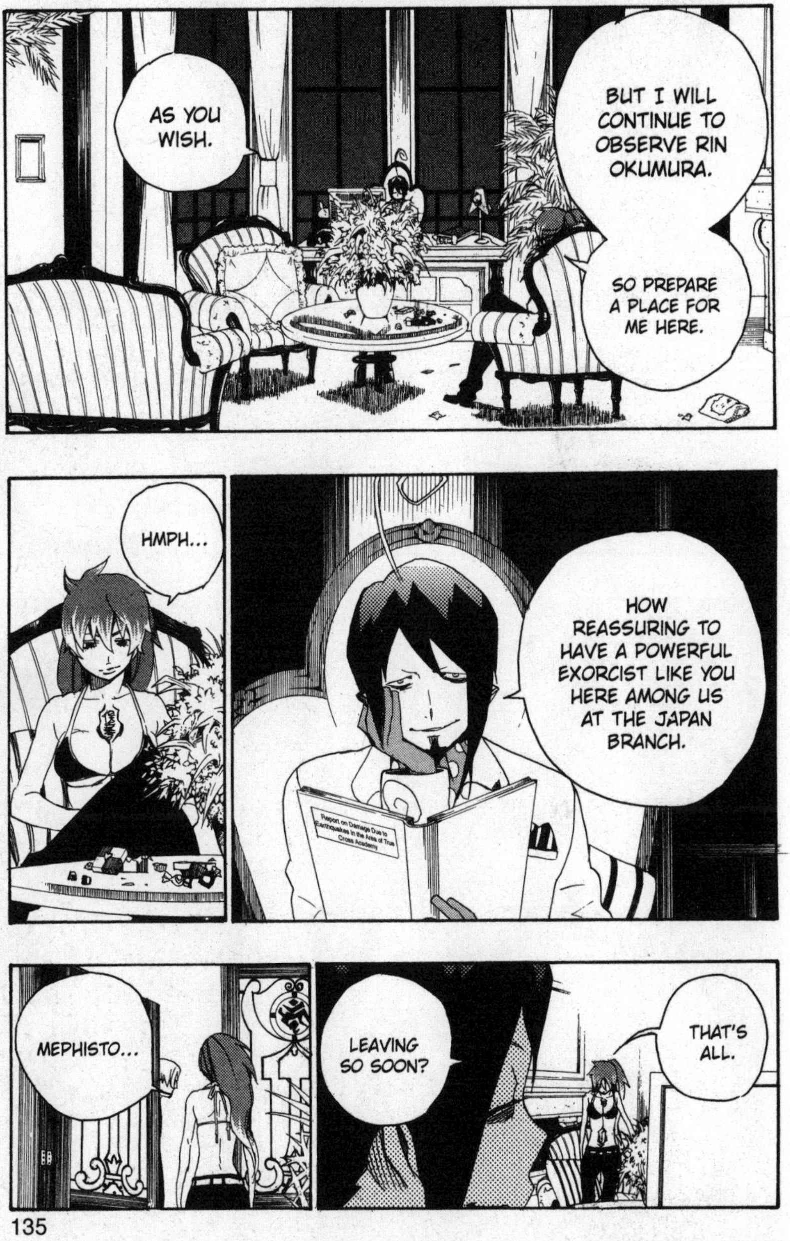
BUT I WILL CONTINUE TO OBSERVE RIN OKUMURA.
SO PREPARE A PLACE FOR ME HERE.
AS YOU WISH.
HOW REASSURING TO HAVE A POWERFUL EXORCIST LIKE YOU HERE AMONG US AT THE JAPAN BRANCH.
Report on Damage Due to Earthquakes in the Area of True Cross Academy
HMPH...
THAT'S ALL.
LEAVING SO SOON?
MEPHISTO...

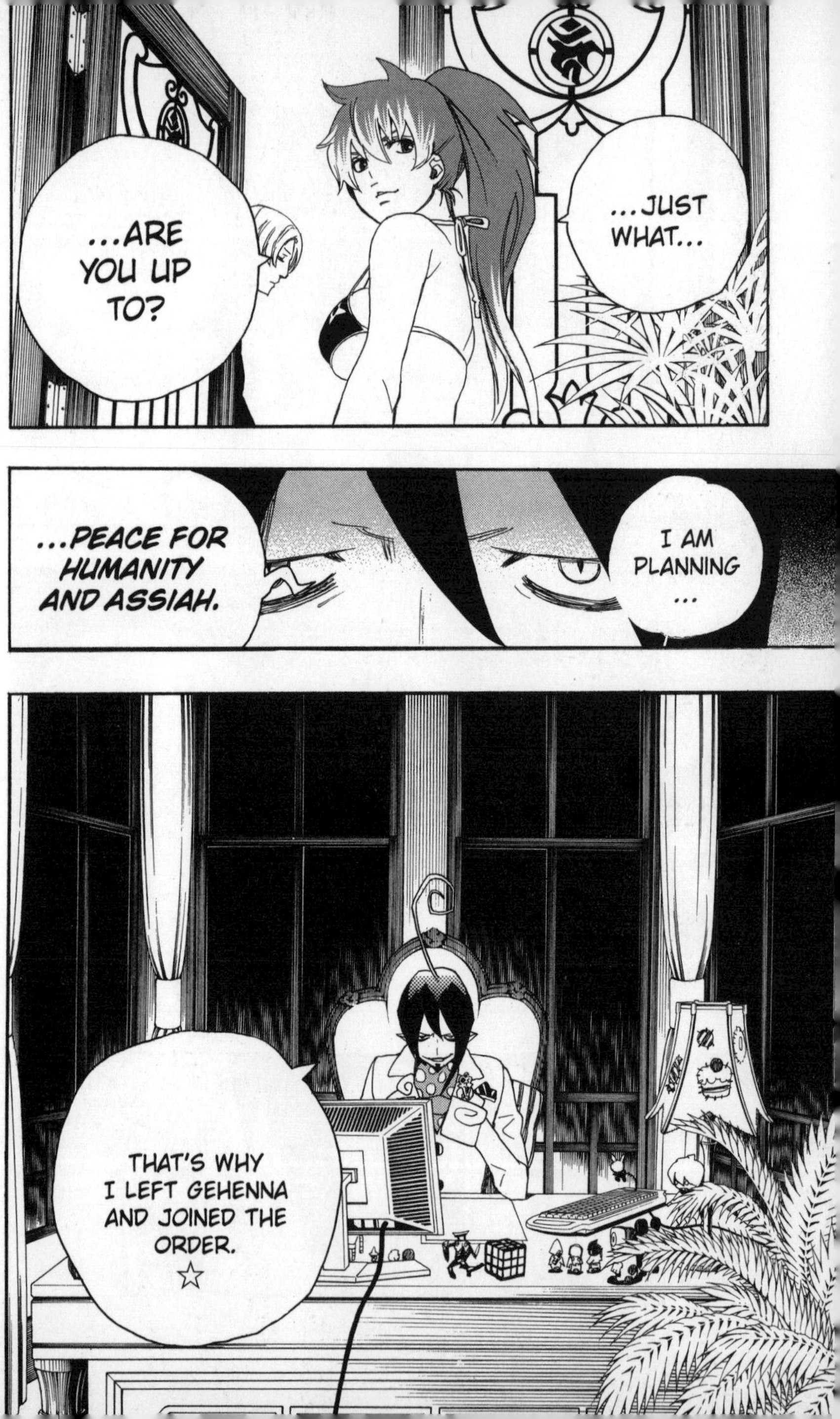
...JUST WHAT...
...ARE YOU UP TO?
I AM PLANNING ...
...PEACE FOR HUMANITY AND ASSIAH.
THAT'S WHY I LEFT GEHENNA AND JOINED THE ORDER. ☆

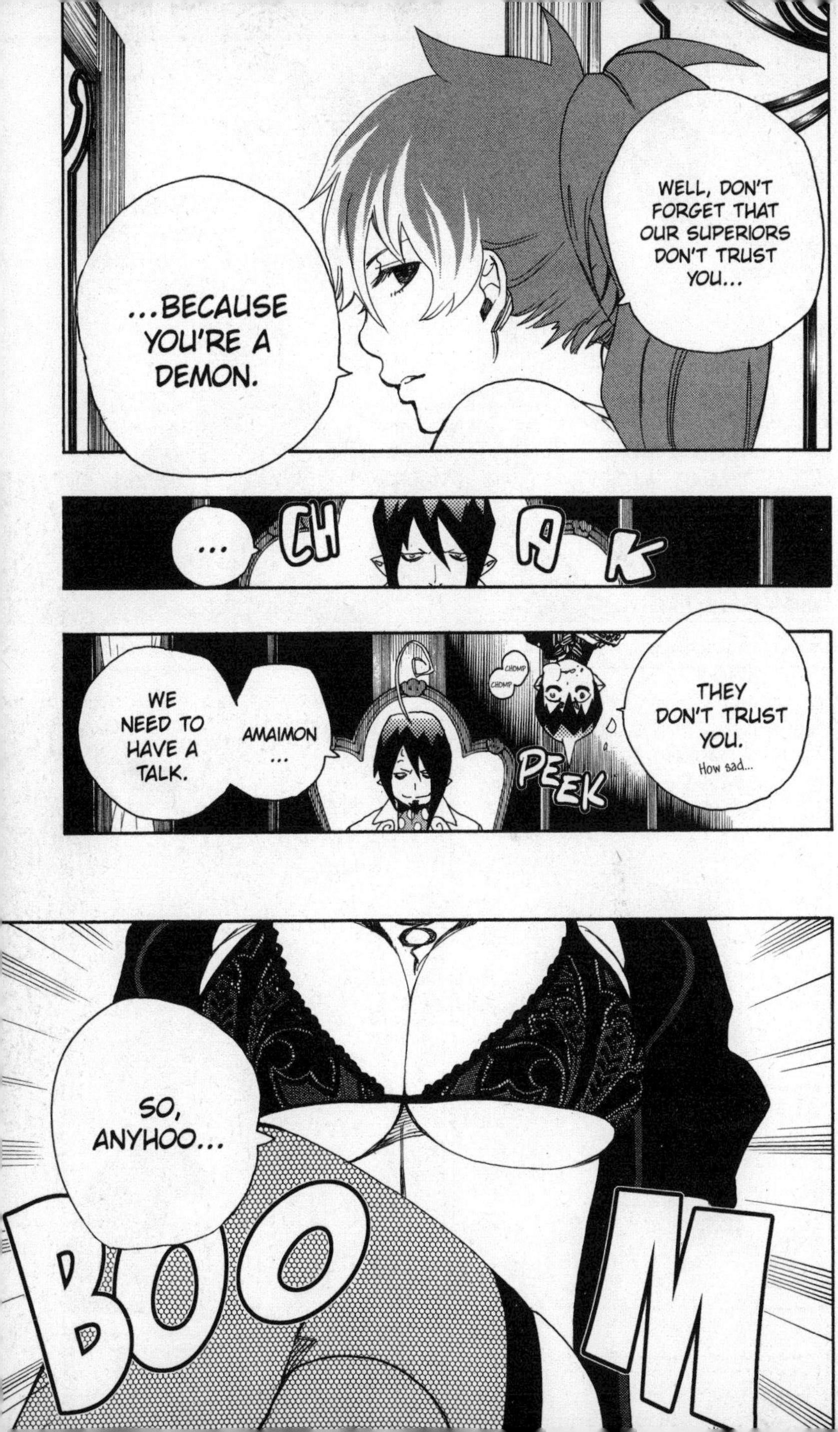
WELL, DON'T FORGET THAT OUR SUPERIORS DON'T TRUST YOU...
...BECAUSE YOU'RE A DEMON.
CHAK
...
THEY DON'T TRUST YOU.
How sad...
CHOMP CHOMP
PEEK
AMAIMON ...
WE NEED TO HAVE A TALK.
SO, ANYHOO...
BOOM

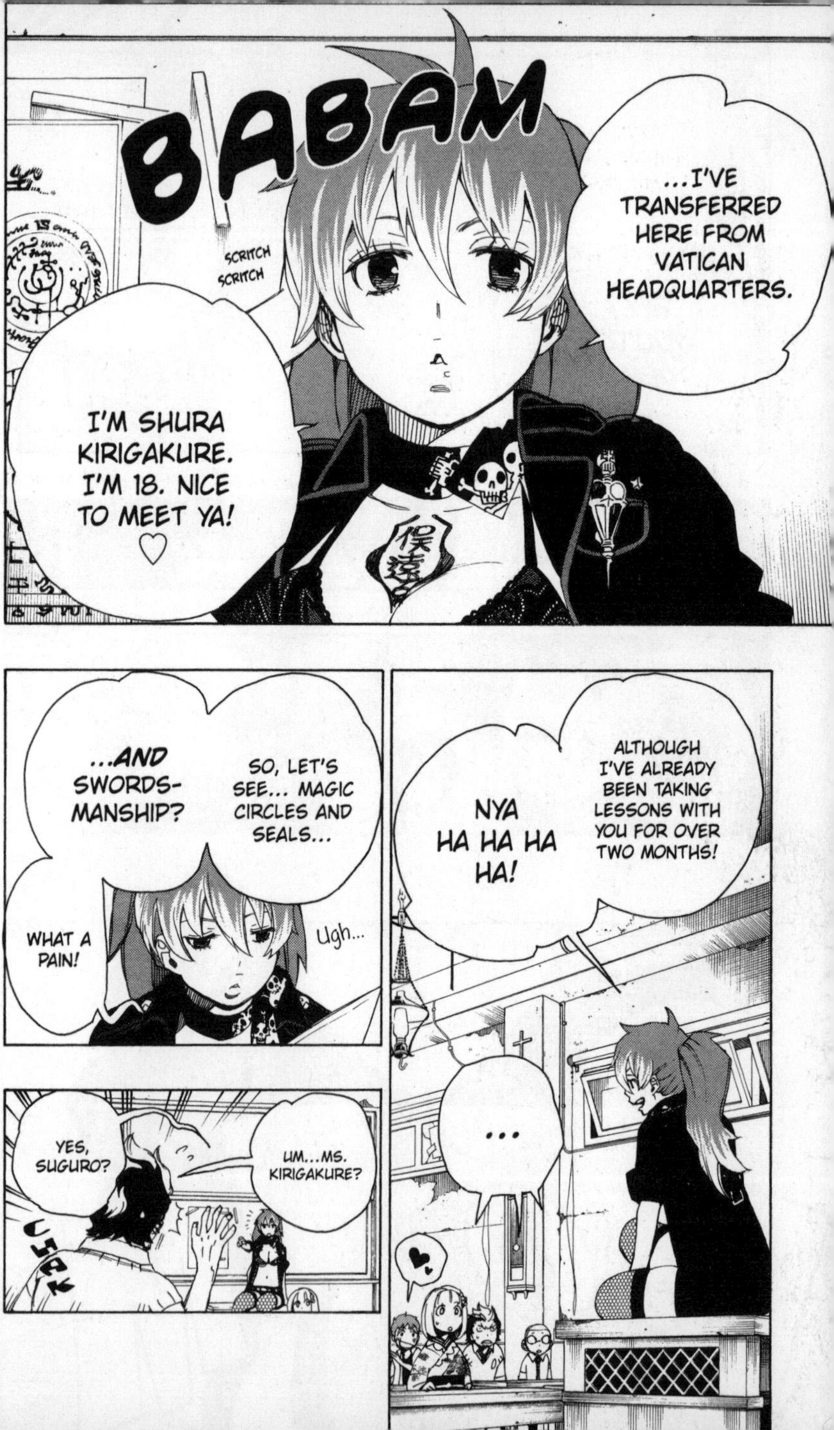
BABAM
...I'VE TRANSFERRED HERE FROM VATICAN HEADQUARTERS.
SCRITCH SCRITCH
I'M SHURA KIRIGAKURE. I'M 18. NICE TO MEET YA! ♡
ALTHOUGH I'VE ALREADY BEEN TAKING LESSONS WITH YOU FOR OVER TWO MONTHS!
NYA HA HA HA HA!
...
SO, LET'S SEE... MAGIC CIRCLES AND SEALS...
...AND SWORDS-MANSHIP?
Ugh...
WHAT A PAIN!
UM...MS. KIRIGAKURE?
YES, SUGURO?

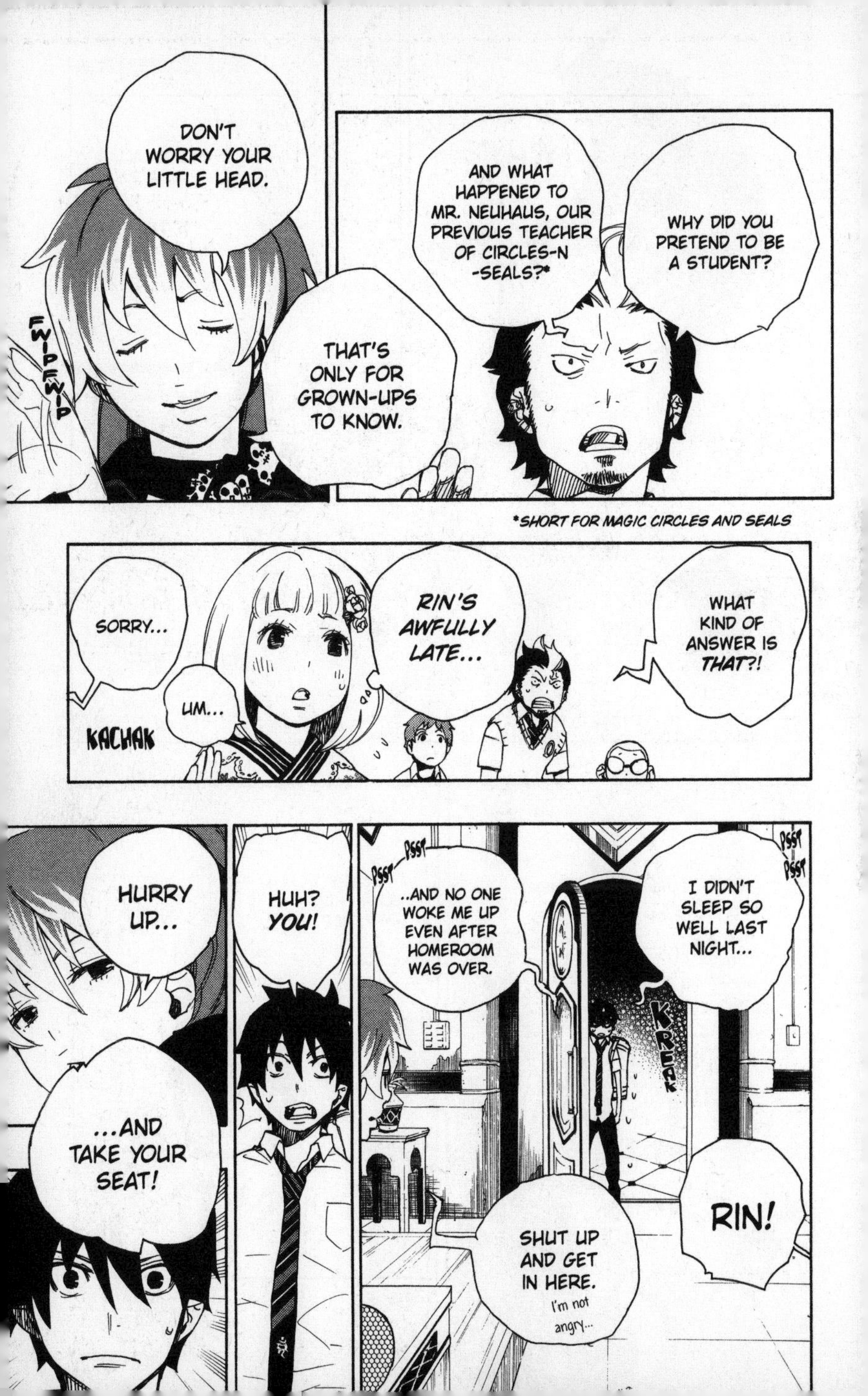
WHY DID YOU PRETEND TO BE A STUDENT?
AND WHAT HAPPENED TO MR. NEUHAUS, OUR PREVIOUS TEACHER OF CIRCLES-N -SEALS?*
DON'T WORRY YOUR LITTLE HEAD.
THAT'S ONLY FOR GROWN-UPS TO KNOW.
FWIPFWIP
WHAT KIND OF ANSWER IS THAT?!
RIN'S AWFULLY LATE...
UM...
SORRY...
KACHAK
PSST PSST
I DIDN'T SLEEP SO WELL LAST NIGHT...
KREAK
RIN!
PSST PSST
..AND NO ONE WOKE ME UP EVEN AFTER HOMEROOM WAS OVER.
SHUT UP AND GET IN HERE.
I'm not angry...
HUH? YOU!
HURRY UP...
...AND TAKE YOUR SEAT!

*SHORT FOR MAGIC CIRCLES AND SEALS

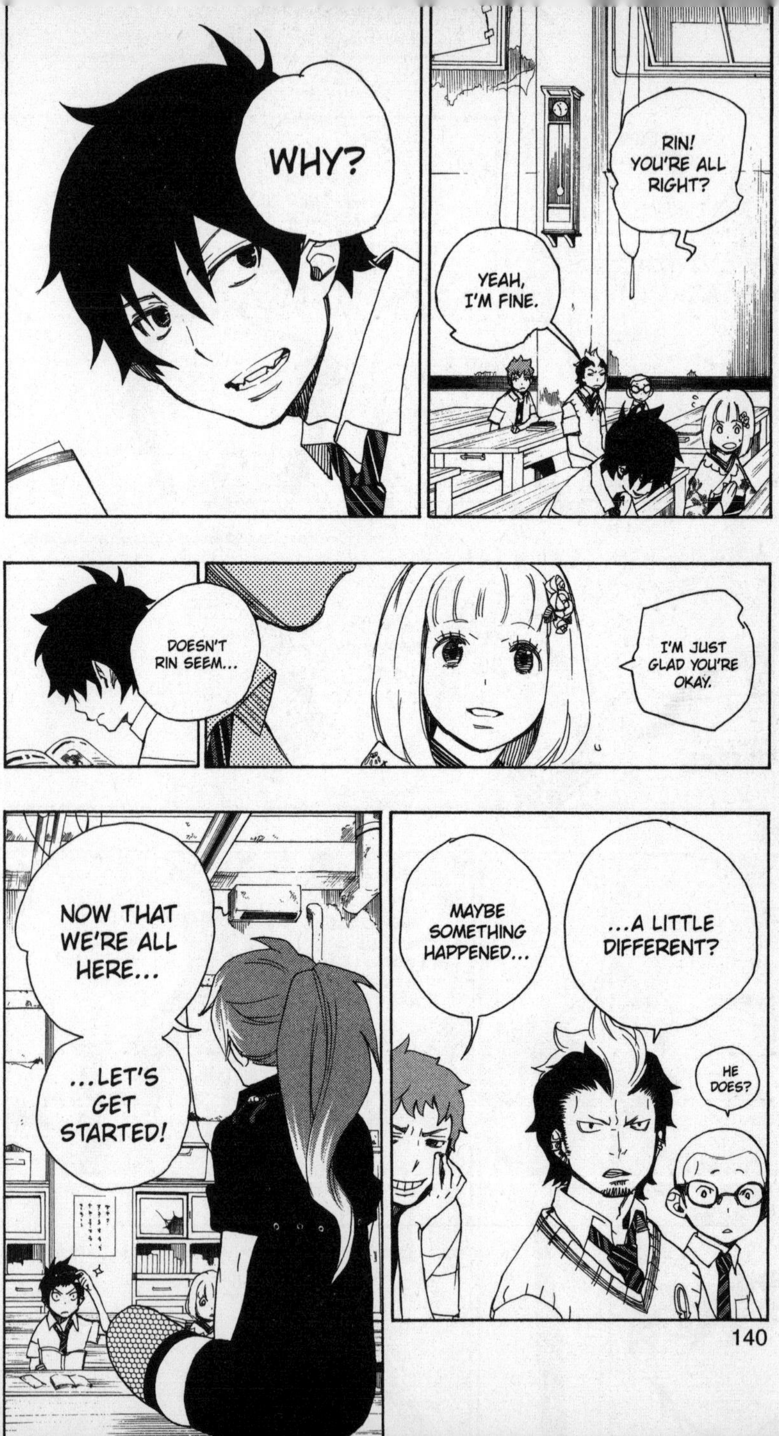
RIN! YOU'RE ALL RIGHT?
YEAH, I'M FINE.
WHY?
I'M JUST GLAD YOU'RE OKAY.
DOESN'T RIN SEEM...
...A LITTLE DIFFERENT?
MAYBE SOMETHING HAPPENED...
HE DOES?
NOW THAT WE'RE ALL HERE...
...LET'S GET STARTED!

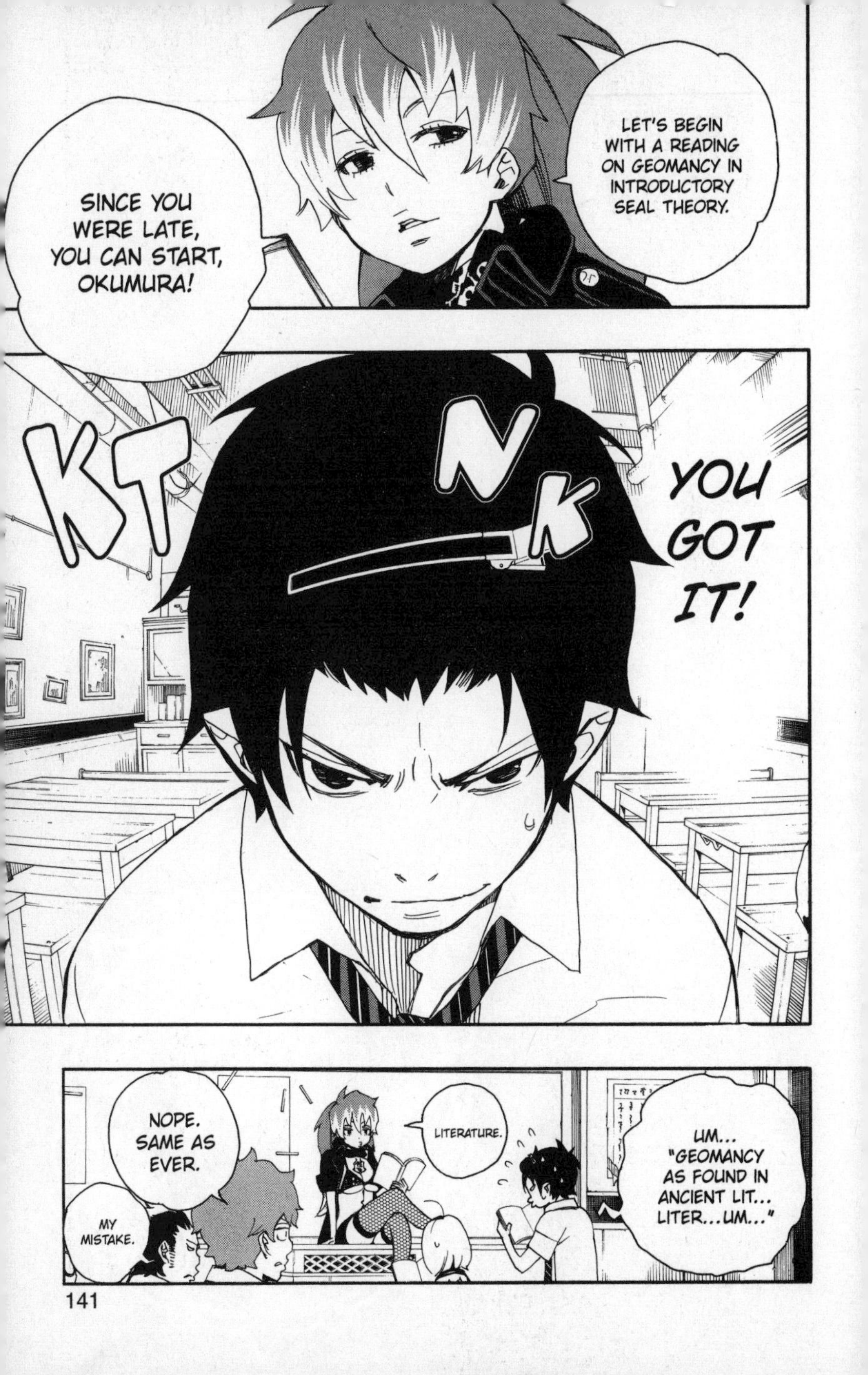
LET'S BEGIN WITH A READING ON GEOMANCY IN INTRODUCTORY SEAL THEORY.
SINCE YOU WERE LATE, YOU CAN START, OKUMURA!
YOU GOT IT!
NK
KT
UM... "GEOMANCY AS FOUND IN ANCIENT LIT... LITER...UM..."
LITERATURE.
NOPE. SAME AS EVER.
MY MISTAKE.

Blue Exorcist Chapter 10 Proof

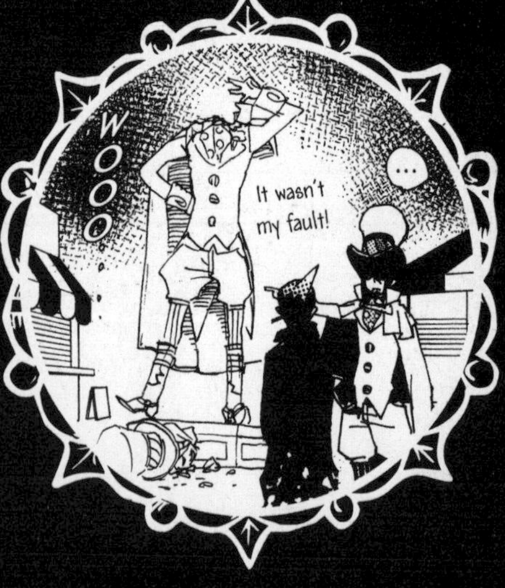
WOOOO
It wasn't my fault!
...

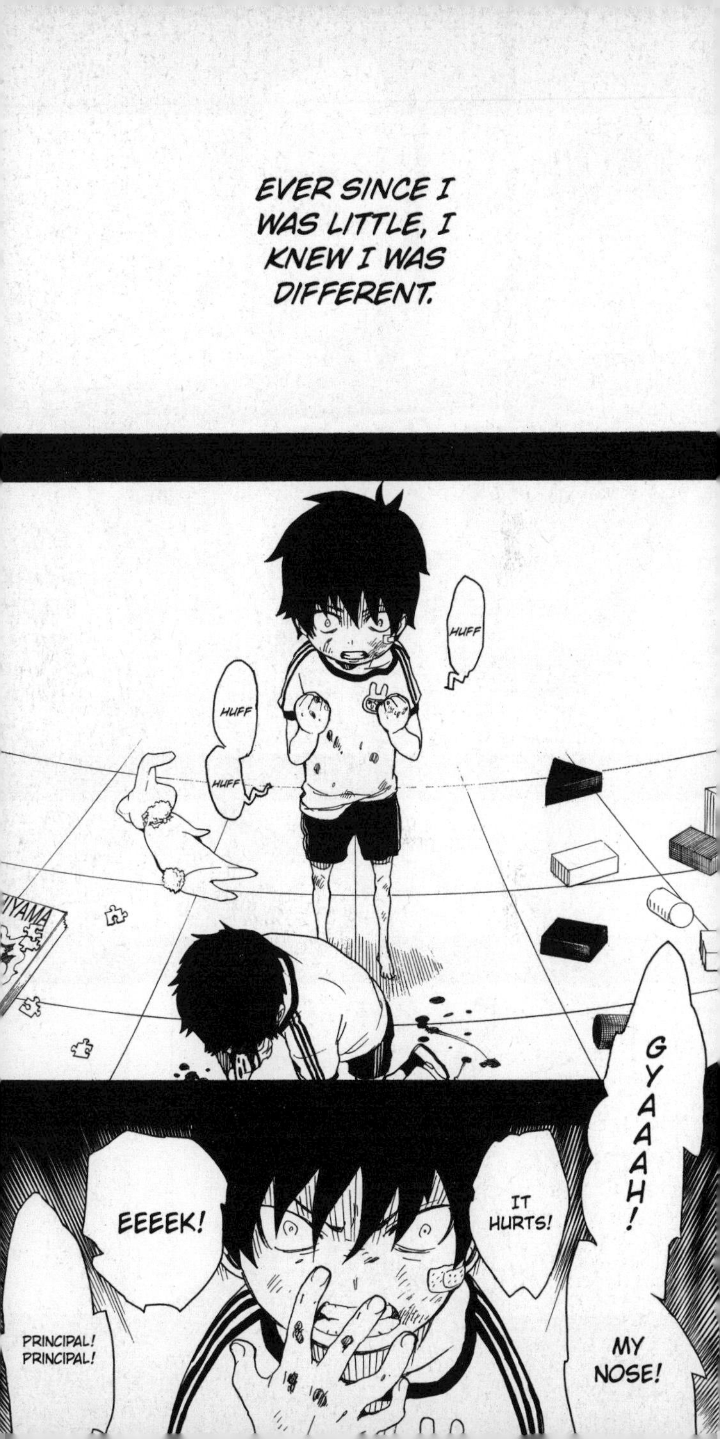
EVER SINCE I WAS LITTLE, I KNEW I WAS DIFFERENT.
HUFF
HUFF
HUFF
GYAAAH!
IT HURTS!
EEEEK!
MY NOSE!
PRINCIPAL! PRINCIPAL!

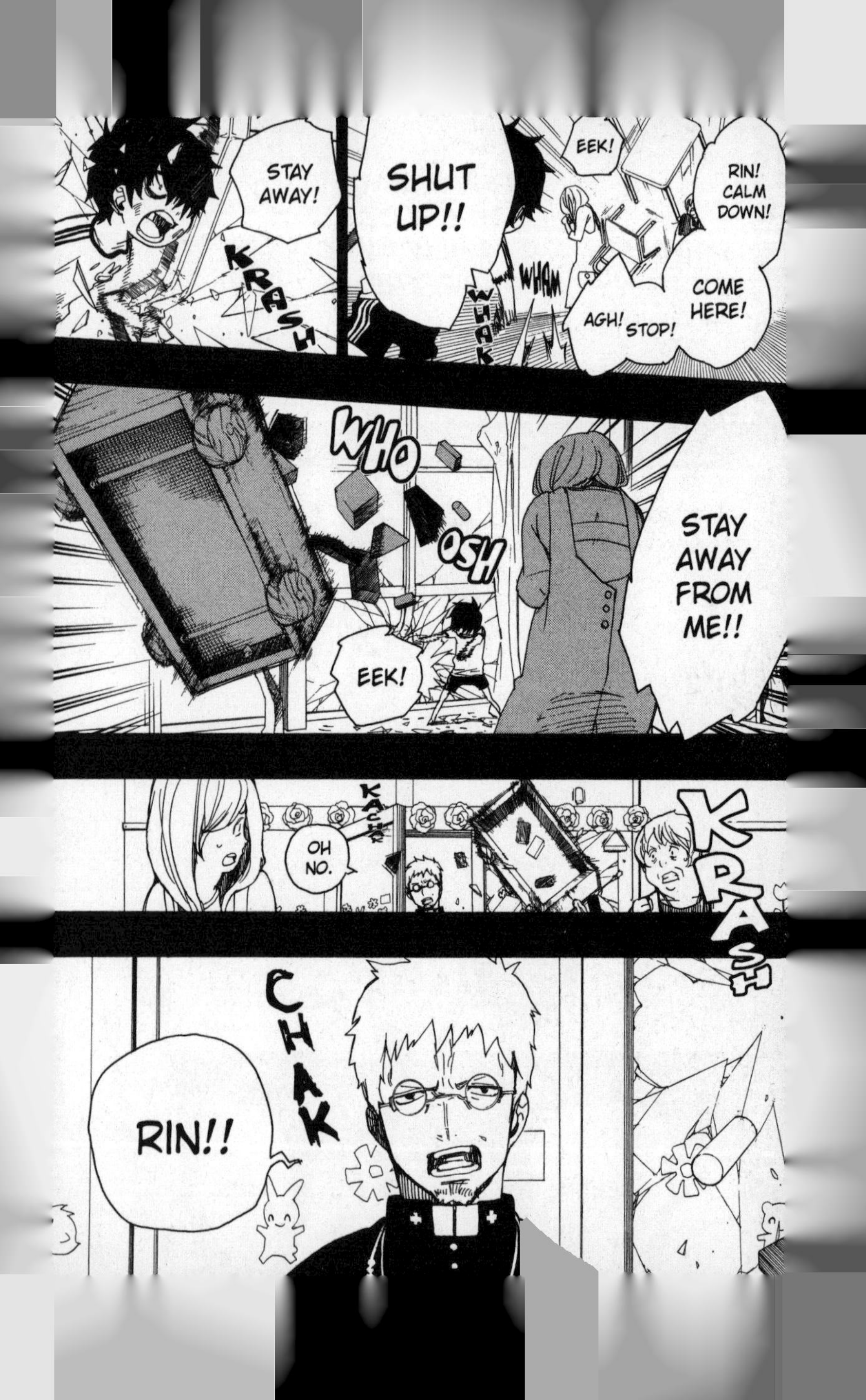
RIN! CALM DOWN!
EEK!
COME HERE!
STOP!
AGH!
WHAM
WHAK
SHUT UP!!
STAY AWAY!
KRASH
STAY AWAY FROM ME!!
WHOOSH
EEK!
KRASH
KACHA
OH NO.
CHAK
RIN!!

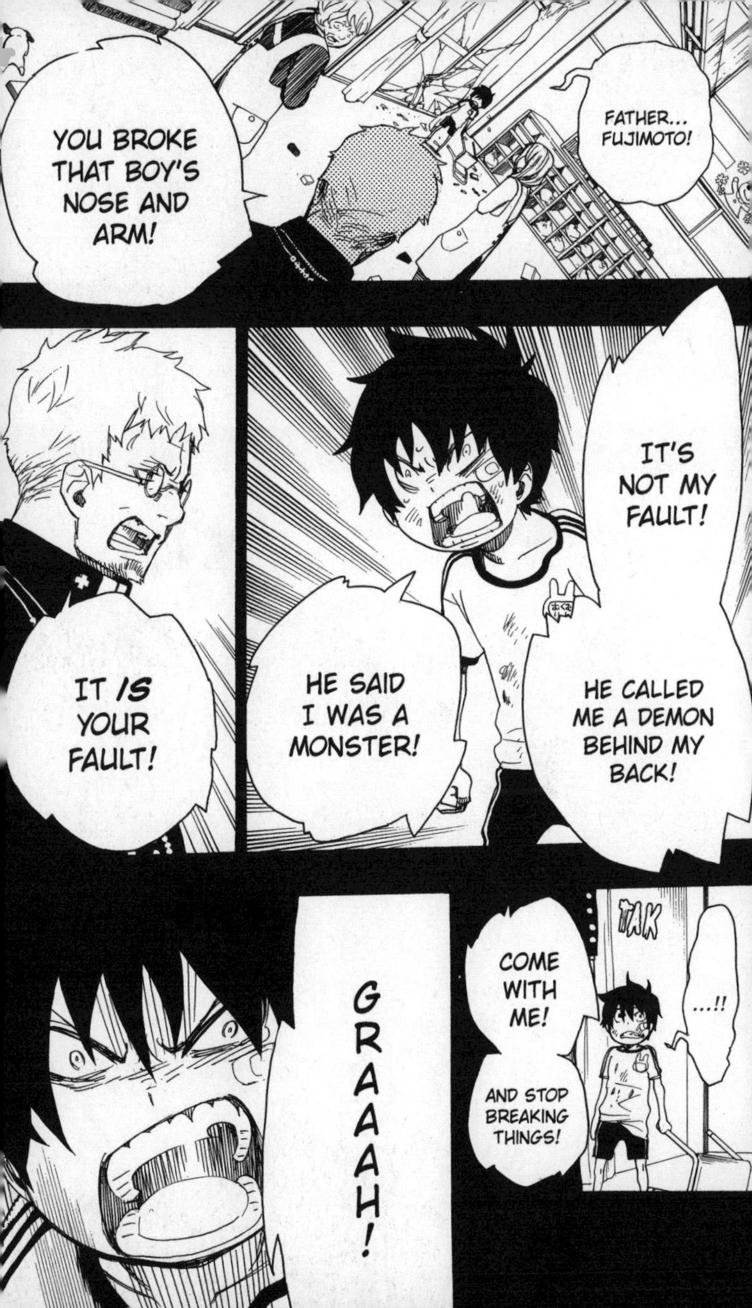
FATHER... FUJIMOTO!
YOU BROKE THAT BOY'S NOSE AND ARM!
IT'S NOT MY FAULT!
HE CALLED ME A DEMON BEHIND MY BACK!
HE SAID I WAS A MONSTER!
IT *IS* YOUR FAULT!
TAK
...!!
COME WITH ME!
AND STOP BREAKING THINGS!
GRAAAH!

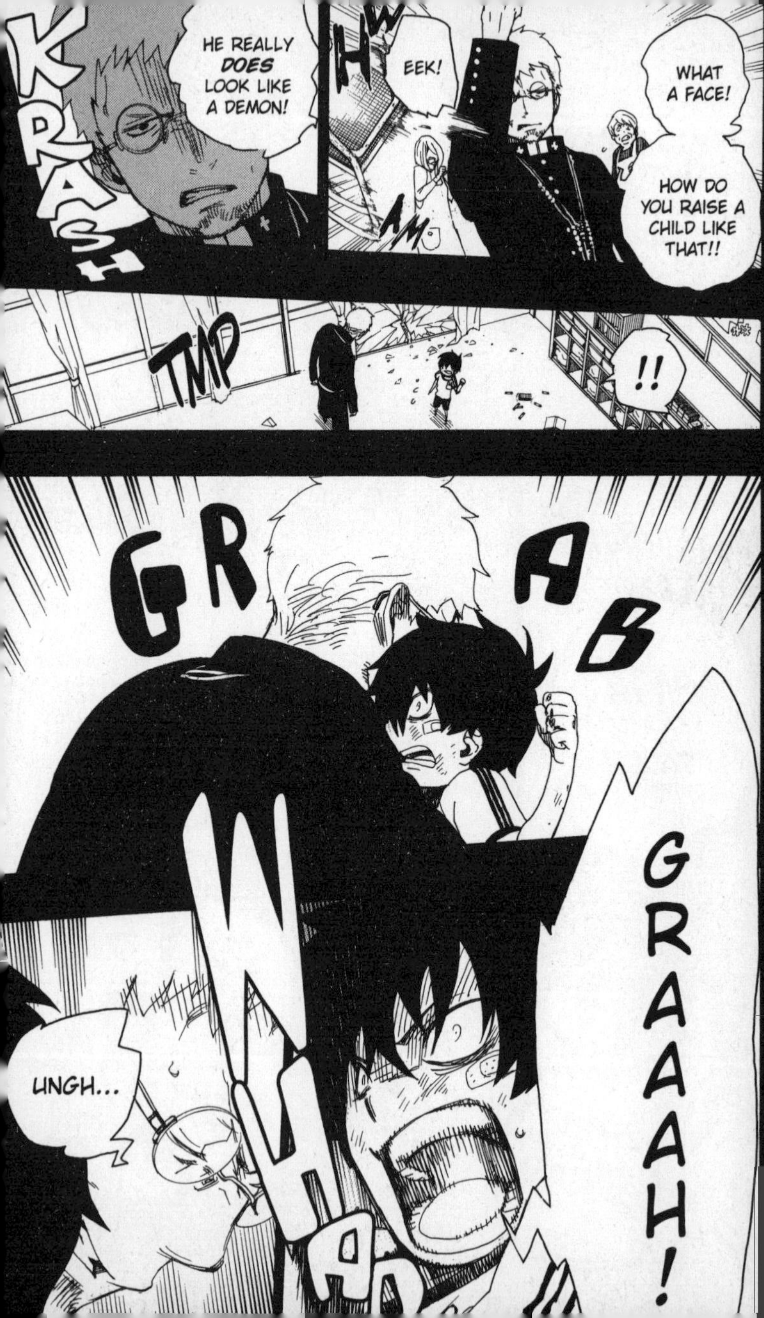
WHAT A FACE!
HOW DO YOU RAISE A CHILD LIKE THAT!!
EEK!
WHAM
HE REALLY **DOES** LOOK LIKE A DEMON!
KRASH
!!
TMP
GRAB
GRAAAAH!
UNGH...

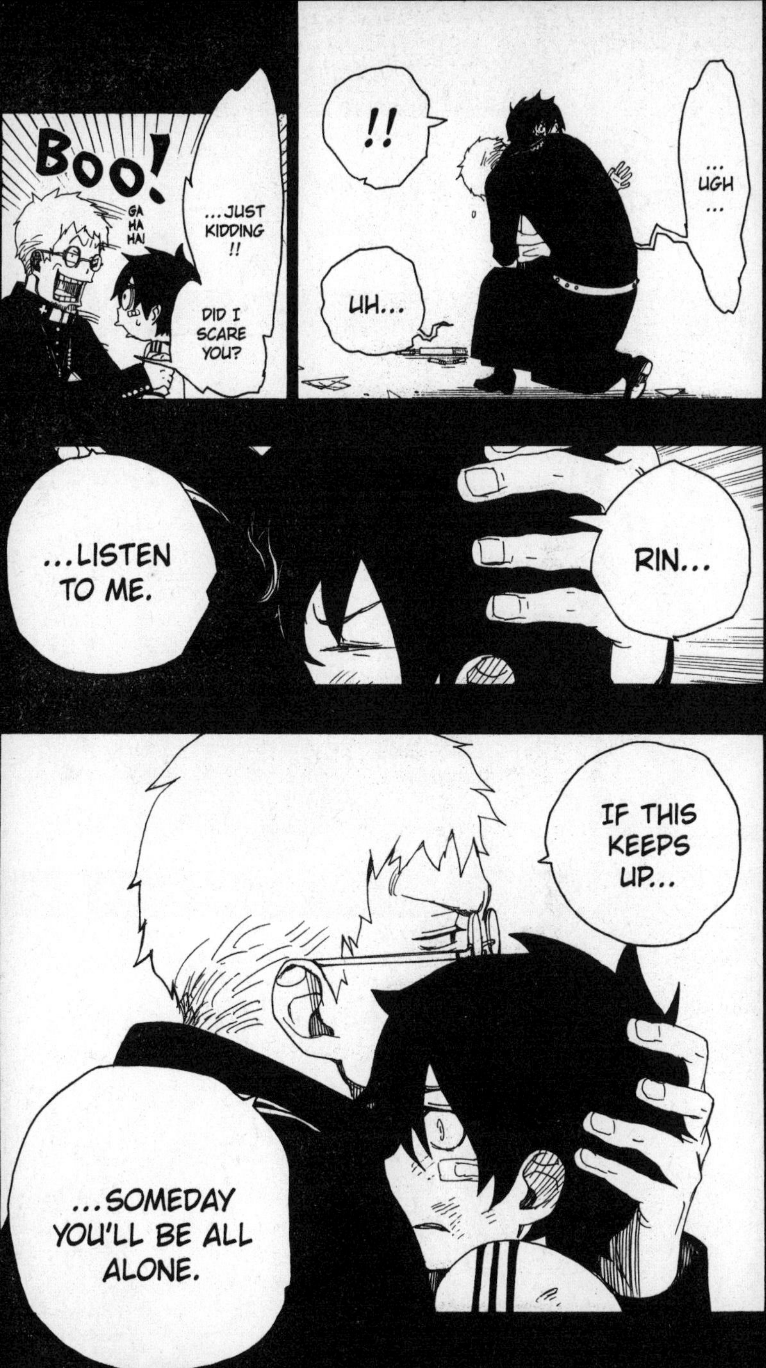
...UGH...
!!
UH...
BOO!
GA HA HA!
...JUST KIDDING !!
DID I SCARE YOU?
RIN...
...LISTEN TO ME.
IF THIS KEEPS UP...
...SOMEDAY YOU'LL BE ALL ALONE.

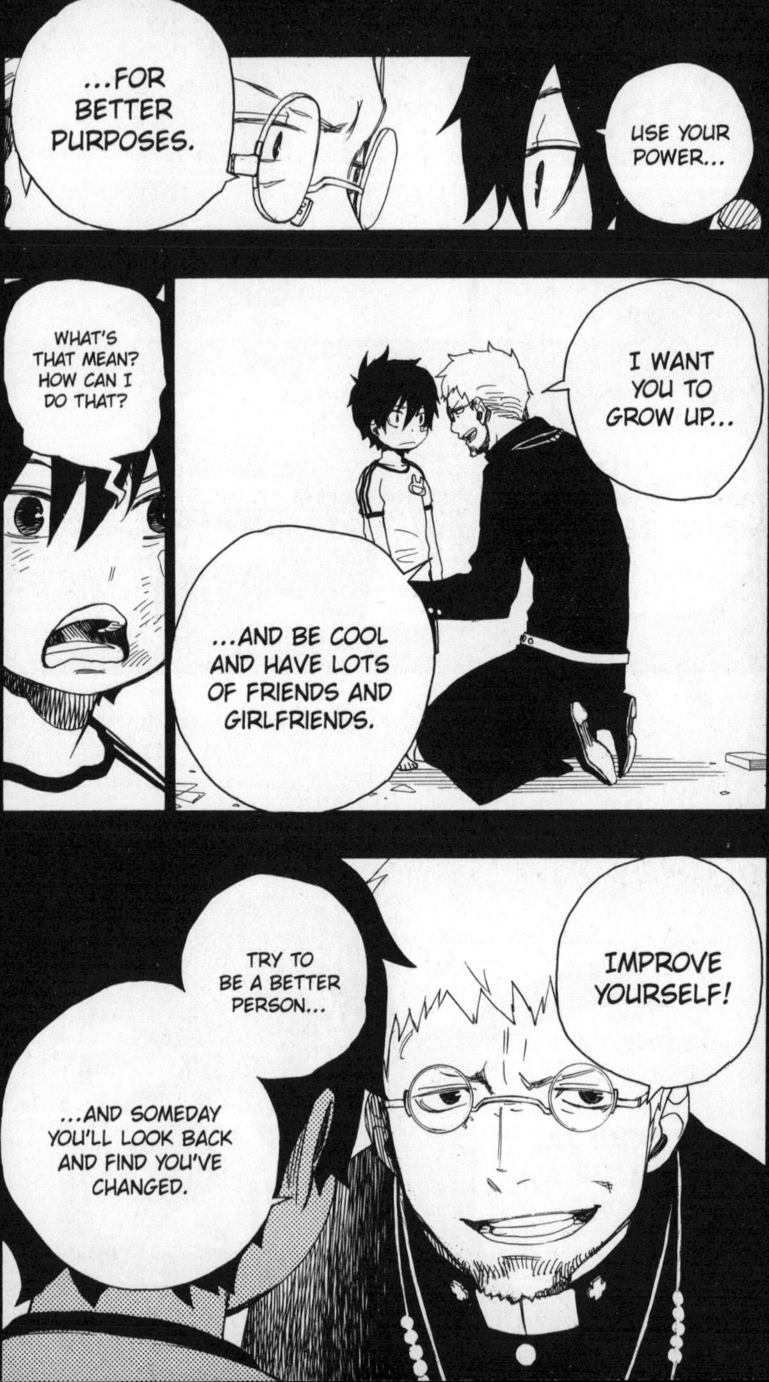
USE YOUR POWER...
...FOR BETTER PURPOSES.
I WANT YOU TO GROW UP...
...AND BE COOL AND HAVE LOTS OF FRIENDS AND GIRLFRIENDS.
WHAT'S THAT MEAN? HOW CAN I DO THAT?
IMPROVE YOURSELF!
TRY TO BE A BETTER PERSON...
...AND SOMEDAY YOU'LL LOOK BACK AND FIND YOU'VE CHANGED.

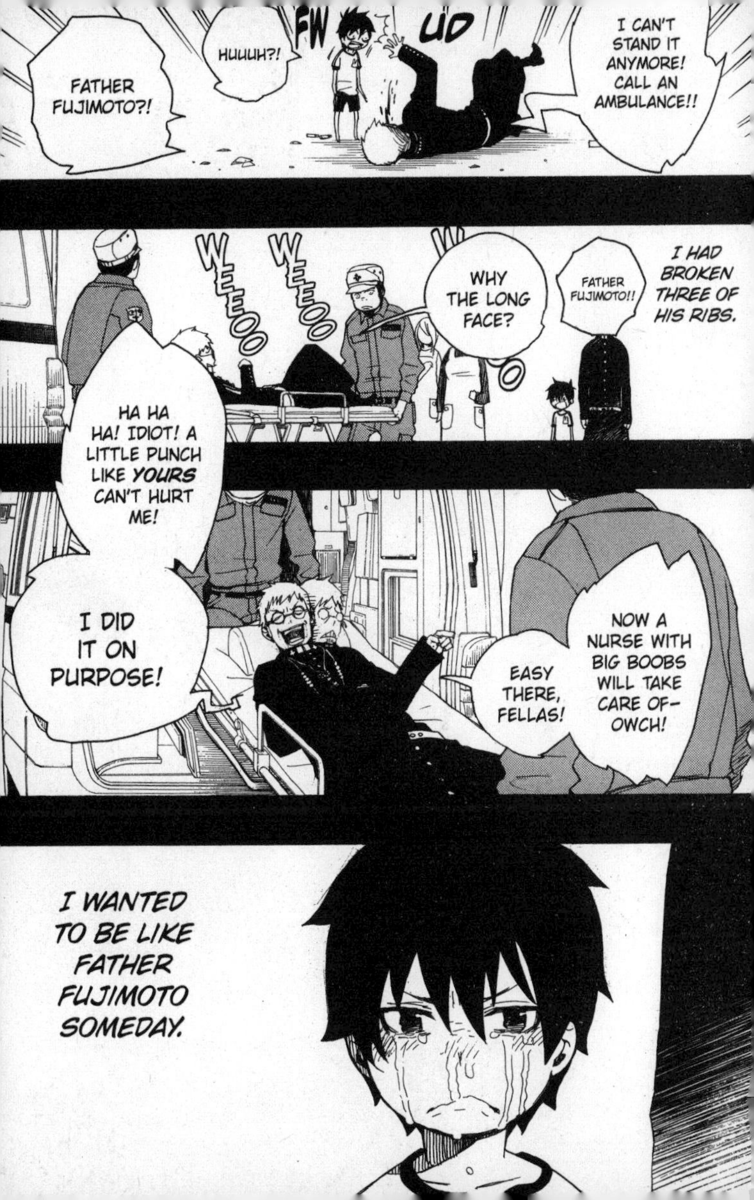
I CAN'T STAND IT ANYMORE! CALL AN AMBULANCE!!
FW UD
HUUUH?!
FATHER FUJIMOTO?!
I HAD BROKEN THREE OF HIS RIBS.
FATHER FUJIMOTO!!
WHY THE LONG FACE?
WEEOO WEEOO
HA HA HA! IDIOT! A LITTLE PUNCH LIKE YOURS CAN'T HURT ME!
NOW A NURSE WITH BIG BOOBS WILL TAKE CARE OF— OWCH!
EASY THERE, FELLAS!
I DID IT ON PURPOSE!
I WANTED TO BE LIKE FATHER FUJIMOTO SOMEDAY.

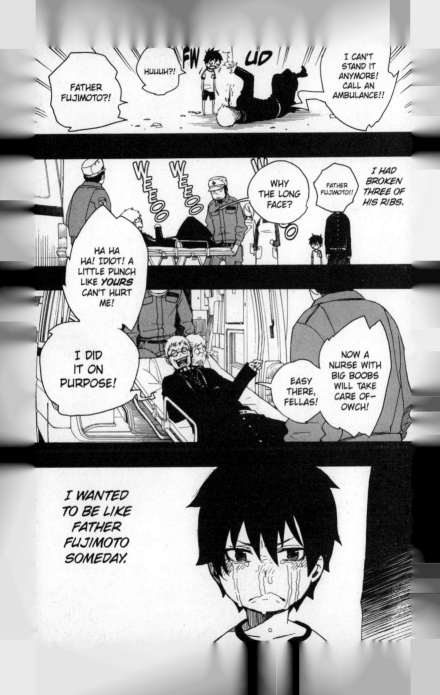

Chapter 11 Fun Camp

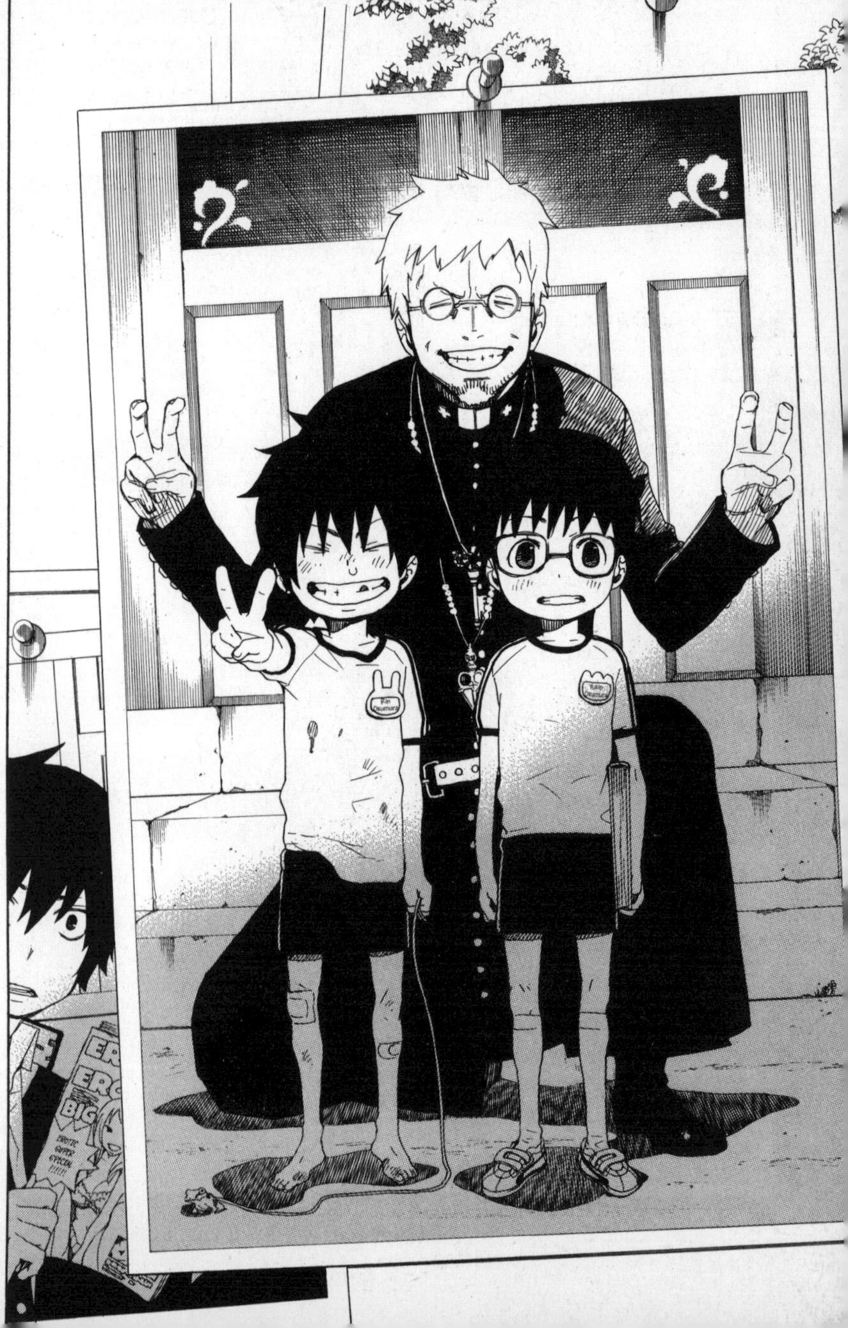

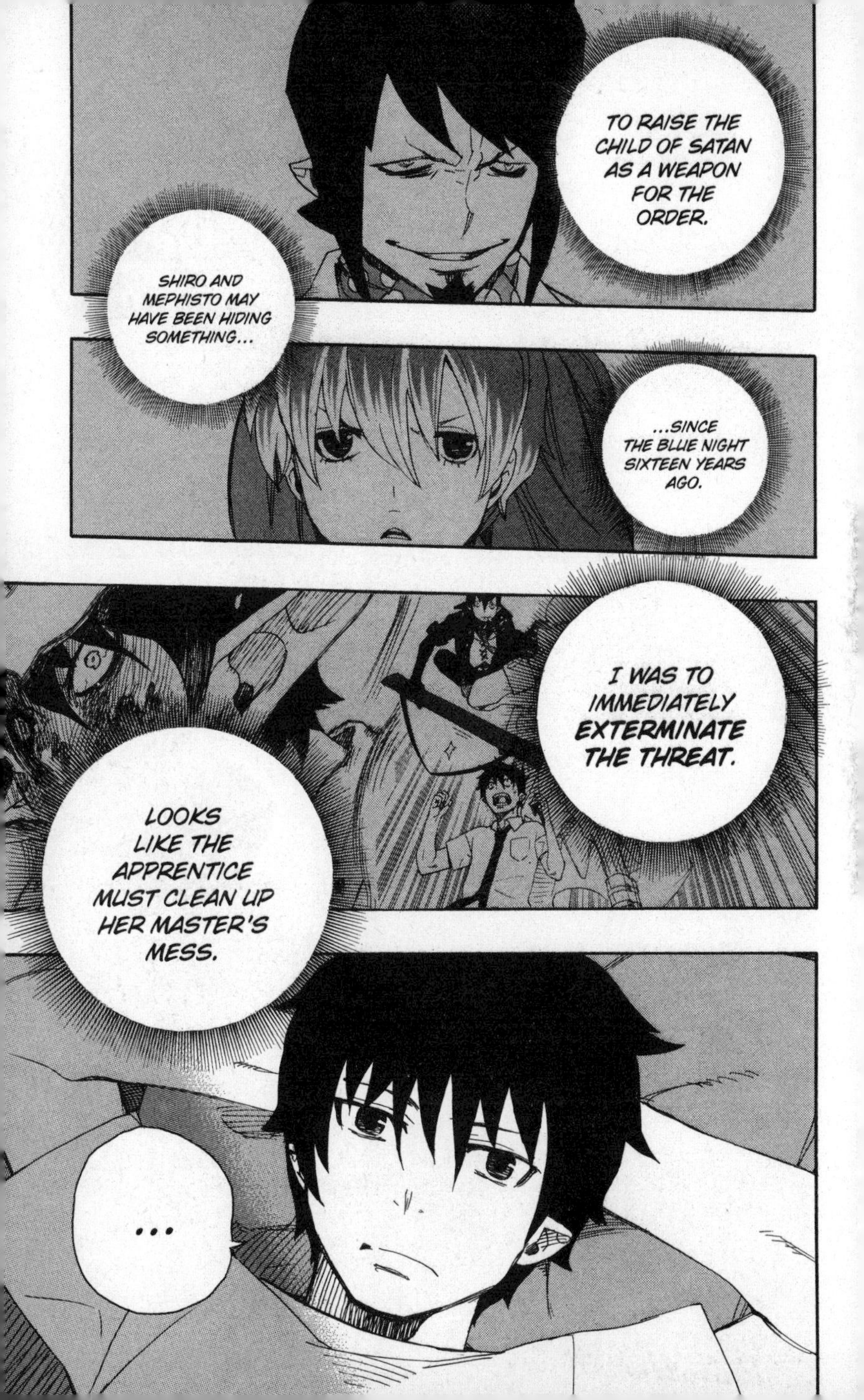
TO RAISE THE CHILD OF SATAN AS A WEAPON FOR THE ORDER.
SHIRO AND MEPHISTO MAY HAVE BEEN HIDING SOMETHING...
...SINCE THE BLUE NIGHT SIXTEEN YEARS AGO.
I WAS TO IMMEDIATELY **EXTERMINATE THE THREAT.**
LOOKS LIKE THE APPRENTICE MUST CLEAN UP HER MASTER'S MESS.
...

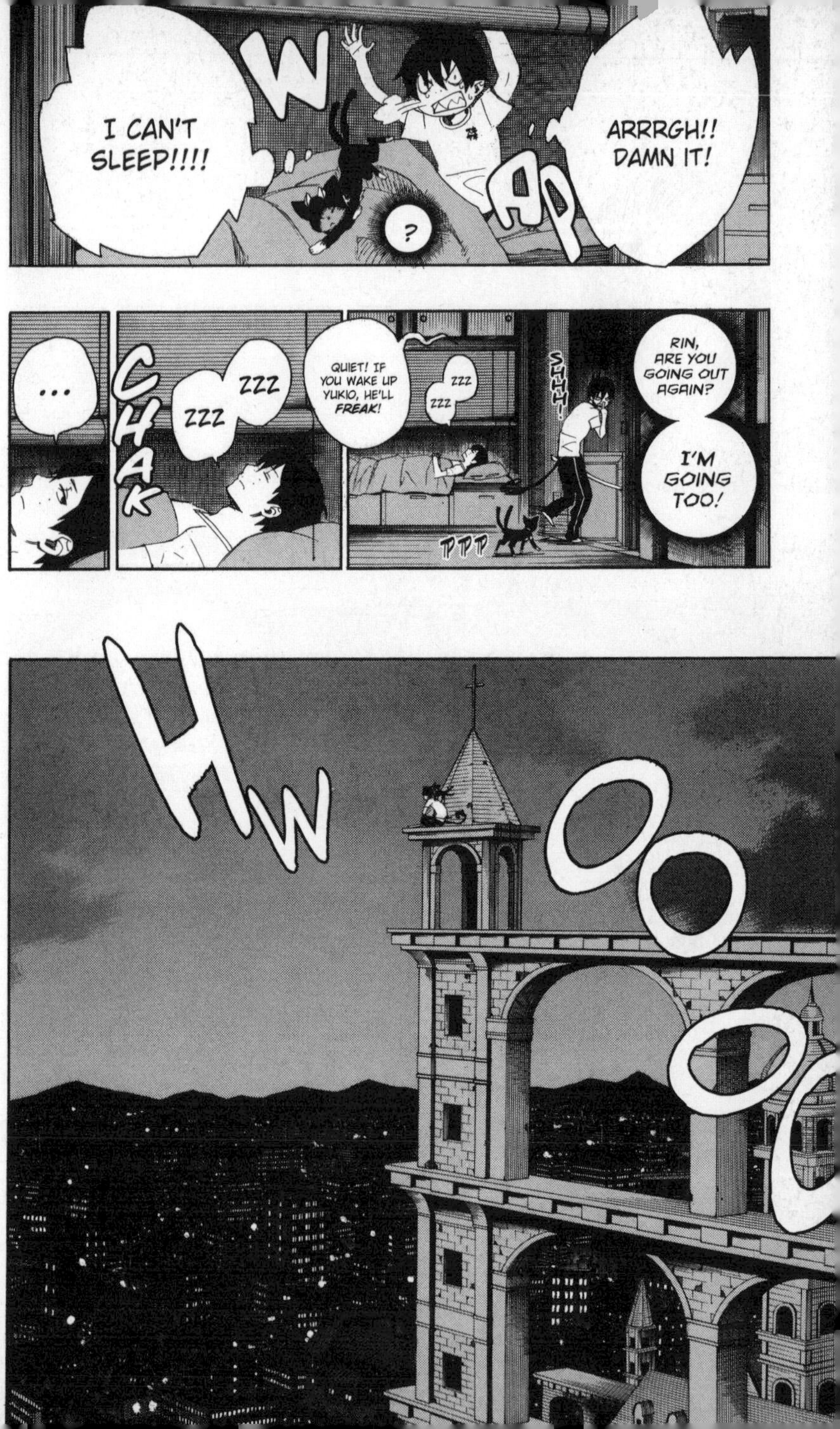
ARRRGH!! DAMN IT!
I CAN'T SLEEP!!!!
WAP
?
RIN, ARE YOU GOING OUT AGAIN?
I'M GOING TOO!
SHHH!
ZZZ
ZZZ
QUIET! IF YOU WAKE UP YUKIO, HE'LL FREAK!
TP TP TP
ZZZ
ZZZ
CHAK
...
HWOOOO

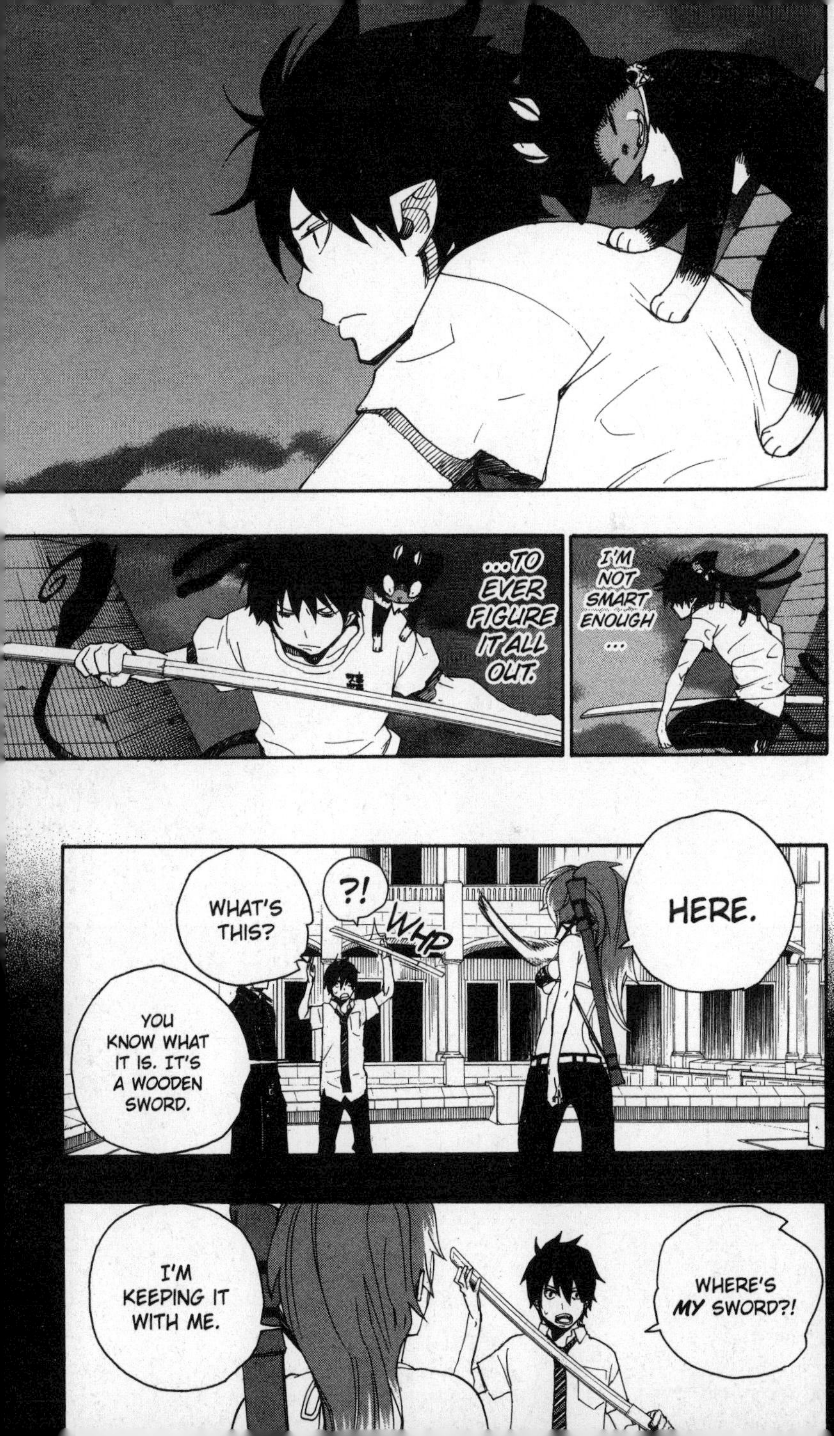
I'M NOT SMART ENOUGH...
...TO EVER FIGURE IT ALL OUT.
HERE.
WHP
?!
WHAT'S THIS?
YOU KNOW WHAT IT IS. IT'S A WOODEN SWORD.
WHERE'S *MY* SWORD?!
I'M KEEPING IT WITH ME.

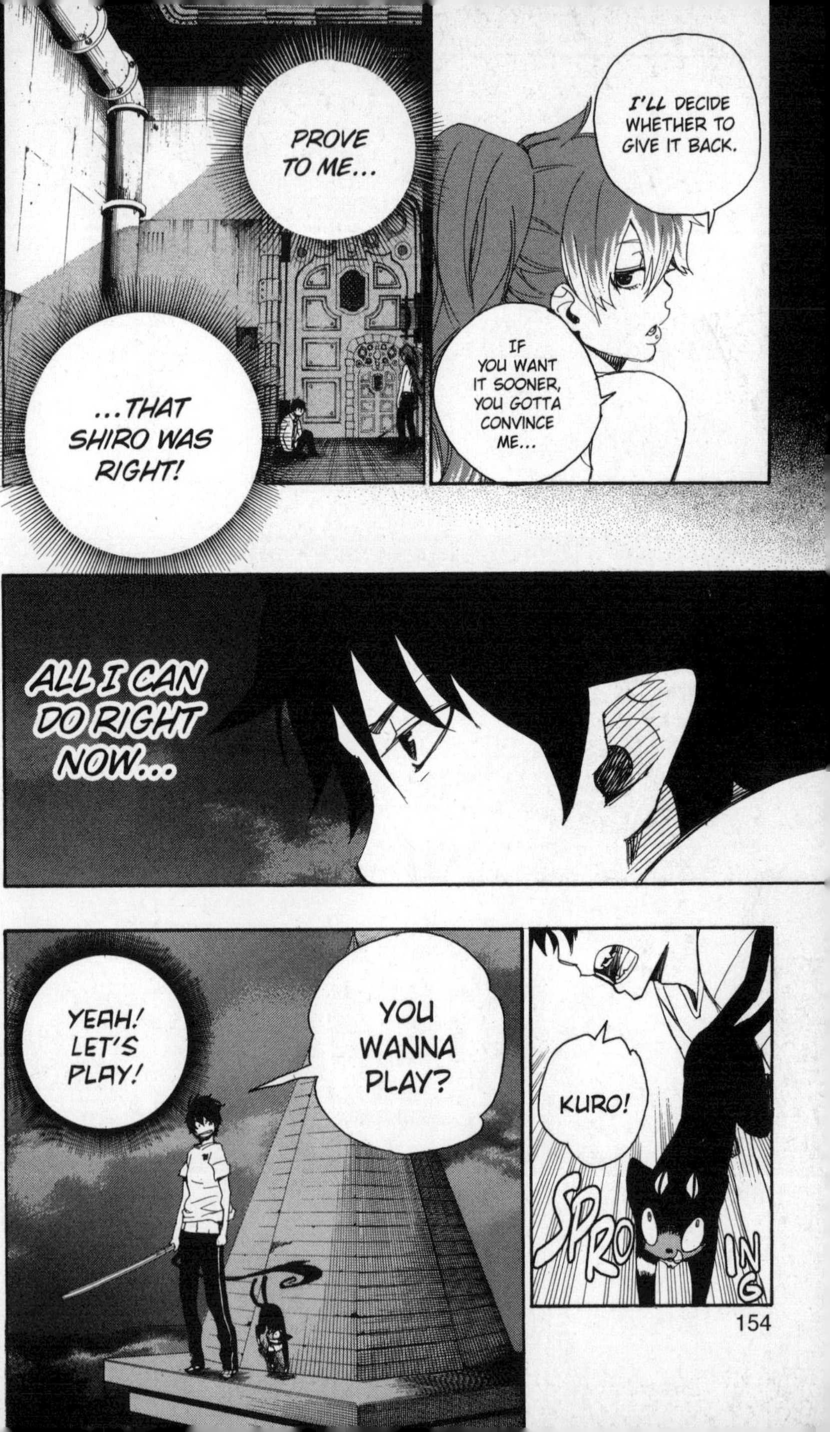
I'LL DECIDE WHETHER TO GIVE IT BACK.
IF YOU WANT IT SOONER, YOU GOTTA CONVINCE ME...
PROVE TO ME...
...THAT SHIRO WAS RIGHT!
ALL I CAN DO RIGHT NOW...
KURO!
SPROING
YOU WANNA PLAY?
YEAH! LET'S PLAY!

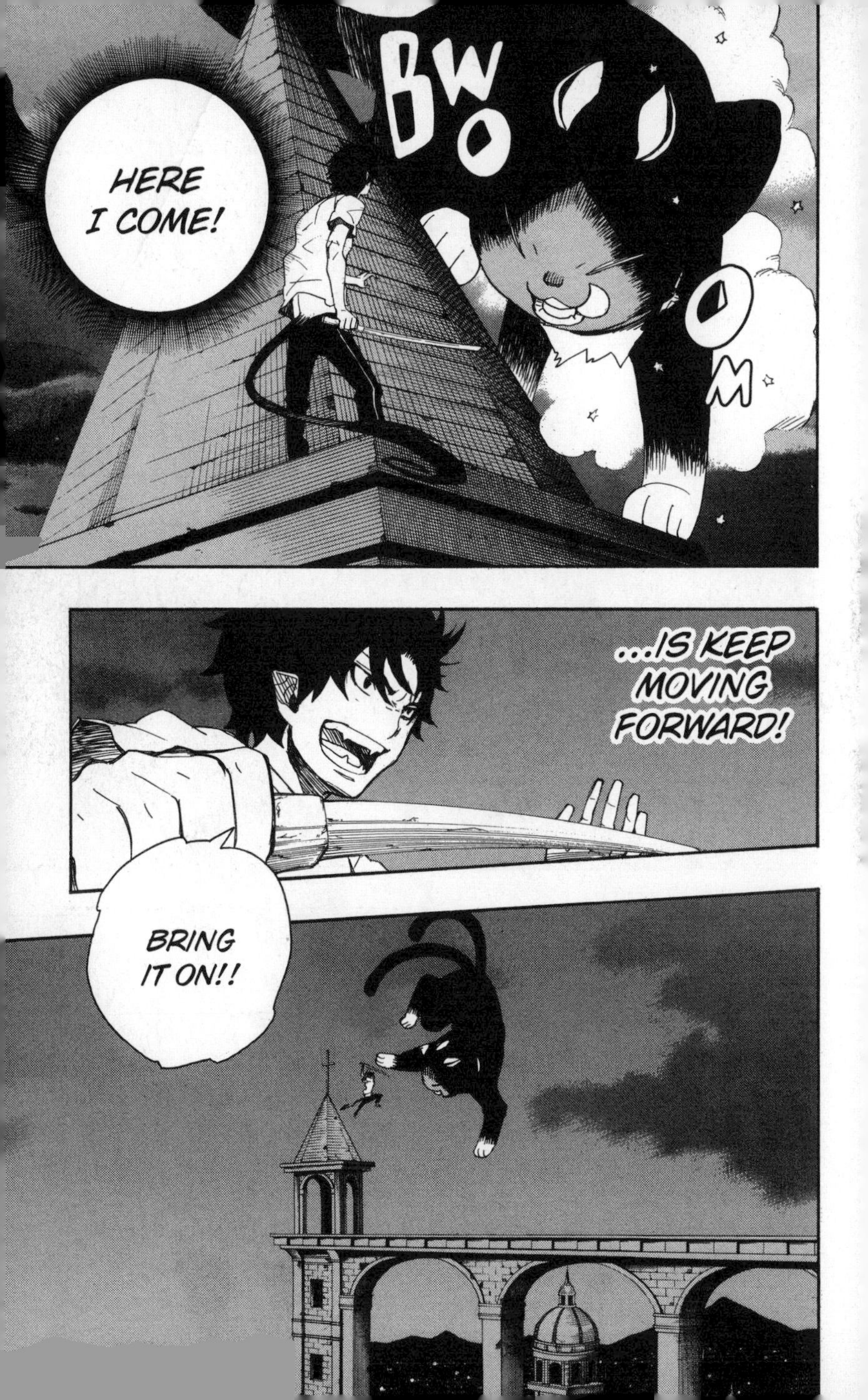
BWOOM
HERE I COME!
...IS KEEP MOVING FORWARD!
BRING IT ON!!

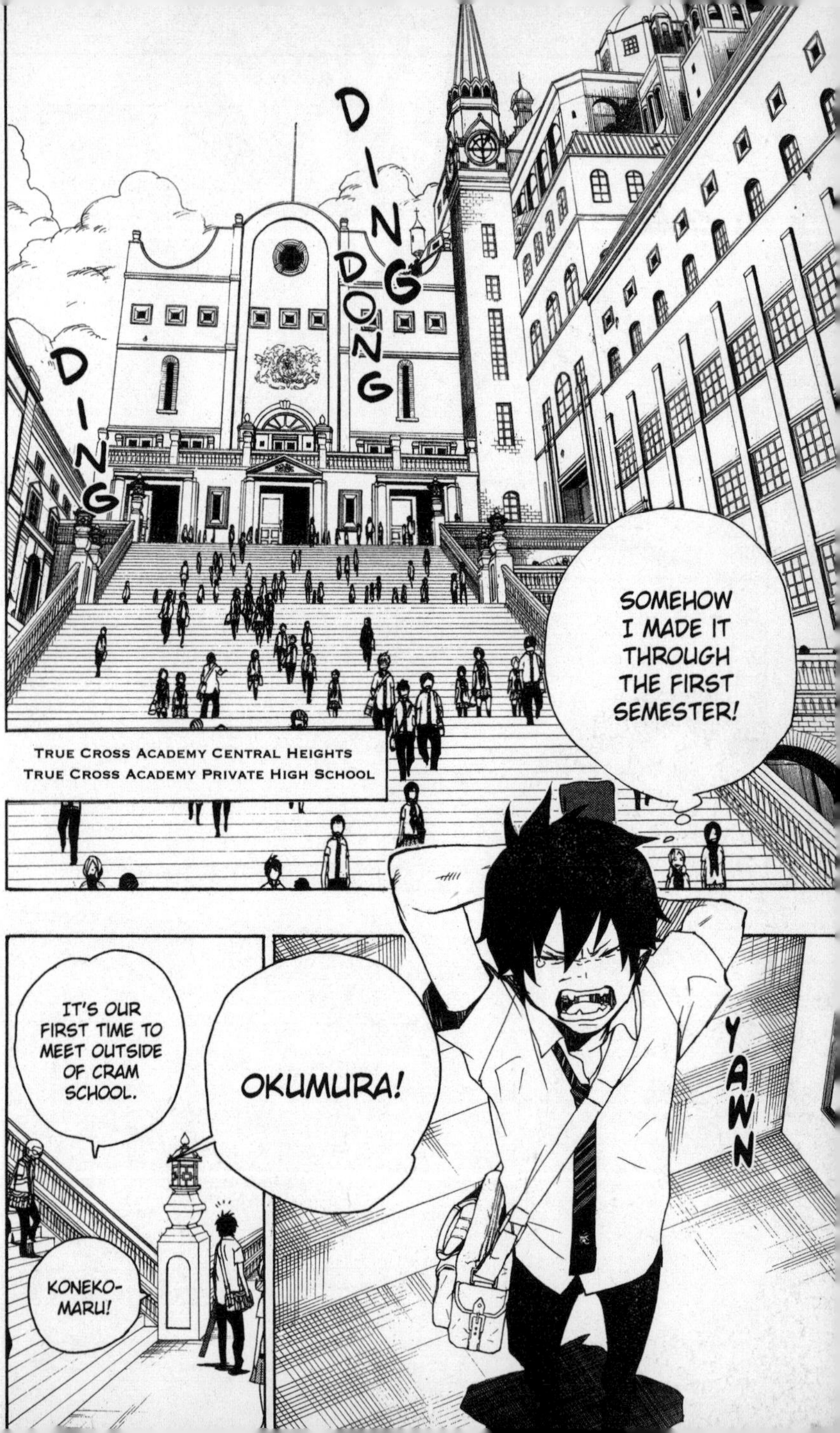
DING DONG
DING
SOMEHOW I MADE IT THROUGH THE FIRST SEMESTER!
TRUE CROSS ACADEMY CENTRAL HEIGHTS
TRUE CROSS ACADEMY PRIVATE HIGH SCHOOL
YAWN
OKUMURA!
IT'S OUR FIRST TIME TO MEET OUTSIDE OF CRAM SCHOOL.
KONEKO-MARU!

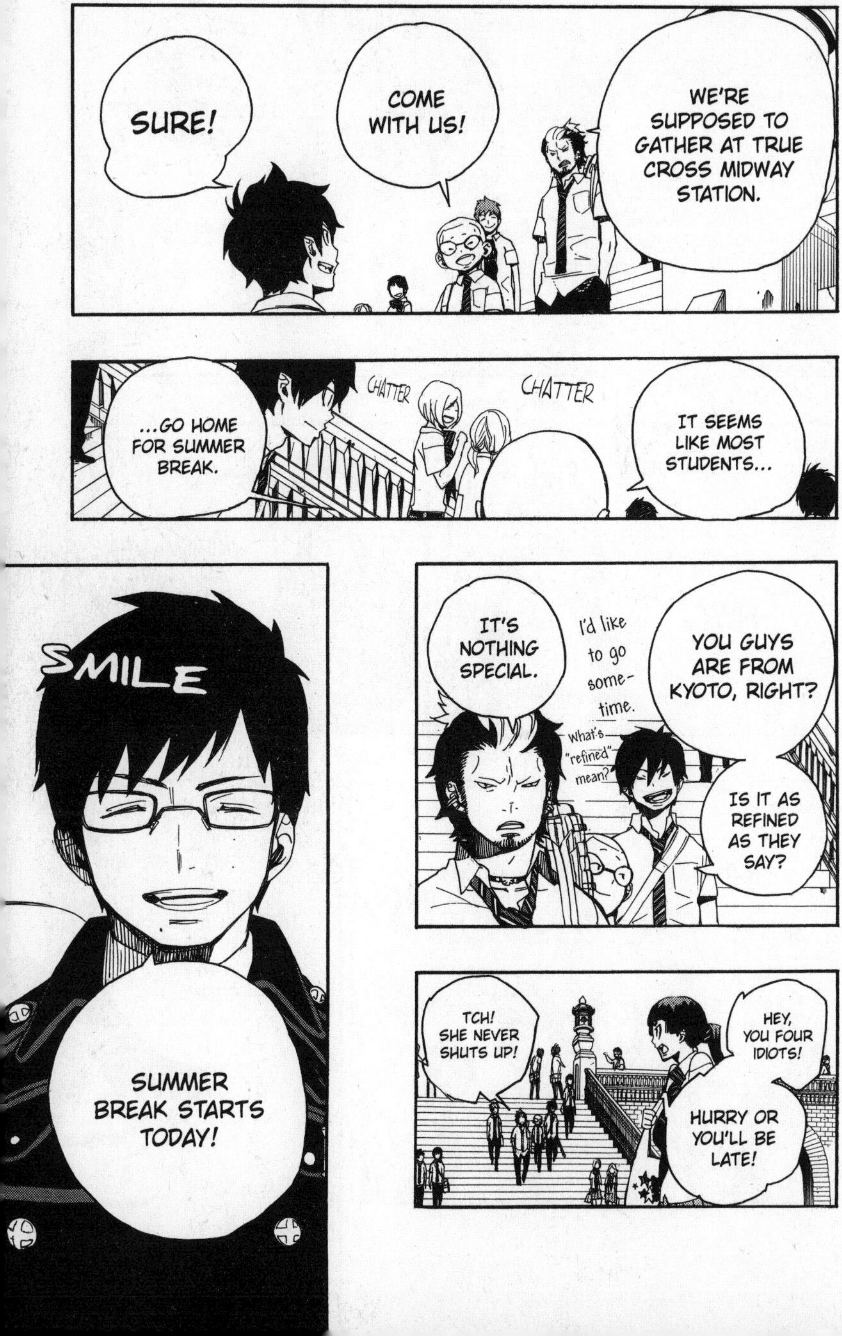
WE'RE SUPPOSED TO GATHER AT TRUE CROSS MIDWAY STATION.
COME WITH US!
SURE!
CHATTER
CHATTER
IT SEEMS LIKE MOST STUDENTS...
...GO HOME FOR SUMMER BREAK.
YOU GUYS ARE FROM KYOTO, RIGHT?
IS IT AS REFINED AS THEY SAY?
I'd like to go some-time.
What's "refined" mean?
IT'S NOTHING SPECIAL.
HEY, YOU FOUR IDIOTS!
HURRY OR YOU'LL BE LATE!
TCH! SHE NEVER SHUTS UP!
SMILE
SUMMER BREAK STARTS TODAY!

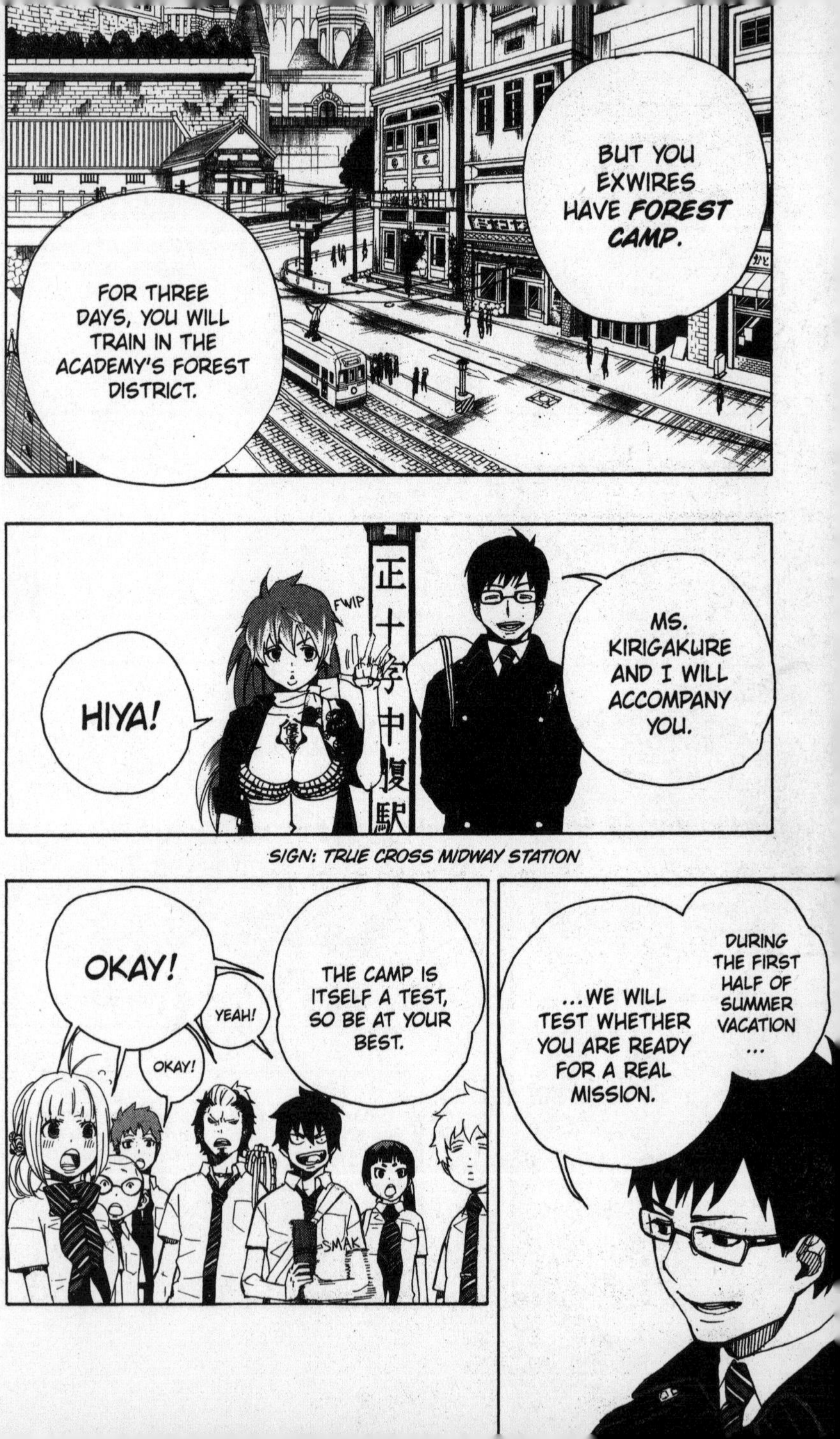
BUT YOU EXWIRES HAVE FOREST CAMP.
FOR THREE DAYS, YOU WILL TRAIN IN THE ACADEMY'S FOREST DISTRICT.
MS. KIRIGAKURE AND I WILL ACCOMPANY YOU.
FWIP
HIYA!
SIGN: TRUE CROSS MIDWAY STATION
DURING THE FIRST HALF OF SUMMER VACATION...
...WE WILL TEST WHETHER YOU ARE READY FOR A REAL MISSION.
THE CAMP IS ITSELF A TEST, SO BE AT YOUR BEST.
YEAH!
OKAY!
OKAY!
SMAK

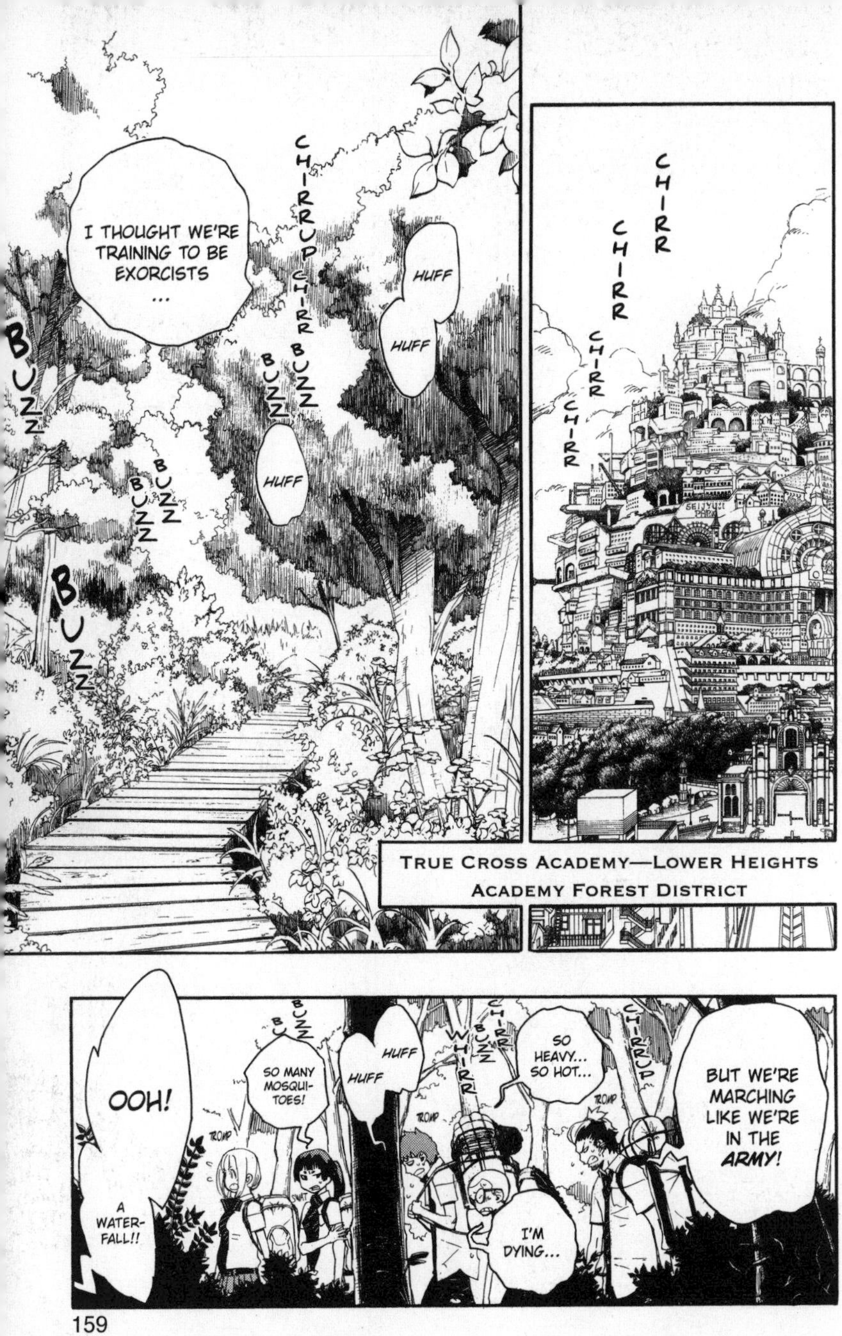
CHIRR
CHIRR
CHIRR
CHIRR
TRUE CROSS ACADEMY—LOWER HEIGHTS
ACADEMY FOREST DISTRICT
HUFF
HUFF
CHIRRUP CHIRR BUZZ
BUZZ
I THOUGHT WE'RE TRAINING TO BE EXORCISTS ...
HUFF
BUZZ
BUZZ BUZZ
BUZZ
BUT WE'RE MARCHING LIKE WE'RE IN THE *ARMY*!
CHIRRUP
SO HEAVY... SO HOT...
TROMP
CHIRR
BUZZ
WHIRR
I'M DYING...
HUFF
HUFF
TROMP
SO MANY MOSQUI-TOES!
BUZZ
SWAT
TROMP
OOH!
A WATER-FALL!!

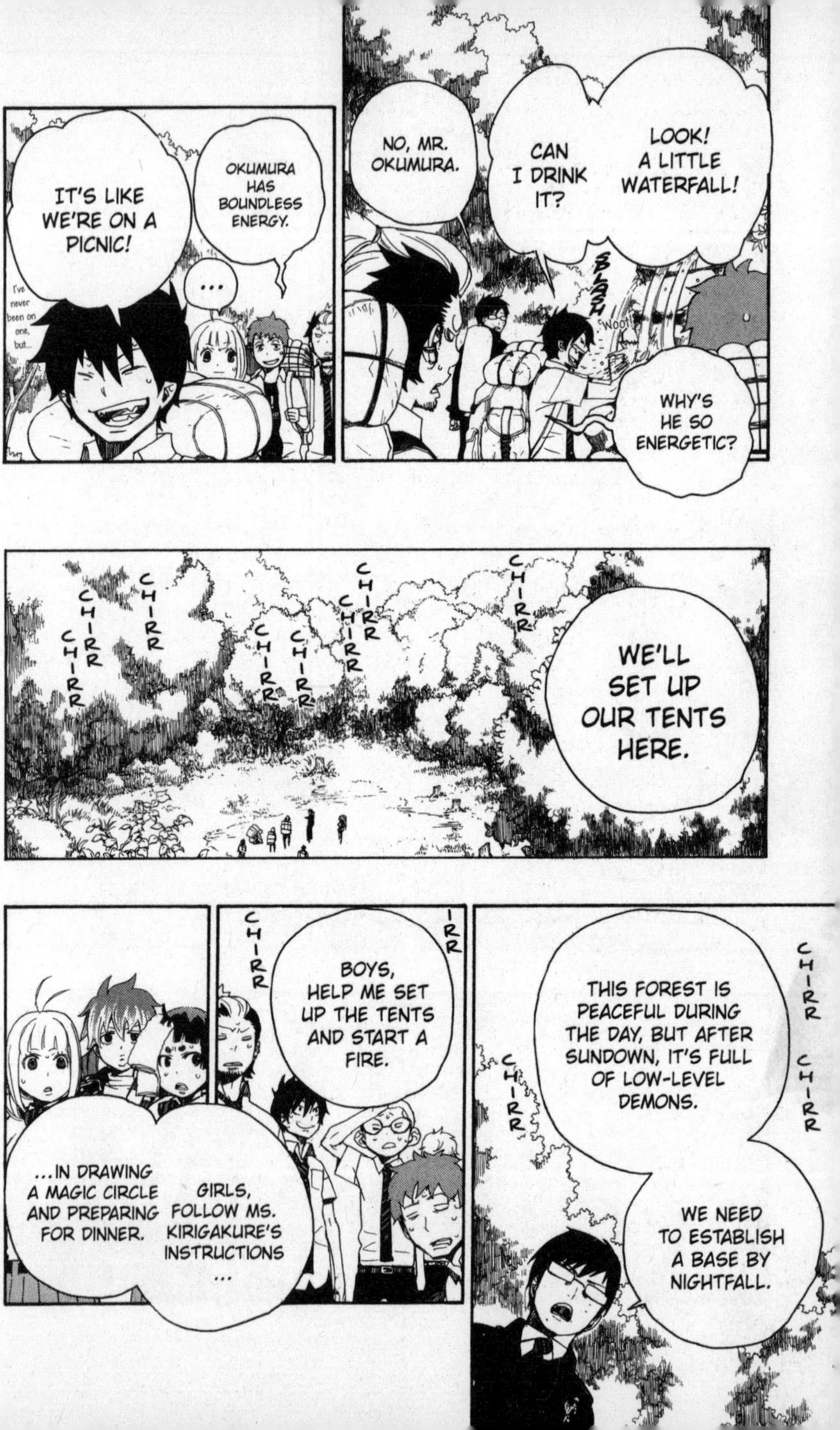
LOOK! A LITTLE WATERFALL!
CAN I DRINK IT?
NO, MR. OKUMURA.
SPLASH
Woof!
WHY'S HE SO ENERGETIC?
OKUMURA HAS BOUNDLESS ENERGY.
IT'S LIKE WE'RE ON A PICNIC!
...
I've never been on one, but...
CHIRR CHIRR CHIRR CHIRR CHIRR CHIRR CHIRR CHIRR
WE'LL SET UP OUR TENTS HERE.
THIS FOREST IS PEACEFUL DURING THE DAY, BUT AFTER SUNDOWN, IT'S FULL OF LOW-LEVEL DEMONS.
CHIRR CHIRR CHIRR
WE NEED TO ESTABLISH A BASE BY NIGHTFALL.
IRR
BOYS, HELP ME SET UP THE TENTS AND START A FIRE.
CHIRR
GIRLS, FOLLOW MS. KIRIGAKURE'S INSTRUCTIONS ...
...IN DRAWING A MAGIC CIRCLE AND PREPARING FOR DINNER.

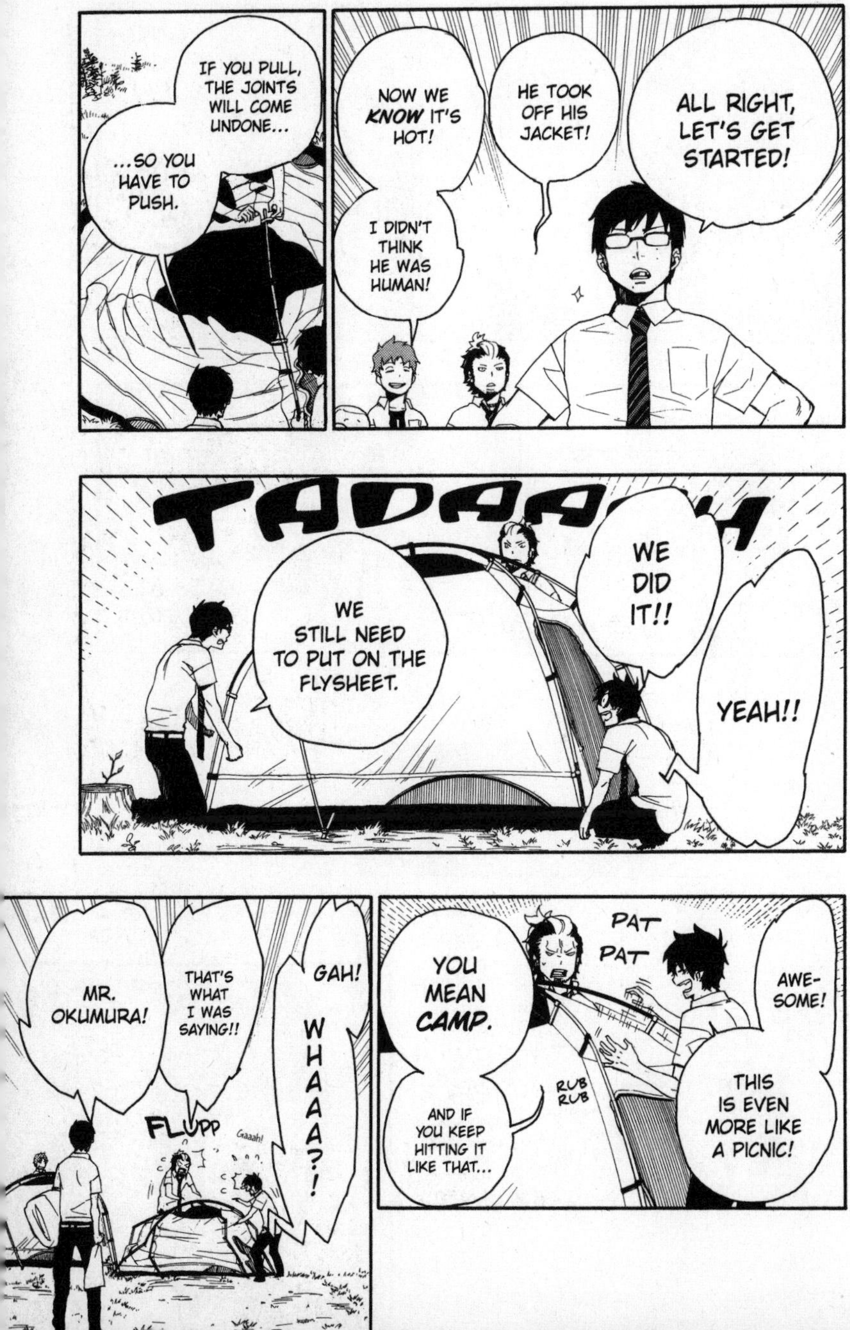
ALL RIGHT, LET'S GET STARTED!
HE TOOK OFF HIS JACKET!
NOW WE *KNOW* IT'S HOT!
I DIDN'T THINK HE WAS HUMAN!
IF YOU PULL, THE JOINTS WILL COME UNDONE...
...SO YOU HAVE TO PUSH.
YEAH!!
WE DID IT!!
WE STILL NEED TO PUT ON THE FLYSHEET.
AWE-SOME!
PAT PAT
THIS IS EVEN MORE LIKE A PICNIC!
YOU MEAN **CAMP**.
RUB RUB
AND IF YOU KEEP HITTING IT LIKE THAT...
GAH!
WHAAAA?!
THAT'S WHAT I WAS SAYING!!
MR. OKUMURA!
FLUPP
Gaaah!

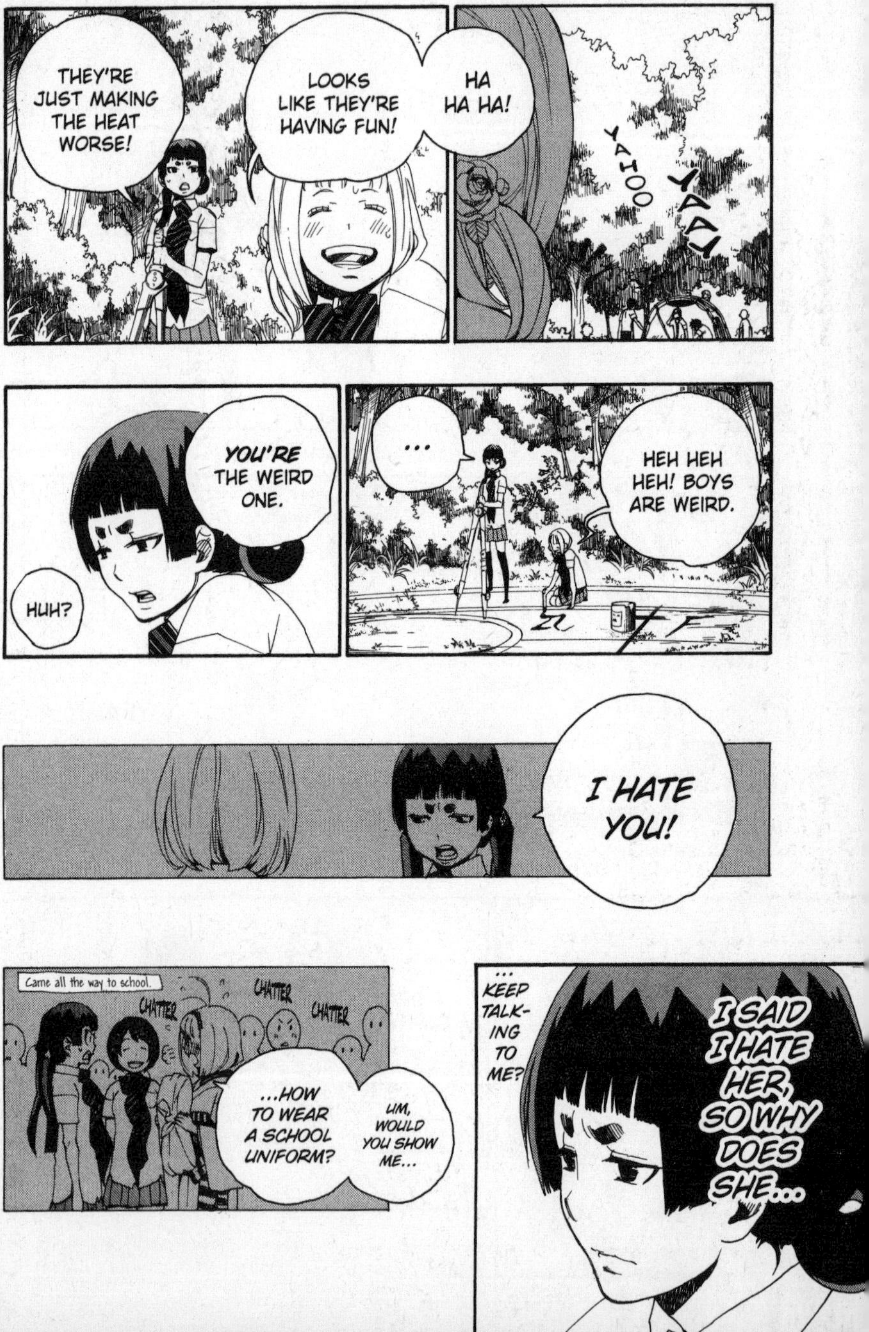
YAAAY
YAHOO
HA HA HA!
LOOKS LIKE THEY'RE HAVING FUN!
THEY'RE JUST MAKING THE HEAT WORSE!
HEH HEH HEH! BOYS ARE WEIRD.
...
YOU'RE THE WEIRD ONE.
HUH?
I HATE YOU!
I SAID I HATE HER, SO WHY DOES SHE...
...KEEP TALKING TO ME?
Came all the way to school.
CHATTER
CHATTER
CHATTER
UM, WOULD YOU SHOW ME...
...HOW TO WEAR A SCHOOL UNIFORM?

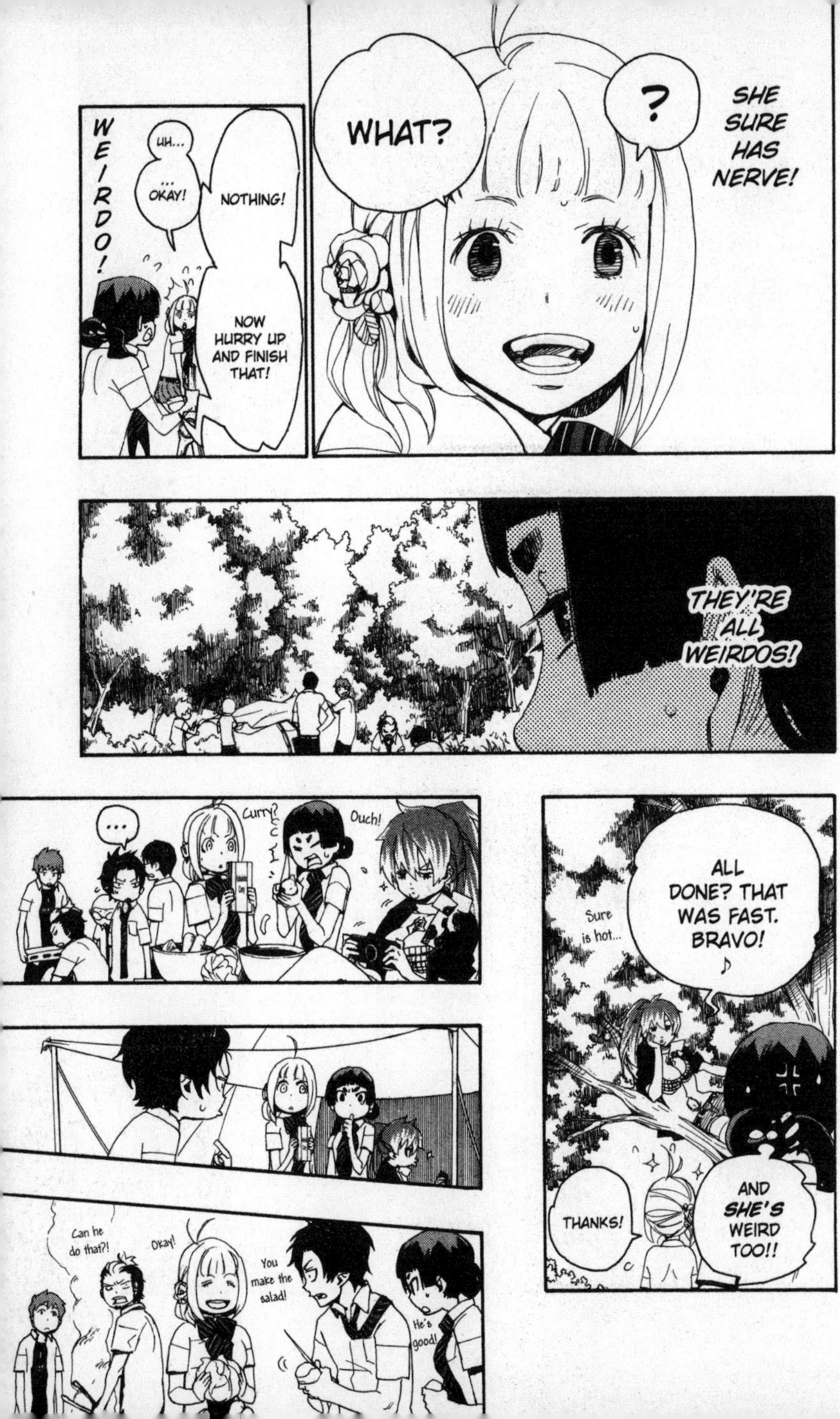
SHE SURE HAS NERVE!
?
WHAT?
NOTHING!
NOW HURRY UP AND FINISH THAT!
UH... ...OKAY!
WEIRDO!
THEY'RE ALL WEIRDOS!
ALL DONE? THAT WAS FAST. BRAVO! ♪
Sure is hot...
AND SHE'S WEIRD TOO!!
THANKS!
Ouch!
Curry?
...
He's good!
You make the salad!
Okay!
Can he do that?!

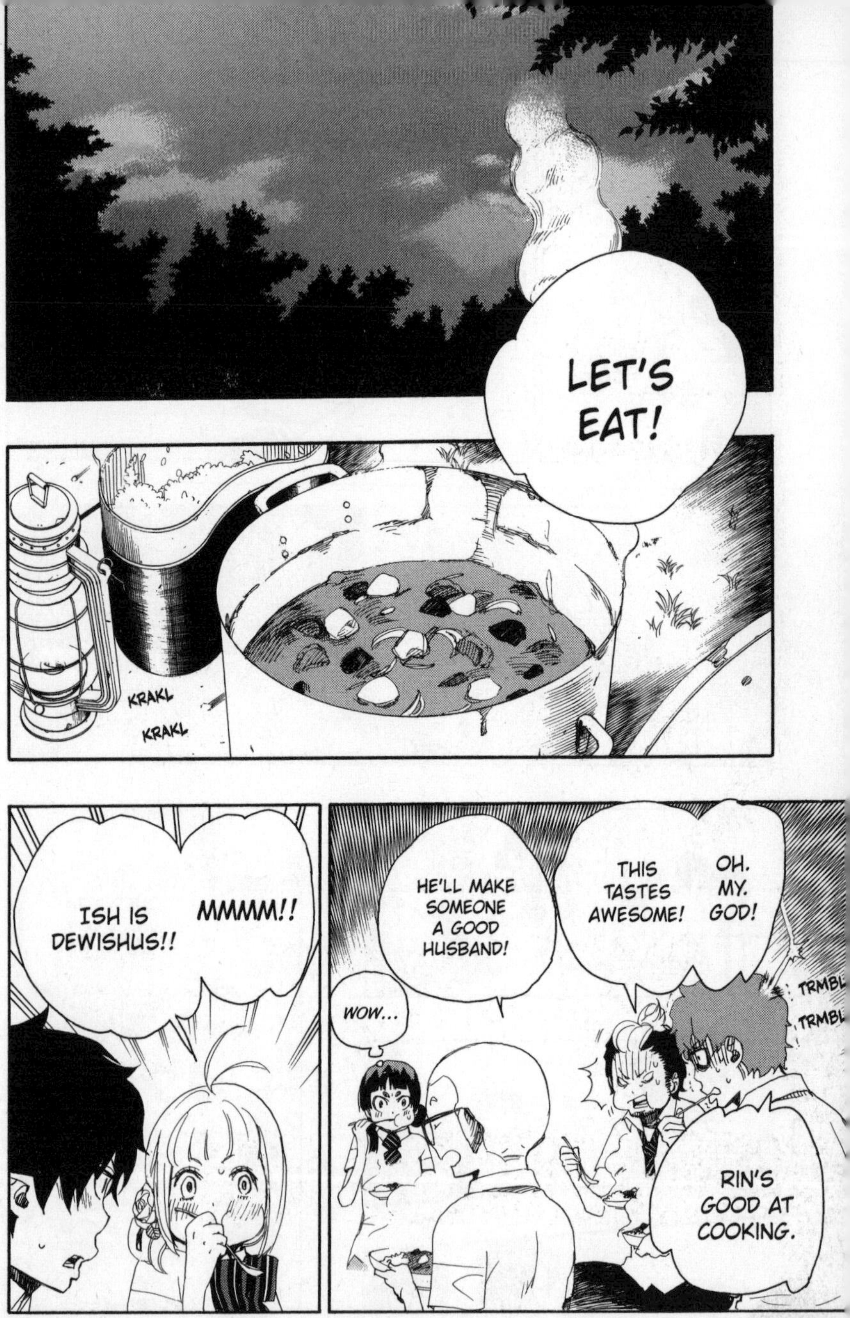
LET'S EAT!
KRAKL
KRAKL
OH. MY. GOD!
THIS TASTES AWESOME!
HE'LL MAKE SOMEONE A GOOD HUSBAND!
TRMBL
TRMBL
WOW...
RIN'S GOOD AT COOKING.
MMMM!!
ISH IS DEWISHUS!!

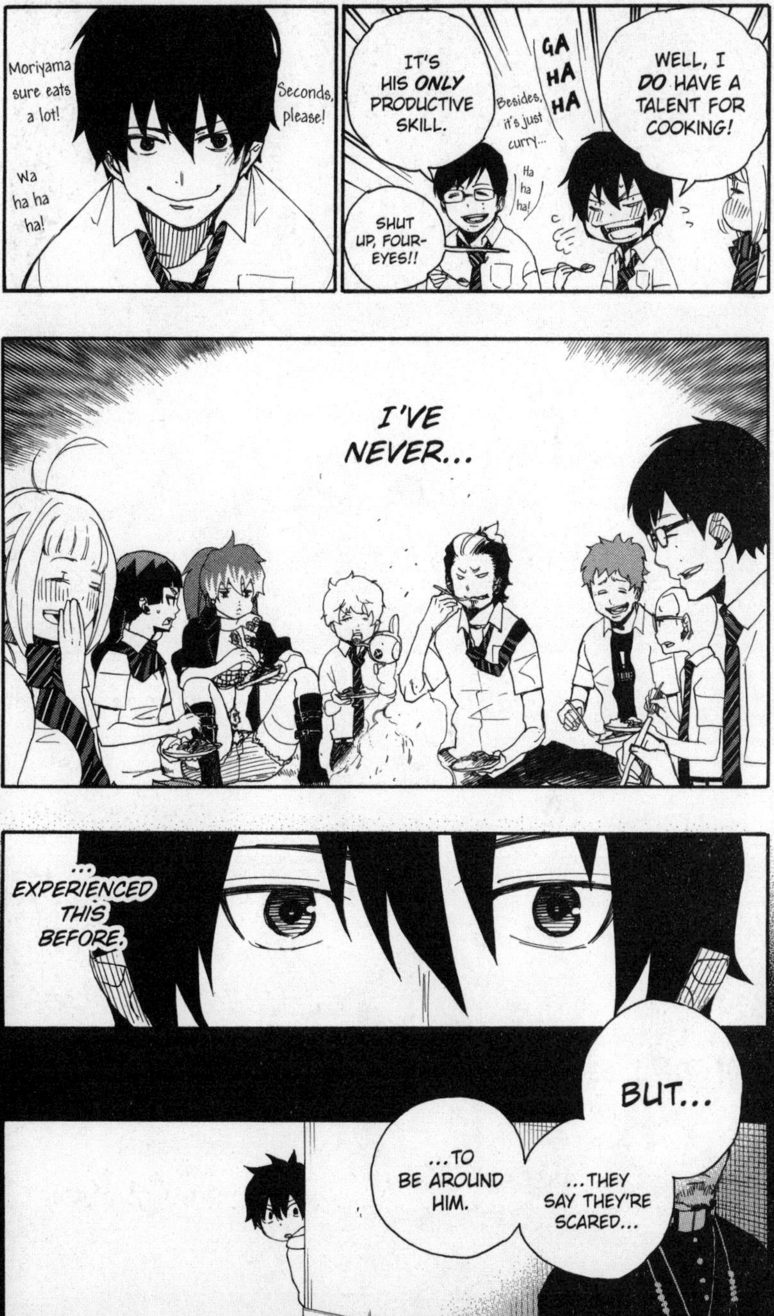
WELL, I *DO* HAVE A TALENT FOR COOKING!
GA HA HA
Besides, it's just curry...
IT'S HIS *ONLY* PRODUCTIVE SKILL.
Ha ha ha!
SHUT UP, FOUR-EYES!!
Seconds, please!
Moriyama sure eats a lot!
Wa ha ha ha!
I'VE NEVER...
...EXPERIENCED THIS BEFORE.
BUT...
...THEY SAY THEY'RE SCARED...
...TO BE AROUND HIM.

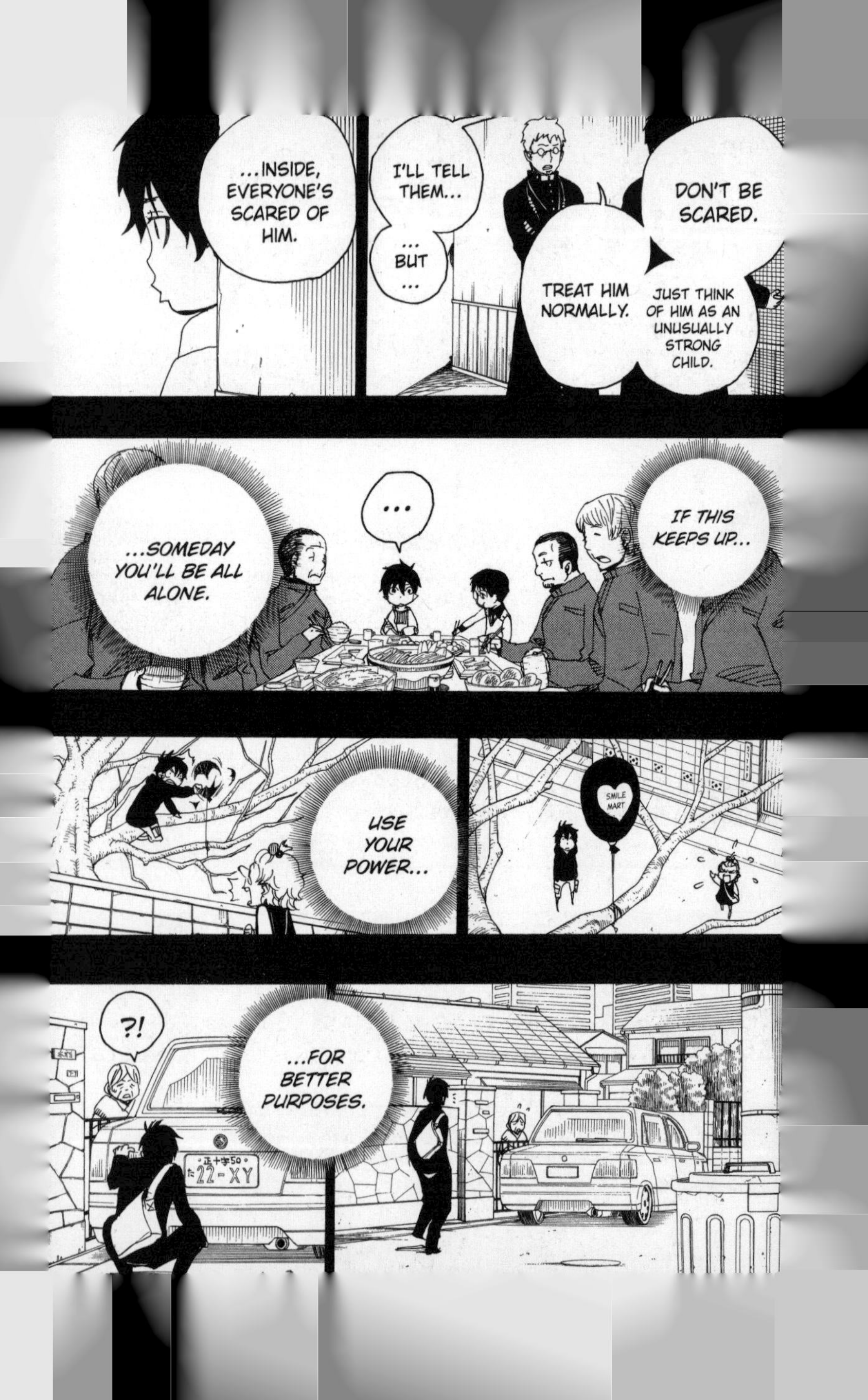
DON'T BE SCARED.
JUST THINK OF HIM AS AN UNUSUALLY STRONG CHILD.
TREAT HIM NORMALLY.
I'LL TELL THEM...
... BUT ...
...INSIDE, EVERYONE'S SCARED OF HIM.
IF THIS KEEPS UP...
...
...SOMEDAY YOU'LL BE ALL ALONE.
SMILE MART
USE YOUR POWER...
...FOR BETTER PURPOSES.
?!
22-XY

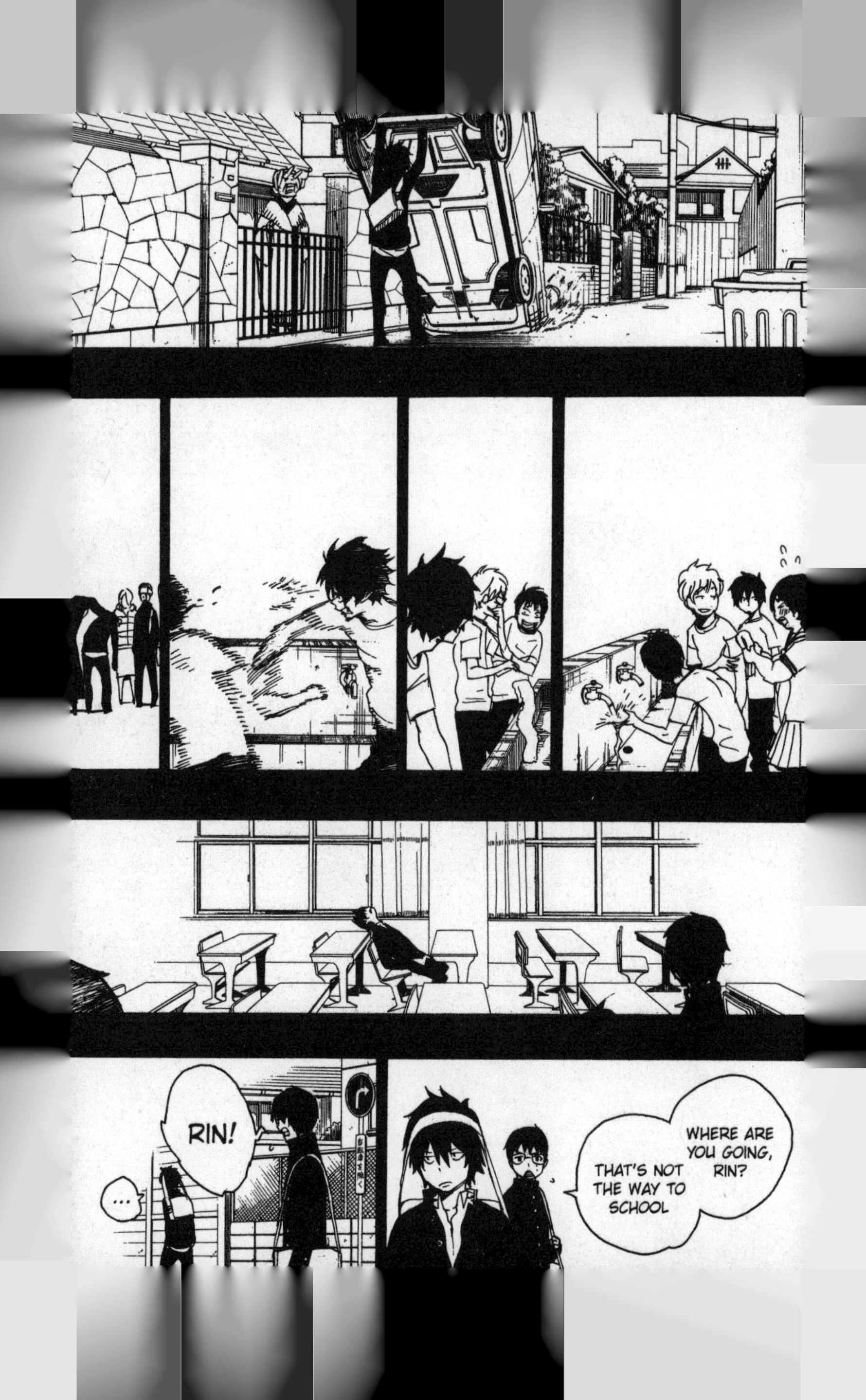
WHERE ARE YOU GOING, RIN?
THAT'S NOT THE WAY TO SCHOOL
RIN!
...

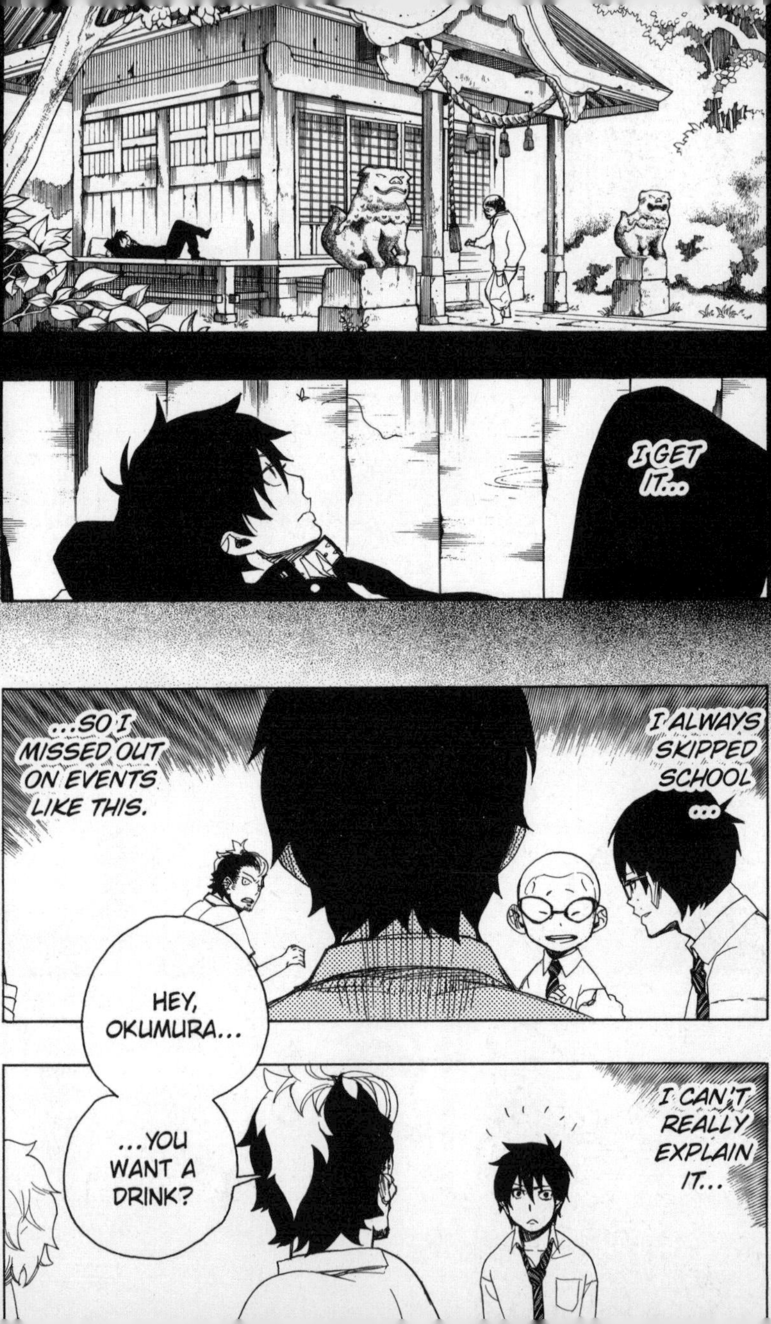
I GET IT...
I ALWAYS SKIPPED SCHOOL...
...
...SO I MISSED OUT ON EVENTS LIKE THIS.
HEY, OKUMURA...
I CAN'T REALLY EXPLAIN IT...
...YOU WANT A DRINK?

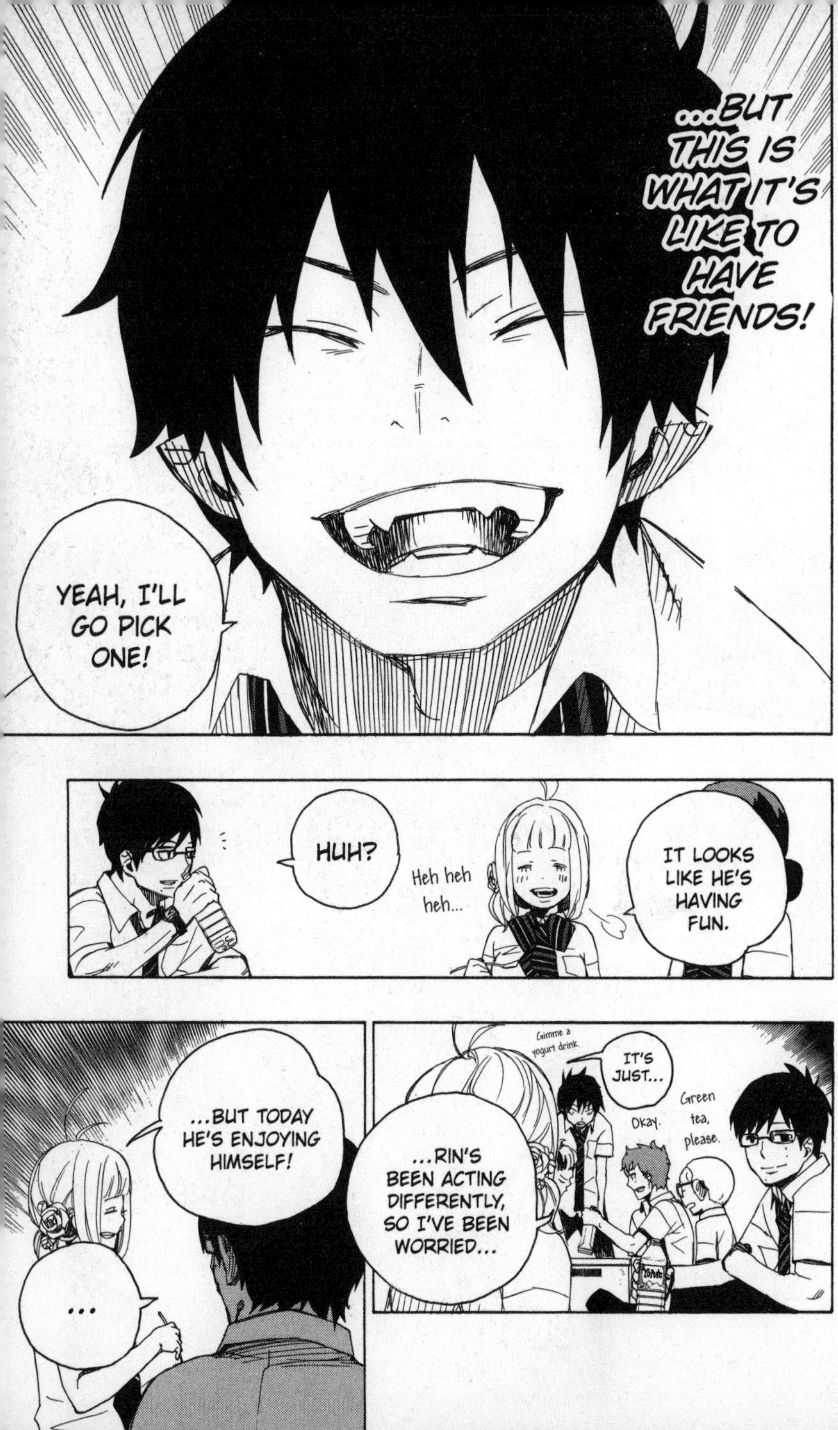
...BUT THIS IS WHAT IT'S LIKE TO HAVE FRIENDS!
YEAH, I'LL GO PICK ONE!
IT LOOKS LIKE HE'S HAVING FUN.
Heh heh heh...
HUH?
Green tea, please.
IT'S JUST...
Gimme a yogurt drink.
Okay.
...RIN'S BEEN ACTING DIFFERENTLY, SO I'VE BEEN WORRIED...
...BUT TODAY HE'S ENJOYING HIMSELF!
...

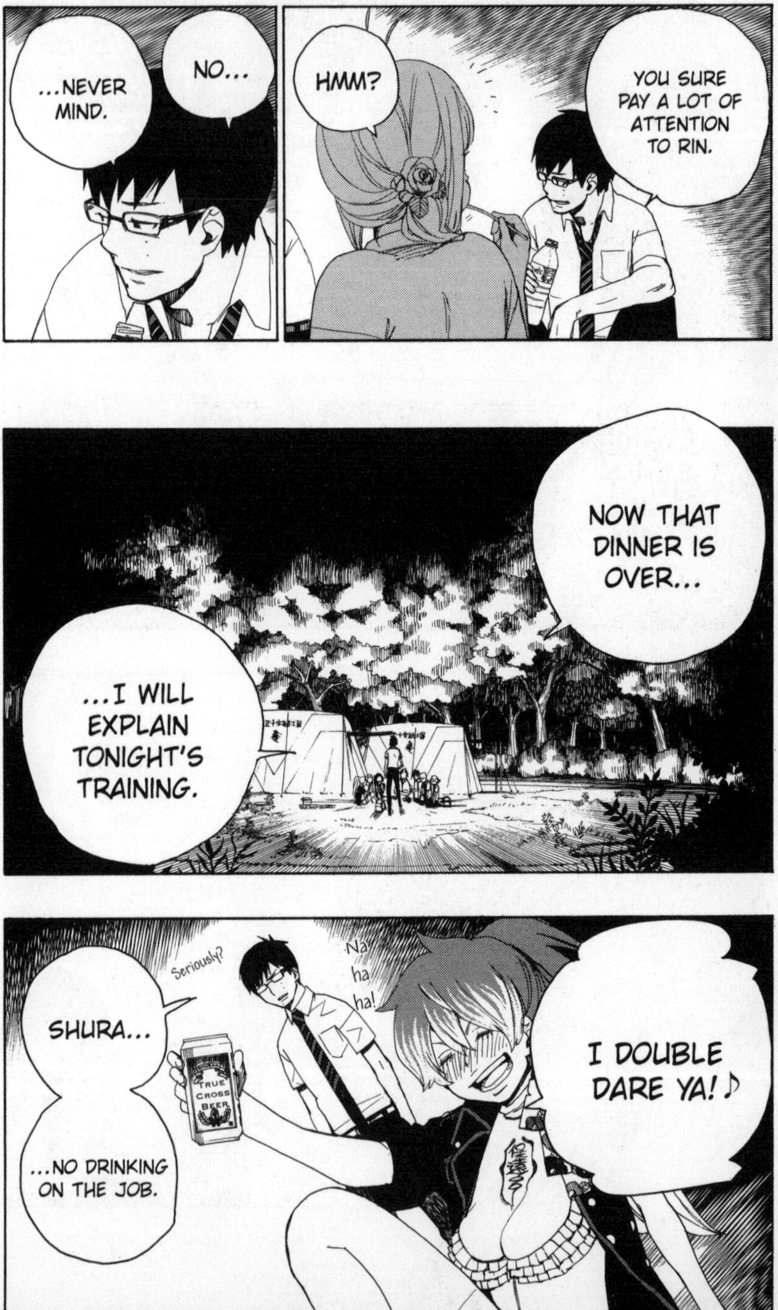
YOU SURE PAY A LOT OF ATTENTION TO RIN.
HMM?
NO...
...NEVER MIND.
NOW THAT DINNER IS OVER...
...I WILL EXPLAIN TONIGHT'S TRAINING.
Seriously?
SHURA...
...NO DRINKING ON THE JOB.
TRUE CROSS BEER
Na ha ha!
I DOUBLE DARE YA!♪

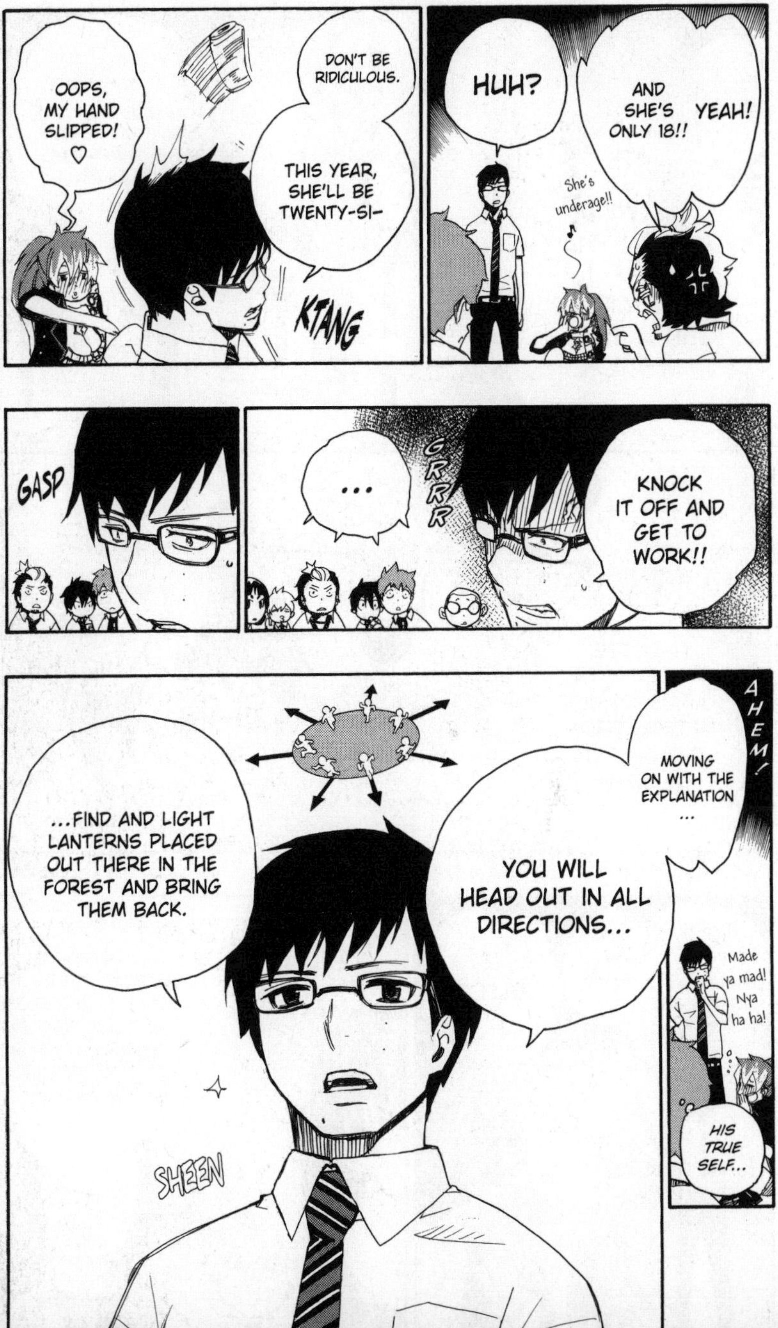
YEAH!
AND SHE'S ONLY 18!!
HUH?
She's underage!!
DON'T BE RIDICULOUS.
THIS YEAR, SHE'LL BE TWENTY-SI-
OOPS, MY HAND SLIPPED! ♡
KTANG
KNOCK IT OFF AND GET TO WORK!!
GRRR
...
GASP
AHEM!
MOVING ON WITH THE EXPLANATION...
Made ya mad! Nya ha ha!
HIS TRUE SELF...
YOU WILL HEAD OUT IN ALL DIRECTIONS...
...FIND AND LIGHT LANTERNS PLACED OUT THERE IN THE FOREST AND BRING THEM BACK.
SHEEN

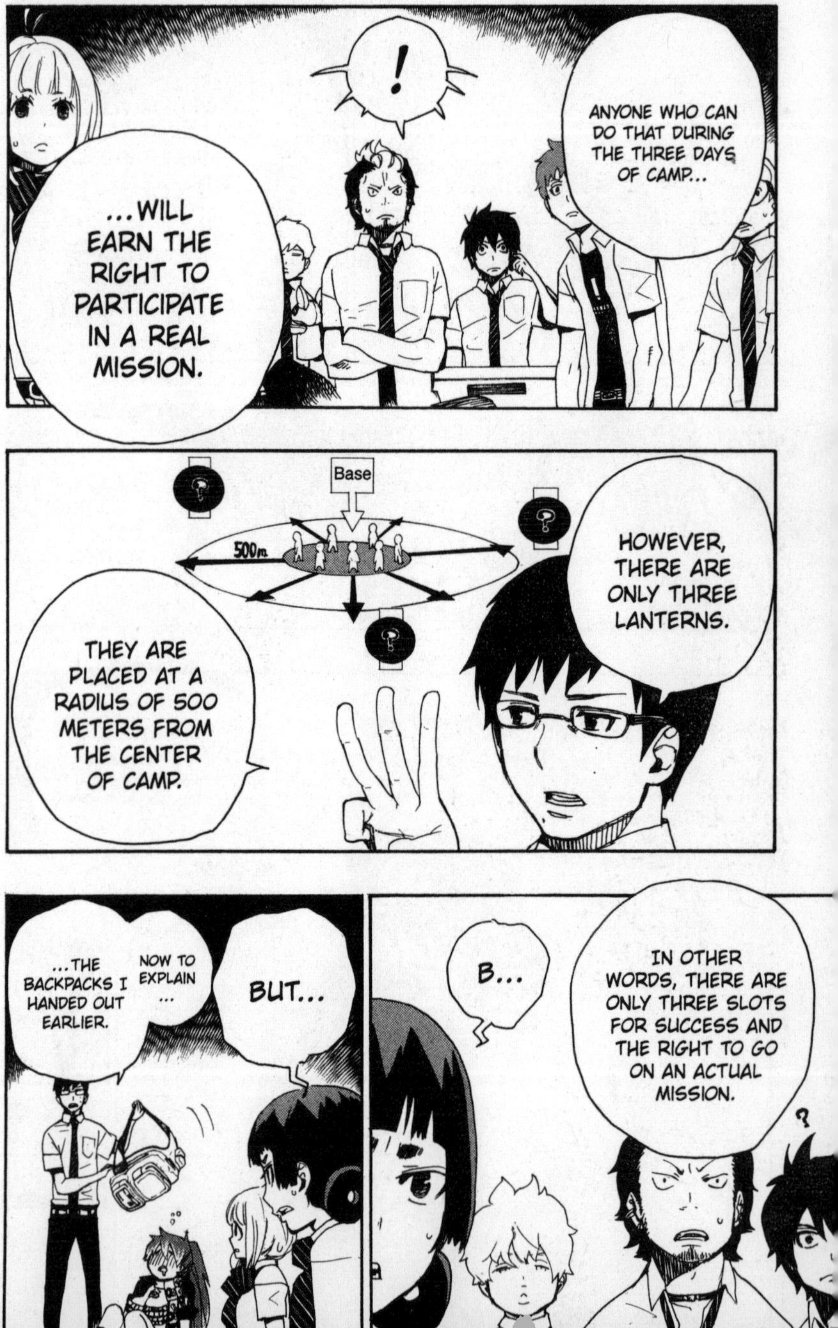
ANYONE WHO CAN DO THAT DURING THE THREE DAYS OF CAMP...
!
...WILL EARN THE RIGHT TO PARTICIPATE IN A REAL MISSION.
HOWEVER, THERE ARE ONLY THREE LANTERNS.
Base
500m
THEY ARE PLACED AT A RADIUS OF 500 METERS FROM THE CENTER OF CAMP.
IN OTHER WORDS, THERE ARE ONLY THREE SLOTS FOR SUCCESS AND THE RIGHT TO GO ON AN ACTUAL MISSION.
B...
?
BUT...
NOW TO EXPLAIN...
...THE BACKPACKS I HANDED OUT EARLIER.

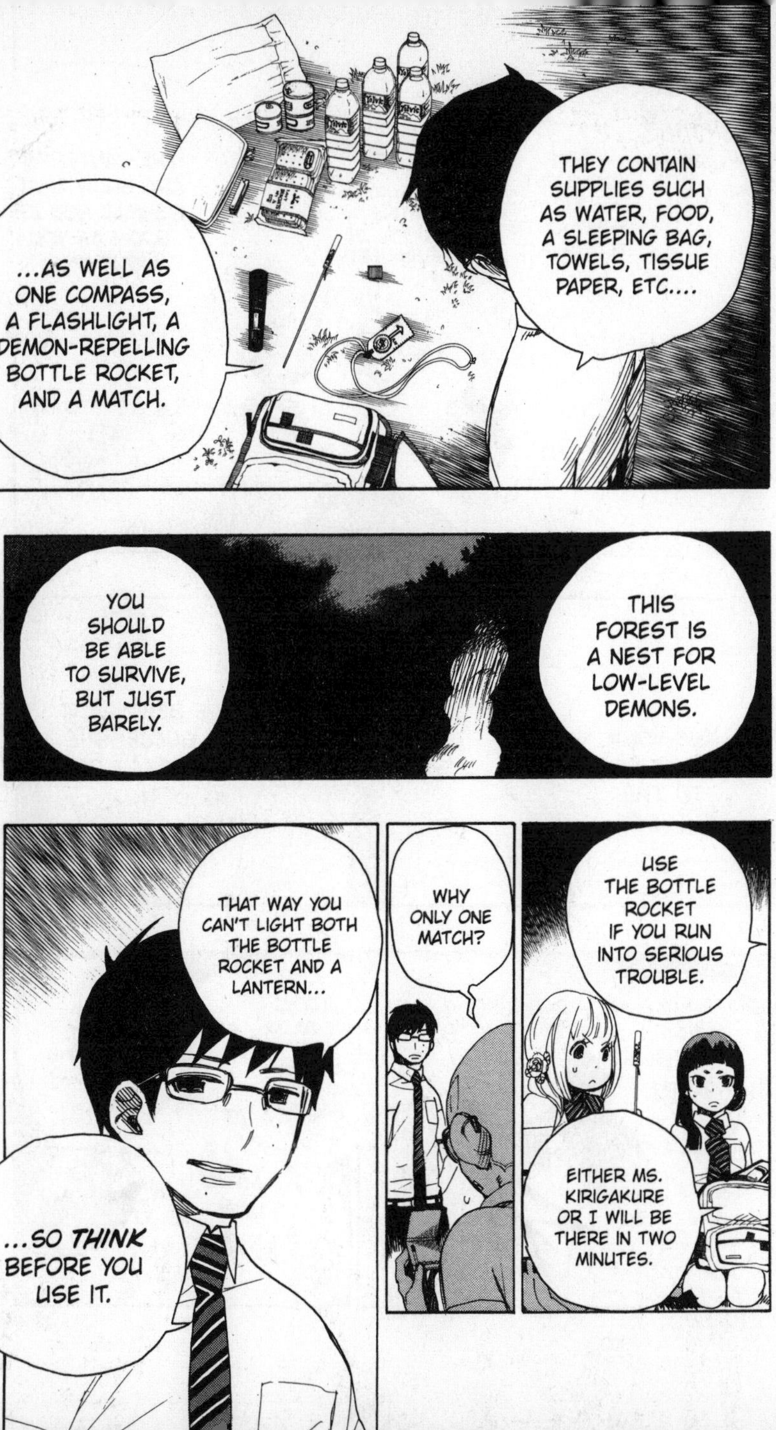
THEY CONTAIN SUPPLIES SUCH AS WATER, FOOD, A SLEEPING BAG, TOWELS, TISSUE PAPER, ETC....
...AS WELL AS ONE COMPASS, A FLASHLIGHT, A DEMON-REPELLING BOTTLE ROCKET, AND A MATCH.
THIS FOREST IS A NEST FOR LOW-LEVEL DEMONS.
YOU SHOULD BE ABLE TO SURVIVE, BUT JUST BARELY.
USE THE BOTTLE ROCKET IF YOU RUN INTO SERIOUS TROUBLE.
EITHER MS. KIRIGAKURE OR I WILL BE THERE IN TWO MINUTES.
WHY ONLY ONE MATCH?
THAT WAY YOU CAN'T LIGHT BOTH THE BOTTLE ROCKET AND A LANTERN...
...SO *THINK* BEFORE YOU USE IT.

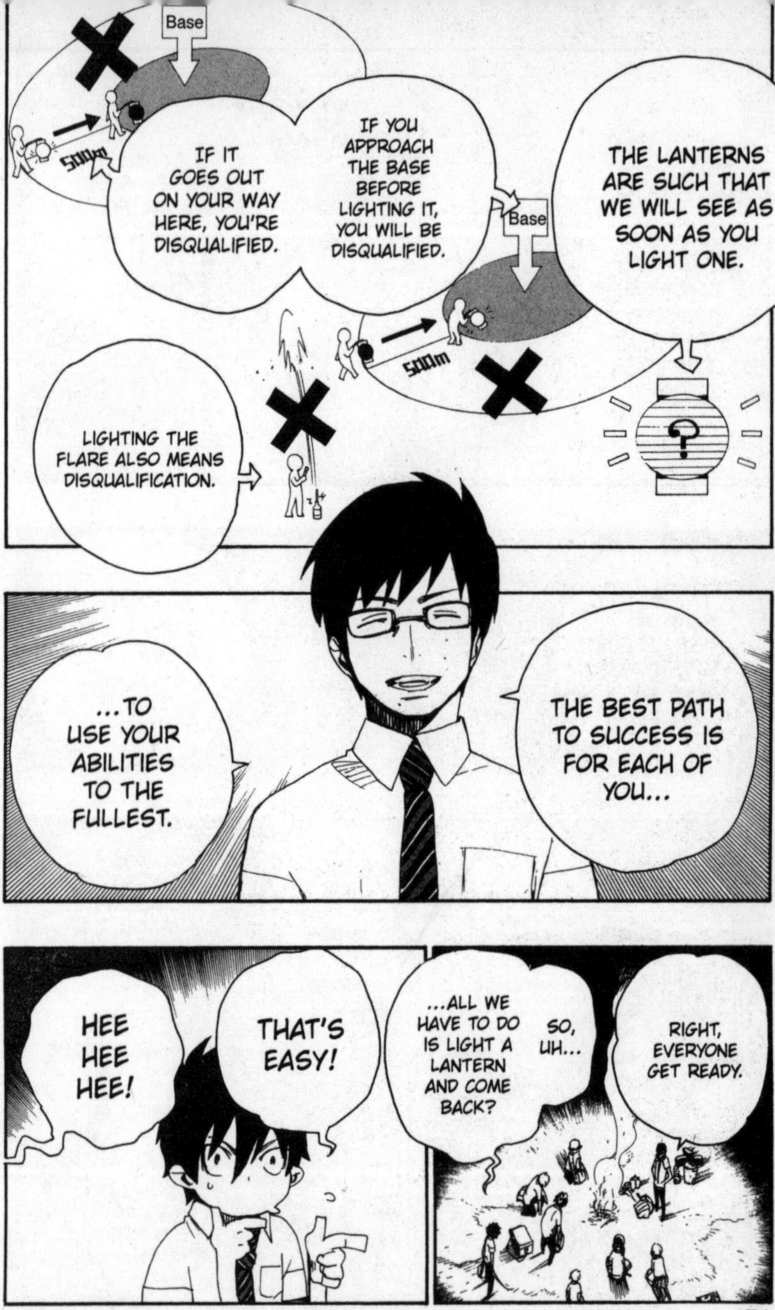
Base
THE LANTERNS ARE SUCH THAT WE WILL SEE AS SOON AS YOU LIGHT ONE.
Base
IF YOU APPROACH THE BASE BEFORE LIGHTING IT, YOU WILL BE DISQUALIFIED.
IF IT GOES OUT ON YOUR WAY HERE, YOU'RE DISQUALIFIED.
500m
500m
LIGHTING THE FLARE ALSO MEANS DISQUALIFICATION.
THE BEST PATH TO SUCCESS IS FOR EACH OF YOU...
...TO USE YOUR ABILITIES TO THE FULLEST.
RIGHT, EVERYONE GET READY.
SO, UH...
...ALL WE HAVE TO DO IS LIGHT A LANTERN AND COME BACK?
THAT'S EASY!
HEE HEE HEE!

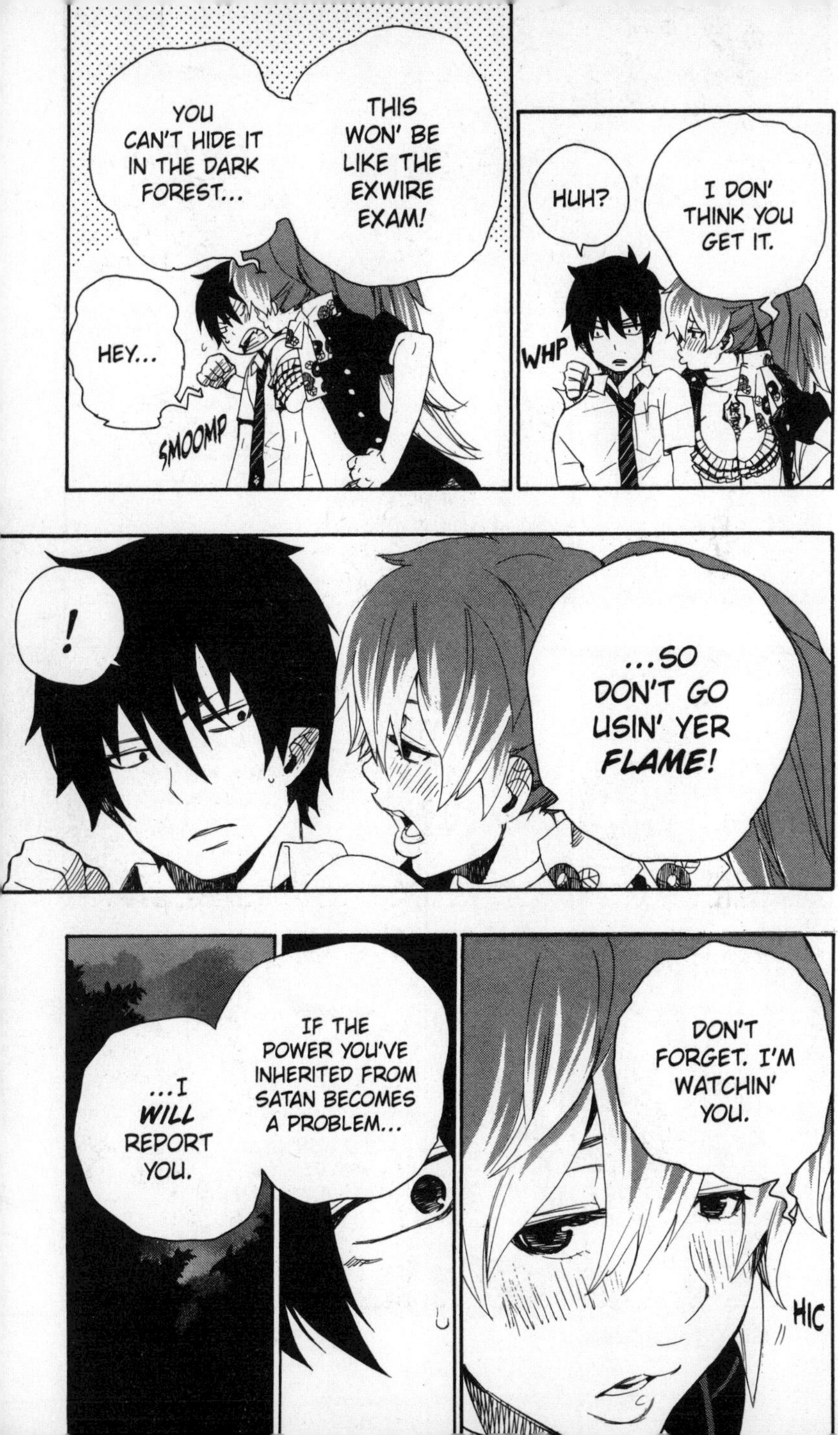
I DON' THINK YOU GET IT.
HUH?
WHP
THIS WON' BE LIKE THE EXWIRE EXAM!
YOU CAN'T HIDE IT IN THE DARK FOREST...
HEY...
SMOOMP
...SO DON'T GO USIN' YER FLAME!
!
DON'T FORGET. I'M WATCHIN' YOU.
HIC
IF THE POWER YOU'VE INHERITED FROM SATAN BECOMES A PROBLEM...
...I WILL REPORT YOU.

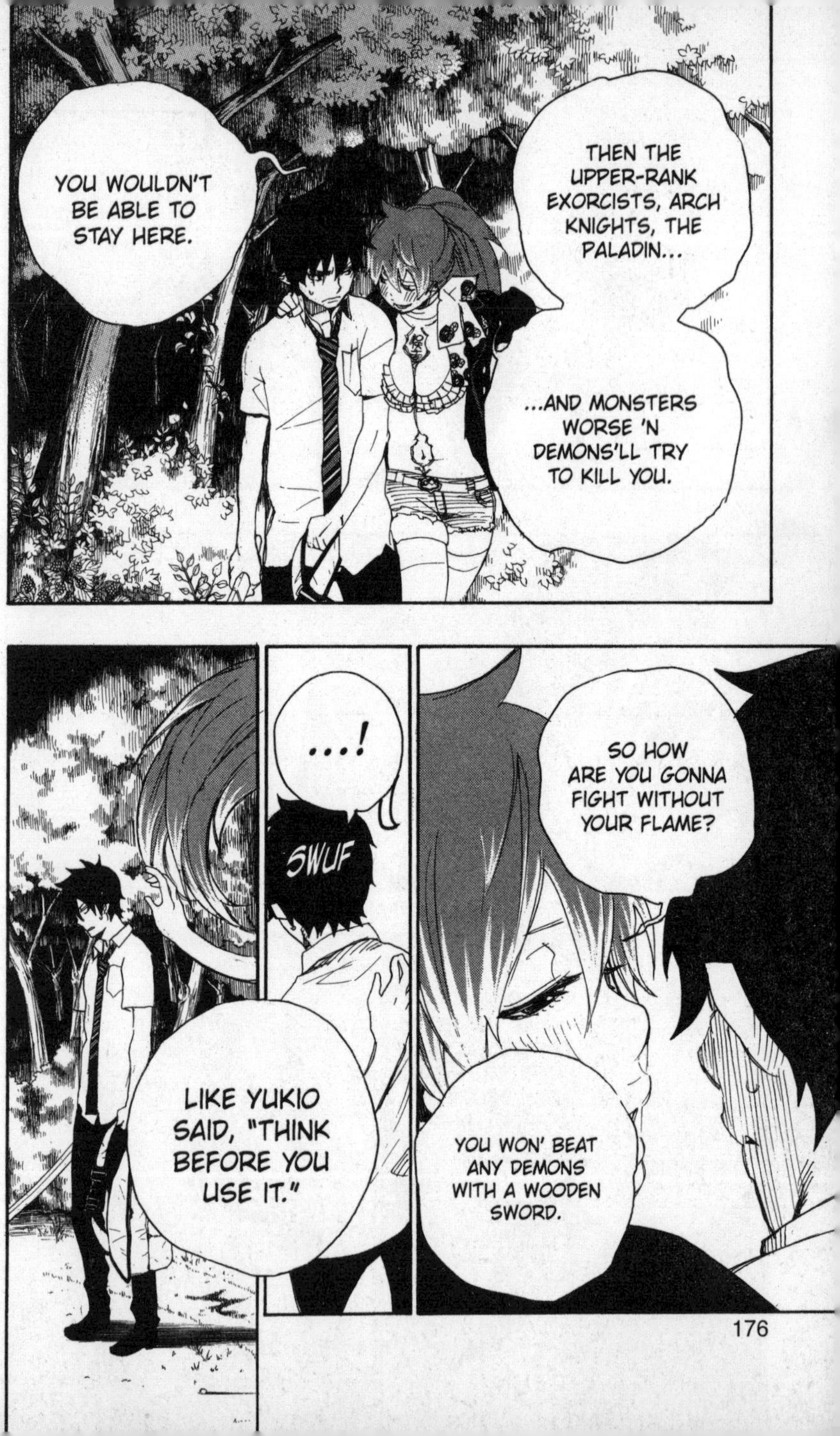
YOU WOULDN'T BE ABLE TO STAY HERE.
THEN THE UPPER-RANK EXORCISTS, ARCH KNIGHTS, THE PALADIN...
...AND MONSTERS WORSE 'N DEMONS'LL TRY TO KILL YOU.
SO HOW ARE YOU GONNA FIGHT WITHOUT YOUR FLAME?
YOU WON' BEAT ANY DEMONS WITH A WOODEN SWORD.
...!
SWUF
LIKE YUKIO SAID, "THINK BEFORE YOU USE IT."

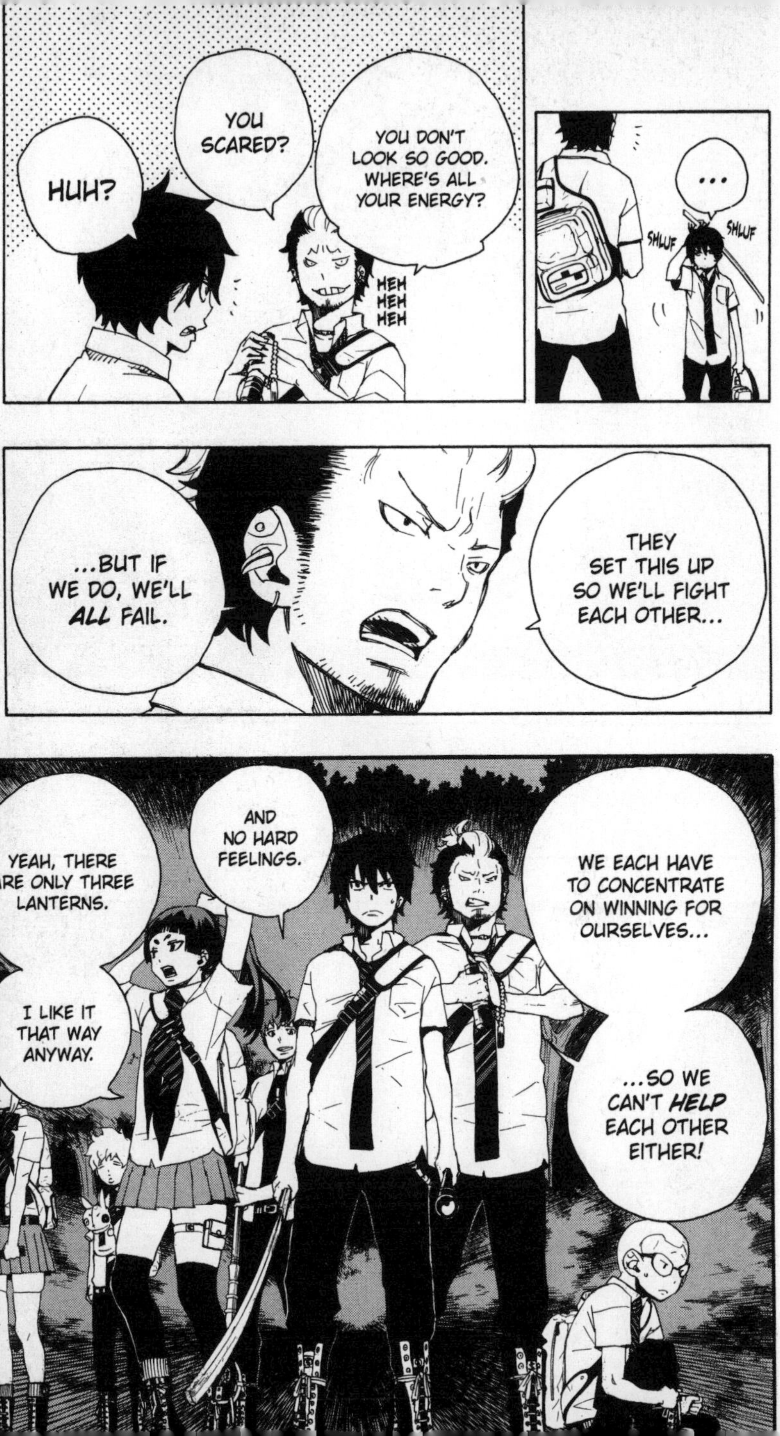
...
SHLUF
SHLUF
YOU DON'T LOOK SO GOOD. WHERE'S ALL YOUR ENERGY?
YOU SCARED?
HEH HEH HEH
HUH?
THEY SET THIS UP SO WE'LL FIGHT EACH OTHER...
...BUT IF WE DO, WE'LL *ALL* FAIL.
WE EACH HAVE TO CONCENTRATE ON WINNING FOR OURSELVES...
...SO WE CAN'T *HELP* EACH OTHER EITHER!
AND NO HARD FEELINGS.
YEAH, THERE ARE ONLY THREE LANTERNS.
I LIKE IT THAT WAY ANYWAY.

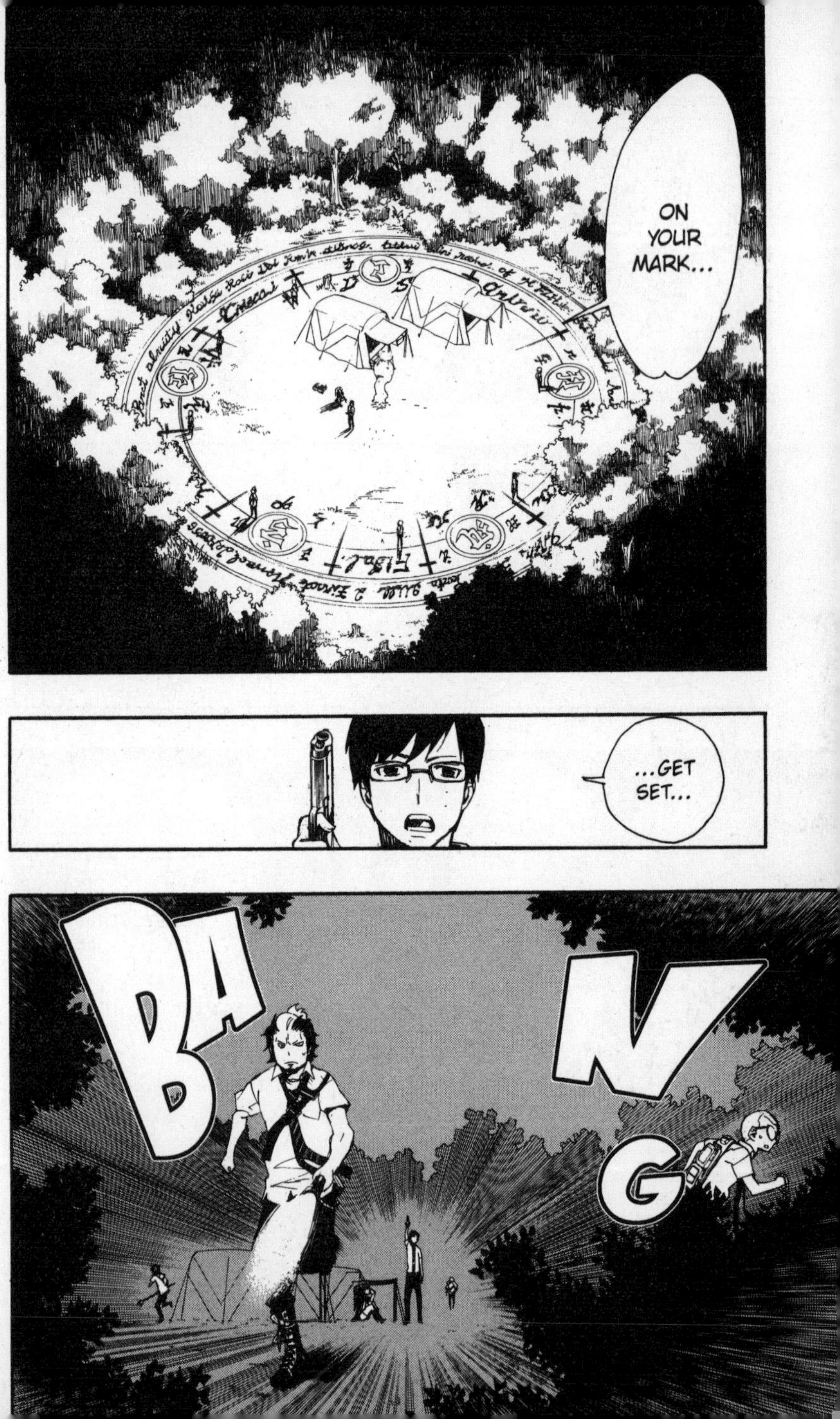
ON YOUR MARK...
...GET SET...
BANG

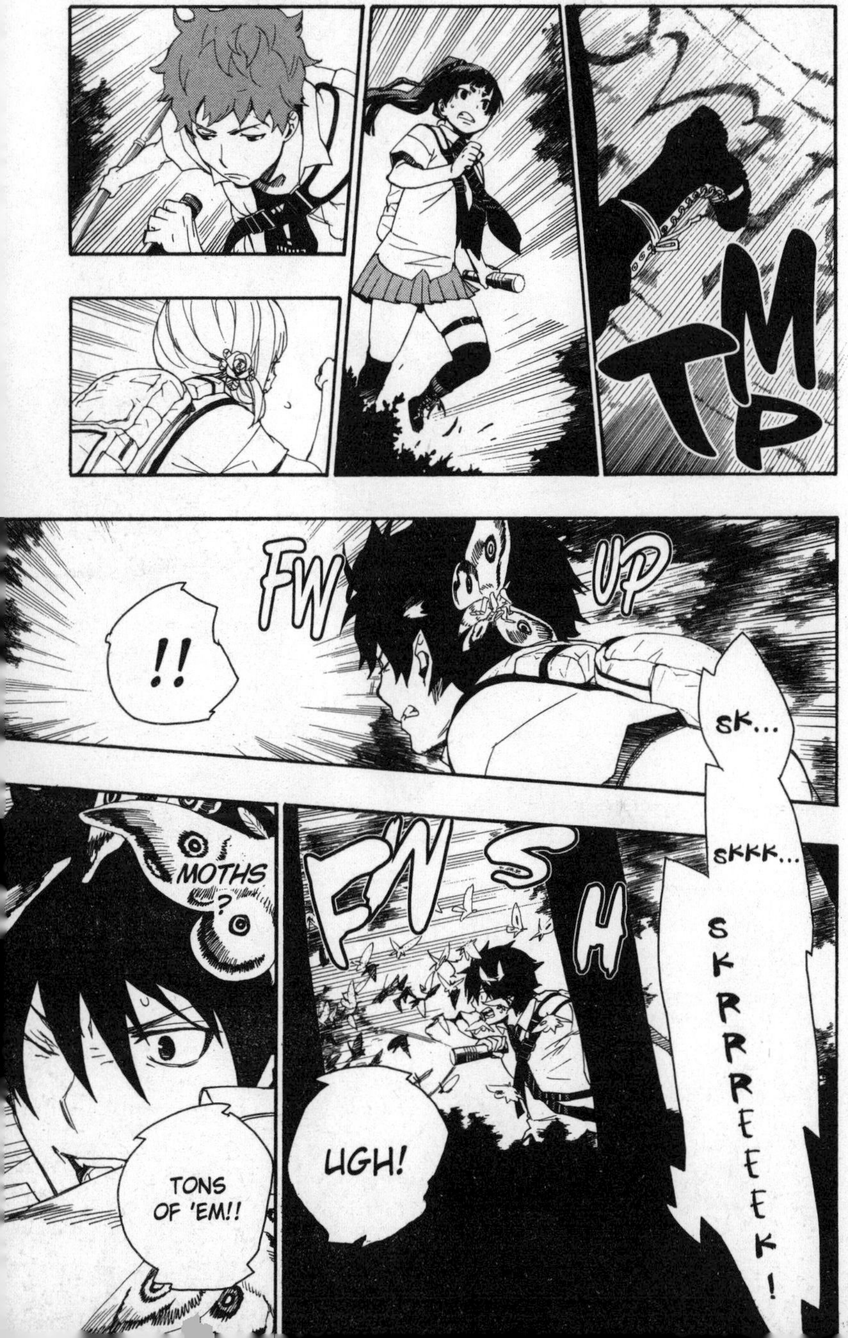
TMP
SK...
FWUP
!!
SKKK...
SKRRREEEK!
FWSH
UGH!
MOTHS?
TONS OF 'EM!!

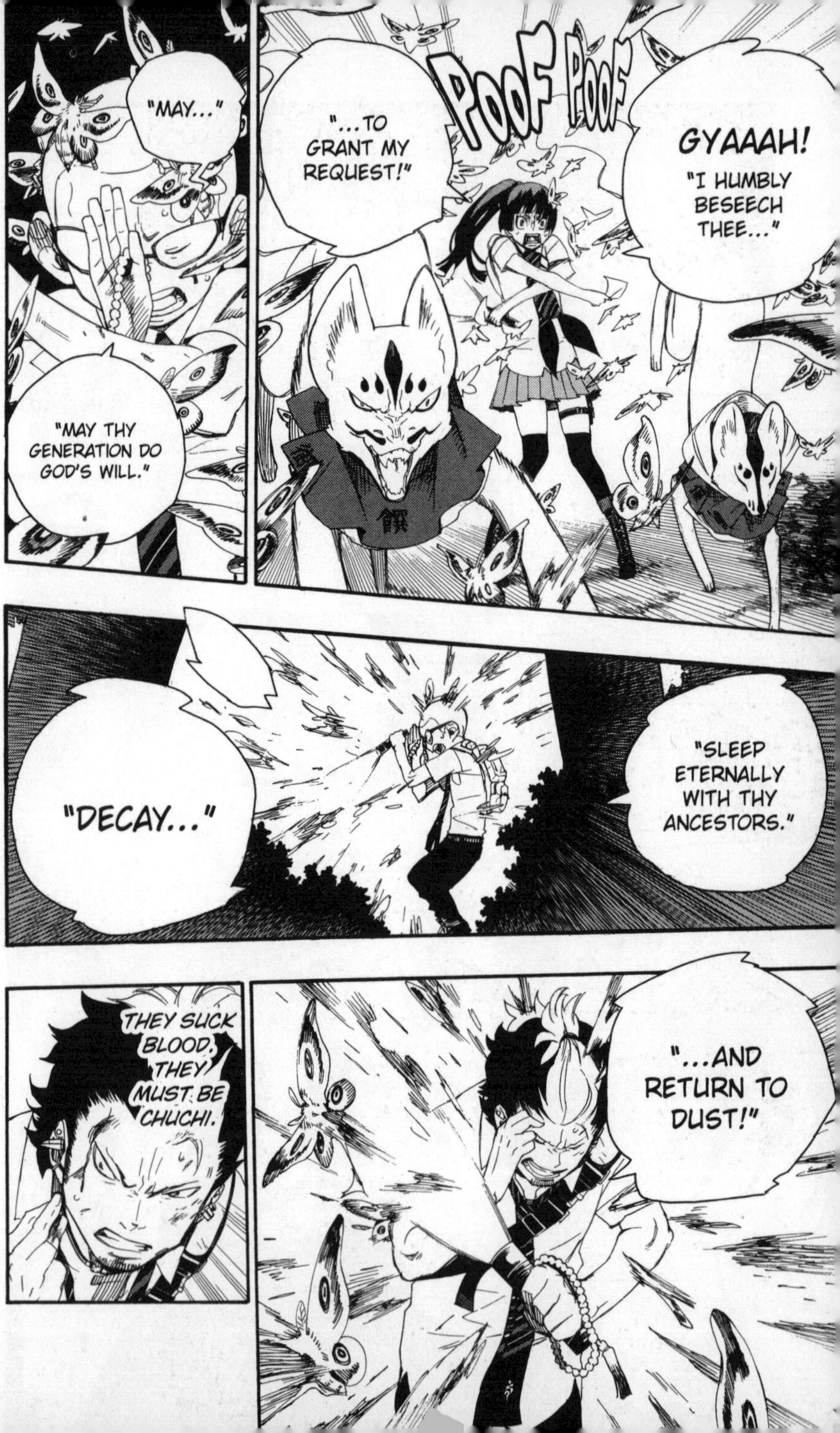
GYAAAH!
"I HUMBLY BESEECH THEE..."
POOF POOF
"...TO GRANT MY REQUEST!"
"MAY..."
"MAY THY GENERATION DO GOD'S WILL."
"SLEEP ETERNALLY WITH THY ANCESTORS."
"DECAY..."
"...AND RETURN TO DUST!"
THEY SUCK BLOOD. THEY MUST BE CHUCHI.

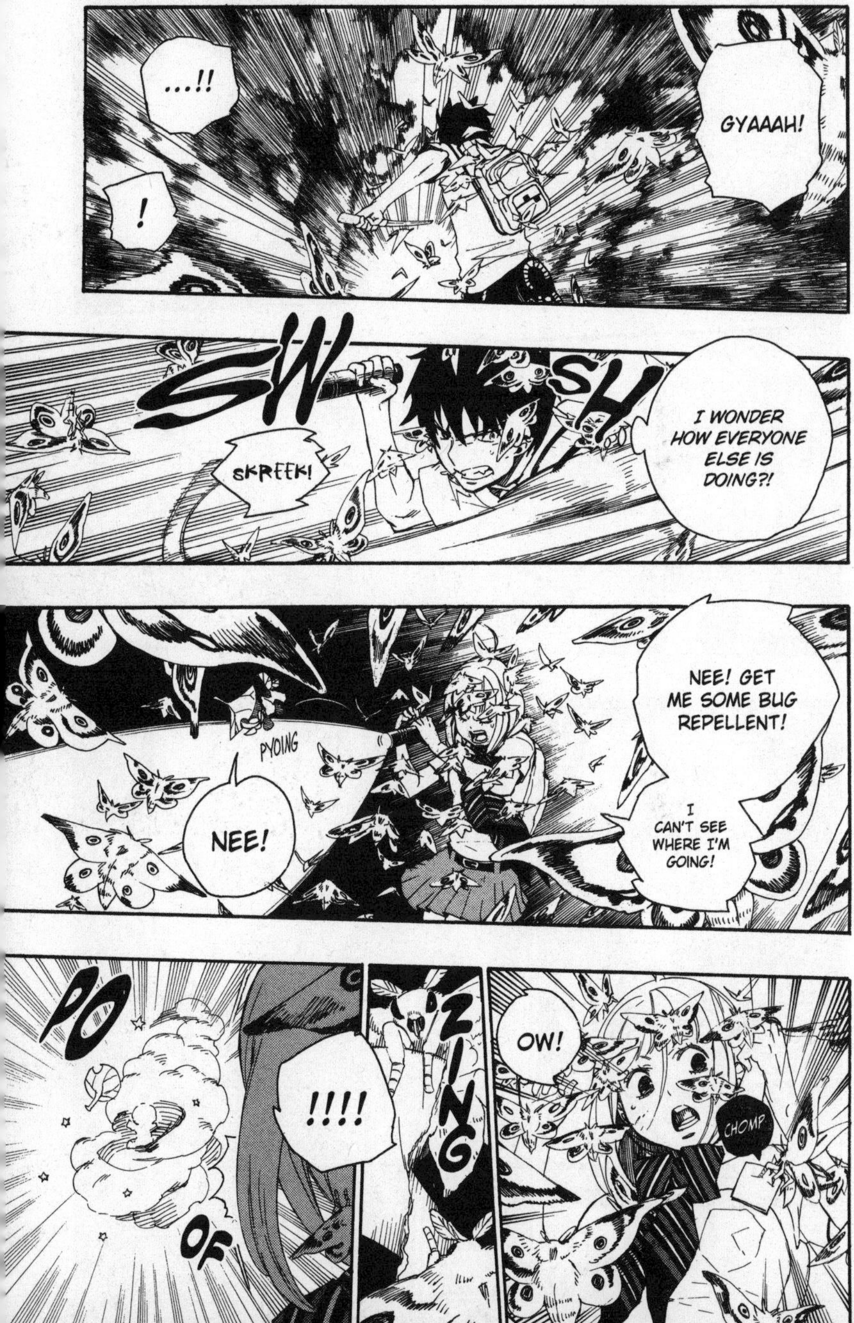
GYAAAH!
...!!
!
I WONDER HOW EVERYONE ELSE IS DOING?!
SWSH
SKREEK!
NEE! GET ME SOME BUG REPELLENT!
I CAN'T SEE WHERE I'M GOING!
PYOING
NEE!
OW!
CHOMP
ZING
!!!!
POOF

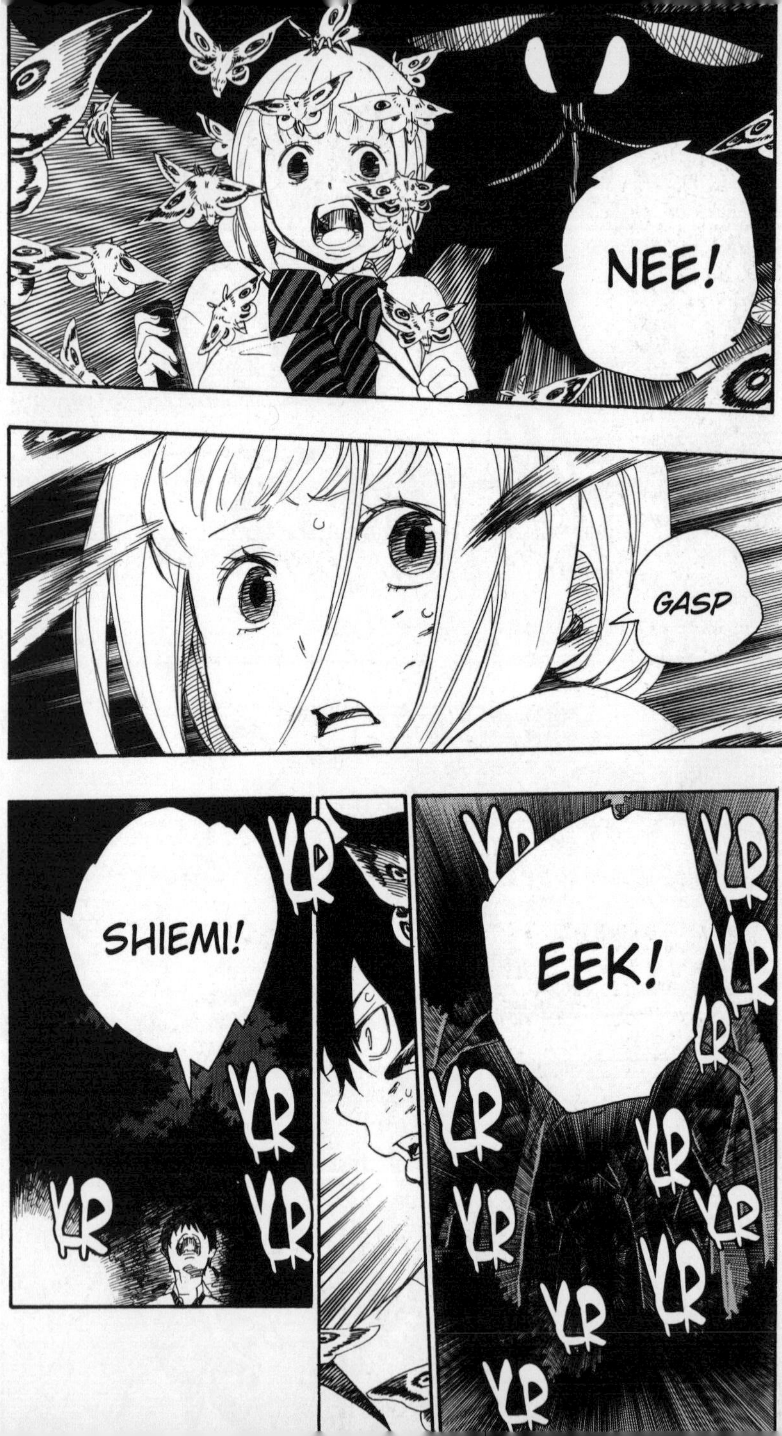
NEE!
GASP
YR YR YR YR YR YR YR YR YR YR YR YR
EEK!
YR YR YR YR
SHIEMI!

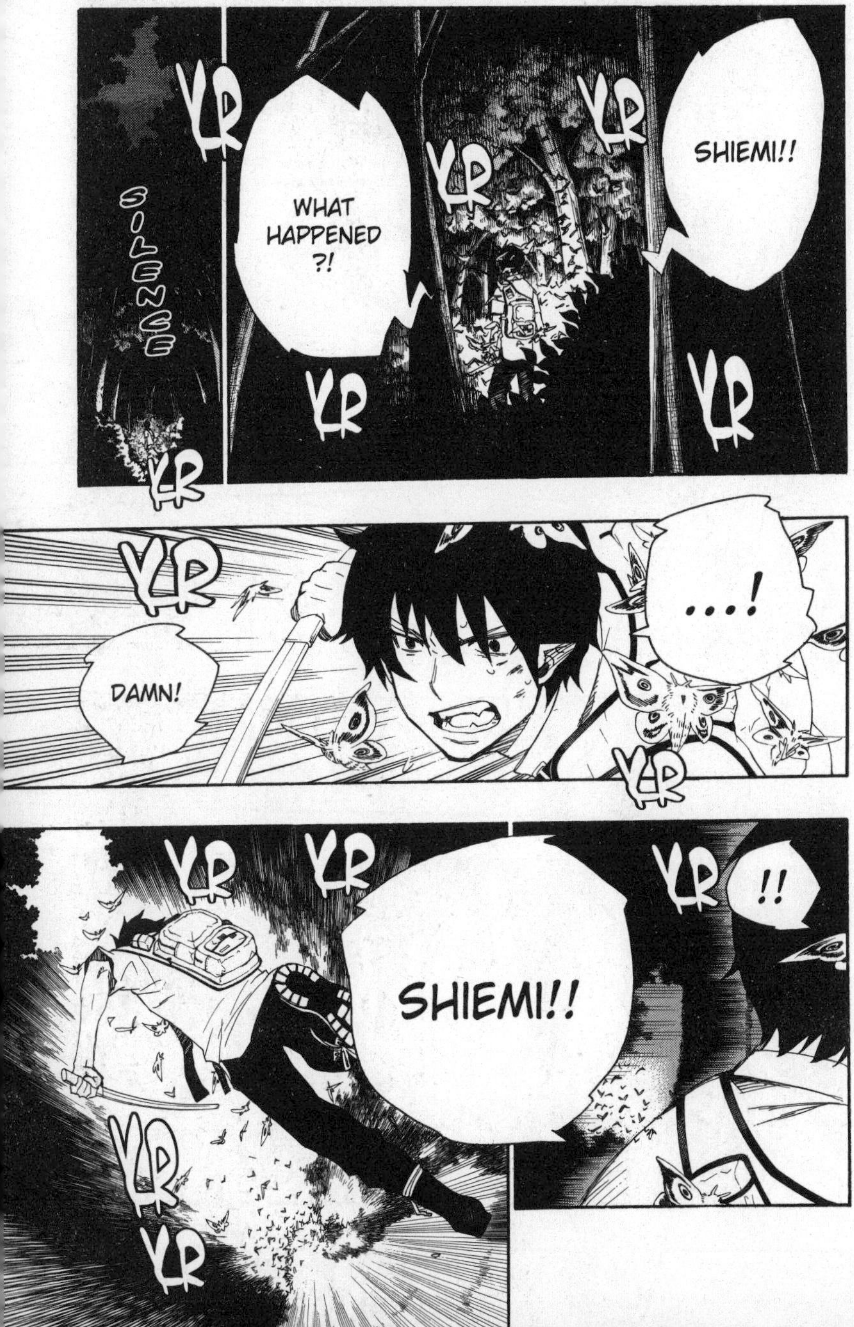
SHIEMI!!
WHAT HAPPENED ?!
SILENCE
...!
DAMN!
!!
SHIEMI!!

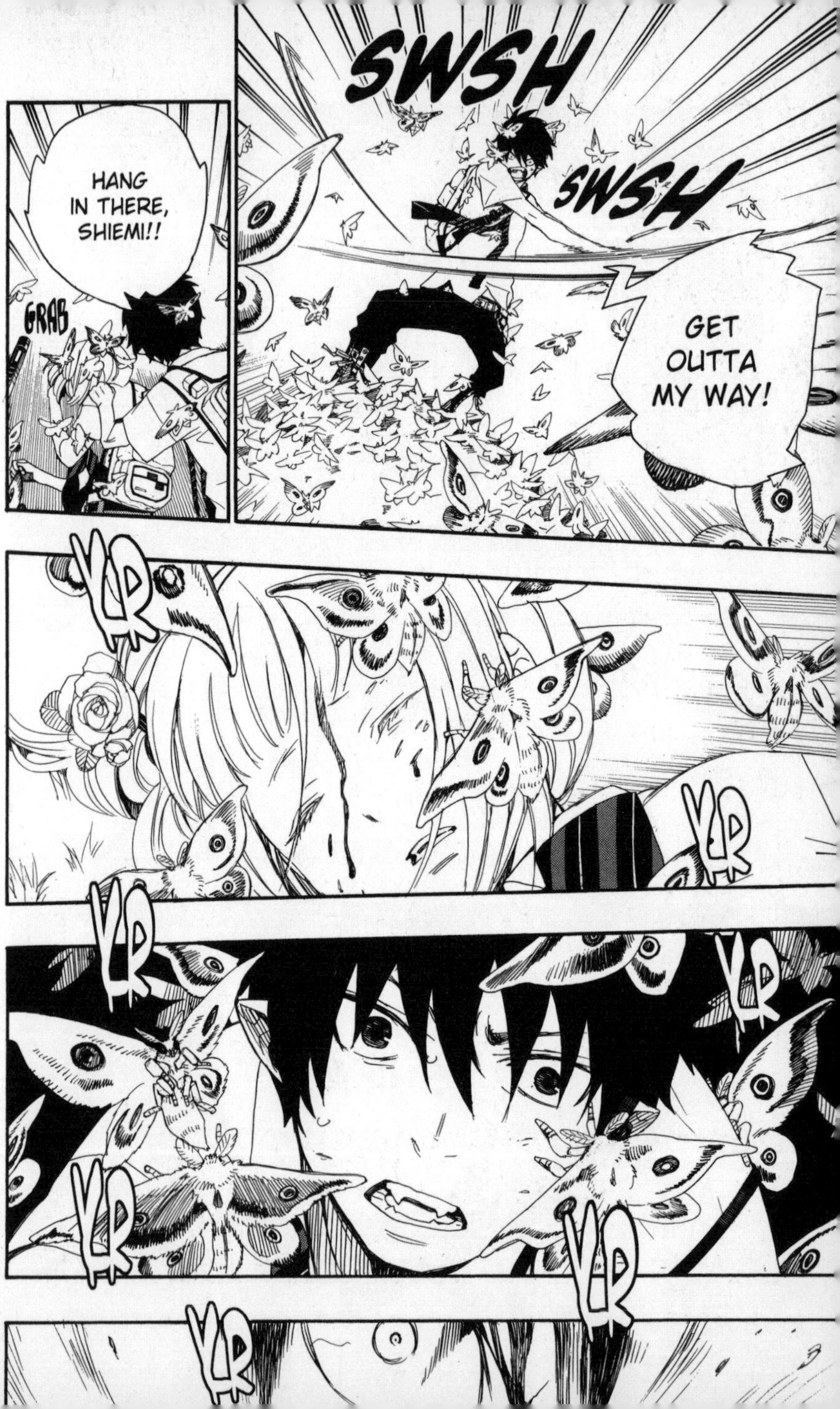
SWSH
SWSH
GET OUTTA MY WAY!
HANG IN THERE, SHIEMI!!
GRAB
VRR
VRR
VRR
VRR
VRR
VRR
VRR

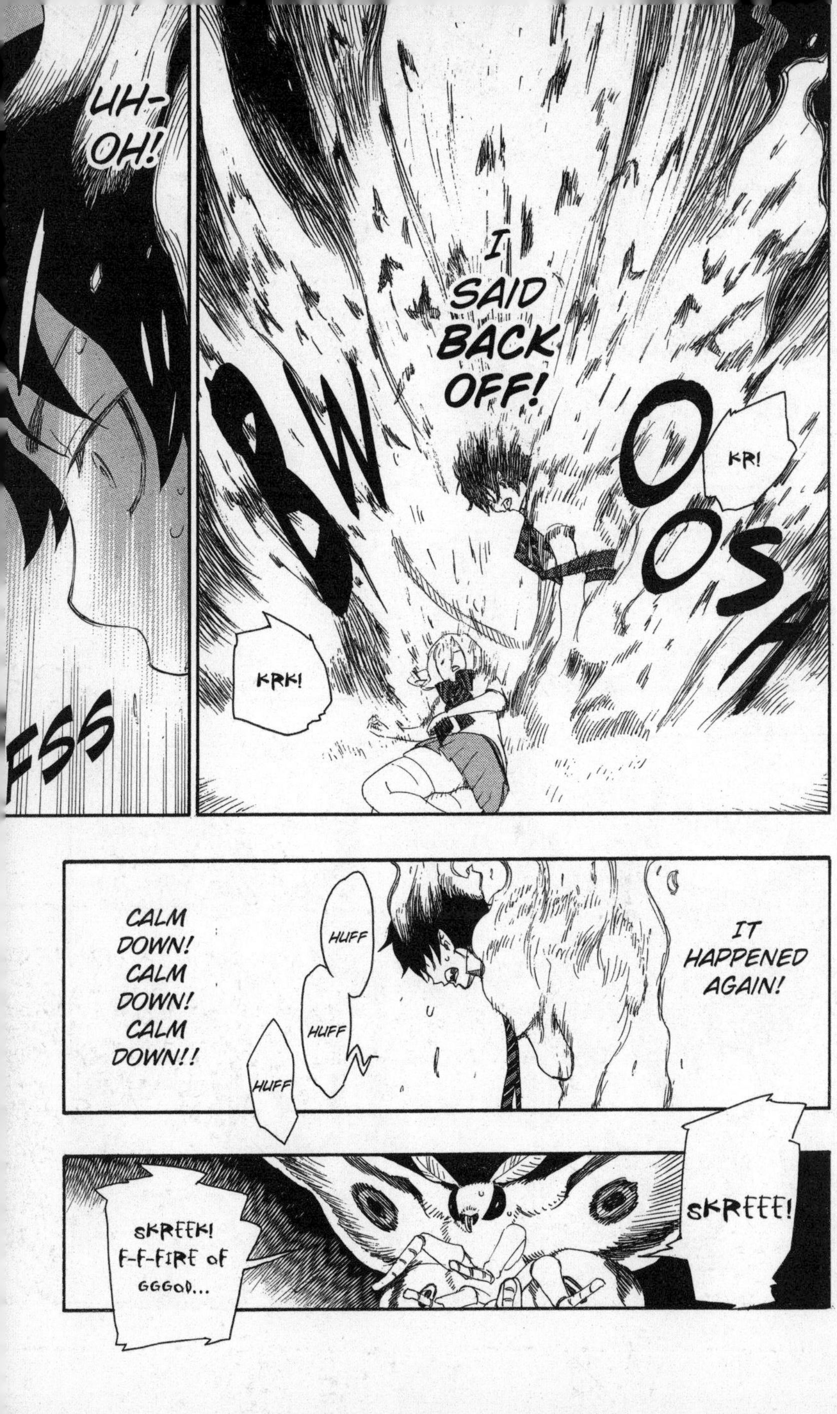
I SAID BACK OFF!
KR!
BWOOSH
KRK!
UH-OH!
FSS
IT HAPPENED AGAIN!
HUFF
HUFF
HUFF
CALM DOWN! CALM DOWN! CALM DOWN!!
SKREEE!
SKREEK! F-F-FIRE OF GGGOD...

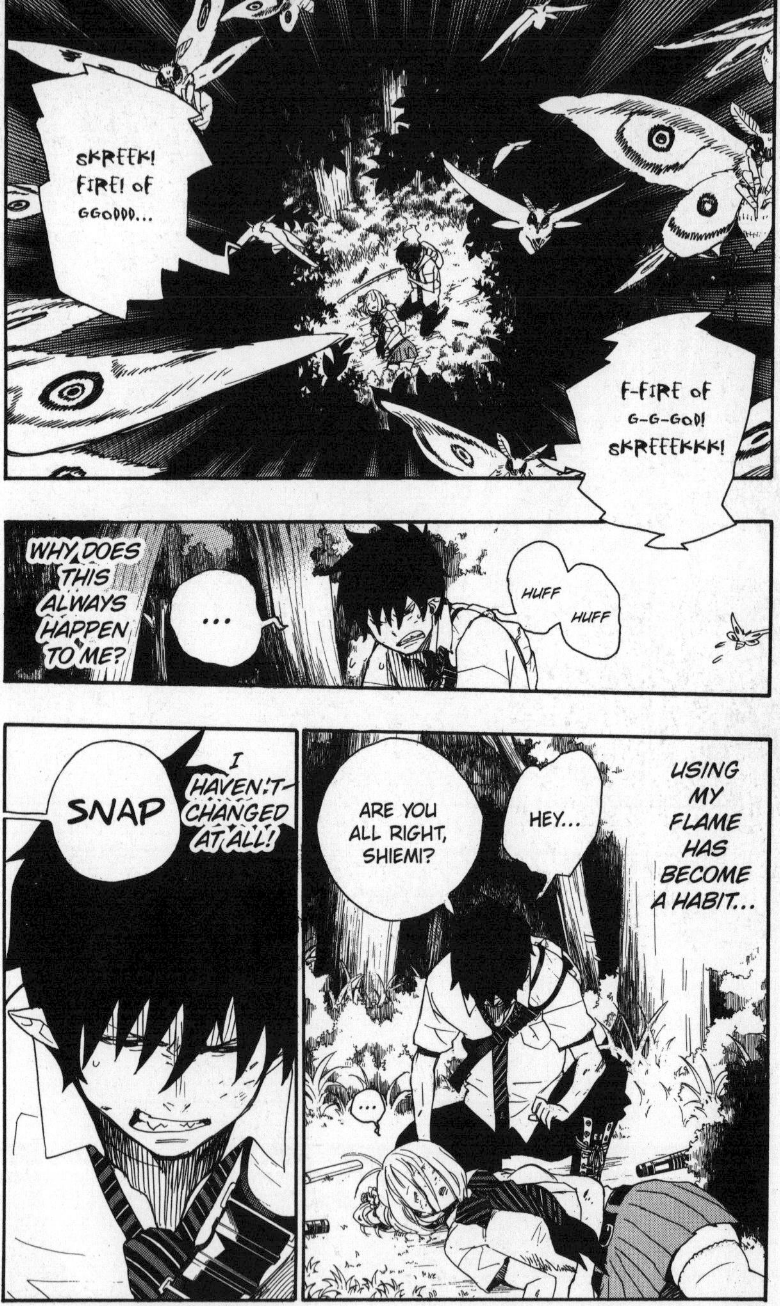
F-FIRE OF G-G-GOD! SKREEEKKK!
SKREEK! FIRE! OF GGODDD...
HUFF HUFF
...
WHY DOES THIS ALWAYS HAPPEN TO ME?
USING MY FLAME HAS BECOME A HABIT...
HEY...
ARE YOU ALL RIGHT, SHIEMI?
...
I HAVEN'T CHANGED AT ALL!
SNAP

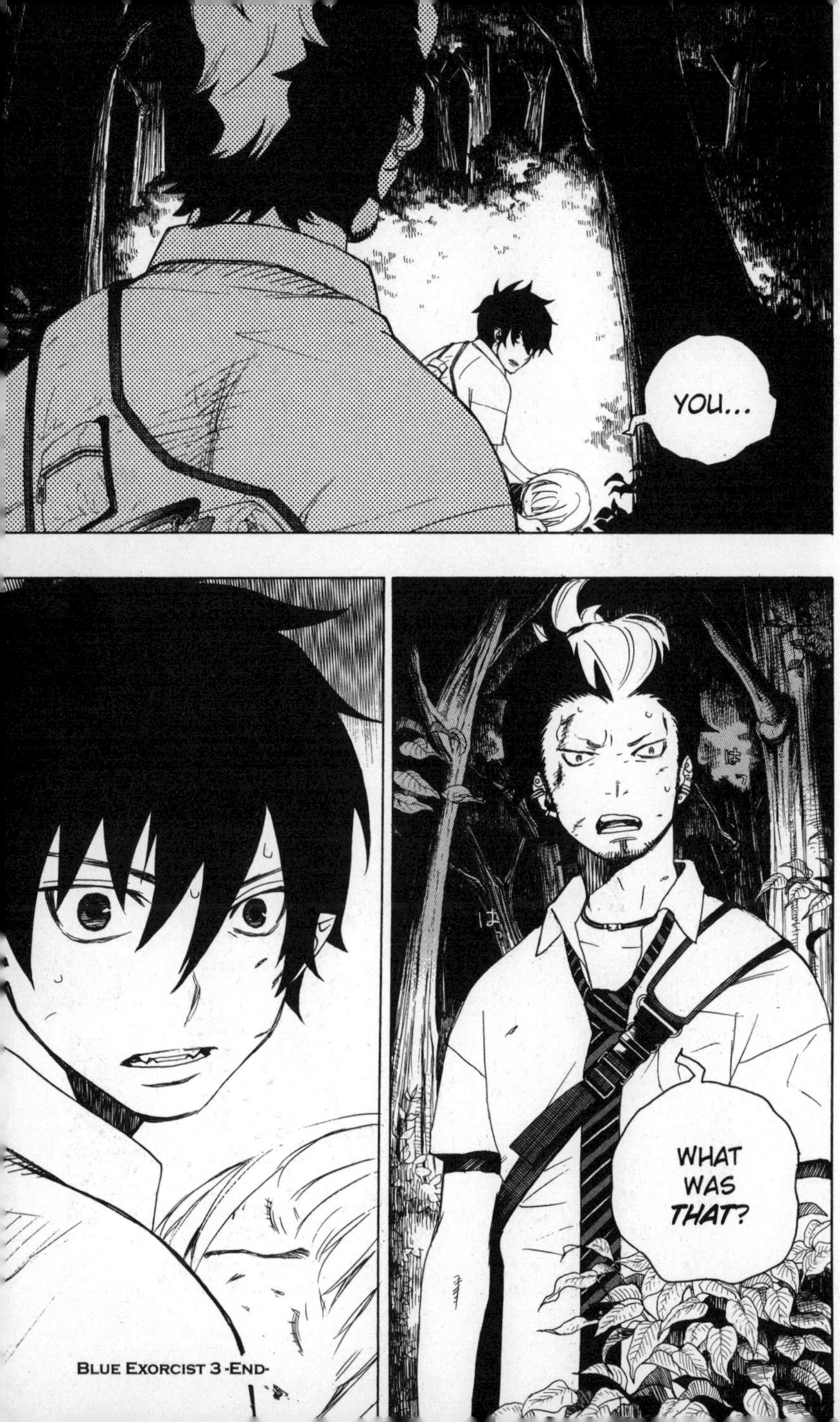
YOU...
WHAT WAS *THAT?*
BLUE EXORCIST 3 -END-

Blue Exorcist Chapter

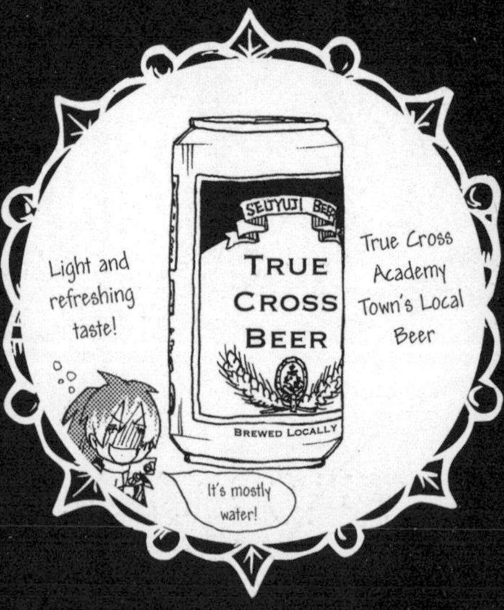
True Cross Academy Town's Local Beer
TRUE CROSS BEER
BREWED LOCALLY
Light and refreshing taste!
It's mostly water!

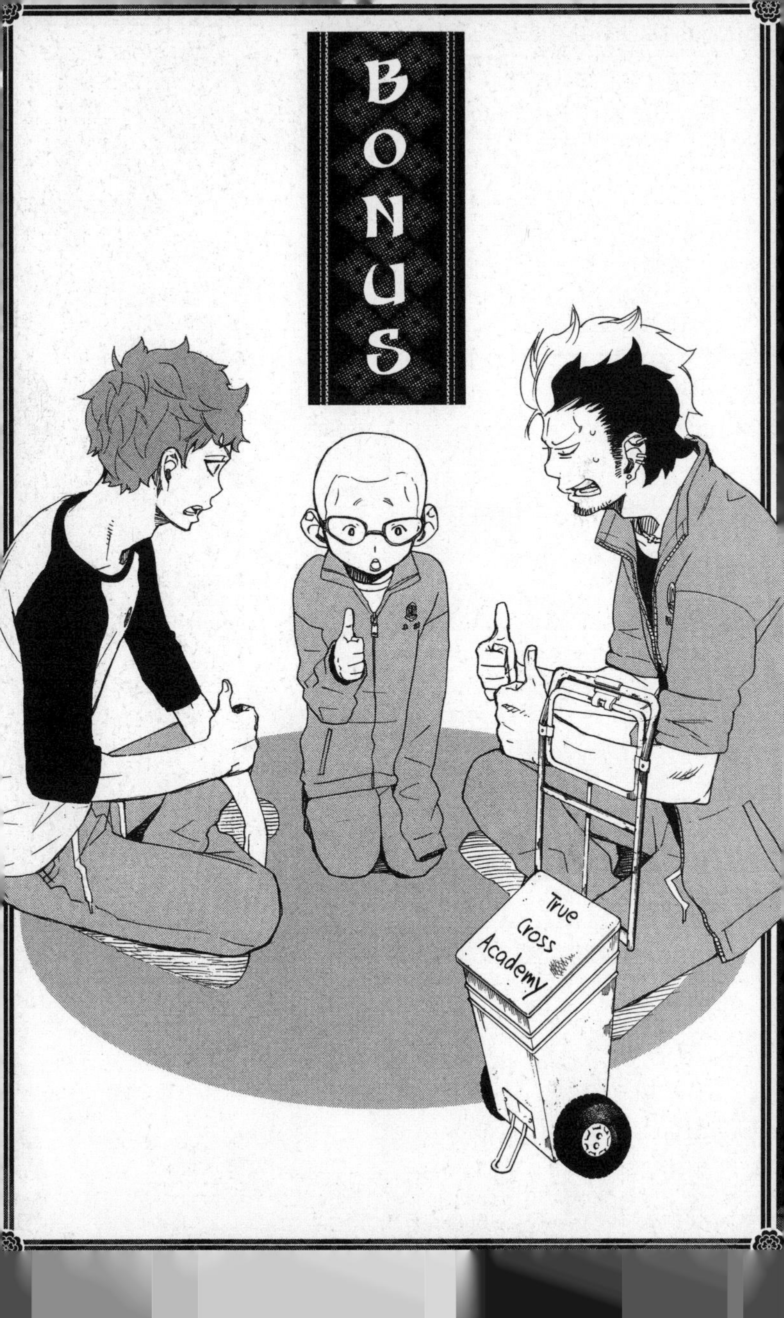
BONUS
True Cross Academy

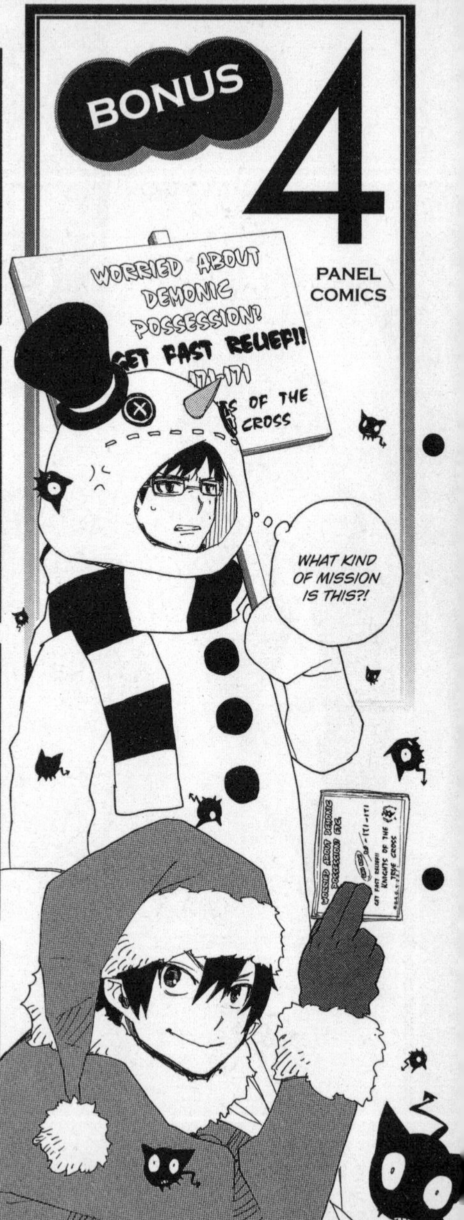
BONUS
4
PANEL COMICS
WORRIED ABOUT DEMONIC POSSESSION? GET FAST RELIEF!!
CROSS
WHAT KIND OF MISSION IS THIS?!

YOU WANNA EMBARRASS ME?!

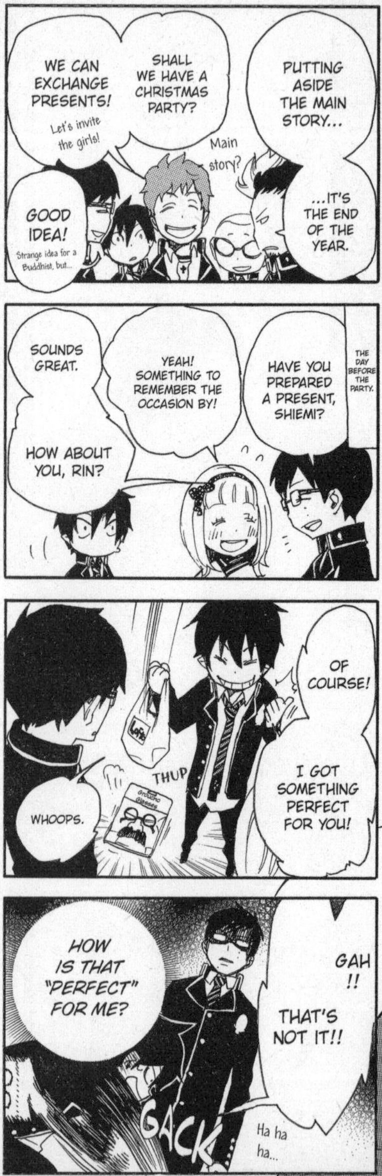
PUTTING ASIDE THE MAIN STORY...
Main story?
...IT'S THE END OF THE YEAR.
SHALL WE HAVE A CHRISTMAS PARTY?
WE CAN EXCHANGE PRESENTS!
Let's invite the girls!
GOOD IDEA!
Strange idea for a Buddhist, but...
THE DAY BEFORE THE PARTY.
HAVE YOU PREPARED A PRESENT, SHIEMI?
YEAH! SOMETHING TO REMEMBER THE OCCASION BY!
SOUNDS GREAT.
HOW ABOUT YOU, RIN?
OF COURSE!
I GOT SOMETHING PERFECT FOR YOU!
THUP
WHOOPS.
GAH!!
THAT'S NOT IT!!
HOW IS THAT "PERFECT" FOR ME?
Ha ha ha...
GACK

I WON'T LOSE!

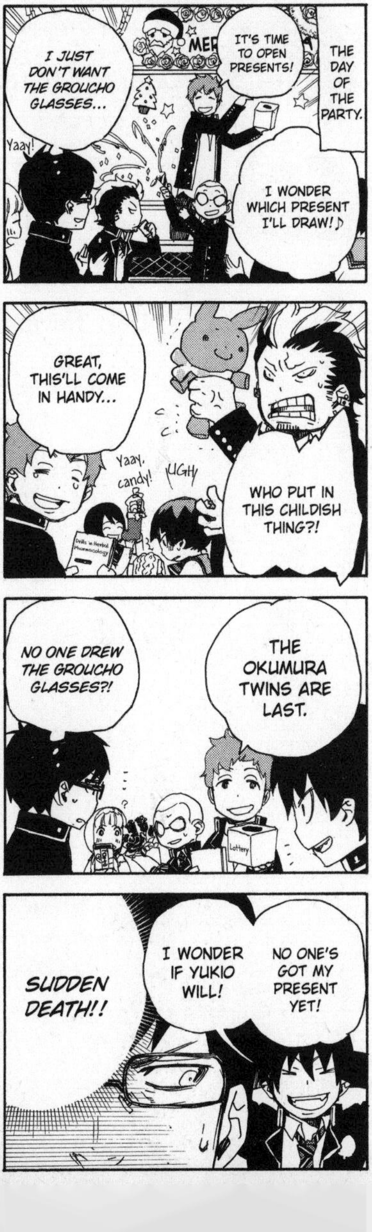
THE DAY OF THE PARTY.
IT'S TIME TO OPEN PRESENTS!
I JUST DON'T WANT THE GROUCHO GLASSES...
I WONDER WHICH PRESENT I'LL DRAW!♪
Yaay!
WHO PUT IN THIS CHILDISH THING?!
UGH
Yaay, candy!
GREAT, THIS'LL COME IN HANDY...
Drills in Herbal Pharmacology
THE OKUMURA TWINS ARE LAST.
NO ONE DREW THE GROUCHO GLASSES?!
Lottery
NO ONE'S GOT MY PRESENT YET!
I WONDER IF YUKIO WILL!
SUDDEN DEATH!!

HAPPY...NEW YEAR!!

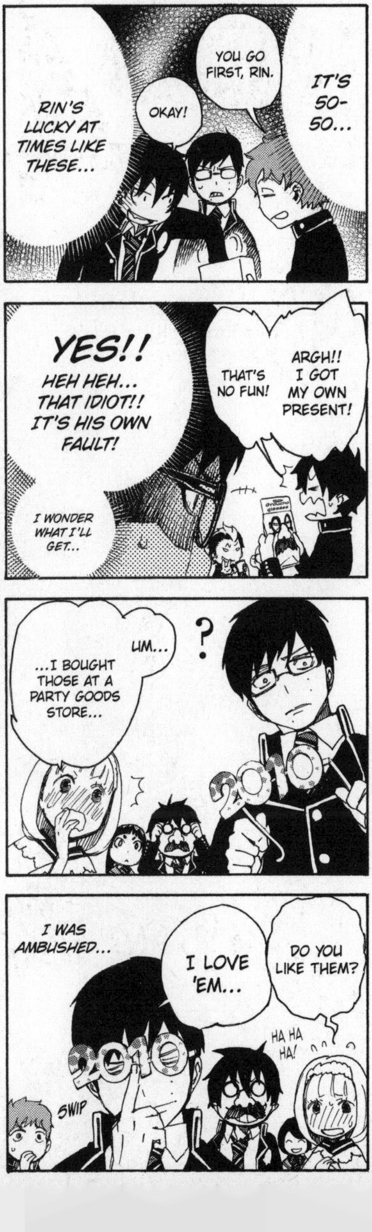
IT'S 50-50...
YOU GO FIRST, RIN.
OKAY!
RIN'S LUCKY AT TIMES LIKE THESE...
ARGH!! I GOT MY OWN PRESENT!
THAT'S NO FUN!
YES!! HEH HEH... THAT IDIOT!! IT'S HIS OWN FAULT!
Groucho glasses
I WONDER WHAT I'LL GET...
?
UM...
...I BOUGHT THOSE AT A PARTY GOODS STORE...
DO YOU LIKE THEM?
I LOVE 'EM...
I WAS AMBUSHED...
HA HA HA!
SWIP

True Cross Academy Exorcism Cram School: Exorcists and Students No. 0011

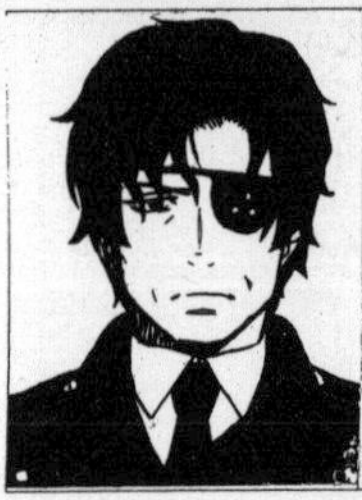

Name	Sex	Age
Igor Neuhaus	Male	39

Status:

Senior Exorcist First Class, Knights of the True Cross
(Titles: Tamer, Doctor, Aria)
Former instructor of Magic Circles and Seals, Year One, Exorcism Cram School

Date of birth
November 13
Blood type
AB
Height
182 cm
Weight
70 kg
Pastimes and talents
Solitaire, jigsaw puzzles
Average hours of sleep per night
3 hours
Favorite food
Beer, sauerkraut
Favorite manga genres (Circle all that apply.)
Battle/action Gags Comedy Romance Horror Suspense/mystery Emotional drama Social drama Other (DOESN'T READ MANGA)
Favorite type of girl
My wife.

Details:

- Always alone
- Currently suspended from teaching at the Exorcism Cram School
- Has ten spare eye-patches with the same design

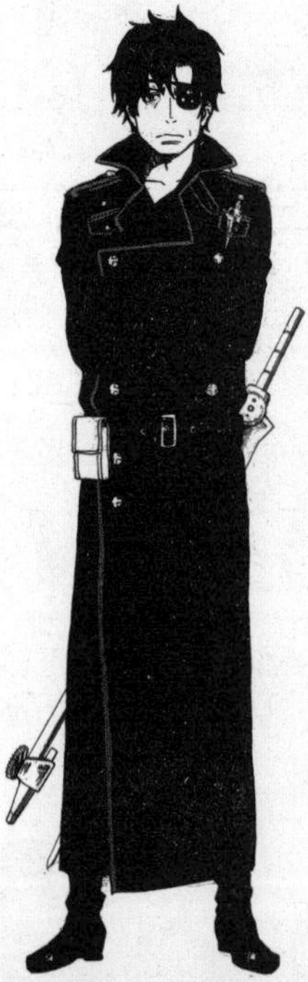

True Cross Academy Exorcism Cram School: Exorcists and Students No. 0012

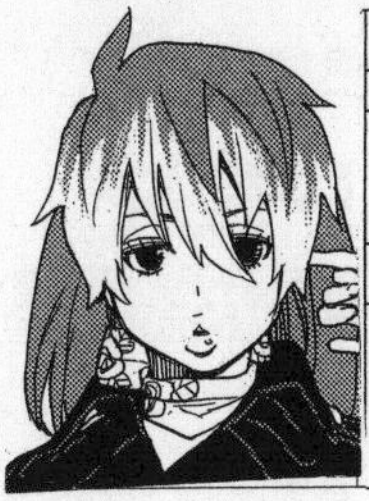

Name	Sex	Age
Shura Kirigakure	Female	18 ♡

Status

Senior Exorcist First Class, Knights of the True Cross (Titles: Knight, Tamer, Doctor, Aria)
Current instructor of Magic Circles and Seals and Swordsmanship, Year One, Exorcism Cram School

Date of birth:	August 8
Blood type	O
Height	169 cm
Weight	That's secret! kg
Pastimes and talents	Foot massages, hot stone spas, bothering animals
Average hours of sleep	8 hours
Favorite food	Her grandmother's herb cookies
Favorite manga genres (Circle all that apply.)	Battle/action Gags Comedy Romance (circled) Horror Suspense/mystery Emotional drama Social drama Other (cat manga, street punk manga)
Favorite type of boy	Strong and collected guys. ♡

Details:

- Wears an F-cup
- A heavy drinker, but can't handle it well. Once she starts, trouble soon follows!

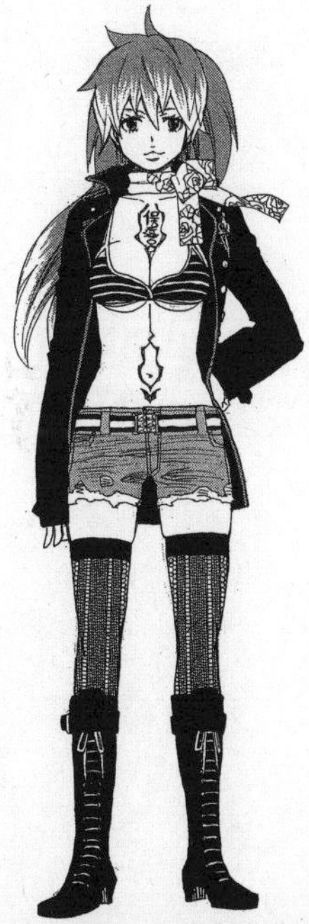

REAPER

FILE 6 · LOW LEVEL

Kin of Egyn, King of Water. Possesses frogs. They exist all over the world in various sizes, but they are all carnivores. In Europe, some grow wings, skip across the water, or generate ultrasonic waves.

BYAKKO

FILE 7 · LOW – HIGH LEVEL

As demons that possess animals and serve as Shinshi (messengers to gods indigenous to Japan), they coexist with humans. Byakko were originally popular in Japan as guardian deities of foods and agriculture. The older ones are intelligent and can understand human language. They will enter into agreements with people. As long as the agreement is kept, they bring benefit, but otherwise, they may inflict harm.

GREENMAN

FILE 8 · LOW – MID LEVEL

Kin of Amaimon, King of Earth. A demon that has possessed an earthen (mud) doll called a golem and then sprouted moss and other plants. They have the power to produce plants from their body in any season. They are peaceful and enjoy basking in the sun. As a side note, a golem made of snow is called a Snowman.

BARIYON

FILE 9

LOW LEVEL

Kin of Amaimon, King of Earth. Bariyons possess rocks and boulders. Most of the time they are motionless and make nonsensical sounds. They're harmless, but if you hold one, it gets heavy and weighs you down. Older and stronger ones may jump on your back and weigh you down.

GHOUL

FILE 10

LOW LEVEL

Kin of Astaroth, King of Rot. A demon that mainly appears in countries where it is customary to bury the dead. It possesses corpses. Ways of driving them away vary according to the customs and beliefs of the country. Cremation is most common in Japan, so they rarely appear anymore. Zombies are a different kind of demon.

GHOST

FILE 11

LOW LEVEL

Kin of Azazel, King of Spirits. A ghost is a demon that inhabits vapor released by the dead bodies of people and animals. Ghosts are often characterized by the emotions the deceased had in life. As with Ghouls, the manner of exorcism depends on the deceased's practices and beliefs in life.

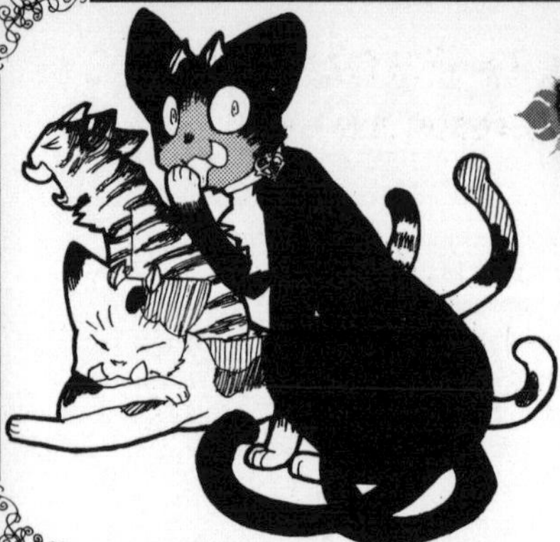

FILE 12 CAT SÍDHE

LOW – HIGH LEVEL

A demon that possesses cats and exists all over the world. In Japan, those that have lived a long time have two tails. They're different from Shinshi, but the older ones are smart and may enter agreements with people and live together with them. For hundreds of years, they may move from house to house as pets.

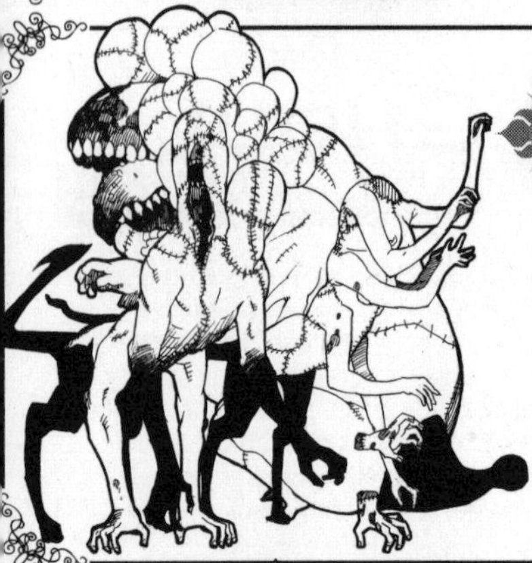

FILE 13 NABERIUS

MID LEVEL

Kin of Astaroth, King of Rot. A demon the ancients made by cobbling together multiple Ghouls for use in fighting against demons. Currently, there are many cases in which they can no longer be kept tame and go wild. For that reason, as well as ethical concerns, making Naberius demons has been forbidden and the technique sealed away.

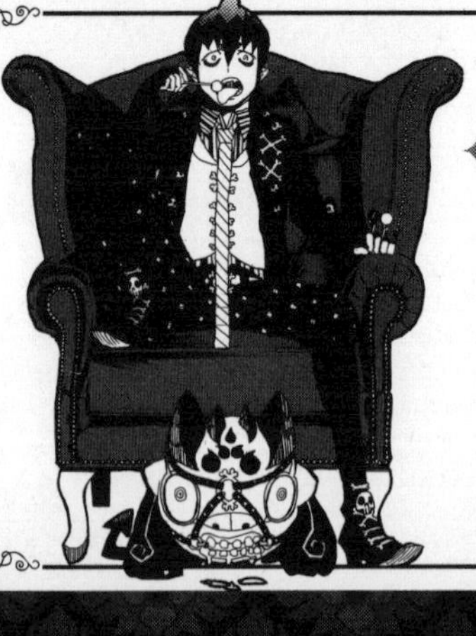

FILE 14 AMAIMON

UPPER LEVEL

A personage of authority in Gehenna who bears the title King of Earth. He is the leader of demons who bear a relation to earth. He has countless names in different lands and different times and is even worshipped as a god in some places. Presently, he occupies the body of a human man and is acclimating to the world of Assiah.

THE PRODUCTION PROCESS

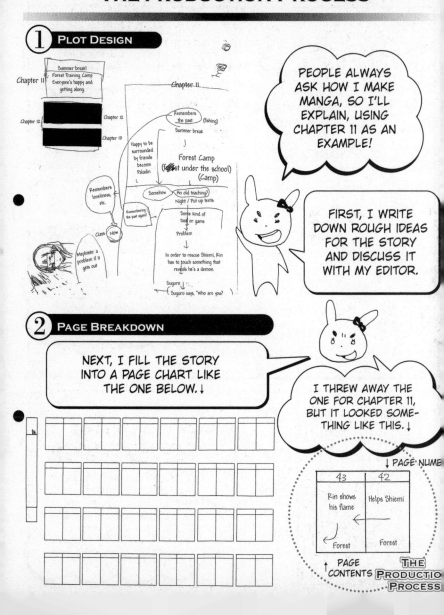

① PLOT DESIGN

Chapter 11
Summer break! Forest Training Camp Everyone's happy and getting along.

Chapter 12.

Chapter 11

Chapter 12

Chapter 13

Remembers the past (fishing)

Summer break
↓
Happy to be surrounded by friends become Paladin

Forest Camp
(forest under the school)
(Camp)

Remembers loneliness, etc.

Somehow An old teaching!

Remembering the past again!

Night / Put up tents
↓
Some kind of task or game
↓
Problem
↓
In order to rescue Shiemi, Rin has to touch something that reveals he's a demon.

Class Now

Mephisto: a problem if it gets out

Suguro ↓ ...
Suguro says, "Who are you?"

> PEOPLE ALWAYS ASK HOW I MAKE MANGA, SO I'LL EXPLAIN, USING CHAPTER 11 AS AN EXAMPLE!

> FIRST, I WRITE DOWN ROUGH IDEAS FOR THE STORY AND DISCUSS IT WITH MY EDITOR.

② PAGE BREAKDOWN

> NEXT, I FILL THE STORY INTO A PAGE CHART LIKE THE ONE BELOW. ↓

> I THREW AWAY THE ONE FOR CHAPTER 11, BUT IT LOOKED SOMETHING LIKE THIS. ↓

↓ PAGE NUMBE

43	42
Rin shows his flame ←	Helps Shiemi
↙ Forest	Forest

↑ PAGE CONTENTS

THE PRODUCTIO PROCESS

3 Layouts

THEN, I LOOK AT THE PAGE CHART AND DRAW LAYOUTS.

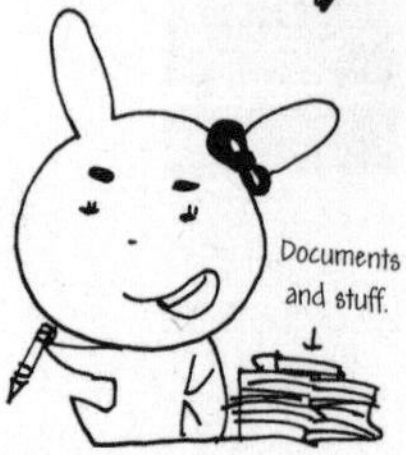
Documents and stuff.

THAT'S WHEN I DECIDE WHAT GOES IN EACH PANEL!

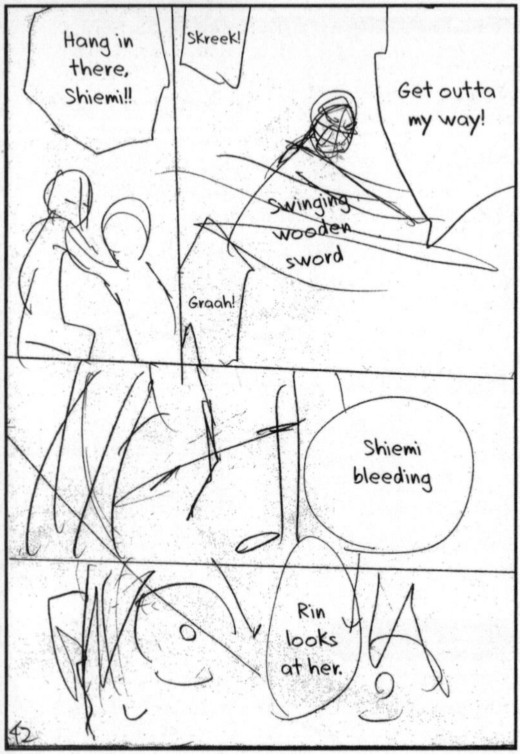
Get outta my way!
Skreek!
Swinging wooden sword
Graah!
Hang in there, Shiemi!!
Shiemi bleeding
Rin looks at her.
42

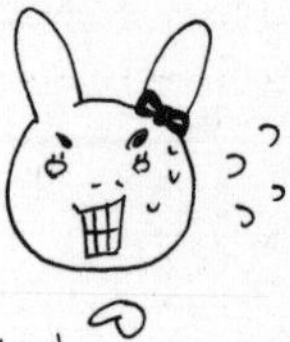
It's hard for the editor!

I ACTUALLY HARDLY EVER DO LAYOUTS WITH ILLUSTRATIONS.

IF YOU WANNA BE A MANGA ARTIST, DON'T FOLLOW MY EXAMPLE!

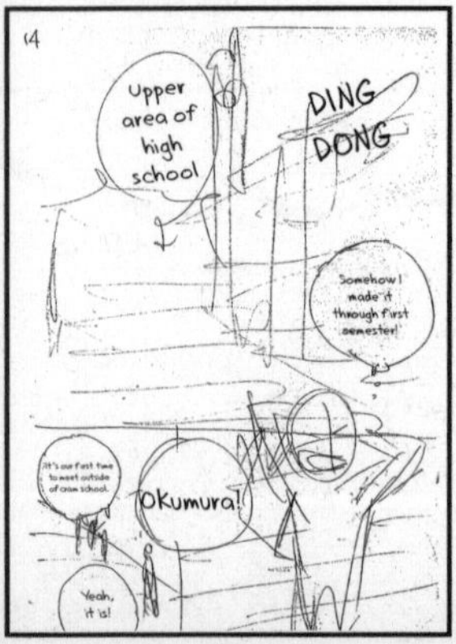
14
DING DONG
Upper area of high school
Somehow I made it through first semester!
Okumura!
It's our first time to meet outside of cram school.
Yeah, it is!

4 Rough Sketches

AFTER MY EDITOR APPROVES THE LAYOUTS, I START THE ROUGH SKETCHES.

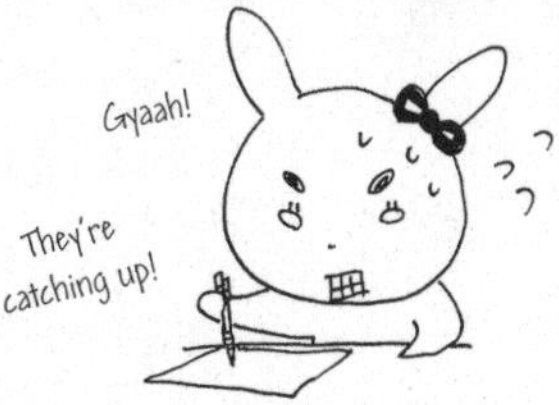

Gyaah!
They're catching up!

MY ART ASSISTANTS ARE BUSILY WORKING AWAY AT THE SAME TIME, AS YOU CAN SEE IN THE BOTTOM LEFT-HAND CORNER... ↙

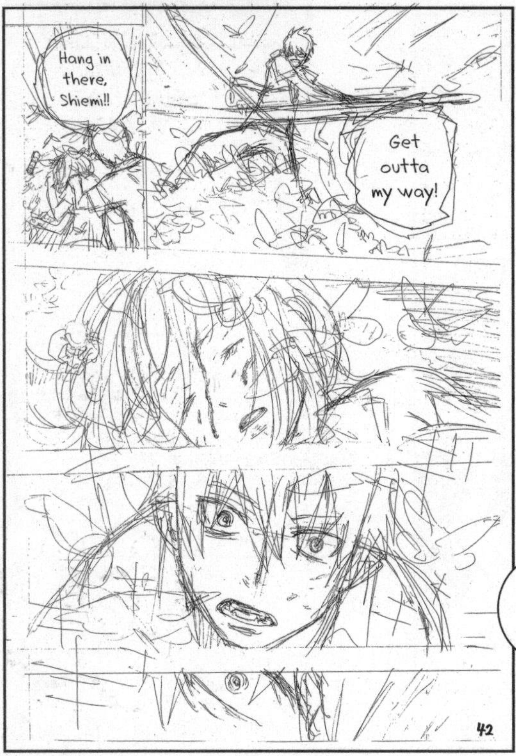

Get outta my way!
Hang in there, Shiemi!!
42

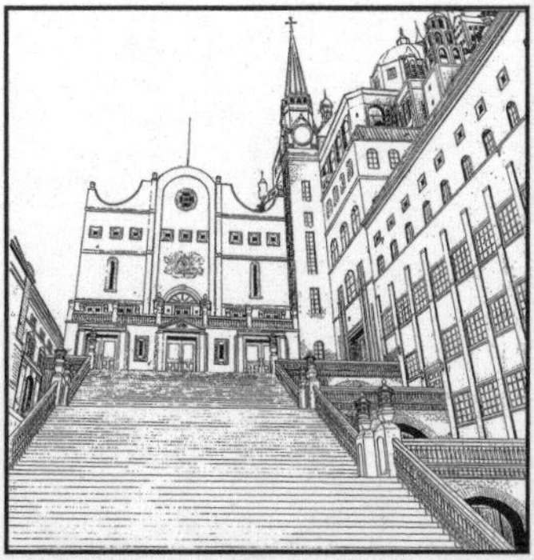

...BEFORE WE INK THE CHARACTERS, WE PUT IN THE BACKGROUND. MY ASSISTANTS DRAW BACK-GROUNDS WE MIGHT WANT TO USE ON SEPARATE SHEETS OF PAPER. →

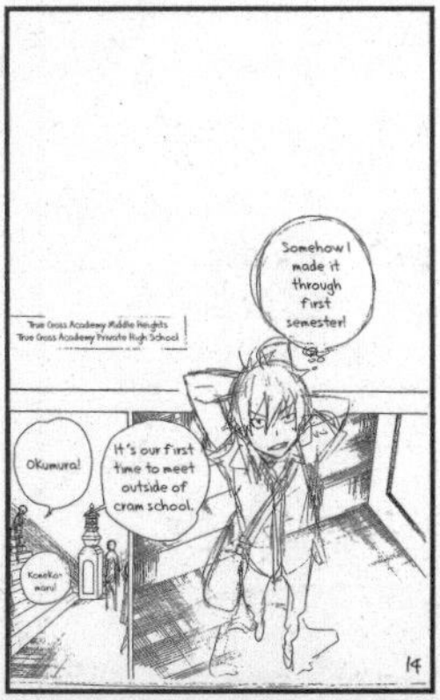

Somehow I made it through first semester!
It's our first time to meet outside of cram school.
Okumura!
14

⑤ INKING

THEN WE INK THE SKETCHES.

...fountain pen!

We ink the characters with a Tachikawa...

I DIDN'T MAKE COPIES OF THE WHOLE PROCESS, BUT HERE'S THE FINAL MANUSCRIPT. WE GO IN ORDER OF BACKGROUND→ CHARACTERS→SOUND EFFECTS→ CORRECTIONS→SCREENTONES.

AS YOU CAN SEE AT THE RIGHT, WE PUT IN THE BACKGROUND AND ADDED THE CROWD OF PEOPLE AND IT WAS DONE. → THE END!

BLUE EXORCIST 3

Art Assistants

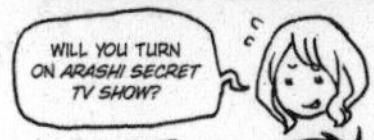
WILL YOU TURN ON ARASHI SECRET TV SHOW?

Shibu-tama

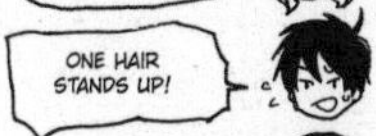
ONE HAIR STANDS UP!

Uemura-san

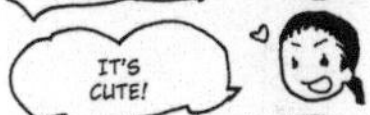
IT'S CUTE!

Kamimura-san

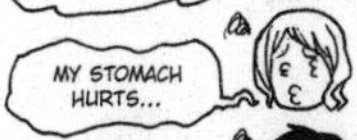
MY STOMACH HURTS...

Tae-chin

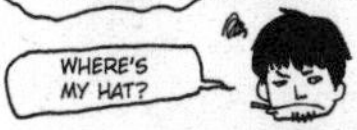
WHERE'S MY HAT?

Kimura-kun

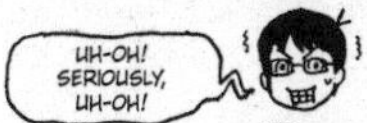
UH-OH! SERIOUSLY, UH-OH!

Hayashi-kun

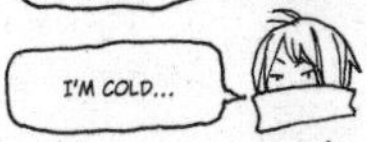
I'M COLD...

Kawamura-san

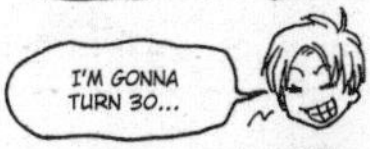
I'M GONNA TURN 30...

Endo-san

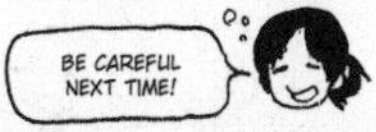
BE CAREFUL NEXT TIME!

Minora

Editor

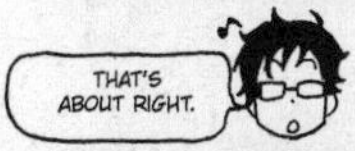
THAT'S ABOUT RIGHT.

Shihei Rin

Graphic Novel Editor

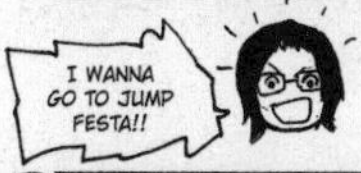
I WANNA GO TO JUMP FESTA!!

Natsuki Kusaka

Graphic Novel Cover Design

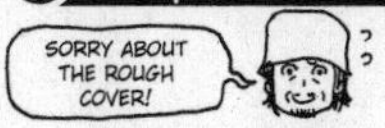
SORRY ABOUT THE ROUGH COVER!

Shimada Hideaki

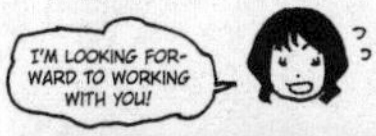
I'M LOOKING FOR-WARD TO WORKING WITH YOU!

Tomoko Hasumi (L.S.D.)

Manga

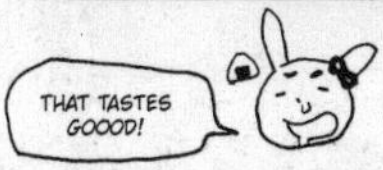
THAT TASTES GOOOD!

Kazue Kato

(in no particular order)
(Note: The caricatures and statements are from memory!)

Be sure to pick up Volume 4!

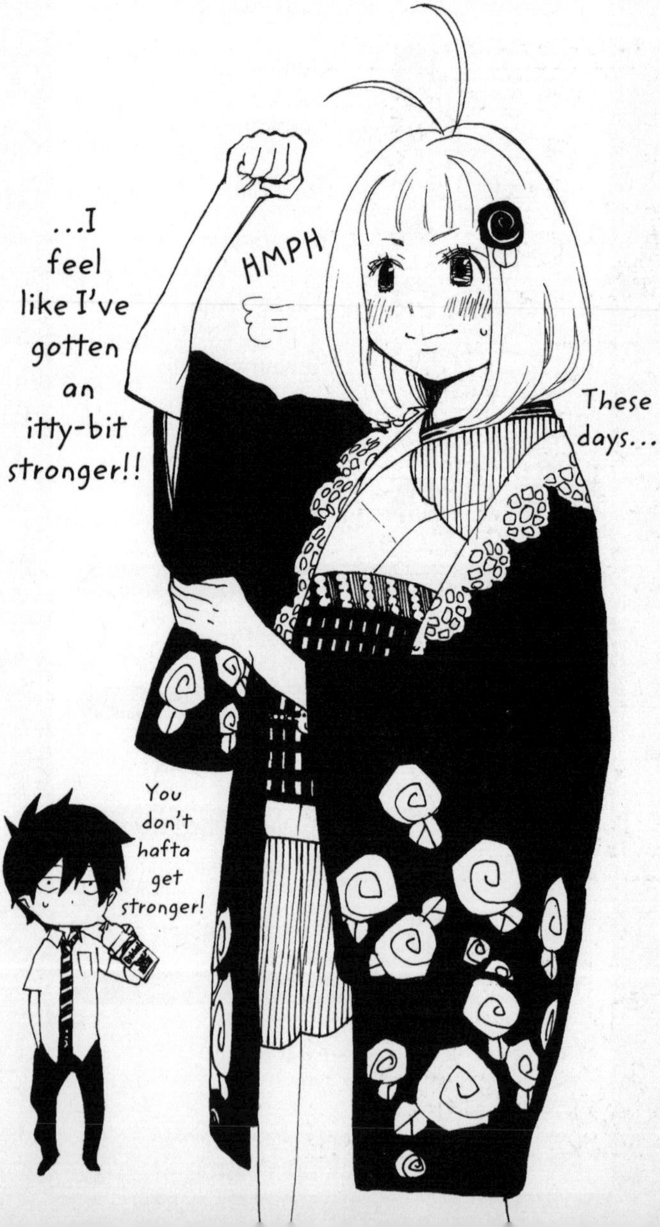
These days...
...I feel like I've gotten an itty-bit stronger!!
HMPH
You don't hafta get stronger!

Imagining the Future

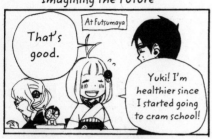

At Futsumaya
Yuki! I'm healthier since I started going to cram school!
That's good.
When I was little, I couldn't eat much...
...so I always caught colds.
Hey, I've got an old photo. Look!
Oh, I'd like to see that...
Ulp!
I... see...!
It doesn't bother me at all.
Huh?

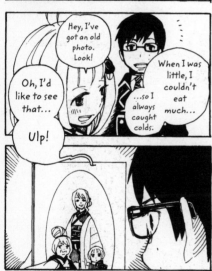

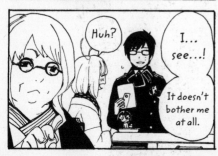

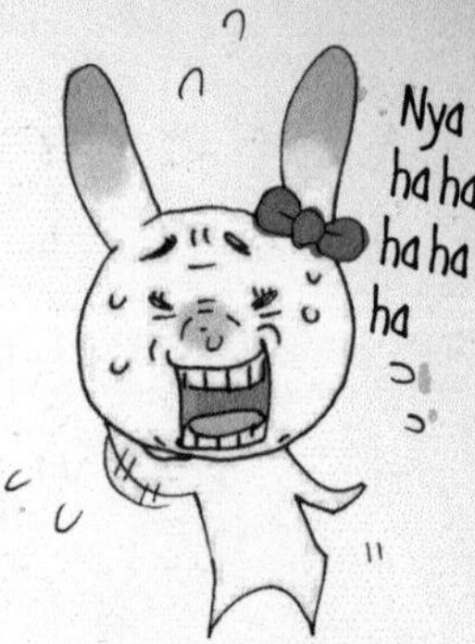
Nya ha ha ha ha ha

KAZUE KATO

I'VE BEEN FREAKING OUT A LOT RECENTLY. I NEED TO DO SOMETHING ABOUT THAT THIS YEAR!

NOW ON TO VOLUME 3!

BLUE EXORCIST

BLUE EXORCIST VOL. 3
SHONEN JUMP ADVANCED Manga Edition

STORY & ART BY KAZUE KATO

Translation & English Adaptation/John Werry
Touch-up Art & Lettering/John Hunt, Primary Graphix
Cover & Interior Design/Sam Elzway
Editor/Mike Montesa

AO NO EXORCIST © 2009 by Kazue Kato
All rights reserved.
First published in Japan in 2009 by SHUEISHA Inc., Tokyo.
English translation rights arranged by SHUEISHA Inc.

Printed in the U.S.A.

Published by VIZ Media, LLC
P.O. Box 77010
San Francisco, CA 94107

10 9 8 7
First printing, August 2011
Seventh printing, January 2015

PARENTAL ADVISORY
BLUE EXORCIST is rated T+ for Older Teen and is
recommended for ages 16 and up. It contains violence,
suggestive situations and some adult themes.
ratings.viz.com

www.viz.com

In the next volume...

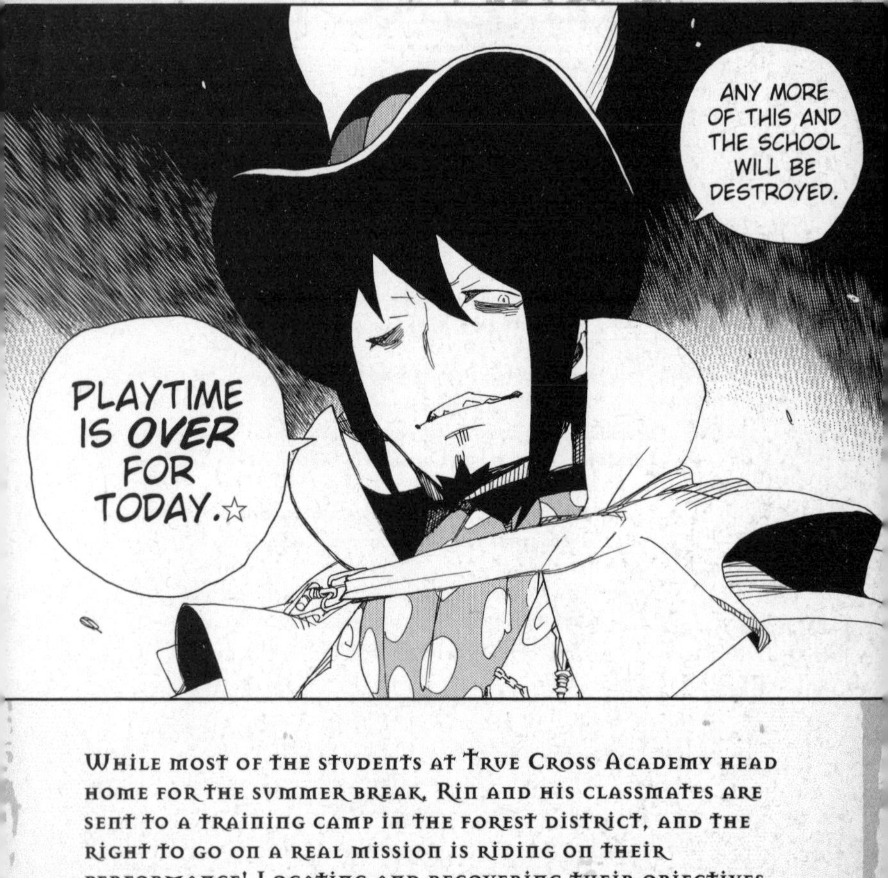
ANY MORE OF THIS AND THE SCHOOL WILL BE DESTROYED.
PLAYTIME IS *OVER* FOR TODAY.☆

While most of the students at True Cross Academy head home for the summer break, Rin and his classmates are sent to a training camp in the forest district, and the right to go on a real mission is riding on their performance! Locating and recovering their objectives in the woods is tough and will require teamwork, skill and more than a little magic, and Rin will have to learn to rely on his friends. But is Mephisto masterminding something behind the scenes?!

Available now!

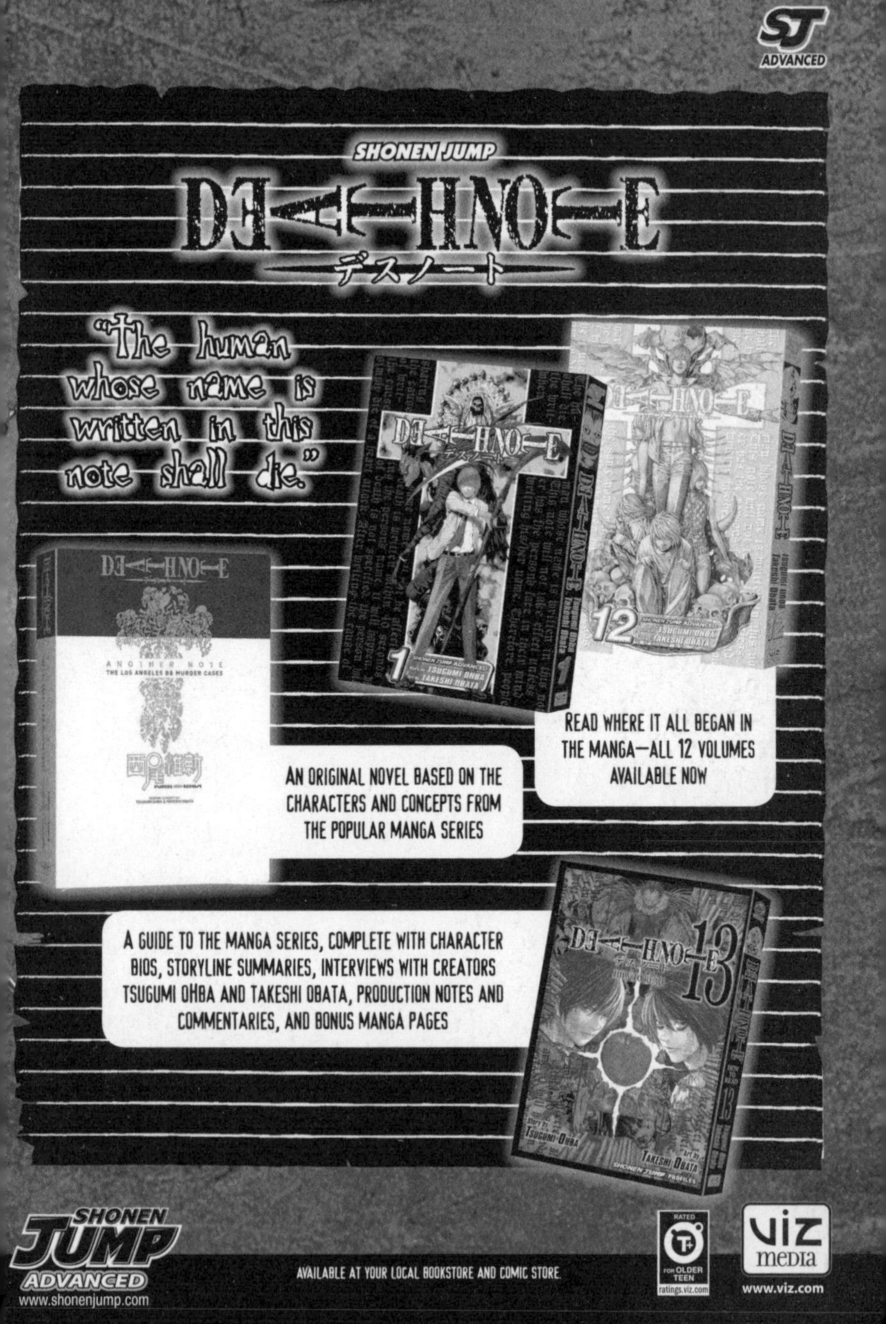
SJ ADVANCED
SHONEN JUMP
DEATH NOTE
デスノート
"The human whose name is written in this note shall die."
READ WHERE IT ALL BEGAN IN THE MANGA—ALL 12 VOLUMES AVAILABLE NOW
AN ORIGINAL NOVEL BASED ON THE CHARACTERS AND CONCEPTS FROM THE POPULAR MANGA SERIES
A GUIDE TO THE MANGA SERIES, COMPLETE WITH CHARACTER BIOS, STORYLINE SUMMARIES, INTERVIEWS WITH CREATORS TSUGUMI OHBA AND TAKESHI OBATA, PRODUCTION NOTES AND COMMENTARIES, AND BONUS MANGA PAGES
SHONEN JUMP ADVANCED
www.shonenjump.com
AVAILABLE AT YOUR LOCAL BOOKSTORE AND COMIC STORE.
RATED T+ FOR OLDER TEEN
ratings.viz.com
viz media
www.viz.com

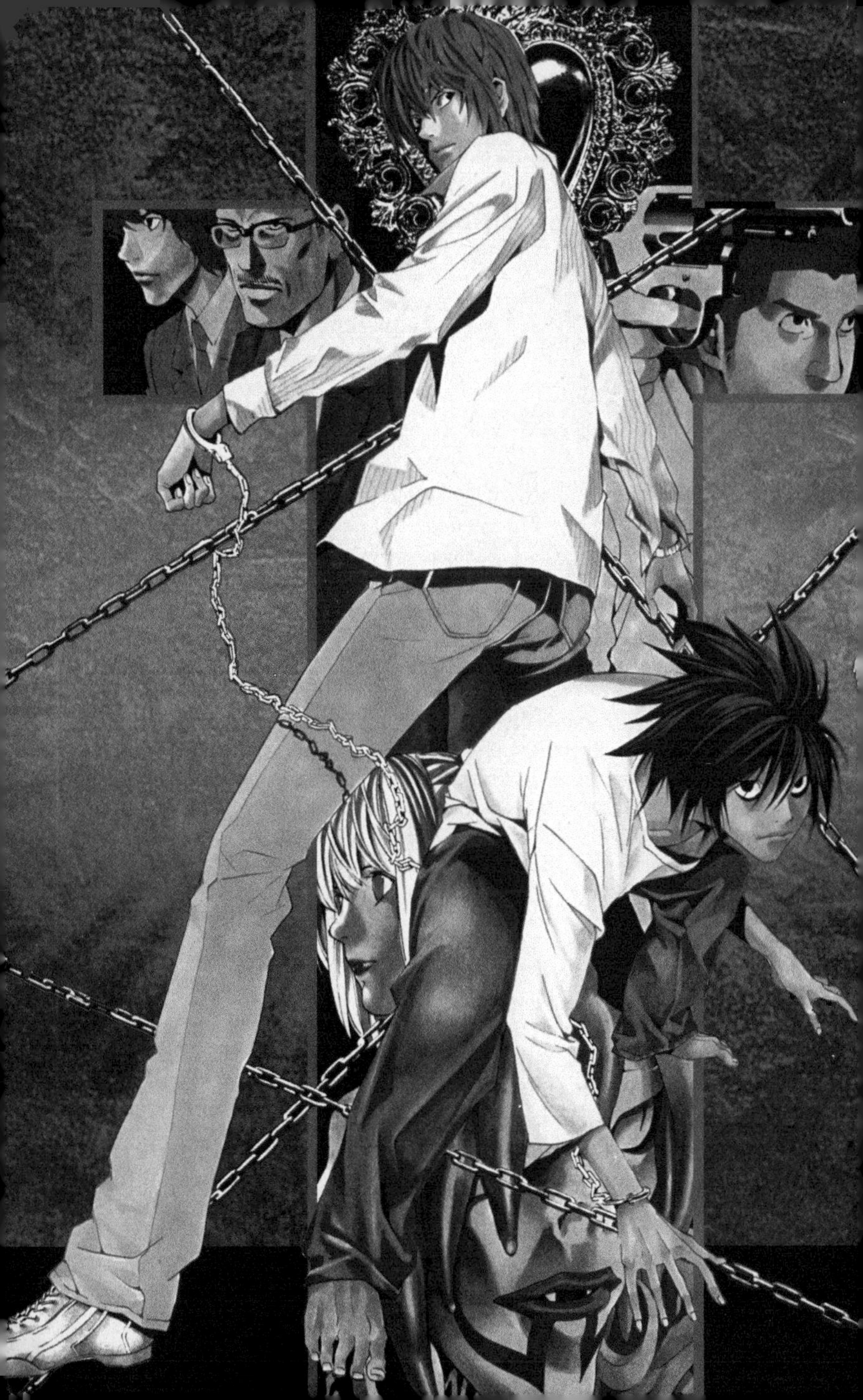

You're Reading in the Wrong Direction!!

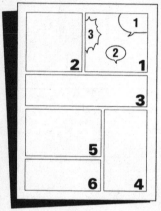

Whoops! Guess what? You're starting at the wrong end of the comic!

…It's true! In keeping with the original Japanese format, **Blue Exorcist** is meant to be read from right to left, starting in the upper-right corner.

Unlike English, which is read from left to right, Japanese is read from right to left, meaning that action, sound effects and word-balloon order are completely reversed… something which can make readers unfamiliar with Japanese feel pretty backwards themselves. For this reason, manga or Japanese comics published in the U.S. in English have sometimes been published "flopped"—that is, printed in exact reverse order, as though seen from the other side of a mirror.

By flopping pages, U.S. publishers can avoid confusing readers, but the compromise is not without its downside. For one thing, a character in a flopped manga series who once wore in the original Japanese version a T-shirt emblazoned with "M A Y" (as in "the merry month of") now wears one which reads "Y A M"! Additionally, many manga creators in Japan are themselves unhappy with the process, as some feel the mirror-imaging of their art skews their original intentions.

We are proud to bring you Kazue Kato's **Blue Exorcist** in the original unflopped format. For now, though, turn to the other side of the book and let the adventure begin…!

—Editor